Women in Weimar Fashion

Screen Cultures: German Film and the Visual

Series Editors:
Gerd Gemünden (*Dartmouth College*)
Johannes von Moltke (*University of Michigan*)

Women in Weimar Fashion

Discourses and Displays in German Culture, 1918–1933

Mila Ganeva

Rochester, New York

Copyright © 2008 Mila Ganeva

All Rights Reserved. Except as permitted under current legislation,
no part of this work may be photocopied, stored in a retrieval system,
published, performed in public, adapted, broadcast, transmitted,
recorded, or reproduced in any form or by any means,
without the prior permission of the copyright owner.

First published 2008 by Camden House
Transferred to digital printing 2009
Reprinted in paperback 2011

Camden House is an imprint of Boydell & Brewer Inc.
668 Mt. Hope Avenue, Rochester, NY 14620, USA
www.camden-house.com
and of Boydell & Brewer Limited
PO Box 9, Woodbridge, Suffolk IP12 3DF, UK
www.boydellandbrewer.com

Paperback ISBN-13: 978-1-57113-516-2
Paperback ISBN-10: 1-57113-516-2
Hardback ISBN-13: 978-1-57113-205-5
Hardback ISBN-10: 1-57113-205-8

Library of Congress Cataloging-in-Publication Data

Ganeva, Mila.
  Women in Weimar fashion : discourses and displays in German
culture, 1918–1933 / Mila Ganeva.
    p. cm. — (Screen cultures: German film and the visual)
  Includes bibliographical references and index.
  ISBN-13: 978-1-57113-205-5 (hardcover : alk. paper)
  ISBN-10: 1-57113-205-8 (hardcover : alk. paper)
  1. German literature—Women authors—History and criticism.
  2. German literature — 20th century — History and criticism.
  3. Fashion in literature. 4. Motion pictures, German — History.
  5. Fashion in motion pictures. 6. Fashion — Germany — History —
20th century. 7. Popular culture — Germany — History — 20th
century. I. Title.

PT405.G334 2008
830.9'355—dc22

2007051303

This publication is printed on acid-free paper.

Contents

List of Illustrations	vii
Acknowledgments	ix
Introduction: On Fashion, Women, and Modernity	1

Discourses on Fashion

1:	The Fashion Journalist: *Flâneur* or New Woman?	21
2:	Fashion Journalism at Ullstein House	50
3:	In the Waiting Room of Literature: Helen Grund and the Practice of Fashion and Travel Writing	84

Displays of Fashion

4:	Weimar Film as Fashion Show	113
5:	The Mannequins	151
6:	Fashion and Fiction: Women's Modernity in Irmgard Keun's Novel *Gilgi*	171

Epilogue	192
Appendix I: Biographical Information on Fashion Journalists and Fashion Illustrators	197
Appendix II: A List of German Feature Films about Fashion from the 1910s, 1920s, and 1930s	203
Works Cited	205
Index	227

Illustrations

1. Ola Alsen. *Reichshandbuch der deutschen Gesellschaft*, vol. 1, 1930 — 22
2. Elsa Herzog. *Reichshandbuch der deutschen Gesellschaft*, vol. 1, 1930 — 23
3. Illustration by Petra [Fiedler]. *Die Dame*, May 1924, no. 16, 15 — 59
4. "The Fashion Staff of *Die Dame*." *Die Dame*, Nov. 1920, no. 4, 8 — 60
5. Fashion illustrator Vally Reinecke. *Die Dame*, Apr. 1921, no. 13, 16 — 61
6. Fashion journalist Lily von Nagy. *Die Dame*, Nov. 1924, no. 3, 5 — 63
7. Fashion illustrator Petra Fiedler in a sweater of her own design. *Die Dame*, Dec. 1927, no. 6, 58 — 64
8. Fashion journalist Anita [Anita Daniel]. *Die Dame*, Jul. 1930, no. 22, 36 — 65
9. Illustration by Ernst Dryden. *Die Dame*, Mar. 1926, no. 13, 5 — 75
10. Page from *Für die Frau*, 1928, no. 5, 11 — 95
11. Page from *Für die Frau*, 1929, no. 6, 8 — 96
12. Asta Nielsen in *Die Geliebte Roswolskys* (Roswolsky's Mistress, 1921) — 115
13. The fashion salon in *Der Fürst von Pappenheim* (Prince of Pappenheim, 1927) — 123
14. Brigitte Helm featured in *Vogue* (German edition), 27 Mar. 1929, 37 — 132
15. Brigitte Helm in *Die Yacht der sieben Sünden* (The Yacht of Seven Sins, 1928) — 133
16. Hilde Zimmermann as a fashion queen. *Elegante Welt*, 12 Jan. 1927, 36 — 136
17. The Award Ceremony for Fashion Queen Hilde Zimmermann. *Der Querschnitt* 1 (Jan. 1927): 71 — 138
18. Brigitte Helm on the second cover in *Elegante Welt*, 16 Sept. 1929 — 140
19. Presentation of fashion for individual clients. *Scherl's Magazin*, Feb. 1930 — 155

20. Fashion show in the display window of a department store. *Scherl's Magazin*, Jun. 1930 — 157
21. Curt Bois surrounded by mannequins in *Der Fürst von Pappenheim* (Prince of Pappenheim, 1927) — 164

Acknowledgments

FROM ITS VERY INCEPTION almost ten years ago, this project has benefited from the support of many people, to all of whom I am deeply grateful. As a doctoral student at the University of Chicago, I was enthusiastically guided by my academic mentors, Katie Trumpener, Miriam Hansen, and Sander Gilman, who steered me toward novel areas of exploration and challenging questions. My friends in graduate school Anke Pinkert, Valentina Izmirlieva, Katia Mitova, Cecilia Novero, Anna Diakow, and Judith Leeb critiqued multiple drafts of chapters. Throughout the years Katie Trumpener, Miriam Hansen, and Anke Pinkert persistently encouraged me to pursue the book project and helped me with advice for rewriting. Many thanks to all of my Chicago friends, especially Vreni Naess and Abby Brown.

During several research trips to Germany I was dependent on the help, knowledge, and responsiveness of numerous people, many of whom became dear friends. Back in 1996 Temby Caprio shared with me her apartment and helpful tips about archival research, while Kerstin Barndt and Johannes von Moltke lent me their expensive camera to take the first photographs of materials at the Kunstbibliothek in Berlin. Some of the images collected at that time appear in this book. Christine Waidenschlager, Gundula Wolter, Patricia Ober, and Katharina Sykora were generous with their time and information about the history of fashion in Berlin. Helmut Lethen has been excited about this project from the beginning and found time to read multiple drafts and give me precious feedback. Philipp Stiasny always managed to discover yet another valuable film source that I did not know about and provided me with photocopies of rare materials. I am grateful to Adelheid Rasche at the Kunstbibliothek in Berlin, Sammlung Modebild-Lipperheidesche Kostümbibliothek, for sharing with me her expert knowledge of fashion history and fashion photography. Many people at the Bundesarchiv/Filmarchiv were always responsive to my inquiries, especially Ute Klawitter, Julika Kuschke, and Maja Buchholz; Barbara Schütz and Evelyn Hampicke retrieved hard-to-find archival footage, screened it with me, and offered valuable insights. Peter Latta and Anett Sawall at the Filmmuseum/Deutsche Kinemathek in Berlin helped me search though the photographic and poster archives. Gundula Weiss and Friedemann Beyer were most helpful with research at the Friedrich Murnau Stiftung in Wiesbaden. During my trips to Germany I could always count on my friends Julia Bertschik, Werner Kindsmüller, Uli Bruckner-Kindsmüller, and Sibylle Lewitscharoff for wonderful dinners, stimulating discussions, and original insights. Julia Bertschik always had invaluable bibliographical references to offer. My biggest debt is to Nathalie Huet and Manfred Flügge for their kind hospitality during many visits to Berlin. Without Manfred's friendship, his generous sharing of research materials about Helen Grund, and the inspiring conversations we have had on literature, culture, and politics, this book would not have materialized.

For the most part this book was written in the United States, and I would like to acknowledge the helpful staffs of the interlibrary loan departments at the University of Chicago, the University of Notre Dame, and Miami University, who diligently supplied innumerable obscure, hard-to-obtain books and microfilms. Special thanks to bibliographer Sem Sutter from the University of Chicago for his help with references. I was inspired to add a new chapter to the book after participating in the German Film Institute workshop "Unknown Weimar" at the University of Michigan in Ann Arbor in the summer of 2004. I am grateful to Eric Rentschler and Anton Kaes and to all the remarkable people I met in Ann Arbor for all their encouragement and feedback.

At my current academic home, Miami University, I enjoy the support of many colleagues. I am particularly grateful to the women's writing group — Mary Cayton, Laura Mandell, Renee Baernstein, Helen Sheumaker, and Judi Hettick — for pushing me to write even during the busiest periods of the school year. Ruth Sanders, Ben Sutcliffe, Ole Gram, Nicole Thesz, Sven Erik Rose, Erik Jensen, and Karen Eng have read various parts of the manuscript at various stages of completion and have offered much-needed feedback. Bob DiDonato has been unwavering in his enthusiasm for the project and has helped me throughout. A semester-long research leave, course releases, two summer grants from Miami University, and Mary Fahnestock-Thomas's editorial help made the completion of the manuscript possible.

At Camden House, this project was embraced by Jim Walker. His belief in the worthiness of the book and his patient editorial work contributed enormously to the improvement of the manuscript. I would like to thank the editors of the series "Screening Cultures," Gerd Gemünden and Johannes von Moltke, for their encouragement throughout the review process and to acknowledge the two anonymous readers for the detailed critical consideration they gave to my work.

I am happy to share the joy of publishing a book with my family and friends in Bulgaria. Sincere thanks go to Christian Takoff, Maria Krasteva, Diana Slavova, and Maya Yordanova. I am deeply grateful for the love and support of my parents, Marina and Mois Aroyo, and my in-laws, Maria, Iordan, Anna, and Georgy Ganev, without whom my summers in the last ten years would not have been as productive. My generous sister, Lora Aroyo, flew across the ocean a few times to be with me, offer help with babysitting, and teach me about electronic images. My best friend, my husband, Venelin Ganev, never ceased to believe in the originality of my work and never tired of reading draft upon draft of chapters. My children, Iori and Marty, have been the most beautiful presence in my life throughout the process of research and writing. It is to them that this book is dedicated.

M. G.
September 2007

Introduction: On Fashion, Women, and Modernity

> I was surprised to discover that the Berlin woman is less conservative [than the modern Viennese woman]. She quickly embraces the new fashions, likes to experiment, and has access to some of the best designer salons.
> — Eva [Ea von Allesch], "Modespaziergang in Berlin" (1920)

> The Berlin fashion season has gone mad — it is not a season any more, but a permanent wave.
> — *Vogue*, German Edition (1928)

THIS IS A BOOK about women's fashions and the various ways they were displayed, worn, created, and discussed in the public sphere of Weimar Germany. It focuses primarily on the years 1918–33 and limits its scope to Berlin and its sartorial practices, because, as the two statements quoted above suggest, it was there and then, in the German metropolis of the 1920s, that the most dazzling spectacles and spirited debates about women's fashion took place. During that long decade Berlin's numerous department stores regularly staged lavish shows in their display windows (Modenschau), organized frequent contests to determine the best model (Modekonkurrenz), and invited their customers to weekly fashion teas (Modentee). If the Berlin woman wanted to look fashionable, she had more choices than ever. If she could afford it, she could place an order for something custom-tailored and imported from Paris or designed in one of Berlin's exquisite fashion salons. Or she could buy a mass-produced knock-off that was less expensive and thus more affordable for the growing numbers of the middle classes. Or — probably the most likely scenario — she could sew her own clothes with the help of sewing patterns and the cheaper synthetic materials that became popular in the 1920s, like rayon and acetate (known as *Kunstseide*, or artificial silk). Finally, whatever their fashion practices, Weimar women got plentiful practical advice, inspiration, and expert guidance: They browsed the dozens of new illustrated magazines to which many female fashion journalists were contributing, or went to the movies to watch films often scripted by fashion journalists and took notice of what their favorite actresses were wearing.

Writing about Weimar fashion means writing about Weimar women. Fashion became central to women's experience of modernity, not only by being such a ubiquitous presence in their everyday lives, but also by allowing them to participate actively in its variegated practices in record numbers, both professionally — as journalists, illustrators, designers, photographers, models, and shop assistants — and for pleasure — as consumers, moviegoers, spectators, or simply window-shoppers. In Weimar Germany fashion was not only, as the conventional wisdom would have it, manipulatively employed by the various mass media — film, magazines, advertising, photography, and popular literature; it also emerged as a powerful medium for the autonomous self-expression of women. They were drawn into an already existing male-dominated philosophical and sociological tradition of debating fashion and modernity, a tradition associated with the names of Georg Simmel, Thorsten Veblen, and Werner Sombart. While the male theorists were abstractly interested in fashion's function within capitalism, their female counterparts in the 1920s were involved — through their writing — primarily in "self-fashioning," that is, creating and interpreting their own fashionable images. In addition to being the principal consumers of fashion, women offered their own original definitions of the categories of fashion and modernity based on immediate experiences and practices of fashion in their everyday lives. For example, female writers and journalists engaged in a challenging self-reflective commentary on the current styles, and by regularly publishing on these topics in the popular press they transformed traditional literary and journalistic genres and carved out a significant public space for themselves. Thus Weimar fashion helped shape a public sphere within which the female practitioners were transformed from objects of male voyeurism into active subjects of the complex, ambivalent, and constantly shifting experience of metropolitan modernity.

Weimar modernity, of which fashion is a key component, is commonly associated with the conditions of urban life that became prevalent in Germany after the First World War. It had its roots in the rapid advance of rationalized modes of work, living, and transportation and was associated with the mass production and mass circulation of goods, services, and images. The increasing democratization of social life, advances in gender equality, and women's increased access to the public sphere also had a strong influence on Weimar modernity. When the monarchy collapsed in 1918, a pluralistic political order was established, a new constitution was passed, and women were granted the right to vote.[1] As a result of a number of economic and social cataclysms in the wake of the war, during the Weimar Republic women also began to enter the work force and public life in greater numbers than ever. According to Frevert, there were almost 1.5 million female white-collar workers in 1925 — three times as many as in 1907 — whereas overall there were over 1.7 million more women in full-time employment than in 1907.[2] Despite persisting patterns of overt and covert discrimination, work outside the home meant increased freedom of movement, as well as more disposable income to spend on personal needs and entertainment. Between 1924 and 1929, in the period of relative material prosperity and economic stability following the implementation of the Dawes plan, women's presence in labor and leisure, in production and consumption, reached a peak.

Among the most visible manifestations of the impact of modernity on daily life were the radical changes in women's fashions. As more women entered into office and service-related professions, they needed clothing that would be both comfortable and presentable all day at the work place and that would also allow them to move around the city on foot or using public transportation. These modern demands were met by the functional styles that spread quickly, not only in Germany but also throughout Europe and North America. Women took off their corsets, cropped their hair, and fell in love with the pageboy haircut (Bubikopf); furthermore, they put on pants or wore dresses with lower waistlines, which suppressed the previously cherished features of sumptuous femininity such as large hips, a slender waist, and a lavish bust. The most provocative change in women's appearance was the shortening of the hem: by 1924, for the first time in the history of Western dress, skirts rose to knee level, and they remained there until the end of the decade. The shortened hemlines showed off legs in flesh-colored, transparent silk stockings, which was another fashion novelty that has persisted up till now. In short, it was during the 1920s that women began to live and dress in a way that we can identify with today. Anne Hollander's succinct characterization of these complex transformations of women's fashion as observed in Paris and New York applies very much to the Berlin fashion scene:

> It was during those brief four years [1924–29] that the new feminine image acquired its final perfection and lasting frame. All the "modern" possibilities for female looks were at last firmly indicated: the visual possibilities for simple, abstract shapes in the design of women's clothes, analogous to those used in male dress; and the possibilities for reduction of the bulk of flesh and hair as well as of fabric, for exposure of skin and indication of bodily movements. The late twenties set the standard for all these, a standard to which subsequent fashion still refers, despite variations in feminine fashion since then.[3]

While the visible changes in fashion during the 1920s have been thoroughly examined by costume historians, another new, "modern" phenomenon of that period has often been overlooked. Hollander calls it "society's heightened self-consciousness and self-descriptiveness" in matters of fashion and defines it as a "new knowledge that the way clothes looked was central to the way life was lived" (110). Indeed, the new styles not only served a functional purpose in the daily lives of the thousands of Weimar women working outside of their homes but also became part of their modern identity as independent subjects and, to a certain extent, a necessity that they could not ignore even if they wanted to. As Siegfried Kracauer emphasized in his 1929 sociological study *The Salaried Masses* (*Die*

Angestellten), quotidian practices such as fashion and sports were shaping the culture of salaried employees in the last years of the Weimar Republic. Without a "pleasant appearance," which included stylish attire, tasteful makeup, and an up-to-date haircut, female office and store employees could not hope to get promoted or even keep their jobs.[4] At the same time women were able to indulge in the new fashions, since they now had income of their own and leisure time to spend at the new venues of mass entertainment — the cinemas, cabarets, dance halls, and beaches in and around Berlin. These changes in work and entertainment patterns help to explain not only why a huge 25 percent of the average income in Weimar Germany was spent on clothing, but also why highly visible 1920s fashions became a central issue in unprecedented public discussions.[5]

The specificity of women's experience of modernity in the Weimar Republic cannot be understood without considering the unique role of Germany's garment industry in the production and dissemination of fashion. If France was best known for its *haute couture*, Germany became famous worldwide for its thriving *Konfektion*, the ready-to-wear clothing industry that was centered in Berlin. As early as the mid-nineteenth century the idea of wearing fashionable clothes spread among the middle and even the lower urban classes, which were growing rapidly in Germany's biggest metropolis. Following the Emancipation Edict of 1812, which granted equal civil rights to Jews in Prussia, trained tailors and salesmen from Brandenburg, Pomerania, Silesia, and East Prussia moved in droves to Berlin in search of employment or to start their own garment businesses. Jewish-owned companies such as Valentin Mannheimer, David Leib Levin, Rudolph Hertzog, and Herrmann Gerson launched a rationalized manufacturing process for men's and women's clothing; they opened salons and department stores that sold not only high-fashion but also mass-produced clothing at fixed sizes and prices.[6] By the mid-1920s Berlin's *Konfektion* was an essential branch of Germany's economy, a leader in domestic sales as well as exports, especially in the area of female clothing (Damenkonfektion).[7] In 1927 there were around eight hundred firms in Berlin specializing in the manufacture and sales of women's ready-to-wear, and *Konfektion* employed over a third of the city's work force, producing fashion for the masses along with exquisite designer clothing. Most of the exports went to the Netherlands, Great Britain, Sweden, Denmark, the USA, and France.

Since the fashion-conscious public liked to take its cue from France, the salons of Berlin's *Konfektion* were geared not only to creating their own lines of high fashion but also to importing, emulating, and adapting Paris styles. Berlin companies sent designers to Paris to observe what women were wearing in fashion shows, on the streets, at the races, and in the theater, and upon their return to Germany, they transformed expensive *haute couture* creations into more affordable, mass-produced, off-the-rack garments with French flair. As it broke down the aura of the unique high-fashion item into the multiplicity of mass-manufactured products, the Berlin *Konfektion* of the 1910s and 1920s came to epitomize many of the commercial, cultural, and national tensions of Weimar Germany — between creativity and business, between elitist exclusivity and mass appeal, between individuality and uniformity. These tensions were also present in other spheres of cultural production credited with democratizing the experience of modernity, such as film, the illustrated press, and popular literature.

If the term "modernity" refers to the material context of the Weimar years, "Weimar modernism" refers to the unique cultural production that came to flourish during the period. Modernist literature, art, photography, film, architecture, and design articulated a wide variety of aesthetic responses to the dramatic effects of modernity on people's lives. During the last twenty years or so the field of German Studies has produced numerous insightful investigations of Weimar modernity and modernism;[8] however, the emphasis has rarely been on fashion alone, because it is generally considered a superficial or ephemeral phenomenon, not a serious expression of modernity like other creative practices such as literature, architecture, film, or fine art.[9] Moreover, fashion is so multifaceted that it is difficult to determine which scholarly discipline may claim the primary right to study it.[10] Fashion can be many things at the same time — an object, a piece of clothing, a combination of textiles and seams — but it is also an expression of individual taste and social status, an interface between the body and its environment, a site for production and consumption. It is an image, a representation, in photographs, drawings, on the silver screen, and described in literature, but it is also a living practice, both spectacular and routine, cyclical and novel, allying itself now with a cosmopolitan spirit, now with nationalist traditions. Women's fashion encompasses an array of heterogeneous everyday practices that inspire, shape, and clarify the emergence of modern agents. In this book I use the analysis of selected representations and discussions of fashion in the pages of the popular press, in literary texts, and in films as a starting point from which to map out a cultural history of Weimar modernity centered around women as fashion journalists, professional models, and avid but critical consumers of fashionable images in the mass media. At the same time I consider unfairly neglected subgenres within Weimar journalism, literature, and film — the fashion column (Mode-Notizen, Modeplauderei), popular novels set in the *Konfektion* milieu, and the fashion farce (Konfektionskomödie) — and reevaluate their relatively marginal status vis-à-vis now canonical works of Weimar modernism.

Among the diverse existing approaches to the study of Weimar modernism, three theoretical studies have offered constant productive dialogue during my effort to define Weimar fashion and fashion practices as central to women's experience of modernity. The first was a direct result of the realization that for too long modernism was associated exclusively with the products of high art and that its study has been kept strictly separate from any interest in popular art or low and mass culture. In his groundbreaking *After the Great Divide: Modernism, Mass Culture, Postmodernism* (1986), Andreas Huyssen points out the historical reasons for excluding the products of commercial mass culture (popular literature, film, illustrated magazines) from the study of canonical modernism: in essence they were seen as inferior, feminine, and threatening. He argues that if we continue to maintain the strict boundary between high art and mass culture, our understanding of modernity and modernism becomes increasingly sterile and incapable of grasping fully the cultural phenomena of our contemporary surroundings.[11] My study of the rise of popular Weimar fashions and fashion practices and their impact on the aesthetics of literary and filmic representation contributes to a new theoretical paradigm, exploring Weimar modernity in the mixed and often contradictory multiplicity of its origins, meanings, and influences rooted in both the vernacular and the avant-garde.

Another approach that has informed my work was first formulated by Patrice Petro in her pioneering monograph on women and melodramatic representation in Weimar Germany, *Joyless Streets* (1989).[12] Both in her reconstruction of historic debates about mass culture and modernism and in her close readings of Weimar cinema, the illustrated press, and photojournalism, Petro consistently draws attention to questions of intertextuality. For example, she always explores the media institutions in Weimar and their various cultural productions (films, texts, images) with an eye to the multiple relationships among them. While her analysis of intertextual connections is geared primarily toward understanding the representations of gender and spectatorship in mass culture, I shift the focus toward a broader cultural-historical reconstruction of women's position as agents of Weimar modernity. Thus my analysis of a heterogeneous body of primary materials — literary texts, journalistic accounts, and films — traces the emerging figure of the fashion practitioner who is not only being observed but is an insightful observer and commentator herself, who is not only a media representation but an influential producer of opinions and shaper of experience as well.

And finally, I have benefited from Janet Ward's more recent *Weimar Surfaces: Urban Visual Culture in 1920s Germany* (2001), which more comprehensively than any other study examines literal and conceptual expressions of *surface* — architecture, advertising, film, and fashion — in Weimar modernity and reassesses them according to their own merits. Ward points out that the Germany of the 1920s offers "a stunning moment of modernity when surface values first ascended to become determinants of taste, activity, and occupation" and that a reengagement with those modern elements would help us understand how they still underpin our contemporary postmodern condition.[13] However, whereas Ward's and Huyssen's approaches are ultimately concerned with Weimar modernism's theoretical connections with postmodernism, I use cultural-historical investigation to focus exclusively on one aspect of surface culture: fashion.

The Pre-Weimar Fashion Debate

Germany has a long tradition of philosophical and sociological reflection on both the history of fashion and the genealogy of modernity. As art and fashion historian James Laver remarks humorously in a preface to one of the numerous German books on the history of dress and manners: "The Germans have a historical spirit developed to a high degree, and everything, even a woman's underwear, must be made to fit into the philosophical framework of their minds."[14] The modern social-philosophical debate on fashion in Europe and the United States was actually shaped toward the end of the nineteenth century and was associated with the well-known names Thorstein Veblen, Georg Simmel, Friedrich Theodor Vischer, and Werner Sombart, and two elements common to their writings are particularly relevant here: all of these male authors identified fashion as a paradigmatic phenomenon of modernity and tied it to the accelerated development of the bourgeois social order and the capitalist economic system. It was primarily in that connection that the undeniable "kinship of modernity and fashion" (die Verwandschaft der Moderne mit der Mode) was noted, a kinship that continues to dominate discourses on fashion.[15] These turn-of-the-century thinkers also launched the enduring tradition of considering fashion a purely feminine activity. While they linked fashion to the sphere of women's culture and women's practical experience, theorizing on fashion remained within the male domain.

It was over the course of the nineteenth century that fashion emerged as the quintessentially modern phenomenon we know today. As society became increasingly industrialized and differentiated, fashion (Mode) developed its own momentum and parted ways with traditional costume (Tracht, Kleidung), which basically served to emphasize and maintain the identity of a group or community. While traditional costume was associated with stability and rarely changed over time, fashion was about perpetual change and the individual's desire to belong to a given social group as well as to appear distinctive within this group.[16] Around 1900 many philosophers, economists, and sociologists recognized that the "modernness" of fashion not only opposed traditional and regional costume but also was tied to the rapid and radical economic developments in society. In his 1902 essay "Economy and Fashion" ("Wirthschaft und Mode") Werner Sombart, for example, insisted on the primacy of economic forces in the creation of the fashion cycle. He called fashion "capitalism's favorite child" and studied its modern essence in connection with the "abundance of goods," "rapid circulation," and "mass consumption" that he observed in contemporary economic life.[17] As an economist Sombart was not only interested in the mechanism of production and profit-making behind the business of women's fashions; he also recognized the "sensual pleasure" of the mass consumer at the turn of the century as a driving force behind the rise of fashion, without, however, exploring the question of women as agents in the fashion system.[18] In 1899 Thorstein Veblen coined the famous term "conspicuous consumption" in part to demonstrate how fashion was intimately related to developments in the bourgeois social order that assigned to men the role of producing wealth and to women the role of demonstrating this wealth in public. According to Veblen, bourgeois women fulfilled this task by constantly wearing fashionable and luxurious clothes that impressed and dazzled observers, while men's costume remained less conspicuous and hardly changed after the late eighteenth century.[19]

Obviously Veblen insisted on a sociological interpretation of the gender distinction within bourgeois fashion: while modern men participated actively in "productive employment" and therefore their sober, dark costumes reflected their involvement in "serious, useful work," modern women were engaged primarily in "conspicuous consumption," and their fashionable attire was the "insignia of leisure" (105–7). But the German sociologist Georg Simmel attempted to provide a more complex — cultural as well as psycho-sociological — explanation of the mutual relationship between modernity, fashion, and women. He continued a German tradition of extensive reflection on fashion from the late eighteenth century onwards: from Kant and his interest in fashion as an anthropological phenomenon, as a "game of imitation," to Friedrich Vischer's influential treatise "Fashion and Cynicism" (*Mode und Cynismus*) in 1879, to Nietzsche's association of modernity with fashion.[20]

Simmel was undoubtedly the most articulate among his contemporaries in elevating fashion from a trivial to a highly symptomatic phenomenon of modern times. His 1901 study "Fashion" ("Die Mode"), included in one of his most popular collections of essays, *Philosophische Kultur* (Philosophical Culture), focused on fashion as a crucial manifestation of modernity overall. At the same time, however, he was interested in defining some gender-based differences in the experience of modernity. Another essay, from 1911 and included in the same volume, "Female Culture" ("Weibliche Kultur"), was dedicated particularly to the discussion of women's place in modern culture, and the two essays set up an enduring theoretical framework for the study of fashion as a manifestation of female modernity.[21]

As Simmel wrote, fashion as a modern phenomenon "stands on the watershed between the past and the future and, as a result, conveys to us, at least while it is at its height, a stronger sense of the present than do most other phenomena."[22] So it is in general well suited to the needs of the modern subject, especially in the metropolis, as a means of effecting social adaptation and social mobility, as well as individual differentiation within a dynamic, rapidly changing urban environment. Yet historically speaking, fashion has generally appealed more to women than to men, and Simmel set out to explain this fact, concluding that women are more interested in fashion because, by participating in it, they compensate for the comparative lack of personal freedom and opportunity for self-improvement inherent in the relative weakness of their social position. Fashion became "a valve, as it were, through which women's need for some measure of conspicuousness and individual prominence finds vent, when its satisfaction is more often denied in other spheres" (196). There is also a biological component to that explanation: since women are more "faithful," "devoted," and "passive" by nature than men (who have more "active," "differentiated," and "fragmented" lives), Simmel argued, their increased interest in fashion provides a needed "balance" between passivity and impassivity, concentration and distraction in their lives (196–97).

In his essay "Female Culture" Simmel provided a more complex explanation of gender-based differences in experience, rooted in his overall understanding of culture. It becomes clear that for him there was no neutral, ungendered culture. It could be either objective, which included all creations of the human mind such as law, art, customs, and religion, or subjective, which related to the individual's participation in objective culture and to the way in which personal growth was fostered by the use of cultural products. He regarded his contemporary objective culture as "thoroughly male," so much so that "deficient performances in the most diverse areas are degraded as 'feminine,' whereas outstanding performances of women are celebrated as 'thoroughly manly.' "[23] The reasons for that state of modern culture lie in a mixture of biological givens and different modes of socialization.

The most interesting and controversial part of this essay deals with the possibility that a distinctive female culture might emerge out of the "objectivation of the female nature" and develop counter to the objective, differentiated male culture, which is more conducive to the realization of male abilities. Given women's different psychological makeup and different experiential reality, Simmel distinguished certain areas in which women can express their feminine creativity — dance, theater, sculpture, medicine, and history — better than any man. And these areas, especially the plastic arts, according to Simmel, have the potential to become the sphere of distinctly female culture.

It is in this connection between Simmel's views on female culture and his views on fashion that both the rich ambivalence and the ultimate flaws of his theories become apparent. Although he demonstrated an acute sensitivity to women's problematic position within modern culture, he was seriously limited in his ability to transcend a biological model of womanhood. He did not fall into the paradoxical trap that many of his contemporaries and even later cultural critics could not escape, namely designating fashion as the sphere of purely female activities and interests and then criticizing women's obsession with fashion as something utterly frivolous, superficial, and trivial. Nevertheless, he saw women generally as a monolithic category, as passive beings rather than active subjects, so that when contemporary bourgeois women did begin to emancipate themselves, he viewed them as partaking equally in the world of men rather than settling for a distinctive sphere of women's culture.[24] He therefore believed that contemporary bourgeois women's increased emancipation and economic independence would lead to an increasing indifference to fashion.[25] "The emancipated woman of the present, who seeks to approach the whole differentiation, personality, and activity of the male sex, lays particular stress on her indifference to fashion," he wrote in "Fashion" (197). Needless to say, history proved him wrong: emancipated women are still interested in and participating in fashion. But it is worth examining Simmel's presupposition in the specific historical context, because it shows that he subscribed at the same time to both a very universal and a very historically specific understanding of the connection between fashion, femininity, and modernity.

At the turn of the century, Simmel was an ardent supporter of the German women's movement to reform contemporary dress (the movement for *Reformkleidung*), which dominated social and aesthetic debates on fashion at the time.[26] The dress-reform movement, which evolved in the 1890s and remained influential throughout the first decade of the twentieth century, consciously defined itself as an adamant "anti-fashion" crusade (Modekritik), rejecting the corset as the most oppressive element of current fashion. This attracted not only the women's movement but also outspoken advocates from two other influential groups: the medical community, concerned with how the corset damaged the women's body, and the artistic community, engaged in a radical aesthetic reform of design. Both groups participated in public fashion debates through studies, pamphlets, treatises, and books.[27] While doctors prescribed the health dress (Gesundheitskleid), which was based on careful consideration of healthy materials and shapes and appropriate length and weight of fabric, artists created the artist's dress (Künstlerkleid) or recommended that women design their own garments (Eigenkleid) to reflect their personal style, following natural body lines and conforming to the practical needs of everyday life.

In all this *fin de siècle* fashion discourse there was a conspicuous lack of female voices. Admittedly, the dress-reform movement did bring about positive changes in women's fashions, but it was men who claimed to have the revolutionary ideas and who had the opportunity to express them publicly. Therefore, turn-of-the-century fashion discourse was emblematic of modernity in being divided between authoritative male voices (the doctors, the artists, and the philosophers) and heterogeneous mass practice (what women actually thought and did about their clothes). These tensions and Simmel's ambivalent views on fashion, women, and modernity foreshadowed some central queries, which were addressed openly for the first time during the Weimar period and which, in a way, we still face today: Must fashion always be considered an instrument of oppression, hence universally despised by women? Or can fashion be viewed as an ambivalent phenomenon of modern times that could possibly constitute a tool for women in their creative search for identity and self-realization? Obviously I tend toward the latter view. The historical analysis and textual examples I present here — relying primarily on popular texts such as pulp fiction and newspaper reports on the latest styles, fashion shows, fashion contests, and so on — demonstrate that fashion for women in Weimar culture was more than just a physical flourish or playful indulgence; it was a multifaceted quotidian experience, sometimes empowering and sometimes limiting, one that generated reflection on modernity and, through the mass media, provided a mode of entry into the public sphere.

Weimar Fashion

This book is divided into two parallel parts, "Discourses on Fashion" and "Displays of Fashion." The first focuses on discussions in the illustrated press, tracing the emergence of the female fashion journalist as both a double of the male *flâneur* and his opposite, and studying how fashion journalism articulated perspectives on modernity. The second offers a kaleidoscopic view into the visual display of fashion and the women who brought it before the public in film, fashion shows, and literature. Throughout, the narrative focuses on Weimar women I call "practitioners of fashion," comprising a diverse group: from authors, reporters, and artists who worked for the fashion press and interpreted fashion for the mass audience, to models and actresses who presented sartorial elegance publicly, to ordinary readers and spectators who were eager to emulate the latest trends, reevaluate them, and adapt them to their own everyday life.

Chapter 1 examines the fashion journalist's affinity with the *flâneur* and the New Woman, conceptual figures traditionally associated not only with particular modes of experiencing early twentieth-century modernity but also with a keen interest in the sartorial codes of society and the various practices of fashion. Gender played a substantial role in establishing the borderline between these figures, for *flânerie*, often equated with certain forms of dandyism, presented a specifically male mode of observation and experience of modernity. The *flâneur*-as-dandy has been persistently defined as the artist and journalist who could capture the essence of modern life, whereas the woman within this paradigm has often been relegated to a place within the work of art. An often ignored and forgotten figure, the female fashion journalist emerged as a peculiar cultural crossbreed or blend of these two types. She was in many respects a New Woman — emancipated, economically independent, with a profession and career of her own — and at the same time a sort of "female dandy" who captivated the public with her extravagant appearance and a "female *flâneur*" (*flâneuse*) who seemed to have mastered the art of astute observation of metropolitan life. But with their texts published regularly in the mass press, fashion journalists demonstrated that they were not mere imitators of the male *flâneur* and dandy. Engaged in a very specific sphere of cultural practices — the promotion of and commentary on fashion for the mass reader — they revealed modernity's specific effect on the everyday lives of German women between the wars.

The print media in Weimar Germany became the site where women's heightened self-consciousness about clothes, hairstyles, and appearance was openly articulated and where many female fashion journalists had successful professional careers. Chapter 2, "Fashion Journalism at Ullstein House," examines the fashion press as a vehicle for women's self-expression in an era of vast modernization and the rise of mass culture, including a closer look at selected periodicals from the Weimar period, their unique institutional politics, and the female fashion journalists who wrote regularly for them. The primary focus is on Ullstein's illustrated magazines *Die Dame* and *Der Uhu*, not only because they present perhaps the richest discursive landscape of Weimar fashion, but also because they bear the strongest testimony to women's increased self-consciousness and self-descriptiveness in matters of fashion. A study of these magazines reveals the extraordinary involvement of Ullstein House as an institution in the creation, distribution, and public discussion of women's fashion and demonstrates how the broader debate on issues such as women's changing and increasingly active role in modern life — as creators rather than followers of aesthetic norms, as subjects rather than objects of visual and textual representation of fashion, as insightful observers, writers, and designers of fashionable images — cannot be separated from the increasing modernization of the mass media in the Weimar Republic.

Chapter 3, "In the Waiting Room of Literature: Helen Grund and the Practice of Fashion and Travel Writing," is a study of the works and career of one fashion journalist whose presence on the German literary and artistic scene from the early 1920s until the mid-1930s demonstrated how professional writing on fashion could turn into an idiosyncratic combination of female *flânerie* and surrealist experimentation. A look at Grund's works expands the canon of texts used in the analysis of modernity and shows how writing on fashion has enriched and transformed popular Weimar genres such as the feuilleton and the travelogue. The last section of this chapter intertwines the narrative of the fascinating final years of Grund's career with an analysis of the idiosyncratic fashion discourse in the Nazi period between 1933 and 1939.

Chapter 4, "Weimar Film as Fashion Show," examines the multiple intermedial and intertextual connections between the institutions of cinema and fashion in two case studies. The first traces the development of a sub-genre of Weimar cinema, the fashion farce (Konfektionkomödie), and its particular way of addressing a predominantly female, lower- and middle-class audience. These films, in which fashion is not only part of a spectacular *mise-en-scène* but also serves as the raw material for the narrative, are set in designer salons and department stores and contain numerous fashion shows. Their protagonists are smart, ambitious, indispensable female mannequins (often called "Konfektionsmädel," "Probiermamsell," "Gelbstern," or "Konfektioneuse") who hope to become actresses or own designer salons themselves. The second case study focuses on Brigitte Helm's star status within German culture and aspects of her on-screen presence that relate to the explicit depiction of and commentary on Weimar's aesthetic practices in the world of clothes and fashion. In documenting and analyzing some of the lost, forgotten, or recently discovered works that make up the genre *Konfektionskomödie*, and in reexamining several well-known films with Brigitte Helm, I propose a reevaluation both of the role of fashion in film and of the "modernity" in which both German cinema and German *Konfektion* came to thrive. Both case studies demonstrate on the one hand how fashion and film, in tandem, guided the audience from the screen to see and experience modern life and how, on the other hand, the visual style of Weimar film was often influenced by popular forms of live entertainment such as the fashion show (Modenschau) and the numerous contests for a fashion queen (Modekonkurrenzen).

Chapter 5 continues to investigate the spectacle of fashion by taking a closer look at the women at the center of fashion shows, namely the mannequins. The preoccupation of the mass media with practices of fashion display during the 1920s testified to the pronounced ambiguity conveyed by the term "mannequin," which was commonly used to designate the artificial reproductions of women's bodies in shop windows (Schaufensterpuppen), but was also sometimes used to refer to the women who offered up their bodies to the ritual of the fashion show in order to assist customers in selecting their clothing (Vorführdamen). The two types of mannequins coexisted in a bizarre dynamic that ranged from an uncanny resemblance between the lifeless and the living to stark contrast and mutual exclusion — all intended to entice more passers-by to stop by the store. It was actually very common for a live person to be made up as an ordinary, inanimate mannequin and "perform" with them in a display window, mimicking the dolls' expressions. This chapter combines a close reading of several literary and journalistic texts that feature mannequins as their protagonists with a historical investigation of Weimar mannequins' social backgrounds, professional careers, and cultural status.

Chapter 6 closes the circle of exploration with a return to the complex relationship between the classical *flâneur* and the modern, fashion-conscious woman. A close discussion of Irmgard Keun's 1931 debut book *Gilgi — eine von uns* (Gilgi, One of Us) revisits the multiple facets of the 1920s experience of fashion and modernity as it is imagined and discussed in the novel. Along with other short stories in women's and fashion magazines of the time, *Gilgi* is a work of fiction that foregrounds convincingly the New Woman's ambivalent position between prescriptive norms and imaginative practices, between emancipatory potential and constricting realities, between the displays and debates of fashion in Weimar Germany.

Notes

[1] Frevert notes the ambiguity of this "superficial modernization": While the feminization of white-collar work was the beginning of real emancipation for women, office work performed by women was subordinate to, less independent, and worse paid than office work assigned to men. See Ute Frevert, *Women in German History: From Bourgeois Emancipation to Sexual Liberation*, trans. Stuart McKinnon-Evans, Terry Bond, and Barbara Norden (Oxford: Berg, 1989), 176–83.

[2] The period of the Weimar Republic is one of the most studied in German history, and the books on it are too numerous to mention here. I find Detlev Peukert's work particularly insightful in its attention to contradictory and crisis-ridden aspects of Weimar modernity. See Detlev J. K. Peukert, *Die Weimarer Republik: Krisenjahre der klassischen Moderne* (Frankfurt am Main: Suhrkamp, 1987); in English, Detlev J. K. Peukert, *The Weimar Republic: The Crisis of Classical Modernity*, trans. Richard Deveson (New York: Hill & Wang, 1989).

[3] Anne Hollander, "Women and Fashion," *Women, the Arts, and the 1920s in Paris and New York*, ed. Kenneth W. Wheeler and Virginia Lee Lussier (New Brunswick: Transaction Publishers, 1982), 117.

[4] *Die Angestellten* was first published in installments in the feuilleton section of the *Frankfurter Zeitung*. The first postwar edition of the text appeared in 1959. See Siegfried Kracauer, *Die Angestellten: Aus dem neuesten Deutschland* (Bonn: Verlag für Demoskopie, 1959). I am referring here to the English language edition: Siegfried Kracauer, *The Salaried Masses: Duty and Distraction in Weimar Germany*, trans. Quintin Hoare (London: Verso, 1998).

[5] Dr. Berthold, *Volkswirtschaft in Zahlen und Bildern: Eine Erinnerung an die Ausstellung im Herbst 1929; Was, wie, wo kauft die Hausfrau?* (Berlin: Reichsverband Deutscher Hausfrauenvereine, 1930), 1 and 4. Quoted in Janet Ward, *Weimar Surfaces: Urban Visual Culture in 1920s Germany* (Berkeley: U of California P, 2001), 86.

⁶ For a historic account of the fashion store Gerson, see Mila Ganeva, "Elegance and Spectacle in Berlin: The Gerson Fashion Store and the Rise of the Modern Fashion Show in the Early Twentieth Century," in *The Spaces and Places of Fashion: 1800–2007*, ed. John Potvin (New York: Routledge, 2008).

⁷ For detailed data on sales and exports, see Erwin Wittkowski, *Die Berliner Damenkonfektion* (Leipzig: Gloeckner, 1928). There are several sources that provide a historical overview of Berlin's *Konfektion*, which was concentrated in a part of the city known as Hausvogteiplatz: see Irene Guenther, *Nazi Chic? Fashioning Women in the Third Reich* (Oxford: Berg, 2004), 78–85; Maria Makela, "The Rise and Fall of the Flapper Dress: Nationalism and Anti-Semitism in Early-Twentieth-Century Discourses on German Fashion," *Journal of Popular Culture* 34.3 (2000): 183–208; Gretel Wagner, "Die Mode in Berlin," in *Berlin en vogue: Berliner Mode in der Photographie*, ed. F. C. Gundlach and Uli Richter (Berlin: Wasmuth, 1993), 113–46; Uwe Westphal, *Berliner Konfektion und Mode, 1836–1939: Die Zerstörung einer Tradition*, 2nd ed. (Berlin: Edition Hentrich, 1992); Christine Waidenschlager, "Berliner Mode der Zwanziger Jahre zwischen Couture und Konfektion," in *Mode der 20er Jahre*, ed. Christine Waidenschlager and Christa Gustavus (Berlin: Wasmuth, 1993), 20–31; Moritz Loeb, *Berliner Konfektion* (Berlin: Hermann Seemann, 1906); Jochen Krengel, "Das Wachstum der Berliner Bekleidungsindustrie vor dem Erstem Weltkrieg," *Jahrbuch für die Geschichte Mittel- und Ostdeutschlands* 27 (1978): 206–37; Christine Waidenschlager, "Aus den Anfängen der Berliner Konfektion," in *Berliner Chic: Mode von 1820 bis 1990*, ed. Christine Waidenschlager and Christa Gustavus (Berlin: Stiftung Stadtmuseum Berlin, 2001), 11–24; and Werner Dopp, *125 Jahre Berliner Konfektion* (Berlin: Ernst Staneck, 1962).

⁸ For example, two recent monographs that focus exclusively on literary texts and films from the Weimar Republic and engage in analysis primarily of social, gender, and sexual identities during the period are Richard W. McCormick's *Gender and Sexuality in Weimar Modernity: Film, Literature and "New Objectivity"* (New York: Palgrave, 2001) and Vibeke Rützou Petersen's *Women and Modernity in Weimar Germany: Reality and Representation in Popular Fiction* (New York: Berghahn, 2001).

⁹ A notable exception is Sabine Hake's pioneering article on women and fashion in Weimar Germany, "In the Mirror of Fashion," in *Women in the Metropolis: Gender and Modernity in Weimar Culture*, ed. Katharina von Ankum (Berkeley: U of California P, 1997), 185–201.

¹⁰ To be sure, given the spectacularity of the clothes from the Weimar period there is no dearth of descriptive (rather than analytical) studies of Weimar fashions, mostly in exhibition catalogues; see for example Waidenschlager and Gustavus, *Berliner Chic: Mode von 1820 bis 1990*, and Gesa Kessemeier's *Sportlich, sachlich, männlich: Das Bild der "Neuen Frau" in den zwanziger Jahren; Zur Konstruktion geschlechtsspezifischer Bilder in der Mode der Jahre 1920 bis 1929* (Dortmund: Edition Ebersbach, 2000).

¹¹ See Andreas Huyssen, *After the Great Divide: Modernism, Mass Culture, Postmodernism* (Bloomington: Indiana UP, 1986), viii–ix.

¹² Patrice Petro, *Joyless Streets: Women and Melodramatic Representation of Weimar Germany* (Princeton, NJ: Princeton UP, 1989).

[13] Janet Ward, *Weimar Surfaces*, 2–3.

[14] See James Laver's preface to Gertrude Aretz, *The Elegant Woman: From the Rococo Period to Modern Times*, trans. James Laver (London: G. G. Harrap & Co., 1932), 4. For a popular history of fashion and manners, see Max von Boehn, *Die Mode: Menschen und Moden im neunzehnten Jahrhundert* (Munich: F. Bruckmann, 1924).

[15] Jürgen Habermas, *Der philosophische Diskurs der Moderne* (Frankfurt am Main: Suhrkamp, 1985), 18, translated by Frederick Lawrence as *The Philosophical Discourse of Modernity: Twelve Lectures* (Cambridge, MA: MIT Press, 1987), 9.

[16] See Georg Simmel, "Die Mode," in *Philosophische Kultur* (Potsdam: Gustav Kiepenheuer, 1911), 31–64. The distinction between *Mode* and *Tracht* was repeatedly brought up in political and philosophical debates in Germany during the 1800s and up until the Nazi period. *Tracht* was considered representative of the German national spirit and was juxtaposed to *Mode*, a synonym for the encroachment of French, American, or Jewish influence into German cultural and economic life, or just a symbol of the corrupting nature of modern civilization. For more on these debates, see Ruth Bleckwenn, "Antimodische Tendenzen in Deutschland," *Waffen- und Kostümkunde* 1 (1977): 66–77. For a vigorous defense of the German *Tracht* and an extremely conservative, nationalistic, and particularly negative assessment of international fashions and ready-made clothes (Konfektion) before the First World War, see the writings of Norbert Stern: *Mode und Kultur* (Dresden: Lemm & Weiss, 1915) and his essays "Weltmode als politisches Machtinstrument," "Mode und Tracht als Gegensätze," and "Praktische Wege zu einer Weltmode" in *Die Weltpolitik der Weltmode* (Stuttgart: Deutsche Verlags-Anstalt, 1915).

[17] See Werner Sombart, *Wirthschaft und Mode: Ein Beitrag zur Theorie der modernen Bedarfsgestaltung* (Wiesbaden: J. F. Bergmann, 1902); reprinted in *Die Listen der Mode*, ed. Silvia Bovenschen (Frankfurt am Main: Suhrkamp, 1986), 81–104; in English, "Economy and Fashion: A Theoretical Contribution on the Formation of Modern Consumer Demand," in *The Rise of Fashion: A Reader*, ed. Daniel Leonhard Purdy, trans. Kelly Barry (Minneapolis, U of Minnesota P, 2004), 310–16.

[18] For a discussion of Sombart's work vis-à-vis the female consumer, see Victoria de Grazia's introduction to *The Sex of Things: Gender and Consumption in Historical Perspective*, ed. V. de Grazia (Berkeley: U of California P, 1996), 1–14.

[19] See Thorstein Veblen, "Dress as an Expression of Pecuniary Culture," in *The Theory of the Leisure Class* (New York: Macmillan, 1899), 103–15. This division of tasks between the genders was reflected in changes within the fashion industry itself in the second half of the nineteenth century. The famous designer Charles Frederick Worth, who is credited with inventing *haute couture*, succeeded in elevating the designer's job to a prestigious and independent male profession. And while the male couturier was transformed from an artisan into a sovereign artist and creator of fashion, the woman became a mere consumer of fashion, albeit at the level of luxury. See Gilles Lipovetsky, *The Empire of Fashion: Dressing Modern Democracy*, trans. Catherine Porter (Princeton, NJ: Princeton UP, 1994), 74–75.

[20] See Friedrich Vischer, *Mode und Cynismus: Beiträge zur Kenntnis unserer Culturformen und Sittenbegriffe* (Stuttgart: K. Wittwer, 1879); in English,

"Fashion and Cynicism," in *The Rise of Fashion: A Reader*, ed. and with an introduction by Daniel L. Purdy (Minneapolis: U of Minnesota P, 2004), 153–62. See also Immanuel Kant, *Anthropologie in pragmatischer Hinsicht. Werke*, 12 (Frankfurt am Main: Suhrkamp, 1964). Nietzsche, who reflected intensively on the essence of modern life, wrote that all modern culture "requires extreme mannerliness and the newest fashions, inward hasty grasp and exploitation of ephemera, indeed of the momentary: and absolutely nothing else! As a result, it is embodied in the heinous nature of journalists, the slaves of the three M's: the moment (Moment), opinions (Meinungen), and fashions (Moden)." See Friedrich Nietzsche, *Sämtliche Werke*, ed. G. Colli and M. Montinari (Berlin: de Gruyter, 1980), 7:817.

[21] Both essays have been discussed extensively in secondary literature, but nearly always separately. See Guy Oakes, "The Problem of Women in Simmel's Theory of Culture," in *Georg Simmel: On Women, Sexuality and Love*, ed. and trans. Guy Oakes (New Haven: Yale UP, 1984), 3–62; and David Frisby and Mike Featherstone's introduction to *Simmel on Culture: Selected Writings*, ed. David Frisby and Mike Featherstone (London: SAGE, 1997), 3–25.

[22] Simmel, "Die Mode," 42. The English translation is from *Simmel on Culture*, 192. Subsequent page numbers given in parentheses in this paragraph refer to *Simmel on Culture*.

[23] Georg Simmel, "Female Culture," in *Georg Simmel: On Women, Sexuality and Love*, 70–71.

[24] Simmel's failure to envisage a possible reconciliation between achieved independence and retained difference was criticized by a friend and contemporary, Marianne Weber, in her 1913 essay "Die Frau und die objektive Kultur" (The Woman and Objective Culture), which was reprinted in Marianne Weber, *Frauenfragen und Frauengedanken: Gesammelte Aufsätze* (Tübingen: Verlag von T. C. B. Mohr, 1919), 95–133. For more on Weber's criticism of Simmel, see Suzanne Vromen, "Georg Simmel and the Cultural Dilemma of Women," *History of European Ideas* 8 (1987): 563–79.

[25] Similar views were not uncommon among Simmel's contemporaries. Regarding the on-going reforms in clothing design as well as women's increasing emancipation, Viennese designer Adolf Loos predicted in 1898 that "velvet and silk, flowers and ribbons, feathers and paints will fail to have their effect. They will disappear." See Adolf Loos, *Spoken into the Void: Collected Essays, 1897–1900* (Cambridge, MA: MIT Press, 1982), 103.

[26] In a newspaper report on the 1896 bourgeois women's congress, which he attended, Simmel seized the occasion to express his unequivocal support for the dress reform. See Vromen, "Georg Simmel and the Cultural Dilemma of Women," 566.

[27] It should be added that the dress-reform movement received support also from a third source, namely the nationalistic cultural critics who saw in the deformities caused by corsets a threat to the health and future of the German nation. See Paul Schultze-Naumburg, *Die Kultur des weiblichen Körpers als Grundlage für die Frauenkleidung* (Jena: E. Diederichs, 1922). For some examples of the medical arguments, see Karl Spener, *Die jetzige Frauenkleidung und Vorschläge zu ihrer*

Verbesserung: Mit 10 Abbildungen im Text (Berlin: n.p., 1897); Heinrich Lahmann, *Die Reform der Kleidung* (Stuttgart: Zimmer, 1898); Carl Heinrich Stratz, *Frauenkleidung und ihre natürliche Entwicklung* (Stuttgart: F. Enke, 1900); and Otto Neustätter, *Die Reform der Frauenkleidung auf gesundheitlicher Grundlage* (Munich: Datterer, 1903). For some representative treatises on dress reform by artists, especially architects and designers, see Henry van de Velde, *Die künstlerische Hebung der Frauentracht* (Krefeld, Germany: Kramer & Baum, 1900); Alfred Mohrbutter, *Das Kleid der Frau: Ein Beitrag zur künstlerischen Gestaltung des Frauen-Kleides* (Leipzig: A. Koch, 1904); Anna Muthesius, *Das Eigenkleid der Frau* (Krefeld: Kramer & Baum, 1903); and Maria van de Velde, *Album moderner, nach Künstlerentwürfen ausgeführter Damenkleider, ausgestellt auf der großen allgemeinen Ausstellung für Bekleidungswesen in Krefeld* (Düsseldorf: F. Wolfrum, 1900).

Discourses on Fashion

1: The Fashion Journalist: *Flâneur* or New Woman?

A GLANCE AT the two thick volumes of the 1930 *Reichshandbuch der deutschen Gesellschaft* (a high-brow, illustrated "Who's Who?" of German society of the late 1920s) will reveal, among the handful of women featured, two representatives of the world of fashion — journalists Ola Alsen and Elsa Herzog.[1] In sharp contrast to all the other photographs in the volume, the studio portraits of Alsen and Herzog show the two women almost full-length; both are stylishly dressed, smile coquettishly at the imaginary audience, and reveal an almost narcissistic pleasure in the spectacle of fashion that they are part of. The photograph of Herzog captures her both in profile and reflected in a mirror, as if she were inspecting her elegant attire: she is holding apart the fur collar of her coat to reveal the soft folds of a shiny evening gown.

In many ways these two fashion writers resemble the film and theater stars featured frequently in the pages of the fashion magazines they edited or contributed to for many years. Indeed, during the 1920s both became media celebrities in the modern sense, embodying, displaying, and performing the styles they wrote about. Alsen was a familiar name to the public as a fashion expert, since she not only wrote regularly for *Elegante Welt* and other mass-circulation magazines and film periodicals of the time (*Moden-Spiegel*, *Sport im Bild*, and *Film-Kurier*), but she was also known to pose as a model for leading Berlin fashion salons.[2] And Herzog had been a staff writer on fashion for *Der Konfektionär* since 1893 and was fashion editor for *Die praktische Berlinerin*, *Die Dame*, and *Die Woche* from 1915 to the late 1920s.[3]

In the early days of the fashion press in Germany — in the late eighteenth and throughout the nineteenth centuries — most of the commentators were men, and it was not until around 1900 that an increasing number of women writers started to work regularly for the fashion pages as reporters or editors, signing their names under the articles and quickly becoming popular with the mass reader. While such texts by male writers — tightly interwoven with Enlightenment philosophy, moral critique, and consumer education — have been scrutinized thoroughly, the writings by female fashion journalists from the decades before and after the First World War have remained a relatively obscure area within German cultural studies of early twentieth century, despite the fact that they offer rare insight into contemporary women's routine practices with regard to fashion, their

Fig. 1: Ola Alsen, *Reichshandbuch der deutschen Gesellschaft*, vol. 1, 1930. Staatsbibliothek Berlin.

specific understanding of modernity, and the daily dilemmas of their modern lifestyle.[4] A closer look at texts by female fashion journalists such as the two prominent society figures featured in the *Reichshandbuch*, in combination with an analysis of these women's public presence, cultural status,

Fig. 2: Elsa Herzog, *Reichshandbuch der deutschen Gesellschaft*, vol. 1, 1930. Staatsbibliothek Berlin.

and specific aesthetic sensibilities, sheds light on the interrelationship between modernity, fashion, and femininity. It reveals, in fact, that Alsen and Herzog, along with other fashion journalists who became quite popular because of their writing, their cultivation of public personae, and their own dandified appearance, can be considered, in Rhonda Garelick's words, "precursors of the modern charismatic media personality."[5]

The female fashion journalist had an affinity with both the *flâneur* and the New Woman, conceptual figures traditionally associated not only with particular modes of experiencing modernity in the early twentieth century but also with a keen interest in the sartorial codes of society and the various practices of fashion. In his writings the *flâneur*, being a man of the crowds and an impervious onlooker, was constantly observing and documenting the metropolitan spectacle of fashion to which he felt perpetually attracted. The New Woman, for her part, was often defined and characterized by the style of her clothing. Since she was present in the public spaces of modern cities in a variety of professional and social roles, she was seen as the personification of the revolutionary changes in women's fashions from the 1880s until the 1920s, when the corset was abandoned, the dresses became shorter and more comfortable to wear, and the pants, suit, and tie were adopted as part of the female wardrobe.

However, there were also definite differences between these related cultural phenomena, largely because of gender. Because of the *flâneur*'s emphasis on aloof independence, provocative individuality, and narcissistic pleasure in being dressed in the latest, finest, and most dazzling garments, *flânerie* has often been equated with certain forms of dandyism, presenting a specifically male mode of observation, self-fashioning, and experience of modernity and leaving no space for women. The *flâneur*-as-dandy has been persistently defined as an artist, writer, or journalist capable of capturing the essence of modern life, whereas a woman within this paradigm is often relegated to a place inside the work of art. She has usually been considered an object of observation, an artistic product, an image to fix and inspire the male imagination. Therefore the late nineteenth-century emergence of the modern New Woman, who rejected the corset and wore reform dress instead, who smoked, enjoyed sports, worked outside the home, and participated more and more in public life, was often perceived as a threat to the traditional gender division and to the very existence of the *flâneur*.

The female fashion journalist appears to have been a peculiar cultural "crossbreed" or blend of the *flâneur* and the New Woman, one who redefined the stereotypical concept of the New Woman as the threatening opposite of the *flâneur*. Rather than an object of representation, an image constructed by society's desires and fears, the fashion journalist represented the female intellectual as an active participant within modern experience. She was indeed in many respects a New Woman — emancipated, economically independent, with a profession and career of her own; at the same time, she was to a certain extent a "female dandy," who captivated the public's attention with her extravagant appearance, and a "female *flâneur*," who had mastered the art of astutely observing metropolitan life. With their texts published regularly in the mass press, however, fashion journalists demonstrated that they were not merely imitators of the male prototypes of the *flâneur* and dandy: engaged in a very specific sphere of cultural practice — commentary on and the promotion of fashion for the mass reader — they revealed modernity's specific effect on the everyday lives of German women between the wars.

The *Flâneur*: Origins, Alignments, and Metamorphoses

The 1893 edition of *Larousse: Grand Dictionnaire Universel* defined the *flâneur* as a loiterer, a fritterer away of time, and emphasized that he could exist only in big cities, but also posited that a *flâneur* could be an artist for whom the urban spectacle provided valuable material for observation.[6] The earliest mention cited by *Larousse* is to Balzac's *Comédie humaine* (1831–47), and the *flâneur* is usually seen as typical of mid-nineteenth-century Paris. An earlier, anonymous, pamphlet from 1806, however, describes a day in the life of a certain M. Bonhomme, a typical *flâneur* of the Bonaparte era, and presents clearly all the primary characteristics of this cultural figure of modernity.[7] In his aimless and solitary sauntering around Paris, M. Bonhomme combines the regularity of a routine — he makes the same rounds day in and day out — with an acute interest in the newest inventions of the modern age, such as the transatlantic telegraph and new building technologies. The *flâneur* represented by M. Bonhomme has a secure income and is seemingly free from familial and work responsibilities. He is keenly interested in dress as a vital component of the urban spectacle and keeps a "little diary recording all the most curious things he had seen and heard during the course of his wanderings."[8] Although by wearing the same brown suit all the time and being generally rather badly dressed he exhibits none of the sartorial characteristics of his successors, and although his relationship to the city lacks the intensity of later *flâneurs*, he nevertheless displays most of the archetypal traits subsequently discussed in the writings of Baudelaire and of twentieth-century theorists of *flânerie* such as Walter Benjamin, Siegfried Kracauer, and Franz Hessel. Most important, the description of M. Bonhomme foreshadowed the *flâneur*'s key future roles of writer, journalist, voyeur, and intellectual-outsider suspended from social obligations.

In her study of nineteenth-century Paris, Priscilla Ferguson traces the metamorphoses of this early *flâneur* against the background of the city's changing political and social configuration from the 1830s until the end of the century. Balzac's *flâneurs* in the *Comédie humaine* celebrate urban enchantment in relatively uncomplicated ways. They are writers as well as readers of the urban text, philosophers and creative artists, and distant observers of city life, but also active participants who are constantly seduced by the urban spectacle. As Ferguson states, "the urban discourse secured in the texts of Balzac and his contemporaries is a discourse of placement, of exploration and explanation," and the role of the *flâneur* was to control through narration the urban spectacle.[9] *Flânerie* became a much more problematical cultural practice by the middle of the century, when Paris was torn down and rebuilt under the aegis of the prefect Haussmann. The urban milieu of the *flâneur* changed radically: the old urban maze of arcades and the cozy street corners were replaced by broad boulevards and fashionable promenades, racetracks and expansive parks, new apartment buildings and impressive department stores. This completely transformed urban landscape necessarily gave rise to a different observer of the city, one whose relationship to metropolitan modernity was marked more by anguish and displacement than by unreserved enchantment.

It is against this changed historical background that Baudelaire's seminal essay "Le peintre de la vie moderne" (The Painter of Modern Life, 1863) is often read. Baudelaire signaled the appearance of the *flâneur* as the new, modern "hero," whose creative energies were still forcefully ignited by the city, but whose blasé attitude connoted not so much superiority as marginality and estrangement.[10] There are, however, two further aspects of this classic treatise that deserve more critical attention. First, Baudelaire merges the *flâneur*, who observes, and the dandy, who displays himself for observation, into one figure, a more complicated cultural phenomenon in our understanding of modernity. According to Baudelaire, it was the dandy who both succumbed to the fascination of the city spectacle and was able to discern the "modern" on its surface was, but he was also an "observer," "idler," "philosopher," and *flâneur*.[11] As an artist, art critic, or writer, he is "looking for that quality which you must allow me to call 'modernity'; for I know of no better word to express the idea that I have in mind. He makes it his business to exact from fashion whatever element it may contain of poetry within history, to distill the eternal from the transitory."[12]

Second, notice the prominence of fashion here as the most striking sign of modernity.[13] Baudelaire marked the beginning of an enduring tradition linking modernity primarily to modes of visual perception centered in a male spectator or artist — the painter of modern life was likened to a "kaleidoscope gifted with consciousness" — and to heightened sensitivity to the superficial, ephemeral, and contingent, the "things even most trivial in appearance."[14] Because Baudelaire viewed fashion as key to interpreting modernity, he insisted that the *flâneur* as artist and as dandy had to be attuned to every minuscule shift in contemporary fashion in order to present a truthful picture of modern life:

> If a fashion or the cut of a garment has been slightly modified, if bows and curls have been supplanted by cockades, if *bavolets* have been

enlarged and *chignons* have dropped a fraction towards the nape of the neck, if waists have been raised and skirts have become fuller, be very sure that his eagle eye will have already spotted it.[15]

Significantly, in Baudelaire's interpretation, the representation of modernity was inseparable from the artist's "eye" for fashion. As a result the practices of fashion became unambiguously gendered: the critical, distanced observation of the fashion spectacle was the male artist's primary tool in his search for modernity, while fashion as a mundane, day-to-day practice and as participation in this urban spectacle came to be defined as a purely feminine occupation. This is a crucial distinction in the tradition of defining modernity, which will be addressed in the last section of this chapter.

Mid- and late-nineteenth-century *flâneurs* and dandies have also been studied in one of their new professional incarnations, as journalists and writers who contributed to a radical change in the hierarchy and structure of literary genres.[16] Urban life and the mass reader in the metropolis generated a demand for different forms of writing gathered under the rubric feuilleton: the gossip column, fashion essays, amusing articles about everyday life, and the serialized novel. Thus, the idle strolls of the *flâneur* suddenly acquired commercial value; in order to secure a living, the *flâneur* and the dandy began to contribute regularly to the rapidly changing and commercialized Parisian press.[17] The *flâneur*-turned-journalist was the man-about-town who recorded the myriad sights and sounds of the city, instilled life into the genre of the feuilleton, and endowed this new kind of literature with inquisitiveness, irony, anecdotal lightness, and melancholy. In short, the *boulevardiers*, as Kracauer calls the dandies and the *flâneurs* of the mid- to late nineteenth century, became "institutionalized" (77).

Both Kracauer and Walter Benjamin point out, however, that as *flânerie* became increasingly affected by mass consumption, the *flâneur*'s pose of aloof detachment, ostentatious inaction, and irony appeared less an extravagance than the expression of a strained relationship with his social environment. *Flâneurs*, always men, were financially dependent on conventional bourgeois society but at the same time lived on its margins; they imagined themselves unsullied by capitalist concerns for money and outside the despised philistine society, but in fact they had become purveyors of commodities in that they were paid to write for the entertainment of the public.

The Return of *Flânerie*: Benjamin, Kracauer, and Hessel

The *flâneur* as a historical personage may have become extinct not long after the demise of his original habitat, the Parisian arcades, in the mid-nineteenth century, but he was nevertheless transformed into one of those mythical figures who have served as a projection screen for continuous reflection on modernity and its origins. Within German culture the *flâneur* became a sort of shorthand for the Berlin myth of the 1920s, representing the city as the locus of cultural vitality, social dynamics, and cosmopolitan glamor. The Berlin *flâneur* has been periodically resurrected in twentieth-century literary and political discourse and seems to thrive particularly at moments of imagined "return"; in fact, as Susan Buck-Morss has pointed out, he has become "more visible in his afterlife than in his flourishing."[18] His first and most spectacular return was in the late 1920s and early 1930s, when the *flâneur* was discussed extensively in the work of German writers and cultural critics such as Walter Benjamin, Siegfried Kracauer, and Franz Hessel. The composite portrait of the *flâneur* that emerges from the works of these three authors helps to elucidate the specific position of the female fashion journalist.

Walter Benjamin (1892–1940) theorized most influentially on the *flâneur*, first in his review of Franz Hessel's collection of essays *Spazieren in Berlin* (Walking in Berlin, 1929). In this piece, titled programmatically "Die Wiederkehr des Flaneurs" (The Return of the Flaneur), Benjamin suggested that in the 1920s *flânerie*, reemerging as a compelling mode of reading and observing the modern metropolis, was already an anachronistic phenomenon. The "endless spectacle of *flânerie*," believed to belong completely to the past, was a phantasm resurrected from nineteenth-century Paris.[19] Yet at the same time, both Benjamin and Hessel found themselves attracted to the *flâneur*, not solely out of nostalgia for an irretrievable past, but because of the perceived heuristic potential of *flânerie*: It constituted a cultural practice using the city as a "mnemonic for the lonely walker," as a site of privileged access to the origins of the present world.[20] Benjamin lauded the *flâneur*'s perceptive sensitivity and the heuristic potential of *flânerie* in general. At the end of his review, he was even tempted to acknowledge certain utopian, redemptive qualities attached to the *flâneur* and to his project of retrieving the past and discerning the essence of the modern from its fading traces and mundane details on the surface of everyday life.[21]

Benjamin's subsequent studies of the *flâneur* chart a rather contradictory and paradoxical trajectory of development.[22] Initially, his concept of *flânerie* was based on a blend of urban figures represented in Baudelaire's poetry and Edgar Alan Poe's short story "The Man of the Crowd." According to that original concept, the fascinated, absorbed, wandering *flâneur* was a "man of the crowd," who found pleasure and exhilaration in observing the spectacle of the street and who could easily mix in and move with the masses. "An intoxication comes over the man who walks long and aimlessly through the streets," wrote Benjamin in *The Arcades Project* (417).[23] By contrast, in the essay "On Some Motifs in Baudelaire" ("Über einige Motive in Baudelaire") Benjamin offered a radically revised definition of *flânerie*: "The man of the crowd is no flâneur. . . . Let many attend to their daily affairs; the man of leisure can indulge in the perambulations of the flâneur only if as such he is already out of place."[24] The man of leisure has retreated from the crowd in the street in an attempt to retain a sense of control over the chaos of the city, and his perspective has changed to that of the man at the window. As an example Benjamin sites E. T. A. Hoffmann's story "Des Vetters Eckfenster" (The Cousin's Corner Window), in which the narrator observes the crowded streets from his window, separated from both enticement and threat by his immobility.[25] With the advance of modernity, the *flâneur* has turned into a detached, aloof, and almost paralyzed observer who likes to maintain his distance from the crowd and who, whenever he ventures into the street, appears out of place and even suspicious.

In all of Benjamin's writings, the *flâneur* remains a complex and overdetermined figure in the prehistory of modernity, a figure drawn from readings of Baudelaire's essays and poetry, Poe's fiction, Balzac and Dickens, Marx's theory of commodity fetishism, and from his own documentary and historical research about nineteenth-century Paris. The *flâneur* is many things at the same time: a historical personage among the inhabitants of nineteenth-century Paris, a representation of an aesthetic sensitivity and of a specific mode of experience, a literary motif, and an embodiment of a modern commodity in its relation to the masses and the literary market. The poet who identified the streets with a cozy interior, who dissolved in the crowds and exposed himself to the shocks of metropolitan experience, was actually engaged in a futile attempt to fill the emptiness and break the isolation that prevailed in the cold world of commodity exchange, rational order, and private interests. In Baudelaire, Benjamin saw the anachronistic, bygone figure of the *bohème* and the dandy, intoxicated by the spectacle of the city and at the same time completely marginalized by rationalized modern life. Finally, some parts of Benjamin's writing on the *flâneur* seem to directly reproach the self-delusions of intellectuals, a reproach some critics believe was aimed primarily at his own contemporaries.[26]

Although Benjamin's reflections on the *flâneur* were rather heterogeneous and contradictory, they contain observations that persisted in all variations of the *flâneur* theme, and they provide a touchstone for a reassessment of his theory of modernity. As Susan Buck-Morss has emphasized in her study on Benjamin, the *flâneur* is consistently considered the "*Ur-form* of the modern intellectual" and the origin of this class of literary producers who, like Benjamin, study modernity in its mundane, mass-cultural, fleeting, and superficial manifestations.[27] It was Benjamin, too, who examined thoroughly the early connection between the perceptive style of the *flâneur* and that of the journalist, and who insisted that journalism was becoming the legitimizing "social foundation" for the practice of *flânerie*.²⁸ Benjamin was interested not only in the mid-nineteenth-century Parisian *flâneur* but also in the modern metamorphoses of this social type in Berlin: In the 1920s and 1930s, the *flâneur* was not (and could not be) a person of leisure but a salaried employee who produced news and literature for information and entertainment: he worked as a reporter-at-large covering the beat, a foreign correspondent, a photojournalist.

Unlike Benjamin, Siegfried Kracauer (1889–1966) was interested in *flânerie* not so much because it was the key to a nineteenth-century genealogy of modernity but because he deemed it a relevant sociological and journalistic practice, an apt "reflective-empirical engagement" with contemporary reality.²⁹ Nevertheless, when he did study nineteenth-century cultural phenomena — as in his major biographical work on Jacques Offenbach — Kracauer offered a similar leftist-Marxist interpretation of the *flâneur*. According to him, the nineteenth-century Paris *flâneur* was "the aimless saunterer who sought to conceal the gaping void around him and within him by imbibing a thousand casual impressions. Shop-window displays, prints, new buildings, smart clothes, elegant equipages, newspaper-sellers — he indiscriminately absorbed the spectacle of life that went on all around him."³⁰ In his texts based on critical observation of big-city life, Kracauer did not play the *flâneur* in the way Benjamin did, yet his cultural-sociological exploration of Berlin and Paris were epistemologically reminiscent of Benjamin's study of the late-nineteenth-century *flâneur*, especially in its concern with the gradual dismantling of those architectural forms, ornaments, and other details that bore witness to the origins of the modern epoch. In his 1932 essay "Straße ohne Erinnerung" (Street without Memory), Kracauer described how all traces of history had been eliminated from a particular street as a result of the continuous renovation, modernization, and mindless monumentalization of the city: "Perpetual change extinguishes the memory of a place. . . . Much of the ornamentation of the houses, which formed a kind of bridge to yesterday, has been knocked away."³¹ So, too, in his famous 1930 essay "Abschied von der Lindenpassage" (Farewell to the Linden Arcade), Kracauer reflected again on the soon-to-be transformed space that was traditionally considered a paradise for the *flâneur*'s inquisitive, slow-paced strolls.³² In the modern city the forces of continuous change erase memory and prevent *flânerie*.

Kracauer was, as Eckhardt Köhn called him, a "metaphysical *flâneur*" who deciphered empirical reality by living in the very middle of it.³³ In 1921 he started working as a journalist with the *Frankfurter Zeitung* (*FZ*); from 1924 until 1930 he was an editor of its feuilleton section, and from 1930 through 1933 he was permanently stationed as a reporter in Berlin. For many years, especially in the second half of his engagement with the *FZ*, Kracauer's publications were based on his exploration of the "surface" and the "superficial," which he found manifested on the streets of Berlin and Paris and in various phenomena of modern mass culture: film, radio, the chorus-line, and metropolitan architecture. His explorations led to what we may now call his "theory of the surface," which became the hallmark of Weimar's *flâneur*-turned-sociologist-of-everyday-life. In the German critical tradition Kracauer's mentor, Georg Simmel (1858–1918), had already established the connection between the man of modern metropolitan experience ("the blasé type") and the "surface" as a methodological tool and diagnostic trope. Simmel's collection of essays, *Philosophische Kultur* (1911), on fashion, flirtation, adventure, the differences between the sexes, and female culture elucidates how rich and complex a reading of surfaces can be.

Simmel's method was both provocative for his time and extremely influential. It consisted in the examination of "the most ephemeral and isolated surface phenomena of life" in order to form a "concept of modern culture."[34] He recognized that the prominence of the surface as the capitalist world became ever more industrialized and urbanized in the late nineteenth century adequately reflected the flattening-out of our perception of people, places, and historical tradition in the modern epoch. Not unlike many contemporary cultural critics, Simmel registered the loss of depth in many aspects of modern life, especially in individuals' relations with each other. The surface was commonly seen as the world of pure appearance, as the opposite of substance. But instead of condemning these phenomena, which other philosophers qualified as the decline of *Kultur* and the rise of *Zivilisation*, Simmel went on to "read" in detail the surface (die Ober-fläche), the upper, visible cover of the surrounding world — street and city life, table manners, clothes and fashions — in order to find out the deeper, underlying social forces of the present and its obscured links to the past and future.

Simmel's disciple Kracauer discovered and explored a different dimension of the surface as a diagnostic tool. In his writings after 1924, the surface metaphor refers less to the dynamics between "superficial" and "real" and more to the dynamics between "superficial" and "deep."[35] As Miriam Hansen has shown, the *Oberfläche* "increasingly loses its prefix and becomes a *Fläche*, a plane of preliminary configurations that require investigation and interpretation. No longer merely tokens of metaphysical decline, such configurations offer crucial insights into the historical dynamics of the present, that is into the present as a part of history."[36] The preface to Kracauer's much-cited essay "The Mass Ornament" contains *in nuce* the methodological approach to such surface investigation: "The position that an epoch occupies in the historical process can be determined more strikingly from the analysis of its inconspicuous surface-level expressions than from that epoch's judgments about itself."[37] According to Kracauer, the people capable of conducting this "surface investigation" in the "loneliness of the large cities" are representative of a new type of intellectuality, and he defines them as "those who wait" (die Wartenden):

> Perhaps the only remaining attitude is one of *waiting*. By committing oneself to waiting, one neither blocks one's path toward faith (like those who defiantly affirm the void) nor besieges this faith (like those whose yearning is so strong, it makes them lose all restraint). One waits, and one's waiting is a *hesitant* openness, albeit of a sort that is difficult to explain.[38]

These are the new "heroes of modern life," who walk in the footsteps of Baudelaire's and Benjamin's *flâneur*s and dandies and are similarly attentive to the myriad stimuli around them, but are less conspicuous, less nostalgic, and more future-oriented.

While Benjamin and Kracauer were becoming increasingly concerned about the "politics of loitering" and reflected continuously on the ideological implications of *flânerie* — whether as an act of individual passive observation it was an adequate response to modern social reality — their contemporary Franz Hessel (1880–1941) elaborated persistently on the aesthetic pleasures of *flânerie* and preferred to reenact nostalgically the postures of nineteenth-century *flâneurs* within the context of Weimar Berlin.[39] Most of his essays and short stories published in the literary periodicals of the 1920s and early 1930s brought back to life the classic Baudelairian *flâneur*: the narrator is inevitably a male observer, a gentleman of leisure, loitering around the city at his own pace, absorbed in the urban spectacle. In Hessel's writings the *flâneur* as a narrator and/or protagonist found his particular delight in practicing a form of walking slowly that appears both naïvely and provocatively anachronistic in a modern urban environment where speed reigns supreme. "To stroll slowly through busy streets is a particular pleasure. The haste of others plays around you like breakers in the surf," wrote Hessel in the opening piece of *Spazieren in Berlin* (1929), the same book that prompted Benjamin to declare the return of the *flâneur*.[40] As he sauntered leisurely, with no concrete purpose ("To be a proper *flâneur*, you can't have anything very particular in mind"), Hessel's *flâneur* quietly resisted the speed, rhythms, and ruptures imposed by modern life and thus stood out as a "suspicious character" (der Verdächtige), an outsider often mistaken for a pickpocket or a secret agent.[41] Intense observation paradoxically combined with passivity and an ostentatious disregard for the pragmatic side of life became staple characteristics of Hessel's *flânerie*; in the world of his texts, leisure (Müßiggang) was elevated to a complex art form, a philosophy of aloof, nostalgic, and definitely apolitical engagement in city realities: "The person taking a walk does not need to take sides, to get involved."[42]

More prominently even than the *flâneurs* in Benjamin's and Kracauer's texts, Hessel's *flâneur* established a notion of modernity divided along gender lines. His protagonists and narrators persistently and emphatically render the reflective and detached mode of experience as male. They imagine themselves in distinct opposition to the women in the city and the occasional female companion. If the "professional idler" appears suspicious on the streets of Berlin because his walk is too slow and not geared toward a concrete goal, the female characters are in a hurry, running errands, concerned about practical aspects of life, or holding a permanent job as in the short story "Das Lederetui" (The Leather Case, 1934): "I have my job. I've got to work in Paris," the female protagonist in the story says.[43] Moreover, Hessel believed that *flânerie* could and should be regarded as a modern art form, even though by the late 1920s it might have appeared outdated. Some of the "benefits" of mastering this art form were laid out in his central theoretical essay "Von der schwierigen Kunst spazieren zu gehen" (On the Difficult Art of Taking a Walk, 1932) and were tied to understanding modernity: "Only the *flâneur* can enjoy and comprehend the time we live in, especially when he is in the grip of this modern rhythm and is constantly pushed to hurry and pursue goals."[44]

The hedonistic aesthetics of this type of *flânerie* emphasized reliance on contingency and the unexpected; a lack of plans, goals, or practical reasons for the walk; and a naïve openness of perception. Hessel was convinced that women particularly needed to learn the proper art of strolling. He observed them rushing to and from work on the streets of Berlin, elegant and self-confident, and he thought that *flanieren* would take the edge off their independent and seemingly ambition-driven behavior. In an open letter "An die Berlinerin" (To the Berlin Woman, 1929) published in the German edition of the fashion magazine *Vogue*, he went so far as to appeal to these women to learn *flanieren* and slow down.[45] Thus Hessel became the most explicit proponent of the view that women were not *flâneur*s, hence could not be regarded as exemplary figures of modern consciousness and modern perception. And it is this gender distinction that has attracted particular attention recently as the *flâneur* has reemerged in the critical discourse on modernity and Benjamin, Kracauer, and Hessel have been reread intensively.

Women in Modernity: The *Flâneuse* and the New Woman

Feminist scholars have been quick to emphasize the predominantly male traits of *flânerie* as an experience of modernity. Critical analyses of the canonical texts on the *flâneur* — Baudelaire's metropolitan poems and his essay on "the painter of modern life," as well as Benjamin's writings — often lead to the conclusion that within the domain of literature, culture, and public life of the nineteenth and early twentieth centuries, a female *flâneur*, a *flâneuse*, is virtually impossible, or at least invisible, her existence precluded by the very definition of *flâneur*. Anke Gleber claims that the impossibility of the *flâneuse* within the nineteenth-century discourses on the *flâneur* is reflected on the linguistic level as well. In the *Larousse* entry quoted earlier, the feminine version of the noun *flâneur* refers not to a person but to an object. The word "flâneuse" designates, we are told, a kind of "reclining chair or a comfortable deck chair" that welcomes its occupant with womanly passivity. In the early twentieth century, the form *Flaneuse* was adopted into German explicitly to designate the female counterpart to the male *flâneur*, but at the same time, *Flaneuse* cannot help but be associated with words such as *Friseuse* (female hairdresser) and *Masseuse* (female massage practitioner) that denote typical and in part sexually suggestive occupations, and thus critics have avoided its use.[46]

The unbounded pursuit of perception, the unimpeded observation and unadulterated pleasure in the sensual stimuli of the street seem to have been reserved for men. Janet Wolff, Griselda Pollock, and Elizabeth Wilson, who all base their discussion of the *flâneur* on Benjamin's definition, have forcefully argued the impossibility of female *flânerie*, or at least the invisibility of women with the leisure to wander, watch, and browse in the streets of the growing European metropolises because of the traditional definition and practice. In "The Invisible Flaneuse" Wolff has declared that "in so far as the experience of the 'modern' occurred mainly in the public sphere, it was primarily men's experience."[47] The problem with this reductive statement, however, results from the fact that Wolff, as well as Pollock and to a certain extent Wilson, conflates the concept of *flâneur* as a fleeting social phenomenon of the mid-nineteenth century period with *flâneur* as a metaphor for the modern artist. The bourgeois man strolling around the city is described as the "archetypal occupant and observer of the public sphere," and his view of and attitude toward the modern urban world is equated with the style of male artists and writers.[48] Thus, according to these scholars women — both in the public spaces of the cities and within works of art — would be reduced to objects of the male gaze, diametrically opposed to the position of the *flâneur*. Rather than taking pleasure in the sights of the urban world around them, they would be looked at, and any attempt to practice unrestricted movement or observation would label them prostitutes.

More recent studies, however, separate the characteristics of *flânerie* from the feminist theory of the controlling male gaze and take into account the transmutations of the *flâneur* concept from the nineteenth into the twentieth century, so the search for alternative, female forms of *flânerie* have been more productive. Anne Friedberg, for example, claims that the rise of department stores and the advance of cinema have finally given middle-class women an opportunity, however limited and however closely connected to consumerism, to roam the cities on their own. Like other new, socially acceptable public activities for women in the late nineteenth century, such as museum visits and tourism, shopping and movie-going have granted women at least an illusion of spacial and temporal mobility, which Friedberg calls "imaginary flânerie" and links to a specifically new form of female subjectivity.[49] Gleber claims that by the beginning of the 1920s female *flânerie* in Weimar Berlin was not just imaginary but real, and films such as Walter Ruttmann's *Berlin, Symphony of the Big City* and urban texts by Weimar women such as Irmgard Keun demonstrated that women had become the subjects of their own perception of metropolitan modernity.[50]

The emerging female *flânerie* at the beginning of the twentieth century coincided with the rise of the New Woman, a highly visible and at the same time controversial cultural figure.[51] The New Woman won ground first in the context of English and American literature and culture of the late 1880s, when the term conjured up an image that combined features of the new fashions embraced by women and characteristics of their changing social status. Affected by the new enthusiasm for sports — skating, tennis, and bicycling — New Women began to wear "pantaloons" and, later, reform dress. At the same time, the term referred to emancipated women of the middle and upper classes who pursued university education, accepted positions in offices and "made their first assault upon the professions entering into competition with man of a new, purely economic kind."[52]

In England in the 1890s, the figure of the New Woman was mediated mostly through literary prototypes and was associated with some striking characteristics of the modern lifestyle: she often smoked in public, for example, and she was frequently equated with the suffragette or the vamp and could be either asexually intellectual or sexually loose.[53] When studied now as a female subject of modernity, she is compared with and usually juxtaposed to another prominent cultural figure of the same period, the English dandy, but in the writings of the dandies themselves — Max Beerbohm, Oscar Wilde, and Aubrey Beardsley — the New Woman was greeted with a mixture of fear and fascination, admiration and contempt. Indeed, she resembled the dandy in many respects: both glorified a self-created personality whose goal was to provoke a reaction in others by the way they dressed and behaved, and both had a penchant for extravagant fashions and were the first to launch them; yet the New Woman was much more vital, active, and self-assertive than the traditional English lady and thus assaulted the supremacy of the male and threatened the reign of the effete dandy.[54]

Somewhat later — in the 1920s — the term *Neue Frau* (the New Woman) came into common usage in German culture, and the stereotype became one of the most prominent symbols of modern times.[55] The illustrated magazines and movies disseminated her image to the mass-media consumers. In films, in photographs, on magazine covers, and in contemporary novels the *Neue Frau* was ubiquitous in the fashion of the time, with her bobbed hair, makeup, skirts above the knees. Her femininity — bust, waist, hips — was made less conspicuous by the cut of her attire, and a whole new erotic allure was based on her legs.

The main explorations of the phenomenon of the German New Woman have been dominated by the assumption that she was primarily a *Kunstprodukt* — an artificial cultural construct — created by the mass media.[56] She was viewed critically either as the modern female consumer of "elegant surface splendor" (films, illustrated magazines, shop windows, fashion), or as a mass-produced object for cultural consumption. Many recent studies have attempted to reconstruct the *Neue Frau*'s experience of modernity on the level of visual representation in the mass media or in terms of consumption patterns of mass-produced images by female readers and spectators. Scholars Maud Lavin and Patrice Petro, for example, have examined how and why the myth of the German New Woman was created and what mechanisms were employed to address and manipulate this audience. Petro analyzes in detail the representation of sexual identity in film and the illustrated press and argues that the liberal and the left-wing press in Weimar Germany promoted their own "one-dimensional types" of the New Woman. The bourgeois press defined her as "middle-class and deeroticized," and the leftist press saw her as "working-class and tragically maternal."[57] Lavin, on the other hand, contends that the essence of the New Woman's experience of modernity can be found in the representation of complexity and ambiguity, arguing that "any attempt to derive a uniform definition of the New Woman results in a disjointed composition of ill-fitting representational fragments," and that in order to capture the New Woman's experience of modernity, one has to see her as "a montage, a juxtaposition of allegorical elements."[58]

It is this search for the ambiguity and complexity, for the disjunctive and unsettling elements in the image of the New Woman, that prompts me to veer away from the now standard interpretation of her as either a "media myth" or a representative of a prevailing type of female consumption of mass culture. There has always been the suggestion that the New Woman figured also as the subject and the agent of modern experience. In Kracauer's essay "Kino in der Münzstraße" the woman appears within the context of mass culture as an observing subject, as the "Wartende" (the one who waits) — the position that Kracauer envisioned as most suitable for the Weimar intellectual:[59]

> A woman stands in front of a movie theater in a fake fur coat, chewing. She is chewing quietly, looking neither right or left, and waiting. She is middle-aged, an ordinary woman with nothing to do, and so she simply stands somewhere by the curb. If no one comes to pick her up and take her into the darkness of the theater, she will keep chewing on the same spot until the sun sinks idly in the west.[60]

In Heide Schlüpmann's reading of Kracauer's essay, the gesture of waiting — this peculiar state of being both enveloped in and strangely detached from the allure of mass-culture's fantasy production or the crowd's gaze — suggests a utopian potential for the female subject; "this waiting could be of ultimate importance," and the figure of the woman that history only glances at in passing could prove to be a central force.[61]

Some theoretical works have already touched upon the fascinating, albeit uneasy, alliance between women and intellectuals in Weimar Germany. In her pioneering essays on the New Woman, Atina Grossmann asserts that this figure was not just a "media myth," a "paranoid fantasy," or a mere "projection of male anxieties and fears," but also "a social reality that can be researched and documented." Grossmann urges fellow cultural historians to begin "to look at the New Woman as a producer and not only as consumer, as an agent constructing a new identity which was then marketed in mass culture, even as mass culture helped to form that identity."[62]

In response to Grossmann, Petro studies the textual constructs of the "New Woman" and how they appealed to female audiences. She sketches out how explanations of the "masculinization" of the New Woman in the pages of an illustrated magazine such as *Die Dame* split along gender lines, for example; while male sociologists, doctors, and psychologists detected in the modern appearance and independent behavior of the New Woman a threat to the traditional — or what they call "natural" — patriarchal order, female contributors to the magazine read into the "outward signs of masculinity" a changed relationship between women's identity and intellectuality. As Vanna Brenner wrote in a 1931 essay in *Die Dame*,

> men have never acknowledged that they are simply unsympathetic to our needs . . . [that] our intellectuality is a form of self-protection against a thousand futile pains. . . . They say "you are simply too intellectual" and thus express what they believe is unnatural or abnormal. For us, however, there remains the consciousness of our intellectuality and of [men's] great misunderstanding.[63]

Although Petro unequivocally sides with Brenner's particular view of women's modernity, namely that the New Woman was none other than the "female intellectual," she is not interested in pursuing some challenging questions that result from that conclusion: In what concrete forms of literary and artistic work did this modern "female intellectuality" crystallize? How did the works authored by "female intellectuals" in the twenties specifically inflect the understanding and interpretation of modernity? And who were these female intellectuals and what are the traces they left in the cultural production of the time?

Scholars Annelie Lütgens and Katharina Sykora point toward answers to these questions.[64] Both authors insist that if we are to redefine women's experience of Weimar urban modernity, we have to move away from the representations found in the seminal texts of male modernists such as Franz Hessel and Walter Benjamin and turn to the literary and artistic production of women themselves. Lütgens finds the richest sources for such studies in the magazines *Die Dame* and *Der Uhu*.[65] There, she contends, aspiring young writers such as Vicki Baum, Mascha Kaléko, Dinah Nelken, Polly Tieck, and many others "find a forum for their short texts in the fashion vignettes [Modenotizen] which are intelligently written, easy to read, and combined with critical commentary [Zeitkritik]."[66] A medium that was open to the female artists of the twenties was fashion design and illustration, a genre featured prominently in the pages of the same magazines.[67]

Let us consider some of the *Mode-Notizen* from *Die Dame* in order to reconstruct the cultural figure of the female fashion journalist as the key to understanding Weimar modernity from a female point of view. It becomes clear from rereading these texts that the fashion journalist can be best described as a combination of the *flâneuse*, the female dandy, the female intellectual, and the New Woman. Yet she gains her independence by means of her conscious efforts to define and negotiate notions such as modernity and modern experience on her own terms.

The Female Fashion Journalist

As we focus on the intricate position of female fashion journalists in the age of emerging mass-culture, we discover that to define fashion as a sphere of women's modernity is actually paradoxical. On the one hand, women commenting regularly on the newest trends in the illustrated magazines continued a tradition of defining modernity through fashion, a tradition that had been established in the mid-nineteenth century, with Baudelaire as its most influential proponent. These women studied modernity in its fleeting, superficial, everyday manifestations. On the other hand, however, by writing, interpreting, and dictating fashion from the pages of the illustrated press, the fashion editors and illustrators implicitly rejected some of the premises of the Baudelairian theory of modernity, namely that women cannot be anything but "the opposite of the dandy," an object rather than a source of critical observation and artistic representation.

Despite the fact that the female journalists for the illustrated, highbrow magazine *Die Dame* did not intend to write a theory of modernity and that their commentary on fashion was couched in the unpretentious style of the women's magazine, they were in fact challenging the domination of fashion from the authoritative perspective of the male *flâneur*. While theorists such as Baudelaire and, later, Benjamin sought modernity in the escalation of superficial changes and viewed fashion mainly as a problem of representation for the artist, female commentators on fashion in the age of mass-culture became more interested in the vantage point of the person wearing and displaying fashionable clothes, namely the modern woman. Like Baudelaire's modern painters, readers of *Die Dame* were urged and taught to select from a variety of fascinating and ephemeral possibilities in order to extract a durable essence designated as "modern." In her regular contributions to the *Mode-Notizen* of *Die Dame*, Johanna Thal insisted that expertise on questions of norm and aesthetic judgment had already shifted from the spectator of women's fashion to the female practitioner of it.[68] As Thal wrote in her 1921 essay "Kritisches über die Mode" (Critical Remarks on Fashion), "It is difficult to generalize about what is beautiful and desirable and what should be avoided, because sartorial beauty no longer depends only on the *judgment of the observer*, but also on the *individuality of the wearer*."[69]

It is no accident that in Thal's statement the noun "observer" is gendered as masculine ("der Beschauer") and "wearer" — as feminine ("die Trägerin"). This choice of words reflects a view of women's clothes and appearance that had been in place for many decades, namely that its paramount function is to delight, please, and stimulate the male gaze. "Show me the man," wrote Baudelaire, "who has never enjoyed, in a wholly detached way, the sight of a beautifully composed attire, and has not carried away with him an image inseparable from the beauty of the woman wearing it, thus making of the two, the woman and the dress, an indivisible whole. . . . Woman . . . carries out a kind of duty in devoting herself to the task of fostering a magic and supernatural aura around her appearance; she must create a sense of surprise, she must fascinate; idol that she is, she must adorn herself to be adored."[70] In view of such prevailing beliefs, Thal's position takes on the character of an indirect polemic against the tendency of those male viewers to offer in the pages of the magazine authoritative and generalized opinions about contemporary women and fashions.

Not unlike the male philosophers of fashion, the female journalists, too, linked modernity with a changed mode of vision resulting from the shock experience of a transformed social reality — crowds, industrialization, the big city. But as Marie von Bunsen reiterated in her numerous essays from the early twenties, there is a stark contrast between the ways in which men and women perceive and experience shocking visual stimuli. Bunsen differentiated between "Männeraugen" (men's eyes) and "Frauenaugen" (women's eyes) and insisted that however receptive and open-minded men might be toward fashion's revolutionary twists and turns, "their eyes always need much more time to adjust to every path-breaking novelty."[71] Later in the decade, commentator Anita Daniel often made a similar point, explaining how women had grown tired of being the leaders in matters of vision and fashion as well as of lifestyle:

> The last two generations of men have been observing passively the development of women. . . . Men have been watching — amused, annoyed, surprised, disturbed, with admiration or rejection, disinterest or unease. While women have changed fundamentally in many ways, men have remained the same. And now men and women have no common language any more.[72]

With this in mind, it is interesting to examine in more detail the position that female journalists envisioned and established for themselves in the ongoing discussion of fashion in the pages of *Die Dame*. Paradoxically, they assumed many of the idiosyncratic characteristics of the male *flâneur*/dandy. After all, it was their professional duty to be passionate observers, sensitively perceptive and linguistically able to convey the slightest nuances of modern dress, since the *Mode-Notizen* were primarily dedicated to descriptions and interpretation of new trends. So female journalists cultivated the dandy's sharp eye for minuscule variations in women's appearance.

Like the Baudelairian *flâneur*, the New Woman appeared "when democracy [was]not yet all-powerful, and aristocracy [was] just beginning to fall."[73] In other words, it was just before and then after the First World War that female fashion journalism in Germany gained prominence and the class boundaries signified by fashionable attire began to blur. Moreover, editors for *Die Dame* such as Elsa Herzog, Johanna Thal, Lily von Nagy, and Stephanie Kaul envisioned their task during the Weimar Republic to be the establishment of a new kind of nobility based not so much on descent or wealth but rather on individual elegance and distinguished taste — a view not unlike that of the classical *flâneur* in nineteenth-century France.

One can also view both the Baudelairean *flâneur*/dandy and the female fashion journalist of the 1920s as a complex and contradictory reaction to what Habermas calls a disintegrating literary public sphere, in which the emergence of a mass press transformed the "reasoning cultural audience" (kulturräsonierendes Publikum) into a "consuming cultural audience" (kulturkonsumierendes Publikum).[74] This process began in France in the mid-nineteenth century, and in Germany it did not reach its zenith until the Weimar Republic. Against the backdrop of an established mass culture, the particular idiosyncrasy of the dandy was his ambivalent relationship to the "crowd"; that is, he both embraced and distanced himself from mass society. On the one hand, he loved and needed the masses and adopted the posture of Narcissus, who, to use Baudelaire's phrase, "contemplates the crowd as though it were a river, offering his own image"; on the other hand, he demonstrated his own deliberate otherness through extravagant clothes and a posture of cool detachment. The dandy felt "a burning desire to create a personal form of originality, within the external limits of social conventions."[75]

This Baudelairian concept of the original self-creation of the male dandy amidst the "rising tide of democracy" may also be applicable to the female writers and artists who contributed to the highbrow fashion magazines in the 1920s. They resembled the *flâneur*/dandy in their modes of self-conception and self-representation on the pages of *Die Dame*, for example, and in their roles in the public sphere and their responses to a society in which the taste of the masses claimed legitimacy. However, they did not remain anonymous and aloof observers of big-city fashions; they became influential public figures personifying the notions of individual, self-invented elegance and dignity. *Die Dame* was distinct from most of the other mass-circulation fashion magazines, in that all of the texts and drawings related to the new trends of the changing seasons were signed by their female authors, so readers became familiar with their names and often addressed specific questions and requests to purchase a pattern (designed or recommended by the fashion experts) directly to them. An influx of such mail prompted *Die Dame* to publish several explicit editorial clarifications that "Ullstein patterns are available only from our vendors and not, as many of our female readers [Leserinnen] have wrongly assumed, from the artists [Künstlerinnen] who signed the drawings."[76]

The question of authorship seemed to be of particular importance for the fashion journalists of *Die Dame*. In a polemical review of an exhibit of arts and crafts and fashion ("Kunsthandwerk und Mode") organized and arranged by the prominent designer Lilly Reich in 1920, a regular editor for *Die Dame*, Edith Wallach criticized the existing practice in the German fashion industry of not crediting designers properly and praised one company that was an exception:

> For the first time now a prominent designer house is demonstrating the courage and sensitivity not to label its creations as its own or as coming from Paris, but to feature the name of the woman artist who designed them. Would a book publisher be ashamed to mention the male artist who illustrated and ornamented a book? No, on the contrary, a publisher is proud to announce the name of a first-rate artist, because it considerably increases the book's value. Similarly, our fashion industry must learn to acknowledge openly and honestly the contribution of the woman designers, because they add to the value of the product.[77]

This passage points to the phenomena discussed in more detail in the next chapter, which draws the "collective portrait" of the women who were professionally involved in fashion for the Ullstein publishing company. For this general introduction of the cultural type, however, it suffices to summarize in broad strokes the position of the fashion journalists and artists (Moderedakteurinnen, Modezeichnerinnen) in Weimar Germany. We see them figuring prominently in public and visibly enjoying the increased publicity. They were photographed for the pages of Ullstein's magazines wearing extravagant costumes and displaying themselves as fashionable models. In so doing they took advantage of the enhanced possibilities of modern mass media — extended use of photographic images and wide circulation. But because they constantly demonstrated an aristocracy based on taste and individual personal style, they assumed the role of a modern female dandy. At the same time, however, they lacked the dandy's provocative stance and ironic disposition, always advocating women's reasonable adjustment to current trends and giving practical advice on how to adapt to fashion's caprices. In the end, the female fashion journalist in Weimar Germany appears to have combined the belated dandy and the emerging modern intellectual. The next chapters pursue this female interpreter of modernity and examine some of her historical and imaginary incarnations.

Notes

[1] Robert Volz and Ferdinand Tönnies, eds. *Reichshandbuch der deutschen Gesellschaft: das Handbuch der Persönlichkeiten in Wort und Bild* (Berlin: Deutscher Wirtschaftsverlag, 1930), 1:19, 735.

[2] See Gretel Wagner, "Die Mode in Berlin," in *Berlin en vogue: Berliner Mode in der Photographie*, ed. F. C. Gundlach and Uli Richter (Berlin: Wasmuth, 1993), 188.

[3] For additional biographical data on Alsen and Herzog and their careers, see Appendix I.

[4] For in-depth discussions of the early fashion press, especially *Journal des Luxus und der Moden* (1786–1827), see Daniel Purdy, *The Tyranny of Elegance: Consumer Cosmopolitanism in the Era of Goethe* (Baltimore: Johns Hopkins UP, 1998); Karin Wurst, *Fabricating Pleasure: Fashion, Entertainment, and Cultural Consumption in Germany, 1780–1830* (Detroit, MI: Wayne State UP, 2005); and Julia Bertschik, *Mode und Moderne: Kleidung als Spiegel des Zeitgeistes in der deutschsprachigen Literatur (1770–1945)* (Cologne: Böhlau, 2005), 49–57. See also Gerhard Goebel, "Mode und Moderne: Der Modejournalist Mallarmé," *Germanisch-romanische Monatsschrift* 28.1 (1978): 36–49, and Margaret Waller, "Disembodiment as a Masquerade: Fashion Journalists and Other 'Realist' Observers in Directory Paris," *Esprit Créateur* 37.1 (Spring 1997): 44–54. Among the very few studies on female fashion journalists, see especially Frauke Severit, *Ea von Allesch: Wenn aus Frauen Menschen werden; Eine Biographie* (Wiesbaden: DUV, 1999), and Paul Michael Lützeler, "Ea von Allesch: Von der femme fatale zur femme emancipée," in *Das Teesdorfer Tagebuch für Ea von Allesch*, ed. P. M. Lützeler (Frankfurt am Main: Suhrkamp, 1995), 190–222. What Lützeler writes about the fashion writer (die Modeschriftstellerin) Ea von Allesch, who worked for the Vienna-based magazine *Die Moderne Welt*, applies to many of the leading female fashion journalists of the 1920s: "For her, however, fashion was not a purely aesthetic issue unrelated to social change, political events, and the changing relationship between the sexes. Her pieces are full of wit and allusions to contemporary events and artistic developments" (Doch Mode war für sie nicht eine von sozialen Wandlungen, von Veränderungen der Beziehungen zwischen den Geschlechtern und von politischen Gegebenheiten zu trennende, rein ästhetische Angelegenheit. Ihre Beiträge sind witzig formuliert, voller Anspielungen auf Zeitgeschichtliches, auf Aktuelles aus der Kunstszene; 202).

[5] Rhonda Garelick, *Rising Star: Dandyism, Gender, and Performance in the Fin-de-Siècle* (Princeton, NJ: Princeton UP, 1998), 3.

[6] "Flâneur," *Larousse: Grand Dictionnaire Universel*, 1893 ed.

[7] My account of this 1806 text is informed by the subtle analyses of Priscilla Parkhurst Ferguson and Elizabeth Wilson. See Ferguson, "The *Flâneur* On and Off the Streets of Paris," in *The Flâneur*, ed. Keith Tester (London: Routledge, 1994), 22–42, and "The *Flâneur*: The City and Its Discontents," in her *Paris as Revolution: Writing the Nineteenth-Century City* (Berkeley: U of California P, 1994), 80–114; and Wilson, "The Invisible *Flâneur*," in *Postmodern Cities and Spaces*, ed. Sophie Watson and Katherine Gibson (Oxford: Blackwell, 1995), 59–79.

[8] See *Le flâneur au salon, ou M. Bonhomme, examen joyeux des tableaux, mêlé de vaudevilles* (Paris: Aubry, 1806), quoted in Wilson, "The Invisible *Flâneur*," 63.

[9] For a more detailed analysis of Balzac's *flâneur*, see Priscilla Parkhurst Ferguson, "The *Flâneur* and the Production of Culture," in *Cultural Participation: Trends since the Middle Ages*, ed. Ann Rigney and Douwe Fokkema (Amsterdam: Benjamins, 1993), 109–24; here, 111–12.

[10] Ferguson argues that Flaubert's 1869 novel *L'Éducation sentimentale* offers another example of the changes in the mid-century *flâneur*. Frederic is a figure of failure, who unlike Baudelaire's *flâneur* is unable to transform his sense of estrangement in the metropolis into a condition for artistic creativity. See Ferguson, *Paris as Revolution*, 94–111.

[11] As Deborah Parsons has pointed out, the urban spectators in Baudelaire are hard to define partly because there have been some "slippages of meaning in translation." Baudelaire does not use the word *flâneur* but "dandy," an English term that was taken up and expanded by the French after the archetypal dandy Beau Brummell fell out of favor in London. If the English dandy was marked primarily by boredom, leisure, and distance, Baudelaire's dandy is often working in the city — as writer, journalist for the feuilletons, or artist — and is exhilarated by the urban spectacle. See Deborah L. Parsons, *Streetwalking the Metropolis: Women, the City and Modernity* (Oxford: Oxford UP, 2000), 20. To avoid confusion, like Parsons I shall use "dandy" for the original aristocratic, English phenomenon, and *flâneur* for Baudelaire's concept.

[12] Charles Baudelaire, *The Painter of Modern Life and Other Essays*, trans. Jonathan Mayne (London: Phaidon, 1964), 27–28.

[13] This aspect has received very little critical attention. One notable exception is Valerie Steele, *Paris Fashion: A Cultural History* (New York, Oxford: Oxford UP, 1988). See especially her chapter on Baudelaire, "The Black Prince of Elegance," 81–96.

[14] Baudelaire, *The Painter of Modern Life*, 27.

[15] Baudelaire, *The Painter of Modern Life*, 28.

[16] See Gerhard Goebel, "Mode und Moderne: Der Modejournalist Mallarmé," in *Der Reisebericht: Die Entwicklung einer Gattung in der deutschen Literatur*, ed. Peter J. Brenner (Frankfurt am Main: Suhrkamp, 1989), 463–89, and John Stokes, "Wilde the Journalist," in *The Cambridge Companion to Oscar Wilde*, ed. Peter Raby (Cambridge, UK: Cambridge UP, 1997), 69–79.

[17] This process was influenced by radical transformations in a public sphere increasingly governed by the mass press. The press reacted to the changes in readers' tastes

and demands with huge transformations in the content of its publications as well as in the method of distribution. Siegfried Kracauer credits Emile de Girardin, publisher of *La Presse*, for initiating the commercialization of the press. Newspapers such as Girardin's drastically reduced their prices, accepted more advertising, became less political, and started to cater to the mass public's growing demand for entertainment. See Siegfried Kracauer, *Orpheus in Paris: Offenbach and the Paris of His Time*, trans. Gwenda David and Eric Mosbacher (New York: Knopf, 1938), 60–78.

[18] Susan Buck-Morss, *The Dialectics of Seeing: Walter Benjamin and the Arcades Project* (Cambridge, MA: MIT Press, 1989), 105. The 1970s and 1980s marked another peak in interest in the *flâneur* that paralleled the boom in restructuring inner-city areas throughout West Germany and a renewal of urban culture; fashion, shopping, entertainment, and pedestrians returned to the attractively designed city centers. Hanns-Josef Ortheil described this late-modern or postmodern West German phenomenon with the words "alles ist Provinz, alles ist Metropole." See Hanns-Josef Ortheil, "Der lange Abschied vom Flaneur," *Merkur* 1 (1986): 30–48. And most recently, in the 1990s, city planners and cultural critics began to envision again (somewhat uncritically and naïvely, one must add) the future of Berlin in forms of the past, particularly in invoking the return of the *flâneur*. For examples of this tendency, see Dieter Hildebrandt, " 'Genieße froh, was du nicht hast': Nie war Franz Hessel aktueller als heute oder warum Berlin der Gegenwart den Flaneur der Vergangenheit braucht," *Die Zeit*, 17 Mar. 1995: 72; Niklas Maak, "Die blauen Enkel: Das neue Berlin sucht seine Zukunft in den Formen der Vergangenheit," *Süddeutsche Zeitung*, 31 Dec. 1998: 23; and Uwe Rada, Die "Rückkehr des Flaneurs," *taz* 26 Jun. 1999: 21.

[19] Walter Benjamin, "The Return of the *Flâneur*," in *Selected Writings*, trans. Rodney Livingstone, ed. Michael W. Jennings, Howard Eiland, and Gary Smith (Cambridge, MA: Harvard UP, 1999), 2:263. In the original German: "Das unabsehbare Schauspiel der Flanerie, das wir endgültig abgesetzt glaubten." See Walter Benjamin, *Gesammelte Schriften*, ed. Hella Tiedemann-Bartels (Frankfurt am Main: Suhrkamp, 1980), 3:194.

[20] Benjamin, "The Return of the *Flâneur*," 262. In the original German: "Die Stadt als mnemotechnischer Behelf des einsam Spazierenden, sie ruft mehr herauf als dessen Kindheit und Jugend, mehr als ihre eigene Geschichte" (Benjamin, *Gesammelte Schriften*, 3:194).

[21] In his own book *Berliner Kindheit um 1900* (Berlin Childhood around 1900, written between 1932 and 1938, first published in 1950), Benjamin offered an example of his own practice of *flânerie* in his hometown of Berlin, using it to bring images of the past into the present.

[22] Benjamin's review of Hessel's book contained some reflections on *flânerie* that were also included in his *Passagen-Werk*; see Benjamin, *The Arcades Project*, trans. Howard Eiland and Kevin McLaughlin (Cambridge, MA: Harvard UP, 1999). In the late 1930s he wrote two essays exclusively on the *flâneur* as part of his book-length study on Baudelaire, *Charles Baudelaire: Ein Lyriker im Zeitalter des Hochkapitalismus* (Charles Baudelaire: A Lyric Poet in the Era of High Capitalism): "Der Flâneur" (The Flaneur), and "Über einige Motive bei Baudelaire" (On Some

Motifs in Baudelaire), the second of which was a significantly revised version of the first in response to criticism by Theodor Adorno. For more on the evolution of the *flâneur* concept in Benjamin, see Parsons, *Streetwalking the Metropolis*, 33–39, and Buck-Morss, *The Dialectics of Seeing*, 303–7.

[23] "Ein Rausch kommt über den, der lange Zeit ohne Ziel durch Straßen marschierte"; see Benjamin, *Gesammelte Schriften*, 5:525.

[24] Walter Benjamin, "On Some Motifs in Baudelaire," in *Illuminations*, ed. Hannah Arendt, trans. Harry Zohn (New York: Schocken, 1968), 172.

[25] See Benjamin, "On Some Motifs in Baudelaire," 173. In the original German: "Hoffmanns Vetter in seinem Eckfenster ist gelähmt."

[26] Buck-Morss, *The Dialectics of Seeing*, 307.

[27] Buck-Morss, *The Dialectics of Seeing*, 304.

[28] Walter Benjamin, *Gesammelte Schriften*, 5:559.

[29] See Miriam Bratu Hansen, "America, Paris, the Alps: Kracauer (and Benjamin) on Cinema and Modernity," in *Cinema and the Invention of Modern Life*, ed. Leo Charney and Vanessa R. Schwartz (Berkeley: U of California P, 1995), 362–402; here, 366. On Kracauer's friendship with Benjamin, see Klaus Michael, "Vor dem Café: Walter Benjamin und Siegfried Kracauer in Marseille," in *"Aber ein Sturm weht vom Paradies her": Texte zu Walter Benjamin*, ed. Michael Opitz and Erdmut Wizisla (Leipzig: Reclam, 1992), 203–21.

[30] Kracauer, *Orpheus in Paris*, 92.

[31] "Der immerwährende Wechsel tilgt die Erinnerung. . . . Man hat vielen Häusern die Ornamente abgeschlagen, die eine Art Brücke zum Gestern bildeten." See Kracauer, *Schriften: Aufsätze (1927–1931)*, ed. Inka Mülder-Bach (Frankfurt am Main: Suhrkamp, 1990), 5/3:172–73.

[32] Kracauer, *Schriften*, 5/2:260–65; an English translation appears in *The Mass Ornament: Weimar Essays*, ed. and trans. Thomas Y. Levin (Cambridge, MA: Harvard UP, 1995), 337–42. A detailed discussion of Kracauer's essays on the city can be found in Henrik Reeh, *Ornaments of the Metropolis: Siegfried Kracauer and Modern Urban Culture* (Cambridge, MA: MIT Press, 2004).

[33] Eckhardt Köhn, *Straßenrausch: Flanerie und die kleine Form; Versuch zur Literaturgeschichte des Flaneurs bis 1933* (Berlin: Das Arsenal, 1989), 238. For other critical analyses of Kracauer's association with and distance from the practice of *flânerie*, see Anke Gleber, *The Art of Taking a Walk: Flanerie, Literature, and Film in Weimar Culture* (Princeton: Princeton UP, 1999), 43–47, and Courtney Federle, "Picture Postcard: Kracauer Writes from Berlin," in *Peripheral Visions: The Hidden Stages of Weimar Cinema*, ed. Kenneth S. Calhoon (Detroit, MI: Wayne State UP, 2001), 39–54.

[34] Simmel, *Philosophische Kultur* (Potsdam: Gustav Kiepenheuer, 1911), 8.

[35] See especially Inka Mülder-Bach, "Der Umschlag der Negativität: Zur Verschränkung von Phenomenologie, Geschichtsphilosophie und Filmästhetik in Siegfried Kracauers Metaphorik der 'Oberfläche,' " *Deutsche Vierteljahresschrift für Literaturwissenschaft und Geistesgeschichte* 61.2 (1987): 359–73; Inka Mülder, *Siegfried Kracauer — Grenzgänger zwischen Theorie und Literatur: Seine frühen*

Schriften, 1913–1933 (Stuttgart: J. B. Metzler, 1985), 86–95; and Miriam Hansen, "Decentic Perspectives: Kracauer's Early Writings on Film and Mass Culture," *New German Critique* 54 (Fall 1991): 47–76.

[36] Hansen, "Decentric Perspectives," 51.

[37] Kracauer, *The Mass Ornament*, 75.

[38] Kracauer, *The Mass Ornament*, 138.

[39] Hessel and Benjamin were close friends and collaborators in the 1920s. In 1926 and 1927 they worked together in Paris on a German translation of Proust's *Remembrance of Things Past* to be published by *Rowohlt*. During the same period Benjamin started preliminary notes on the *Arcades Project* (*Passagen-Werk*). For reflections on their friendship, see Benjamin's letters to Gershom Scholem from 18 September 1926, to Theodor Adorno from 31 May 1935, and to Gretel Adorno from 1 November 1938 in *The Correspondence of Walter Benjamin 1910–1940*, ed. Theodor W. Adorno, trans. Manfred R. Jacobson and Evelyn M. Jacobson (Chicago: U of Chicago P, 1994), 304, 488, and 579. See also Bernd Witte, *Walter Benjamin: An Intellectual Biography*, trans. James Rolleston (Detroit, MI: Wayne State UP, 1991), 144–45.

[40] "Langsam durch belebte Straßen zu gehen, ist ein besonderes Vergnügen. Man wird überspielt von der Eile der anderen, es ist ein Bad in der Brandung." See Franz Hessel, *Ein Flaneur in Berlin* (Berlin: Das Arsenal, 1984), 7. Reprint of *Spazieren in Berlin* (Leipzig: Dr. Hans Epstein, 1929) 7. All references are to the 1984 edition.

[41] Hessel, *Ein Flaneur in Berlin* 145, 7–11.

[42] "Er [der Spaziergänger] braucht nicht einzutreten, er braucht sich nicht einzulassen." See Hessel, "Von der schwierigen Kunst spazieren zu gehen," *Literarische Welt* 8.6 (1932): 3–4; reprinted in *Ermunterung zum Genuß: Kleine Prosa*, ed. Karin Grund and Bernd Witte (Berlin: Brinkmann & Bosse, 1981), 53–61. Since the rediscovery of Hessel's writings by literary scholars in the 1980s and 1990s, numerous studies have appeared that analyze his concept of *flânerie* in great detail, pointing out that it lacks political engagement or sociological inquisitiveness. As Anke Gleber observes, the narrator in Hessel's texts accepts everything that he sees "without passing aesthetic or ideological judgment," and thus the realities of labor and politics in Berlin of the late 1920s and early 1930s are left out of the picture. See Anke Gleber, *The Art of Taking a Walk*, 82. Eckhardt Köhn, too, finds Hessel's "aestheticist perception" problematic, because it often borders on political naiveté. See Eckhardt Köhn, *Straßenrausch:*, 192. For more on the aestheticist roots of the nostalgic *flâneur*, see Eva Banchelli, "Zwischen Erinnerung und Entdeckung: Strategien der Großstadterfahrung bei Franz Hessel," in Opitz and Plath, *"Genieße froh, was du nicht hast,"* 105–16.

[43] Franz Hessel, "Das Lederetui," *Die Dame*, Sept. 1934, no. 22, 23–24; repr. in *Ein Garten voller Weltgeschichte*, ed. Bernhard Echte (Munich: dtv, 1994), 68–73. For additional examples of female characters in Franz Hessel's prose who serve as opposites to the *flâneur* because they are employed or pursuing practical tasks, see "Leichtes Berliner Frühlingsfieber," in *Nachfeier*, 62 and "Der Verdächtige" in his *Spazieren in Berlin*, 7–11.

⁴⁴ "Gerade wer — fast möchte ich sagen: nur wer flanieren kann, wird danach, wenn ihn dieser berühmte Rhythmus packt und eilig, konstant und zielstrebig fortbewegt, diese unsere Zeit umso mehr genießen und verstehen." See Hessel, *Ermunterung*, 54.

⁴⁵ Hessel wrote: "Verweile doch . . . Nicht so faustisch, Fräulein! Bitte flaniere. Das ist ein Fremdwort und wird ein fremder Begriff bleiben, bis du dich so bewegst, daß ein neues Wort von deinem schönen Gange redet. Lustwandeln ist zu langsam und kleinstädtisch. Berlinerin, schaff' ein neues Wort. Mach ein Korso aus deinem westlichen Boulevard Tauentzienstraße-Kurfürstendamm. Noch ist er Stockung und Häufung, noch ist er voreilig. Schöne Berlinerin, sei gelassen." See Franz Hessel, "An die Berlinerin," *Vogue*, 13 Mar. 1929, 25; repr. in Hessel, *Ein Garten voller Weltgeschichte*, 26–28.

⁴⁶ See Gleber, *The Art of Taking a Walk*, 172.

⁴⁷ Janet Wolff, "The Invisible *Flâneuse*: Women and the Literature of Modernity," *Theory, Culture and Society* 2/3 (1985): 37. See also Wolff, "The Artist and the *Flâneur*: Rodin, Rilke, and Gwen John in Paris," in *The Flâneur*, ed. Keith Tester (London: Routledge, 1994), 111–37, and Priscilla Parkhurst Ferguson, *Paris as Revolution*, 80–114.

⁴⁸ See Elizabeth Wilson, "The Invisible *Flâneur*," *The New Left Review* 191 (1992): 93.

⁴⁹ Anne Friedberg, *Window-Shopping: Cinema and the Postmodern* (Berkeley: U of California P, 1993), 38. On women's window-shopping and women's mobility in the city, see also Christopher Prendergast, *Paris and the Nineteenth Century* (Oxford: Blackwell, 1992), 34.

⁵⁰ See Gleber, *The Art of Taking a Walk*, 171–213.

⁵¹ The term the "New Woman" was coined in England by writer Sarah Grand in her 1894 essay "The New Aspect of the Woman Question," which spurred numerous spirited responses until the phrase was ubiquitous. See Carolyn Christensen Nelson's introduction to *A New Woman Reader: Fiction, Articles, and Drama of the 1890s*, ed. C. C. Nelson (Toronto: Broadview P, 2001), ix.

⁵² See James Laver, *Taste and Fashion: From the French Revolution until Today* (New York: Dodd, Mead & Co., 1938), 93.

⁵³ For a detailed overview, see Andreas Höfele, "Dandy und New Woman," in *Die "Nineties": Das englische Fin-de-siècle zwischen Dekadenz und Sozialkritik*, ed. Manfred Pfister and Bernd Schulte-Middelich (Munich: Francke, 1983), 147–61.

⁵⁴ For a discussion of these points, see Joseph Stein, "The New Woman and the Decadent Dandy," *Dalhousie Review* 55.1 (1975): 54–62. See also Teresa Mangum, "Style Wars of the 1890s: The New Woman and the Decadent," in *Transforming Genres: New Approaches to British Fiction of the 1890s*, ed. Nikki Lee Manos and Meri-Jane Rochelson (New York: St. Martin's P, 1994), 47–66.

⁵⁵ For a comparison of the English and German New Woman, see Carol Diethe, "Nietzsche and the New Woman," *German Life and Letters* 48 (1995): 428–40.

⁵⁶ This argument is made by Hanne Loreck, "Das Kunstprodukt 'Neue Frau' in den zwanziger Jahren," in *Mode der 20er Jahre*, ed. Christine Waidenschlager and Christa Gustavus (Berlin, Tübingen: Wasmuth, 1993), 12–19.

⁵⁷ See Patrice Petro, *Joyless Streets: Women and Melodramatic Representation of Weimar Germany* (Princeton: Princeton UP, 1989), 79–139.

⁵⁸ Lavin thus proceeds to analyze Hannah Höch's photomontages, demonstrating how they challenge and unsettle various stereotypes of Weimar women. See Maud Lavin, *Cut with a Kitchen Knife: The Weimar Photomontages of Hannah Höch* (New Haven: Yale UP, 1993), 4.

⁵⁹ See Heide Schlüpmann, "Die nebensächliche Frau: Geschlechtsdifferenz in Siegfried Kracauers Essayistik der zwanziger Jahre," *Feministische Studien* 1 (1993): 38–47.

⁶⁰ "Vor dem Kinoportal steht eine Frau im imitierten Pelz und kaut. Lautlos kaut sie, sieht weder nach links noch nach rechts und wartet. Sie ist in mittleren Jahren, eine gewöhnliche Frau, die nichts zu tun hat und darum einfach irgendwo am Straßenrand stehen bleibt. Wenn nicht einer kommt und sie ins dunkle Kino mitnimmt, kaut sie sicher noch bis in die Nacht hinein am selben Fleck, und die Sonne zieht unverrichteter Dinge ab." Siegfried Kracauer, "Kino in der Münzstraße," in *Straßen in Berlin und anderswo* (Frankfurt am Main: Suhrkamp, 1964), 95.

⁶¹ "Das Nebenbei wird gar nicht selten die Hauptsache." See Schlüpmann, "Die nebensächliche Frau," 45–46; see also Kracauer, "Berliner Figuren: Das Nummernmädchen," in *Straßen in Berlin und anderswo*, 154.

⁶² See Atina Grossmann, "Girlkultur or Thoroughly Rationalized Female: A New Woman in Weimar Germany?" in *Women in Culture and Politics: A Century of Change*, ed. Judith Friedlander et al. (Bloomington: Indiana UP, 1986), 64.

⁶³ Vanna Brenner, "Gnädige Frau, Sie sind zu intellektuell," *Die Dame*, Apr. 1931, no. 14, 42–44. Quoted in Petro, *Joyless Streets*, 124–27.

⁶⁴ See Katharina Sykora, "Die Neue Frau: Ein Alltagsmythos der zwanziger Jahre," and Annelie Lütgens, "Passantinnen/Flaneusen: Frauen im Bild großstädtischer Öffentlichkeit der zwanziger Jahre," in *Die Neue Frau: Herausforderung für die Bildmedien der zwanziger Jahre*, ed. Katharina Sykora et al. (Marburg: Jonas Verlag, 1993), 9–24 and 107–18 respectively.

⁶⁵ Both magazines were owned by the publishing conglomerate Ullstein. For detailed discussion, see chapter 2.

⁶⁶ Lütgens, "Passantinnen/Flaneusen," 117.

⁶⁷ On women as fashion illustrators, see Christa Gustavus, "Lieselotte Friedlaender und der 'Modenspiegel,'" in Waidenschlager and Gustavus, *Mode der 20er Jahre*, 36–39, and Sabine Runde, *Welt ohne Alltag: Modegraphik der 20er Jahre von Annie Offterdingen* (Frankfurt am Main: Das Museum, 1986). On Weimar women in photography, see the excellent volume *Fotografieren hieß teilnehmen: Fotografinnen der Weimarer Republik*, ed. Ute Eskildsen (Düsseldorf: Richter, 1994).

⁶⁸ See Appendix I for biographical details on the female journalists mentioned here.

⁶⁹ "Es läßt sich schwer verallgemeinern, was schön und wünschenswert und was abzulehnen ist, denn Schönheit der Kleidung hängt nicht mehr nur vom Urteil des Beschauers, sondern auch von der Individualität der Trägerin ab." Johanna Thal, "Kritisches über die Mode," *Die Dame*, Nov. 1921, no. 4, 13; emphasis mine.

[70] Baudelaire, *The Painter of Modern Life*, 27.

[71] Marie von Bunsen, "Männeraugen und Frauenaugen," *Die Dame*, May 1919, no. 16, 2.

[72] Anita, "Lebensstil 1930," *Die Dame*, Apr. 1930, no. 19, 18, and "Die bevorstehende Männeremanzipation," *Die Dame*, Feb. 1928, no. 10, 14.

[73] Baudelaire, *The Painter of Modern Life*, 27.

[74] A similar thesis is discussed in detail in one of the few German studies on the dandy: see Sebastian Neumeister, *Der Dichter als Dandy: Kafka, Baudelaire, Thomas Bernhard* (Munich: Wilhelm Fink, 1973), 40–71. Habermas's sociological treatise on the public sphere is found in *Strukturwandel der Öffentlichkeit* (Berlin: Luchterhand, 1971), 23–30.

[75] Baudelaire, *The Painter of Modern Life*, 27–28. For an illuminating analysis of the self-fashioning of the dandy, see Ellen Moers, *The Dandy: Brummell to Beerbohm* (New York: Viking P, 1960), 271–83.

[76] See *Die Dame* issues 20, 21, and 22 from 1919.

[77] "Zum erstenmal hat hier ein großes Schneideratelier den Mut und das Feingefühl, nicht seine Schöpfungen als alleiniges eigenes Produkt oder gar als 'Pariser Modell' hinzustellen, sondern wie es sich gehört, auch den Namen der schmückenden Künstlerin zu nennen. Würde ein Verleger oder ein Buchbinder sich schämen, den Künstler, der sein Einband . . . zeichnete und das Buch mit Ornament und Zeichnung schmückte, zu verheimlichen? Mit Recht nennt er im Gegenteil den Namen des erstklassigen Künstlers, weil er selbstverständlich hierdurch den Wert des Buches bedeutend hebt. In gleicher Weise muß allmählich unsere Modenindustrie gewöhnt und erzogen werden, nicht keusch der mitzeugenden Künstlerin, sondern sich frank und frei zu ihr zu bekennen, weil hierdurch der Wert der eigenen Arbeit erhöht wird." See Edith Wallach, "Kunsthandwerk und Mode," *Die Dame*, Mar. 1920, no. 11, 29.

2: Fashion Journalism at Ullstein House

ON JANUARY 29, 1933, on the eve of one of the most fateful days in German history, the day on which Hitler was appointed Chancellor, the huge banquet halls of Berlin's Zoological Gardens were hosting the annual Press Ball. As described by Hermann Ullstein, a participant and one of the most influential figures of the German press, this was the culminating event of the capital's social life. All halls were packed with "illustrious peoplee . . . : ministers of state, politicians, members of Parliament and the press, artists, poets, and the intellectual leaders of both the theater and film worlds." Before Ullstein proceeded with the insider's succinct analysis of the press "dancing on the edge of the volcano," he took a moment to describe a glittering facet of this annual gathering and to make a peculiar observation:

> The men [are] wearing multicolored uniforms with rows of medals, or evening dress with white ties, and the women [are] in dazzling evening dress. Indeed, it does not occur to one of these society ladies to appear in anything but fashion's last creation. For such is the tradition of the Press Ball. Nor will their ambition be satisfied until they have read in the morning papers a detailed description of their appearance by a leading fashion expert.[1]

This cursory remark, coming from one of the masterminds of the modernized, highly popular, and commercially prosperous illustrated press, deserves more than passing attention. On the one hand it describes the enormous scale of the spectacle known as the Press Ball: organized traditionally in Berlin since 1872, it was an event attended sometimes by close to 6000 guests, and it was eagerly anticipated and widely covered in the press, which characterized it as "the high point of social life," "the big theater of fashion," and "the biggest fashion show."[2] On the other hand, Ullstein's remark emphasizes that the real, physical public space in which women paraded their fashionable outfits was really nothing without the imaginary public realm of the print media, where women's heightened self-consciousness about clothes, hairstyles, and general appearance was openly articulated. Women's reading and writing on fashion was arguably as essential a facet of their experience of fashion as the actual display of it in public. It was the numerous illustrated women's and fashion periodicals, including Ullstein's own *Die Dame* and *Der Uhu*, that served as a large public mirror to the fashionable attire of "society ladies" — the wives and daughters of prominent political and intellectual leaders, and theater and movie stars — and at the same time gave inspiration and practical advice to the mass audience. The scope and influence of the fashion press between 1918 and 1933 were remarkable. In Berlin alone there were over 90 periodicals, including the fashion supplements to the daily newspapers, which covered various social gatherings of the upper class, from the Press Ball to the numerous fashion shows (Modenschau, Modentee, Modekonkurrenz).[3] The fashion press informed the public about what was worn at the races and at the theater (both on-stage and in the audience), how the movie stars dressed, what was appropriate to wear for any imaginable social occasion, and what the newest fashions in the mountain and seaside resorts were.

Moreover, the fashion press emerged as a forum for the broader debate on issues such as women's changing role as active participants in modern life, as creators rather than followers of aesthetic norms, as subjects rather than objects of the visual and textual representation of fashion, and as insightful observers, writers, and designers of fashionable images. This new feature of the fashion press cannot be separated from the process of modernization and transformation of the public sphere by the mass media that took place in the first third of the twentieth century. In this context the Weimar fashion press in particular emerged as a niche in mass culture that served as a women's public sphere (Frauenöffentlichkeit), a sphere in which women openly began to participate as agents and in which specifically female attitudes toward modernity were intensively negotiated in the public discourse.[4] A close reading of the texts written by female fashion journalists not only demonstrates how fashion constituted a sphere of discursive practices in which women were able to discuss the female experience of modernity on their own terms; it also elucidates the definition of "modernity" advanced by the regular female editors of the various magazines, which in many cases differed significantly from the views prevailing among contemporary male philosophers, writers, and historians.

This chapter examines the fashion press as a vehicle for women's self-expression during an era of vast modernization and the rise of mass culture, taking a closer look at selected periodicals from the Weimar period, the unique institutional politics in place, and female fashion journalists. The primary focus is on Ullstein's illustrated magazines *Die Dame* and *Der Uhu*, not only because they present perhaps the richest discursive landscape of Weimar fashion, but also because they bear the strongest testimony to women's increasing self-consciousness and self-descriptiveness in matters of fashion. As an institution Ullstein House was extraordinarily involved in the creation, distribution, and public discussion of women's fashion.

"Teaching Women How to Look Chic"

After the First World War Ullstein was one of the "public sphere's preeminent institutions," whose development exemplified what Habermas defines as a structural transformation of the "public sphere in the world of letters" into a "pseudo-public or sham-private world of culture consumption." As we will see, the transformation of the "culture-debating public" (kulturräsonierende Öffentlichkeit) into a "culture-consuming public" (kulturkonsumierende Öffentlichkeit) was paralleled by an opening up of a public space in which women were involved not only as mass consumers but also as agents of cultural production.[5]

The rise of this massive Berlin-based publishing conglomerate took place in the last quarter of the nineteenth century, when the first giant newspaper trusts were founded in Europe and the United States.[6] During the Weimar Republic Ullstein was the largest publishing empire in Germany. It owned nineteen newspapers and magazines (including the mass-circulating and enormously popular *Berliner Zeitung am Mittag*, the *Berliner Illustrirte Zeitung*, the *Berliner Morgenpost*, and the *Vossische Zeitung*), launched a mass-market book division, and ran a huge advertising agency as well as news and photo services.[7] Along with the two other media giants in Berlin after German unification in 1871, Scherl and Mosse, Ullstein quickly embraced modern strategies of production and marketing that assured spectacular and lasting economic success.[8] The company learned to address its large and mostly metropolitan reading public deliberately as "depoliticized consumers."[9] In the 1890s it began to offer subscriptions at low monthly rates and opened the pages of its publication to massive advertising. Although in its first decades of existence Ullstein House was actually following effective marketing strategies developed by August Scherl and Rudolf Mosse in the 1880s, it surpassed its competitors soon after the turn of the century.

Two aspects of Ullstein's history are particularly pertinent here: the publishers' deliberate and self-conscious self-alignment with the spirit of modernization and the representation of modernity, and their persistence in creating a unique institutional framework that enabled Weimar's New Woman to assume the role of intellectual — an active participant in modernity. And both of these aspects are best exemplified by the history of Ullstein's engagement with fashion and its division for fashion publications (der Modeverlag). "We Ullsteins, [were] heralded for our reputation for modernism," wrote Hermann Ullstein. He was the youngest of the five brothers who inherited the publishing empire founded by Leopold Ullstein in 1877 (*RF*, 22).[10] During the 1920s Hermann was in charge of the magazine division of the house and of advertising, and hence responsible for its radically modern appearance. He directed the monthlies, fashion papers, sewing patterns, and magazines for children — the *Berliner Illustrirte Zeitung* (*BIZ*), *Querschnitt*, *Die Dame*, *Der Uhu*, *Blatt der Hausfrau*, and *Der heitere Fridolin* — and part of his task was "to find new slogans for the various publishing projects" (*RF*, 67–68). Vicki Baum, one of the most famous editors hired by Hermann Ullstein, characterized him as having an extraordinarily "keen sense for sales propaganda, packaging, and slogans."[11]

To modernize the mass media meant, as Ullstein put it, to abandon "the drowsy atmosphere of the old century" and the narrow "local horizon" and to keep pace with the "new rhythm of life" (*RF*, 91). From Scherl's *Die Woche* Ullstein learned that "the main purpose of the illustrated magazine was no longer to illustrate the text but to allow events to be seen directly in pictures, to render the world comprehensible through the photograph." This belief led him to develop the weekly *Berliner Illustrirte Zeitung* (acquired in 1894) as the acknowledged prototype of commercially successful and aesthetically appealing photojournalism on a large scale (*RF*, 85).[12] Kurt Korff, editor in chief for the *BIZ* and primarily responsible for the invention of the new, popular format of the "picture-story," argued that the triumph of Ullstein House's innovative photojournalism was comparable to the concurrent popularity of film: "At a time when life 'through the eyes' began to play a larger role, the demand for visuals became so strong that they alone could function as news. That meant a completely new attitude toward pictures. It is no coincidence that the cinema and the *Berliner Illustrirte Zeitung* developed more or less in tandem."[13]

Liberal views, modernist claims, cosmopolitanism — all came together to further consumerist strategies yielding high profits. Fundamental to Ullstein's success and appeal was the publishers' belief that entertainment should tap into two powerful resources, advanced technology and the mass public's desire for distraction and pleasure, and the key was engagement with fashion. It demonstrated the publisher's persistent and genuine commitment to modern business practices as well to offering women unprecedented participation in the public sphere in the context of a booming mass culture. In 1905 the firm bought "an insignificant periodical for housewives" from a small publisher named Friedrich Schirmer and continued to publish it as *Das Blatt der Hausfrau*. Several years later another low-profile magazine, the *Illustrierte Frauen-Zeitung*, was acquired by Ullstein and reappeared, in a new guise, in 1912 as *Die Dame*. Transformed under the ambitious guidance and unwavering marketing intuition of Hermann Ullstein, both magazines achieved, each in its own way, unprecedented success with large female audiences across age and class boundaries. The company considered them "our fourth success" — alongside the daily *Berliner Morgenpost* and *Berliner Zeitung am Mittag*, and the weekly *Berliner Illustrirte Zeitung* — and regarded the fashion publications division (der Modeverlag) as its "most valuable trump" (*RF*, 101).[14]

Ullstein realized that for the vast majority of low- and middle-class women fashion had come to represent the spirit of modern times in the most palpable way. A new venture was added to the recently acquired *Blatt der Hausfrau*: "a real dressmakers' workshop employing some fifty accomplished women dressmakers [turned] out patterns for readers who wished to make their own clothes." "Fashion designs for women who made their own clothes," he wrote, "did more good for all concerned than boring advice on how to remove stains or clean carpets. Teaching people how to look chic without spending large sums of money had a greater power of attraction" (*RF*, 103). Readers would request patterns for the dresses they liked in the magazine, and the patterns were made according to the customers' own measurements. This practice yielded unexpected success and popularity, and the company was inundated with more orders than it could handle. The solution came from a young employee, Francis Hutter, who suggested that the company should keep patterns in various standard sizes in stock.[15] Thus, the famous Ullstein sewing patterns ("Ullstein-Schnitte") were launched and became, according to Hermann Ullstein, "the strangest mass-produced merchandise imaginable" (*RF*, 105–6). About two thousand different patterns a year were produced; they were carried by most German department stores, selling for a mark each and bringing significant profit to the company.

Das Blatt der Hausfrau and the pattern business were conceived with a view toward instilling and cultivating in wide groups of bourgeois female consumers a consciousness of their modern, middle-class identity. Fashion magazines and patterns were nationally and internationally promoted as "indispensable for the modern working woman" and advanced a concept of her as "rational," "thrifty," "self-tailored," and "independent in most money-spending decisions."[16] Evidently this advertising tactic worked. By the late 1920s the magazine was reaching half a million readers, and the sale of patterns ran into the millions every year. According to numerous contemporary accounts, one particular slogan for the patterns quickly became a household word and was even parodied in the cabarets:

> Be thrifty, my honey,
> Ullstein patterns save money![17]

Ullstein's other women's magazine, the more high-brow and sumptuously illustrated *Die Dame*, broadened the publisher's appeal to a wide public of working women, promoting a notion of the "modern" associated with ideas of worldliness, sophistication, and a cosmopolitan spirit. Defined by Hermann Ullstein as an "ultramodern social magazine of women's fashions" and widely advertised as Germany's only illustrated publication "of international repute," *Die Dame* was actually read not just by "spoiled" bourgeois women of high class and distinguished taste. As Maud Lavin and Patrice Petro have shown, most Ullstein periodicals reached several classes of readers, so it is difficult to define with any precision the class of readership based solely on the content of the publications.[18] Although *Die Dame* regularly featured lavishly illustrated upscale fashion, including essays and plentiful photographs of foreign countries, exotic places, and exciting national and international society events, this did not mean that its readers were only rich women who could afford luxurious attire or leisure trips abroad. A further component of its commercial success and immense popularity was its self-promotion as a product combining the mundane world of women's fashions with the more urbane, intellectual world of literature and the arts.[19] For most of its readers the fashion magazine represented primarily a vehicle of entertainment and fantasy, an imaginary mirror in which women envisioned themselves as attractive, elegant, self-confident individuals.

Yet *Die Dame* was by no means without rivals. It was competing for the female public with *Elegante Welt* (1912–62), a magazine of similar format and equally high circulation figures, as well as with the extravagant *Styl* (1922–24), the high-brow *Die deutsche Elite* (1924–30), *die neue linie* (1929–33), which was modernist in its design and concept, and the ambitious if short-lived German edition of *Vogue* (1928–29).[20] There were also popular fashion supplements to the high-circulation daily newspapers (Modebeilagen), namely *Der Moden-Spiegel* (supplement to the *Berliner Tageblatt*, 1921–33) and *Für die Frau* (supplement to the *Frankfurter Zeitung*, 1926–34). Although all of these magazines covered similar topics — women's fashions, society events, theater, film, the arts, dance — *Die Dame* remained unsurpassed, because it maintained a high level of technological innovation and performance, including layout, photography, and illustration, and at the same time exerted intellectual appeal due to its formidable literary component. Along with *Der Uhu* and the *BIZ*, *Die Dame* attracted the biggest names in literature and art across a broad political spectrum.[21] Ullstein House, unlike the publishers of other, more politicized, illustrated magazines, treated the literary text first of all as a sellable, attractive commodity. As Kurt Tucholsky remarked on his work for various Ullstein periodicals: "At Ullstein I have the comfortable feeling that he is buying a commodity; no one has ever tried to influence me, nor has Georg Bernhard or anyone else ever threatened my freedom."[22]

Here we arrive at an important and perhaps the most ambivalent characteristic of Ullstein's contribution to the rise of mass media. As much as it defined and aggressively promoted modernity in terms of leveling notions of "high" and "low" culture and embracing technological innovation with the ultimate goal of reaching an ever larger public, including a female public, Ullstein's illustrated press continued to sustain in its own way the distinction between higher and lower intellectual pretension, between more and less "serious" types of intellectual activity. This ambivalence is most apparent in the publisher's institutional policies concerning the sphere of women's and fashion publication.

Consider, for example, Hermann Ullstein's own attitude toward the women's magazines and the sewing-pattern business that he was in charge of. According to his memoir, the sphere of fashion and advertisement constituted for him a source of "relaxation after much more intellectual efforts"

(*RF*, 107–8). This condescending evaluation of the importance and status of fashion was reflected in his overall judgment of the role of women in the public sphere the publishing conglomerate had been opening up and actively expanding ever since the end of the nineteenth century. Ullstein House was consistently proud of the high number of female workers it employed, because it saw itself as a benefactor of women's welfare in an age when more and more women were compelled and/or eager to join the work force. By 1904, around two thousand delivery women (Botenfrauen) were working for the publishing house and "laid the *Morgenpost* on the breakfast table of half a million people" every morning. Ullstein even emphasized the important social effect of his company's policies: "Working for no more than two hours a day, these women earned as much as a hundred marks a month, a substantial addition to their income" (*RF*, 83–84).

So the picture that emerges from the reconstruction of Ullstein's institutional policies is rich in interesting contradictions. On the one hand women were discovered as one of the most powerful and promising consumer groups, and dreams of elegance, higher self-esteem, and luxury were served to them in huge doses. On the other hand, Ullstein blamed the "politically inexperienced" women readers for falling prey to "stupid demagogic slogans" spread by the nationalist press (*RF*, 165). But most evocative of the double standard with which the prominence of women and fashion in the public sphere was evaluated was the status of the female journalists, designers, and editors — in short, of the female intellectuals within the Ullstein media empire. The most significant breakthrough for women in the professional arena came after 1918, when the number of female journalists and writers who contributed to Ullstein's magazines and newspapers increased dramatically. A long-time editor for Ullstein, Hedda Pänke characterized the publishing empire as a "springboard for female talents" and as a key Weimar institution that opened up publishing opportunities for numerous aspiring young authors, including Nelly Sachs, Irmgard Keun, Polly Tieck, Gabriele Tergit, Vicki Baum, Marieluise Fleißer, Ruth Landshoff, Regina Ullmann, Gina Kaus, Dinah Nelken, and Dora Benjamin.[23]

A Collective Portrait of Ladies

In her memoirs, *It Was All Quite Different,* Vicki Baum recounts a remarkable story: after she had "published six books, written two more, and thrown away maybe a dozen," she wrote a letter to a friend at Ullstein and humbly asked to be taken on as an apprentice:

> My vague idea was that it could not be too hard to become a fashion designer. Why not, indeed, after all the things I had created out of those

navy blue hand-me-downs? Somewhere I had read that fashion designers earned good money, but I would have gratefully accepted any kind of job in the buzzing Ullstein beehive. Among other assets I mentioned that I could type at fair speed, though in my own hit-and-miss two-finger method. On the debit side I confessed "no shorthand," but I added that I would gladly learn quickly if necessary. Or maybe they needed a music critic? Someone who knew the stage inside-out? Perhaps a reliable secretary? . . . Perhaps they could use me as an assistant in the corner for recipes, advice to housewives and mothers?[24]

To her delight — she was so eager to leave provincial Mannheim — the young writer was invited for an interview, and this is how she prepared for it:

I filled a large drawing pad with designs for all sorts of attire, from alluring negligees to street-, house-, and afternoon dresses, to elaborate evening gowns. I added patterns for embroideries and fabrics, sofa pillows, lampshades, and for good measure some furniture sketches I had discussed with the owner of a large furniture plant. . . . I remember especially drawing a tableau in which I tried to combine all my ideas: elegant ladies in various dresses and fashionable tea gowns or simple smartly-tailored outfits, with or without hats, standing, sitting, or leaning amid a super-abundance of pillows, lampshades, and other accessories, all looking something like the Tower of Pisa, as the entire drawing had the same slant as my handwriting. Not one of my modish creatures stood straight.[25]

Baum's recollection is particularly helpful for rethinking the myth of the New Woman and her ties to modernity. On the one hand this quotation highlights an emerging rupture in the sociological structure of Weimar society. Middle-aged and middle-class women demonstrated new, emancipated life-styles and modern cultural practices in a variety of traditionally male-dominated fields such as journalism, photography, and design. According to Atina Grossmann, bourgeois New Women during the Weimar years profited from a fortuitous, albeit brief, historical encounter of conventional class privileges — comfortable home, domestic help, a nanny for the children — with radically expanding opportunities for professional self-realization.[26] At the same time, however, the types of jobs imaginable and available to well-educated middle-class women were still, as Baum put it, "some kind of apprenticeship" — marginal in comparison to what was perceived as "mainstream" intellectual endeavor, rather trivial, repetitive, and not truly creative. This paradox, explored in more detail below, was at the heart of Ullstein's unique economic success and sense of modernness.

Ullstein took enormous pride in its encouraging attitude towards women as professional journalists and used it to promote itself as modern and progressive. The anniversary volume *Fünfzig Jahre Ullstein, 1877–1927* features the photographs, names, and titles of the various women editors for Ullstein periodicals, accompanied by the following commentary:

> On the editorial staff of the periodicals women quickly grew more prominent. Their number grew in proportion to the publications dedicated primarily to feminine interests. Today the company is unimaginable without the numerous women colleagues in the different fields. Of the many, only a few can be mentioned here.[27]

Of the women who worked for Ullstein House, only the names of those who successfully pursued a literary career — which was regarded as prestigious — and published best-selling books survive in public memory, most prominently Vicki Baum, and, to a lesser extent, Ola Alsen. The majority of the female editors were never mentioned in contemporary encyclopedias such as the *Reichshandbuch der deutschen Gesellschaft*, and very little biographical information about them is obtainable.[28] Still, they acquired the status of role models in the eyes of the magazine readers, so it is worthwhile to resurrect the names of these women, to reconstruct a collective cultural portrait of them, and to shed light on their long-standing intellectual presence and how they were portrayed visually in the pages of Ullstein's periodicals.

Most of the female journalists mentioned in the anniversary volume were working for the women's and travel sections of the daily press or for specialized women's magazines, a fact in line with a well-documented general trend among female Weimar journalists. According to the report of the International Work Office (Internationales Arbeitsamt) from 1928, most women in journalism specialized in thematic spheres such as "fashion, hygiene, household, women's issues, and sometimes in literary and art criticism."[29] Very few of them were able to penetrate the male-dominated sphere of political reporting.[30] The internal editorial hierarchy at Ullstein and in other publishing houses compels us to agree with Almut Todorow's characterization of this phenomenon as a "ghettoization" of women in the journalistic profession.[31]

A closer look at the history of *Die Dame*, however, reveals that both the public status and the image of the female intellectual underwent an uneven development during the Weimar Republic. From 1919 until 1926 most original fashion layouts and cover pages were created by female designers and artists such as Erica Mohr, Hanna Goerke, Martha Sparkuhl, Julie Haase-Werkenthin, Gerda Bunzel, and Steffie Nathan. In 1923 Petra Fiedler, the daughter of the well-known modernist architect Peter Behrens, joined the designers' team, and her association with the magazine proved to be the longest and perhaps most successful.

The fashion designers (Modezeichnerinnen) were assigned to draw original models based on impressions gathered during shows at prominent Berlin fashion houses, and around 1924, designer Vally Reinecke began

Fig. 3: Illustration by Petra [Fiedler]. *Die Dame*, May 1924, no. 16, 15. Kunstbibliothek, Staatliche Museen zu Berlin.

traveling frequently to Paris fashion shows and created her own regularly appearing page, "Was ich in Paris sah." The fashion layouts and especially the magazine covers before 1926 do not portray the New Woman as a symbol of cold, masculine uniformity as one might expect. Steffie Nathan's covers from 1923 and a variety of layouts by Fiedler and Haase-Werkenthin were

Fig. 4: "The Fashion Staff of *Die Dame*": fashion artist Martha Sparkuhl (top left), fashion artist Julie Haase-Werkenthin (bottom left), the head of the fashion department Johanna Thal (right). *Die Dame*, Nov. 1920, no. 4, 8. Kunstbibliothek, Staatliche Museen zu Berlin.

Unsere Modezeichnerin Vally Reinecke.
Aufnahme von Becker & Maaß.

Fig. 5: Fashion illustrator Vally Reinecke, *Die Dame*, Apr. 1921, no. 13, 16. Kunstbibliothek, Staatliche Museen zu Berlin.

typical in presenting the modern and fashionably dressed woman (within the limits of stylized fashion drawing) as a person with individualized taste, posture, and gestures. The reader encounters her in a variety of outdoor and mostly metropolitan settings: in the busy street, at the train station, next to a car, at a crowded beach resort, or against a backdrop of modernist façades. Whenever the female fashion model is featured in a domestic interior, we find her engaged in an intellectual activity: perched on a ladder browsing through a huge collection of books, or reading in front of the fire while her male companion has fallen asleep.

At the same time, topical commentaries on fashion (Mode-Notizen) — meticulous descriptions and detailed interpretation of the latest trends in clothes, fashionable accessories, and hairstyles — ran in every issue of *Die Dame*. Unlike similar sections in other fashion periodicals, Ullstein's

Mode-Notizen were always properly signed with the names of the female fashion journalists: Elsa Herzog, Johanna Thal, Stephanie Kaul, Julie Elias, Ruth Goetz, Anna Paula Wedekind-Pariselle, Lily von Nagy.[32] Readers not only quickly became familiar with the names of the women engaged professionally with the creation and interpretation of fashion but also got to see their photographs frequently in the pages of the magazine. As early as 1920 *Die Dame* published three large photographs by the famous Karl Schenker in which fashion journalist Johanna Thal and designers Martha Sparkuhl and Julie Haase-Werkenthin posed as models. Also included were designer Vally Reinecke, not to mention Gerda Bunzel (in her new car) and Erica Mohr, wearing fashionable outfits and posing artistically for the camera. On the occasion of Erica Mohr's death in 1923, the magazine dedicated a whole page to its "valued contributor," featuring again her photograph and a selection of her fashion layouts, illustrations, and other drawings. Later in the decade, photographs of the designer Petra Fiedler and the fashion journalist Lily von Nagy (who was also famous for winning a number of international beauty contests) appeared quite often in *Die Dame*.[33] The first two photographs of Petra Fiedler appeared in 1927 with the following captions: "Our colleague, the painter and fashion artist Frau Petra, at a masquerade ball," and "The fashion artist Petra Fiedler in a pullover of her own design"; a third one appeared in 1929 where she is photographed in a fashionable cap with her dog.

Such examples, not to be found in any other fashion magazine of the Weimar Republic, demonstrate that Ullstein was consistent in its unique policy of honoring female fashion journalists and designers as role models and granted them a social status comparable to that of other prominent women whose photographs appeared in the pages of *Die Dame* — wives of renowned politicians, writers, and artists, as well as theater celebrities, singers, dancers, and movie stars. In fact, during the 1920s there were very few professional models who posed for fashion photographs, a role performed largely by movie stars and society ladies wearing designer clothing.[34] The photographs of Ullstein's fashion journalists do not show the clichéd image of the New Woman — very young and conspicuously androgynous. On the contrary, the reader sees middle-class and middle-aged women who demonstrate their modernness by emphasizing individuality rather than uniformity. Posing in outfits designed by themselves, the journalists and designers in the photographs also affirmed the notion that "fashionable" did not imply extravagant and luxurious (as was mostly the case when movie stars were featured in the pages of *Die Dame*) so much as self-made, professional. The careers of these female fashion journalists and illustrators and their presence on the pages of the magazine are in fact emblematic of widespread changes for a whole generation of Weimar women. What Ute Eskildsen notes about female photographers and photojournalists also applies to a great extent to the fashion journalists and

Fig. 6: Fashion journalist Lily von Nagy posing for *Die Dame*. *Die Dame*, Nov. 1924, no. 3, 5. Kunstbibliothek, Staatliche Museen zu Berlin.

Fig. 7: Fashion illustrator Petra Fiedler in a sweater of her own design. *Die Dame*, Dec. 1927, no. 6, 58. Kunstbibliothek, Staatliche Museen zu Berlin.

Auf vielseitiges Verlangen: Unsere Mitarbeiterin „Anita", die Verfasserin der Aufsatzreihe „Lebensstil 1930". Fot. Rolf Mahrenholz.

Fig. 8: Fashion journalist Anita [Anita Daniel]. Photograph published upon numerous requests from readers who were following her series of articles "Lifestyle 1930." *Die Dame*, Jul. 1930, no. 22, 36. Kunstbibliothek, Staatliche Museen zu Berlin.

designers: most of them belonged to the generation born in the late 1880s or early 1890s, and many came from conventional, well-to-do bourgeois, often Jewish, families. Lured by economic freedom, artistic and intellectual challenge, mobility, and the public exposure of the profession, these Weimar women turned fashion into an "instrument for individual flexibility and personal exploration of their environment."[35]

Yet at the same time, even when they were allowed much professional discretion and received high praise for their work in women's magazines, the "global" and "more serious" tasks of running the magazines and setting up the overall marketing policy and artistic production were left to men. When Hermann Ullstein appointed Kurt Korff as a chief editor of *Die Dame*, he did so because he "discovered that no one of the opposite sex could have been better suited for the position" (*RF*, 87). Also, a distinct shift in the politics of the magazine occurred in the second half of the twenties, when Viennese designer Ernst Dryden was named chief artistic director for the fashion section of *Die Dame*.[36] After 1926 he was permanently located in Paris, whence he sent drawings of models he saw at fashion shows, extensive commentaries, and a large number of covers; by the end of his association with *Die Dame*, in 1933, many of the previously well-known names of female journalists and designers such as Vally Reinecke, Gerda Bunzel, and Anna Paula Wedekind-Pariselle had faded away. The popular rubric *Mode-Notizen* continued in a truncated and marginalized form, completely overshadowed by Dryden's essays, sent directly from the capital of fashion. Petra Fiedler, Steffie Nathan, and Julie Haase-Werkenthin, who had been celebrated in the first half of the decade as creators of original styles and cover pages, were assigned to work primarily in the patterns area, which did not enjoy the same distinction and eminence as the department concerned with original fashion drawings.

By 1927 the photographs of "our valued female fashion editors and illustrators" (Moderedakteurinnen und -zeichnerinnen) had virtually disappeared from the pages of *Die Dame*; their original work was given less and less visible space in the magazine, while Dryden's drawings and essays reinforced on a mass scale the myth of a New Woman as a symbol of uniformity and cold, haughty, unattainable elegance. His fashion layouts denied the individualization of modern women, showing geometrical silhouettes arranged in a chorus line. In his presentation, women's experience of fashion seemed completely detached from the experience and understanding of everyday life and carried the markers of a self-centered arrogance that invited many critics of the New Woman to misunderstand and condemn her as too masculine or too intellectual.

The institutional policies at Ullstein during the late 1920s and early 1930s were marked by the emergence of a new distinction between the regular "fashion editors" and the more prominent "writers," although both groups of women wrote about the same things: clothes, fashionable accessories, manners, women's issues. On the one hand, as the previously quoted reminiscence by Baum about her own start at Ullstein House makes clear, fashion in the context of Ullstein's modernized, mass-circulating press provided many opportunities for a large number of young women who aspired to professional careers as writers and artists. Most of all, especially in the first half of the 1920s, it gave them unique access to public life. In short essays, fashion vignettes, and drawings, and through their own images appearing in numerous photographs, they interpreted (and literally demonstrated) the specific meaning of modern times to modern women, emphasizing such qualities as individuality, professional engagement in the public sphere, and self-made elegance. On the other hand, especially from 1927 to 1933, specific hierarchies surfaced within the women's public sphere of fashion. Although it was open to women's issues and proud of the invaluable work of its female fashion editors, Ullstein House consciously maintained the rigid distinction between its "new, truly original stars," namely bestselling writer Vicki Baum and journalist Anita Daniel, and the "older, more ordinary stars," the fashion editors and fashion designers. As Vicki Baum recalls, editor Korff was always very careful to keep her and her "charming, elegant colleague Anita apart from the coarser-grained ladies of the fashion department and their garment-industry jargon."[37]

What Is Modern? The Response of the Fashion Editors

Despite the limitations imposed on Ullstein's female writers, the fashion editors managed to contribute something more to the Weimar era than just detailed descriptions of the day's fashions. Especially in the first half of the 1920s they persistently attempted to transform the question "What is fashionable?" (Was ist modisch?) into the question "What is modern?" (Was ist modern?). Their writings in response to that question constitute a unique discussion and conceptualization of modernity from a woman's point of view. In a large number of essays published throughout the 1920s, regular fashion editors for *Die Dame*, such as Herzog, Thal, Kaul, and von Bunsen attempted to historicize the current trends of fashion and to interpret their specifically experiential aspect. The "modern woman," with all the radical changes in her appearance, was repeatedly construed as the product of a major socio-historical disruption, namely the First World War. As many of the journalists claimed, the simplified, loose-fitting cut of dresses, with the shorter hem exposing the legs, and the new aesthetic ideal of slenderness and functionality were a natural consequence of a transformed social and economic situation for women. During and after the war they were dealing with an extreme fabric shortage (Stoffknappheit) and severe economic inflation, while simultaneously gaining unprecedented social and professional mobility. Women went out to work en masse in factories and offices and had to use public transportation. All of these new experiences not only caused radically innovative clothing styles and practices to emerge but in a way also guaranteed the irreversibility of the aesthetic and social changes that took place. As fashion editor Elsa Herzog wrote, "The saying that women belong at home is long out-moded. The war made women independent, with the result that they can move freely in public without risking discredit."[38]

Most of the paragraph-long socio-historical prefaces to the actual description of fashion in the *Mode-Notizen* were obviously prompted by the negative publicity surrounding postwar fashions. Fashion journalists referred repeatedly to the war experience and its impact on women's lifestyles in order to rebuff criticism of the new fashions and to argue that the clock could not be turned back. Marie von Bunsen detected "not an ordinary storm, but a hurricane" of disapproving responses and bad publicity, and she undertook to clarify again and again the historical connection that most male fashion commentators did not see or did not want to accept: "Apparently there is still insufficient understanding of the connection — the symbolic embodiment and manifestation — between the world in crisis and such clothing."[39] Such lack of understanding of the historical necessity and practical considerations behind new clothing styles was evident even in the pages of *Die Dame*, most prominently in the essays by male experts in "more serious" fields such as history and art. In his 1919 essay "Pagen" (Pages), for example, cultural critic and historian Hans von Kahlenberg dwelt at length on the increasing masculinization of women's appearance in the course of the last century, though he admitted that for the modern woman there was indeed no way back. At the same time he evoked the distressing experience of the recent war and economic crisis, but only to depict it as a male trauma that needed to be remedied by a return to the feminine: "The connection between our origins and our past must be maintained at all cost. [Women] need hearts, soft hands, and lips that can be silent and offer comfort. Much patience, much wisdom, self-forgetfulness. Don't look so belligerent! We have just come from war. We need peace."[40]

Throughout the 1920s this side of the discussions about fashion was permeated by fear that "external masculinization" of dress and hairstyle was leading directly to an "internal masculinization" of women. Although it is not entirely clear what was meant by "internal masculinization," the term was mainly associated with women's higher self-confidence, greater independence, and mobility outside the domestic sphere.[41] "Sociologists and moral philosophers fear that outer masculinization could be followed by inner masculinization," wrote an anonymous fashion editor for *Der Uhu*, who emphasized, however, that such fears did not deter women from bobbing their hair or wearing short skirts, because this was a "thoroughly practical and healthy fashion."[42] Thus it became a common rhetorical gesture in the *Mode-Notizen* written by the regular fashion editors to fend off attacks against fashion trends that might be interpreted as further steps toward masculinization. As pants became fashionable around 1925, fashion journalist Lily von Nagy sought to preempt anticipated criticism: "Wearing trousers no longer represents the embarrassing transgression of a woman into a sphere hitherto closed to her: the sphere of masculinity! . . . It is rather an expression of the new trend of our times to regard a woman's physical beauty as understood, regardless of its clothing."[43] If for Kahlenberg women's appearance was to soothe and delight men's eyes, and therefore contemporary fashions presented a threatening experiment or capricious aberration, the female fashion journalist interpreted them as an expression of women's newly gained "ability to look" at their own bodies — not as symbolic objects, but as natural "corporality." One could also view Nagy's comment as consistent with the second set of concepts to which women's modernity was linked, namely individuality and autonomy in aesthetic taste and choice.

Female fashion journalists were astonishingly persistent in explaining to their readers throughout the 1920s that fashion should not be viewed as a set of norms to be followed by all who would like to appear fashionable. They rather shared the belief that fashion reflected an ever-changing configuration of women's feelings, desires, and ambitions: "Fashion is the barometer that most precisely registers psychic trends."[44] Therefore, the modern woman — a reader and practitioner of fashion — aided by the fashion expert — the female fashion journalist who deciphered and mediated the readings of the "barometer" — no longer appeared as an object of the norm but as its coauthor and creator.

The editors of *Die Dame* frequently used the *Mode-Notizen* and especially their long introductory paragraph to define the category "modern" in terms of a specifically female experience of contemporary realities. Johanna Thal was one of the regular editorial staff members who was prominently engaged in clarifying the difference between what was just "fashionable" (modisch) and what was essentially "modern" for the German woman. As early as 1919 in an essay entitled "Puppen und Frauen" (Dolls and Women), she noted that the traditional saying about beautiful women "She has a doll's face" or "She looks like a doll" was becoming outdated. She used this observation as a starting point for a discussion about women and fashion:

> This comparison is not modern. Because such faces are out of fashion, for women and for dolls. Today we women have our individuality, which describes the spirit of the independent woman and has begun to influence her appearance as well. Fashion in its many forms supports this drive for individuality; every woman can dress differently and still be in fashion.[45]

The alignment of the dramatic changes in women's postwar fashions with the spirit of modernity was a persistent leitmotiv in articles by Thal and other female journalists in Ullstein's magazines. More specifically, women's modernity would very often be defined, in Thal's words, as "pursuit of individuality" (Streben nach Eigenart), which finds one of its concrete and most noticeable expressions in the varying styles of fashion. Again and again the fashion journalist would urge female readers not to follow blindly the fashion trends presented and explained at length in the magazines but to make their own personal choices according to their own sense of the modern: "Real fashion sense is present only in people who also have world sense, as we now call the feeling for everything modern. . . . Every lady can dress according to her own taste if she is sensitive to the modern world."[46]

The modern cult of individuality as seen here in the practice of fashion also became evident in the work done by sociologists, social workers, and feminist activists in the 1920s on a variety of problems related to the life experience of the modern woman. In 1931 a large volume entitled *Die Kultur der Frau: Eine Lebenssymphonie der Frau des XX. Jahrhunderts* (Feminine Culture: A Life Symphony of the Twentieth-Century Woman) was edited and published by Ada Schmidt-Beil. Over seventy female scholars, journalists, and other professionals contributed articles on topics ranging from aesthetics to politics, from sexuality to social work. Particularly interesting are a few articles that touch upon the link between modernity and fashion. A common thread weaving through two introductory and programmatic essays — one by the sociologist Dr. Marianne Weber and the other by the fashion journalist Charlotte Wilke — is an insistence on the fact that the modern woman had emerged and asserted herself as an "individualized person" (individualisierter Einzelmensch).[47] Women's individuality, as Marianne Weber contended, is qualitatively different from Georg Simmel's conceptualization of the female role as complementary to the male rationalized sphere of "objective achievements" (sachliche Leistung). It is rather a product of changing social realities — work outside the home (aushäusige Arbeit) and radically new forms of life outside the family (ganz neue, außerfamiliäre Lebensformen).[48] In a similar vein, in her excursus on "Mode, Frauentyp und Zeitgeist" (Fashion, Type of woman, and the Spirit of the Times), Charlotte Wilke concluded that "today's woman has achieved an enviable state even in her outer appearance: she wants neither to imitate men nor to oppose them by denying her femaleness; rather, she has found her own type by dressing in different ways, depending on what she is doing."[49]

The assertion of a strong sense of individuality and the legitimacy of autonomous choices through the practice of fashion in the early 1920s was demonstrated concretely when the institution of *haute couture* failed in its campaign to reverse the trend of shorter skirts and hair.[50] A magazine such as *Die Dame*, and especially the strong position of its vocal fashion journalists, contributed much to the triumph of customers' preference for functionality over the industry's attempts to impose a lavish and impractical style of dress. A series of articles published in 1921, most prominently "Die Bilanz der Mode" and "Die nächste Modelinie," had warned readers of *Die Dame* that leading French designer houses planned to reintroduce the corset, because the new fashions made the female body appear particularly "formless." While fashion journalists were often ardent promoters of *haute couture*'s creativity (their task, after all, was to train readers in the code of fashion and the rapid variation of seasonal collections), starting in the early 1920s they were also convinced that women as consumers are and should be ultimately guided by their newly gained modern experience. In a reaction to frequent reports in French magazines that corsets and long skirts were on their way back into fashion, one journalist for *Die Dame* dismissed the likelihood of such a trend and denounced it as a "skillful advertisement for corset manufacturers and tailors." She openly pooh-poohed a "radical overturn of woman's street silhouette," because "the taste of the modern woman for youthful and sporty clothes and her steady presence and mobility in public spaces" could not be reversed.[51]

A comparison of most of *Mode-Notizen* of the early 1920s with the authoritative opinions of then well-known historians and cultural critics shows that individuality had become a contentious issue. Renowned male commentators such as writer Friedrich Freksa and costume historian Max von Boehn were granted considerable space in the pages of *Die Dame* to discuss the phenomenon of fashion within a broader, cultural-historical frame; their task and ambition was to enlighten women, and thus their essays assumed a didactic or patronizing tone.[52] Consider, for example, Friedrich Freksa's 1918 essay "Mode, Tracht und Möbel" (Fashion, Traditional Costume, and Furniture). In many ways its rhetoric reflects the common nostalgia of many conservative cultural critics for the times preceding the industrial revolution and the concomitant rise of fashion — in other words, for traditional women's dress rather than frequently changing fashion. Freksa expressed opinions that were diametrically opposed to female fashion journalists' notions of what was individualized, personal, and, for that matter, modern. For Freksa, it was traditional costume (Tracht) rather than fashion (Mode) that expressed a woman's individuality, because it stood for a stable set of clothing rather than permanent change and unpredictability: "Only clothes in which the wearer can always move comfortably become an expression and constituent of the personality."[53] And since men's attire hardly changed from the nineteenth to the early twentieth century, Freksa was primarily addressing women's fashions, attacking the modern phenomenon of frequent, unpredictable changes of style. In conclusion he denied women any decision in matters of fashion and envisioned them more as the objects of existing rules rather than subjects or creators of new norms: "Still, we should not blame women when they follow fashion. A new costume will emerge again, just not until their homes are filled with better-built furniture of a more lasting design." Like many other male commentators on women's fashion, Freksa was obviously not interested in the notion of women's growing sense of individuality and independence as a factor in the formation of contemporary styles of dress.

The emphasis on individuality as the most characteristic aspect of women's experience of modernity cannot be fully understood without considering another feature in the development of postwar fashions, namely their democratization. All commentators on modern fashion agreed that the striving for functionality and simplicity in the twenties accomplished a leveling of women's fashions across class lines. "The democratic principle of the last years," wrote Stephanie Kaul, "found in fashion its utmost and final expression. There was an effort to create a fashion that would make the most elegant lady and the most ordinary girl appear equally well and fashionably dressed."[54] The point was made again and again that the silhouette of the little shop girl could hardly be distinguished from that of a well-to-do aristocrat. But in the discursive context of *Die Dame* the terms "individualization" and "democratization" were not lacking a certain ambiguity. On the one hand the publisher's leading positions in the business of producing and selling affordable sewing patterns and in the advertising of off-the-rack clothing (Konfektion) demonstrated its firm commitment to the process of democratization. The rise of both industrial clothing production and the mass-circulation press made dressing in the fashion of the day possible for a broad social group by facilitating the imitation of fashionable models and making them affordable. But on the other hand, much of the fashion coverage for *Die Dame* was designed to feature the production of the other branch of the clothing industry, *haute couture*. *Die Dame*, as well as other comparable fashion magazines, celebrated the French couturiers as modern artists, geniuses, and unchallenged arbiters of elegance. Paradoxically *haute couture*, aided by the popular illustrated press and large-scale clothing manufacturers, managed to achieve two mutually incompatible things: it transformed women into mass consumers of luxury and male couturiers from artisans into sovereign artists. *Haute couture* played a contradictory role, both revolutionizing and patronizing, and this role informed not only the image of the New Woman but also the ambivalence of the fashion debate in Weimar Germany.

It is worth making a short digression at this point to look at the concrete ways in which *haute couture* so powerfully influenced women's imagination and self-conception. The institution of *haute couture* was based in Paris and represented by such prestigious design houses as Worth (est. 1857), Rouff (1884), Paquin (1891), Doucet (1880), Lanvin (1909), Chanel (1919), and Patou (1919). Just before and then after the First World War, these "unrivaled laboratories for novelty," as one historian calls them, revolutionized the experience of fashion in major ways.[55] Regular fashion shows with live mannequins were introduced between 1908 and 1910, then spread quickly to the big cities of Europe, including Berlin, and became both an authentic public spectacle and a cornerstone in the careful institutionalization and orchestration of mass consumption in the industrial age. The manufacturing companies represented at the seasonal shows bought models and the right to reproduce them in simplified versions that could then be purchased at the cities' department stores.[56]

Fashion designers from *Die Dame* were also present at the shows — until 1923 mainly at the one organized by the Berlin fashion salons (Modehäuser), and after 1923 also at the Parisian shows. They collected impressions, took notes, made sketches, and published dozens of their original drawings in the pages of the bi-weekly magazine. Thus the fashion press played a major role as *haute couture* carefully steered consumers through theatrical display and fanciful advertisement. But the seduction process also worked by perpetuating a new myth of individuality and originality, and by instilling what Lipovetsky succinctly defines as "new dreams of an ephemeral harmony between one's inner self and one's outward appearance."[57] If the leading fashion designers perceived themselves as the creators of an individualized fashion ("There ought to be as many models as there are women," declared Paul Poiret), *Die Dame*'s leading experts on fashion interpreted these models as giving concrete form to women's individuality and their desire for personal metamorphosis.[58]

In light of these historical observations, the journalists' assertion of women's sense of individuality and freedom of choice through fashionable attire appears more ambivalent than at first glance. On the one hand it is hard to ignore the fact that concrete trends and practices in the twenties represented a radical break with tradition and more than at any other time were determined by women customers and their choices rather than by *haute couture*. This point was reiterated again and again by the fashion journalists:

> We are accustomed to Paris determining new fashions. . . . That depends on pattern makers, fabric manufacturers, and great designers — always men making the decisions. Now it seems as if women — not even those occupationally concerned with fashion, but the typical women-on-the-street in Paris — are taking the lead.[59]

They seemed to agree in general that in modern times, "not just the inclinations of the tailoring firms, but those of women themselves were becoming decisive."[60] Yet at the same time, as *haute couture* and its eloquent promoters the fashion journalists emphasized individuality and autonomy, they reacted against the modern leveling of women's personal appearance in the process of the democratization of fashion. If signs of social difference and class hierarchy were obscured in the age of affordable, mass-produced fashionable clothing, the loss had to be compensated for by particular emphasis on originality and personal identity.

Thus fashion's modernity was interpreted as an irrevocable break with century-old aesthetic traditions and cultural practices on the one hand, and on the other as a reaffirmation of the primordial requirement for feminine beauty under the guise of individuality. This dual understanding is reflected with astonishing clarity in the fashion debate around 1929, when images of seductive and lush femininity were restored to women's fashion, at least in evening dress. If we trust the detailed descriptions of the trend provided by Stephanie Kaul and Johanna Thal for the readers of *Die Dame*, skirts and hair became longer, rich ornamentation reappeared, and the cut of dresses emphasized rather than obscured the natural form of the female body. All these changes were interpreted precisely as a reaction against the previous tendency to democratization and simplification. As Kaul wrote,

> After years of the strictest simplicity of line and economy of materials, after seasons of puritanical moderation, clothes are finally again being designed according to individuality rather than type. The new fashions make the girl into a lady — an individual lady who has freed herself from vulgarity, conformity, and standardization.[61]

In the early 1930s the tone of the fashion debate in *Die Dame* and in Ullstein's other illustrated magazines lost most of its sense of celebrating modernity. Although the come-back of explicit femininity primarily affected evening dress, while day-time attire remained as functional and practical as it was before, the fervor of the discussion intensified, and fashion was again used as an occasion to comment on issues such as women's experience of modernity, this time from a different point of view. As Ernst Dryden, the editor in chief of the fashion section of *Die Dame*, contended, "fashion has not become so extreme as some prophets claim with unconcealed horror. The long dress, in which [women] detect an anachronistic threat against [their] freedom and public activity, is worn solely in the evening."[62] But at the same time, it can hardly be overlooked that Dryden's colleagues Thal and Kaul were particularly vocal in defense of the new trends. They rushed to generalize that the rebirth of feminine fashions was the ultimate expression of an "awakened maternal sensibility" ("das mütterliche Gefühl ist wach geworden"), of a "desire for deeper spirituality" ("Wunsch nach vertiefter Geistigkeit"), and of a longing for a more stable gender identity, and they reiterated this position in numerous essays published after 1929.[63]

Still, *Die Dame* preserved the tradition of presenting a picture of diversity. Around 1926 it allowed one of its younger and more open-minded fashion journalists, Anita, to start an editorial column of her own. Not infrequently, Anita's texts had provocative overtones of dissent, especially during and after 1929, when most fashion commentaries grew more and

Fig. 9: Illustration by Ernst Dryden. *Die Dame*, Mar. 1926, no. 13, 5. Kunstbibliothek, Staatliche Museen zu Berlin.

more conservative. While other fashion experts were preoccupied with deciphering the significance of the alleged return of the feminine ideal, Anita dismissed such rhetoric as overblown and appealed to readers to look around and realize that neither the "overtly fashionable girl" (mondänes Girl) nor the "stylish gentlewoman" (die Dame) existed in reality. Such an observation led to a new definition of women's modernity that was neither reduced to the effects of mass fashion nor abolished by recent developments toward a more individualized, personalized, overtly feminine style:

> The fashionable woman as reflected until a short time ago in the imagination of the world around us was a fairy-tale phenomenon.... Fashionable is no longer modern.... The most recent version of a modern

woman is a kind of wonder of the world. She can do everything. . . . She doesn't want to represent; she wants to experience. And how she does that is her own private matter. There are no longer any fashionable women, just modern women.[64]

Anita recognized the intense projection of imaginative qualities and symbolic meanings onto fashion and juxtaposed that process with women's "real" experiences, occasioning a look back at the fashion debate of the 1920s, which may serve to conclude our discussion of fashion and women's modernity.

The numerous essays published by the regular fashion journalists for *Die Dame* over the course of the twenties reflected two trends in the conceptualization of fashion in the emerging age of mass culture. First, in the wake of the First World War fashion gave women palpable experience of professional activity, of social and class mobility, and facilitated the rise of woman as an "individualized personality" with autonomous aesthetic choices. This interpretation, which prevailed in the *Mode-Notizen* from 1918 to 1924, sent a covert emancipatory message to readers, affirming a directly positive, even celebratory embrace of modernity and reinforcing a confident, albeit illusory, belief that innovation stems from one's own ability and will rather than from ancestral laws or the genius-designer. Second, however, at the same time that they destabilized traditional class divisions, modern Weimar fashions, especially of the late 1920s and early 1930s, paradoxically accentuated the division between men's and women's appearance as never before, especially in the way the sexes presented themselves. The fashion debate in *Die Dame* seemed to suggest that despite the new democratized, modern practices in the Weimar Republic, fashion continued to be interpreted by many male fashion writers as a feminine passion reflecting women's timeless infatuation with clothes, beauty, and appearances.

Notes

[1] Herman Ullstein, *The Rise and Fall of the House of Ullstein* (New York: Simon and Schuster, 1943), 3–4. Further references to this work will be given in the text using the abbreviation *RF* and the page number. For another description and a more critical cultural commentary on the famous Press Ball as part of Berlin's social life, see Bernard von Brentano's feuilleton piece "Masken und Menschen," first published in the *Frankfurter Zeitung*, Abendblatt, 11 Feb. 1926, and reprinted in Bernard von Brentano, *Wo in Europa ist Berlin: Bilder aus den zwanziger Jahren* (Frankfurt am Main: Insel Taschenbuch, 1993), 42–44.

[2] See Gretel Wagner, "'Die Nacht der schönsten Roben': Modische Eindrücke vom Berliner Presseball," in *Der Bär von Berlin: Jahrbuch des Vereins für die Geschichte Berlins* 49 (2000): 81–96. According to Wagner, it was not until 1886

that the Press Ball became an annual event. No balls were held during the First World War, between 1915 and 1918.

[3] For an overview of the fashion magazines, see Gretel Wagner, "Die Mode in Berlin," in *Berlin en vogue: Berliner Mode in der Photographie*, ed. F. C. Gundlach and Uli Richter (Berlin: Wasmuth, 1993), 113–46.

[4] For a discussion of the term "Frauenöffentlichkeit," see Sigrid Weigel, "Frauen und Öffentlichkeit: Von den Um- und Irrwegen des Weibes aus den männlichen Räumen zum Ort der Frau," and Ruth-Esther Geiger, ". . . Im verschärften Maße, eine Frauenfrage: Partei- und unabhängige Frauenpresse in Weimar," in *Sind das noch Damen? Vom gelehrten Frauenzimmer-Journal zum feministischen Journalismus*, ed. R.-E. Geiger and S. Weigel (Munich: Frauenbuchverlag, 1981), 7–12 and 163–74.

[5] See Jürgen Habermas, *The Structural Transformation of the Public Sphere*, trans. Thomas Burger and Frederick Lawrence (Cambridge, MA: MIT Press, 1991), 181, 158–59.

[6] Habermas mentions Hearst in the United States, Northcliffe in Great Britain, and Ullstein and Mosse in Germany as the most striking examples of the processes of concentration and centralization of the press. These developments were marked by a commercialization of the press, a blurring of the line separating the private and the public sphere, and a leveling of the distinction between "high" and "low" literature. See Habermas, *The Structural Transformation*, 181–96.

[7] For comprehensive overviews of Ullstein's history before 1945, see Lynda J. King, *Best-Sellers by Design: Vicki Baum and the House of Ullstein* (Detroit, MI: Wayne State UP, 1988), 45–71; Peter de Mendelssohn, *Zeitungsstadt Berlin: Menschen und Mächte in der Geschichte der deutschen Presse* (Berlin: Ullstein, 1969); and Maud Lavin, *Cut with a Kitchen Knife: The Weimar Photomontages of Hannah Höch* (New Haven: Yale UP, 1993), 51–61.

[8] Along with the biggest advertising agency, Rudolf Mosse (1843–1920) founded the Mosse publishing group, one of Ullstein's main competitors, in 1872. Its flagship publication was the *Berliner Tageblatt* (together with the *Frankfurter Zeitung* the major liberal newspaper in Germany), and it owned also the *Berliner Morgenzeitung*, the *Volkszeitung*, and the *8-Uhr-Abendblatt*. August Scherl (1849–1921) founded his printing and publishing house in Berlin in 1883 and later published the *Berliner Lokal-Anzeiger*, the *Berliner Abendzeitung*, and the *Neueste Berliner Handels- und Börsennachrichten*. In 1899 he launched the illustrated *Die Woche*, followed by *Der Tag* in 1900 and *Gartenlaube* in 1904. After a financial crisis in 1914, Scherl lost control of the newspapers and printing operations, which were acquired by Alfred Hugenberg (1865–1951). In the 1920s and early 1930s the conservative "Hugenberg Konzern" included UFA (feature-film and newsreel production, distribution, and financing, and a chain of cinemas) and Scherl (over 300 daily and weekly newspapers, magazines, technical periodicals, film and radio journals, directories and tourist guides, and book publishing).

[9] See Peter Fritzsche, *Reading Berlin, 1900* (Cambridge, MA: Harvard UP, 1996), 73.

[10] Hermann Ullstein (1875–1943) joined the company in 1902 and fled Germany in 1939, first for England and eventually for New York, where he died the year his

memoirs were published. These memoirs, *The Rise and Fall of the House Ullstein*, trace in detail how the publishers' embrace of American culture and business practices, their devotion to the most advanced means of mass communication, and their liberal political positions were firmly tied to their modernist self-identity.

[11] Vicki Baum, *It Was All Quite Different: Vicki Baum's Memoirs* (New York: Funk & Wagnalls, 1964), 259.

[12] From the second half of the 1920s until 1933, the average circulation of the *BIZ* was around 1,750,000. In 1926 *Ullstein* began to report its notarized circulation figures in a special publication called *Ullstein Berichte*, and in January 1927 circulation levels for the *BIZ* reached 1,563,880; in 1929 1,883,010; and in January 1931 1,753,580 readers. See *Ullstein Berichte*, Jan. 1927, 9–10; Jul. 1929, 7; and Jan. 1931, 7 and 10–11.

[13] "In einer Zeit, in der das Leben 'durch das Auge' eine stärkere Rolle zu spielen anfing, war das Bedürfnis nach visueller Anschauung so stark geworden, daß man dazu übergehen konnte, das Bild selbst als Nachricht zu verwenden. Das bedeutete eine vollkommen neue Einstellung dem Bilde gegenüber. Es ist kein Zufall, daß die Entwicklung des Kinos und die Entwicklung der *Berliner Illustrirten Zeitung* ziemlich parallel laufen." Kurt Korff, "Die 'Berliner Illustrirte,'" in *Fünfzig Jahre Ullstein, 1877–1927* (Berlin: Ullstein, 1927), 297–302; here, 290. Korff and Kurt Szafranski, in charge of the entire magazine department, left Germany in 1933 and created the new magazine *Life* for Henry Luce, the publisher of *Time*.

[14] Within just a few years — from the end of the First World War until 1927 — the circulation of *Das Blatt der Hausfrau* rose from about 30,000 to 500,690. See *Ullstein Berichte*, Jan. 1927, 8.

[15] Hutter made a brilliant career at the company. He became the manager of the entire distribution system and ended up as one of the most successful directors. In 1914, Hutter left *Ullstein* for the United States, where he became one of the directors of McCall's Patterns. See Ullstein, *The Rise and Fall*, 104–5.

[16] See the self-promoting essays "Die Dame: Die Gesellschafts-Zeitschrift vom internationalen Ruf" and "Das Blatt der Hausfrau: Das Fachblatt für den modernen Haushalt; Einzige regelmäßig erscheinende Zeitschrift der Ullstein-Schnitte," in *Der Verlag Ullstein zum Weltreklamekongress: Berlin 1929* (Berlin: Ullstein, 1929) n.p.

[17] "Sei sparsam, Brigitte/Nimm Ullstein-Schnitte!" See Ullstein, *The Rise and Fall*, 104; translation by Hermann Ullstein.

[18] Lavin, *Cut with a Kitchen Knife*, 55–59; Petro, *Joyless Streets: The Weimar Photomontages of Hannah Höch* (New Haven: Yale UP, 1993), 110–39.

[19] See Gretel Wagner, "Zeitschriften à la mode," in *Europäische Moderne: Buch und Graphik aus Berliner Kunstverlagen, 1890–1933*, ed. Lutz S. Malke et al. (Berlin: Dietrich Reimer Verlag, 1989), 191–204; here, 193–95, and Anthony Lipman, *Divinely Elegant: The World of Ernst Dryden* (London: Pavilion, 1982), 92. In her memoir, Vicki Baum writes that "the best, most advanced authors of those days were published at *Ullstein*'s. They brought to us their bitter, postwar, postrevolution, disillusioned humor, and their burning idealism in spite of everything." See Baum, *It Was All Quite Different*, 259. This view was also confirmed

by a contemporary participant in the fashion press, Gerd Hartung (1913–2003), a fashion and graphic designer for *Die Dame* and *die neue linie* in the 1930s, whom I interviewed in the summer of 1996. He used an expressive metaphor from the language of fashion — "halbseiden," that is, fifty-percent silk, dubious — to characterize the other fashion magazines competing with the *Die Dame*. See also, "Chronist des Chic: Das Stadtmuseum zeigt eine Hommage an den Modezeichner Gerd Hartung," *Der Tagesspiegel*, 7 Jul. 2004.

[20] *Styl* was the monthly publication of the *Verband der deutschen Modeindustrie* and was sponsored by leading German designer houses, such as H. Gerson, Mannheimer, E. Mossner, M. Gerstel, Regina Friedländer, and Martha Löwental. The goal of the organization was to elevate the prestige of German designers and promote a national style in fashion.

[21] Authors as diverse as Kurt Tucholsky and Alfred Döblin, Thomas Mann and Max Osborn, Lion Feuchtwanger and Bertold Brecht, Else Lasker-Schüler and Carl Zuckmayer, Stefan Zweig and Robert Walser regularly contributed short stories and articles to these magazines. The publisher's reputation for being open-minded and liberal does not sufficiently explain this phenomenon.

[22] "Ich habe bei Ullstein das mir sehr angenehme Gefühl: er kauft eine Ware, niemals hat eine Beeinflussung stattgefunden, niemals hat mir [Georg] Bernhard oder irgend ein andrer jemals meine Freiheit angetastet." Quoted in Almut Todorow, "Frauen im Journalismus der Weimarer Republik," *Internationales Archiv für Sozialgeschichte der deutschen Literatur* 16.2 (1991): 98.

[23] See Hedda Pänke, "Frauen als Mitarbeiter und Leser," in *Hundert Jahre Ullstein, 1877–1977* (Berlin: Ullstein, 1977), 376; Petra Budke and Jutta Schulze, eds., *Schriftstellerinnen in Berlin, 1871–1945: Ein Lexikon zu Leben und Werk* (Berlin: Orlanda Frauenverlag, 1995); and Todorow, "Frauen im Journalismus," 88–95.

[24] Baum, *It Was all Quite Different*, 260–61.

[25] Baum, *It Was all Quite Different*, 261.

[26] Anita Grossmann, "Berufswahl — ein Privileg der bürgerlichen Frauen," in Eskildsen, *Fotografieren hieß teilnehmen*, 8–12.

[27] "Frauen haben im Redaktionsstab der Zeitschriften rasch an Bedeutung gewonnen. In dem Maße, wie hier Blätter entstanden, die sich vorwiegend weiblichen Interessen widmeten, wuchs auch ihr Kreis. Heute ist der Verlag ohne die reiche Zahl weiblicher Mitarbeiter auf den verschiedenen Gebieten nicht zu denken. Aus der großen Schar können nur wenige erwähnt werden." See Gustav Willner, "Das Tagewerk der Abteilungen," in *Fünfzig Jahre Ullstein, 1877–1927*, 333.

[28] The publishing house kept a rich archive of personnel files of its employees, but it was "cleansed" in 1934 of all Jewish-related material, and apparently all data pertaining to Jewish employees were destroyed. When the headquarters of the company in the Kochstraße were hit by a bomb on February 3, 1945, all the remaining personnel files disappeared in the flames and rubble. Valuable information about the lives and the professional accomplishments of many of Ullstein's fashion editors and illustrators was lost. Much of the photographic archive, however, remained intact.

29 *Lebens- und Arbeitsbedingungen der Journalisten: Studien und Berichte*, Reihe L. (Geistige Arbeiter), vol. 2 (Geneva: Internationaler Arbeitsamt, 1928), 30; quoted in Todorow, "Frauen im Journalismus," 92–93. For more on the socio-historical aspects of female journalism during the Weimar Republic, see Adolf Dresler, *Die Frau im Journalismus* (Munich: Knorr & Wirth, 1936), 10–12, and Heinz Barth, "Kein ordentlicher Beruf," in *Hundert Jahre Ullstein, 1877–1977*, 349.

30 For more on the difficulties female journalists encountered when attempting to establish themselves as political analysts and foreign affairs correspondents, see Margret Boveri, *Verzweigungen: Eine Autobiographie*, ed. Uwe Johnson (Munich: Piper, 1977).

31 Todorow, "Frauen im Journalismus," 94.

32 In my archival research on Weimar's famous fashion journalists, I was unable to discover much biographical or bibliographical data on these women. See Appendix I.

33 As is the case for so many female fashion journalists, very little is known now about these women designers, who obviously enjoyed considerable publicity in the early 1920s. Although the names and photographs of Gerda Bunzel, Erica Mohr, Martha Sparkuhl, and Vally Reinecke are frequently present in the pages of every issue of *Die Dame* during the first half of the 1920s, virtually no biographical information about them is available now. Steffie Nathan (who signed her drawings with her first name only), an illustrator and fashion designer for *Die Dame*, *Der Uhu*, and *Styl* throughout the Weimar period, is mentioned only in passing in a book about the artist Albert Schäfer-Ast, because she was married to him. See G. Pommeranz-Liedtke, ed., *Albert Schäfer-Ast, 1890–1951: Gedächtnis-Ausstellung* (Berlin: n.p., 1952), 8. For more on Petra Fiedler and Vally Reinecke, see Appendix I.

34 According to Marion Beckers and Elisabeth Moortgat, modeling for fashion photographs was not a glamorous profession in the 1920s. It was usually young women, "budding actresses or extras who had been gripped by film fever," who agreed to pose as models for very little money (2 to 5 marks per dress or clothing item; 25 per published photograph). "There was not training for photo models," Beckers and Moortgat write, "and finding jobs for models came under the white-slave trade laws." See Marion Beckers and Elisabeth Moortgat, *Yva: Photographien, 1925–1938/Photographies, 1925–1928* (Berlin: Das Verborgene Museum, 2001), 151–52. There were, however, professional models (Mannequins) hired and trained to display clothes for the clients of designer houses and department stores and to perform at various fashion shows. They were considered very low on the social scale. For more on the mannequins, see chapter 5.

35 Ute Eskildsen, "A Chance to Participate: A Transitional Time for Women Photographers," in *Visions of the "Neue Frau": Women and the Visual Arts in Weimar Germany*, ed. Marsha Meskimmon and Shearer West (Aldershot, UK: Scholar P, 1995), 62–63.

36 In stark contrast to the paucity of biographical material on the majority of the female fashion experts, the life and work of Ernst Deutsch (1887–1938), who called himself Dryden after 1916, has been examined in numerous studies and exhibits. He was a well established Viennese fashion designer and illustrator, and later was also known as a costume designer for Marlene Dietrich. See René

Gohnert, "Klassiker deutscher Gebrauchsgrafik," *Neue Werbung* 37.3 (1990): 30–33; Lipman, *Divinely Elegant*, 92–6; Bernhard Denscher, *Tagebuch der Straße* (Vienna: Kunstpresse, 1988), Peter Noever, ed., *Ernst Deutsch-Dryden: en vogue!* (Vienna: MAK, Österreichisches Museum für angewandte Kunst, 2002) and Angele Zobl, ed., *Von Wien bis Hollywood: Die Blüte der Mode-Illustration und Werbegrafik: Ernst Deutsch-Dryden (1887–1938) und Max H. Lang (1901–1984)* (Salzburg: Verlag für Kunst und Kultur, 1990).

[37] See Baum, *It Was All Quite Different*, 278. Unlike Vicki Baum, who now counts as one of the best-studied female authors of popular fiction from the Weimar Republic, Anita Daniel (1893–1978) is virtually unknown. From 1925 until 1933, Daniel (who signed her humorous poetry, sarcastic commentaries, and witty essays only with her first name) published in almost every issue of *Die Dame* on topics such as fashion trends and women's emancipation. The publication of her photograph in the pages of *Die Dame* in 1930 "upon numerous requests from our readers" testifies to the tremendous popularity of her writings. For more biographical and bibliographical information on Anita Daniel, see Appendix I.

[38] "Längst ist der Spruch, die Frau gehöre ins Haus, überholt. Der Krieg hat die Frau selbständig gemacht, so daß sie sich in der Öffentlichkeit frei bewegen kann, ohne dafür Mißkredit zu gelingen." See Elsa Herzog, "Mode-Notizen," *Die Dame*, Oct. 1918, no. 2, 18. See also Elsa Herzog, "Die Mode im Frühjahr 1919," *Die Dame*, Mar. 1919, no. 12, 16; Marie von Bunsen, "Kriegszeit und Mode," *Die Dame*, Feb. 1920, no. 10, 21; H. W., "Die Bilanz der Mode," *Die Dame*, Aug. 1921, no. 20, 14; Johanna Thal, "Kommt ein Modeumschwung?" *Die Dame*, Aug. 1922, no. 22, 55; and Stephanie Kaul, "Zur Psychologie der neuen Mode," *Die Dame*, Oct. 1929, no. 1, 82–83.

[39] "Anscheinend hat man nie genügend den Zusammenhang, die symbolische Verkörperung und Veranschaulichung der Weltkrisis durch eben diese Kleidung beachtet." See Marie von Bunsen, "Kriegszeit und Mode," 21.

[40] "Die Verbindung mit dem Ursprung und der Vergangenheit muß unter allen Umständen aufrechterhalten werden. [Die Frau] braucht ein Herz, weiche Hände, Lippen, die schweigen können und trösten können. Viel Geduld, viel Weisheit, Selbstentsagung. Schau nicht gar so kämpflustig drein! Wir kommen vom Kampf. Wir brauchen den Frieden." See Hans von Kahlenberg, "Pagen," *Die Dame*, Aug. 1919, no. 21, 11.

[41] Patrice Petro discusses in detail the public's preoccupation with the allegedly "masculinized" image of the New Woman. "Masculinization" in the context of Weimar theorists' debate, as Petro extrapolates from articles in *Die Dame* and the *BIZ*, is linked to the "unnatural," to rejection of motherhood and traditional marriage. She, however, does not refer to any texts in the same magazines that dissent from the view of the New Woman as "masculinized." See Petro, *Joyless Streets*, 79–139.

[42] "Soziologen und Moralphilosophen befürchten, daß der äußeren Vermännlichung auch eine innere Vermännlichung folgen würde." "Der siegreiche Bubikopf," *Der Uhu*, Dec. 1925, 89.

[43] "Es [das Kleidungsstück, die Hose] ist nicht mehr das peinliche Abirren der Frau in eine Sphäre, die ihr nun mal verschlossen ist: die Sphäre der

Männlichkeit! . . . Es ist viel mehr ein Ausdruck des neuen Zuges, der durch die Zeit geht, die Körperlichkeit der schönen Frau als etwas Selbstverständliches zu betrachten, gleichviel in welchem Gewand." See Lily von Nagy, "Die Frau im Pyjama," *Der Uhu*, Mar. 1925, 48–52.

44 "[Die Mode] ist das Barometer, das die seelischen Unterströmungen mißt und haargenau registriert." See Stephanie Kaul, "Die frauliche Mode," *Die Dame*, Nov. 1929, no. 4, 90.

45 "Dieser Vergleich is unmodern. Denn diese Gesichter sind außer Mode, bei Frauen und bei Puppen. Wir Frauen haben heute unsere Individualität, die dem Geiste der selbständigen Frau entspricht und auf ihr Äußeres übergangen ist. Die Mode mit ihren vielfachen Formen unterstützt dieses Streben nach Eigenart; jede Frau kann sich im Rahmen der Mode individuell kleiden." See Johanna Thal, "Puppen und Frauen," *Die Dame*, Dec. 1919, no. 6, 7–8.

46 "Das richtige Modegefühl ist nur bei Menschen vorhanden, die auch Weltgefühl haben, wie wir das Gefühl für alles Moderne nennen. . . . Jede Dame kann sich persönlich kleiden, wenn sie überhaupt modern empfindet." See Johanna Thal, "Modische und unmodische Beobachtungen," *Die Dame*, Jan. 1924, no. 8, 8–9.

47 See Marianne Weber, "Das alte und das neue Frauenideal," in *Die Kultur der Frau*, ed. Ada Schmidt-Beil (Berlin-Fronau: Verlag für Kultur und Wissenschaft, 1931), 21.

48 Weber, "Das alte und das neue Frauenideal," 22.

49 "Die Frau der Gegenwart hat auch in ihrem äußeren Gewand ein durchaus erstrebenswertes Stadium erreicht: sie will weder den Mann imitieren noch sich in einen betonten Gegensatz zu ihm stellen durch Leugnung ihres weiblichen Geschlechtscharacters; sondern sie hat ihren durchaus eigenen Typ gefunden, indem sie sich je nach ihrer Tätigkeit verschieden kleidet." See Charlotte Wilke, "Mode, Frauentyp und Zeitgeist," in *Die Kultur der Frau*, ed. Schmidt-Beil, 41.

50 For a detailed historical account of *haute couture*, see Anny Latour, *Kings of Fashion*, trans. Mervyn Savill (London: Weidenfeld & Nicolson, 1958), 188–89. In the chapter "A Century of Fashion" in his study, which is devoted to the rise of modern fashion, Gilles Lipovetsky analyzes the emergence of *haute couture* and of the couturier-creator in the second half of the nineteenth century. *Haute couture* attributed to the designer the status of the modern artistic "genius." As the institution of *haute couture* was established, the couturier was transformed from an artisan into a sovereign artist, while the woman became a mere consumer of luxury. According to Lipovetsky, the early 1920s presented the first encounter of high fashion with the era of mass consumption and communication. See Gilles Lipovetsky, *The Empire of Fashion: Dressing Modern Democracy*, trans. Catherine Porter (Princeton, NJ: Princeton UP, 1994), 55–87.

51 H. W., "Die nächste Modelinie?" *Die Dame*, Jul. 1921, no. 20, 14.

52 The condescending tone of the these male experts is particularly striking in the case of Otto Flake, who began his article on abstract art with the following sentence: "Eine Zeitung wie *Die Dame* ist nicht der Ort, um die Philosophie einer Kunstbewegung zu geben; es genügt, die Leserin mit denjenigen Gesichtspunkten bekannt zu machen, die den Gegensatz der neuen Richtung zu der bisherigen

Kunstübung erkennen lassen." See Otto Flake, "Abstrakte Künstler," *Die Dame*, Apr. 1919, no. 14, 4.

[53] "Nur Gewänder, in denen sich die Träger dauernd bequem bewegen, werden zum Ausdruck und zum Bestandteil der Persönlichkeit." Friedrich Freksa, "Mode, Tracht und Möbel," *Die Dame*, Nov. 1918, no. 3, 4–5.

[54] Stephanie Kaul, "Zur Psychologie der neuen Mode," 82–83.

[55] Lipovetsky, *The Empire of Fashion*, 56. See also Ingrid Loschek, *Die Mode im 20. Jahrhundert: Eine Kulturgeschichte unserer Zeit*, 5th ed. (Munich: Bruckmann, 1995).

[56] For an extended discussion of the origins of the fashion show, see chapter 4.

[57] Lipovetsky, *The Empire of Fashion*, 78.

[58] Paul Poiret, *Kings of Fashion: The Autobiography of Paul Poiret*, trans. Stephen Haden Guest (Philadelphia: J. B. Lippincott, 1931), 148. A similar point is made by Roland Barthes in *The Fashion System* (1967), trans. by Matthew Ward and Richard Howard (New York: Hill and Wang, 1983), 254–55.

[59] "Wir sind gewohnt, daß Paris die neue Mode bringt. . . . Dahinter steht der Musterzeichner, der Stofffabrikant, der große Couturier — also immer sind es Männer, die diktieren. Diesmal scheint es, als ob die Frau, nicht einmal die beruflich mit der Mode verhaftete, sondern die Pariserin schlechthin den Ton angibt." See Ruth Ludwig, "Die Pariserin als modernes Kunstwerk," *Die Dame*, Jan. 1929, no. 7, 53–54.

[60] "Nicht nur der Wunsch der Schneiderfirmen, sondern der Frauen selbst wurde entscheidend." See Stephanie Kaul, "Die frauliche Mode," 90.

[61] "Nach Jahren strenglinigster Einfachheit und größter Zurückhaltung im Stoffverbrauch, nach vielen Saisons einer puritanischen Genügsamkeit werden diesmal zum erstenmal wieder Kleider geschaffen. . . . Die Individualisierung der Mode kommt an Stelle der Typisierung. . . . Die neuen Modelle machen aus dem Girl eine Dame. Die individuelle Dame, die sich freigemacht hat von der Allgemeinheit, Typisierung und Normisierung." See Stephanie Kaul, "Zur Psychologie der neuen Mode," 82.

[62] Ernst Dryden, "Rechtfertigung der Mode," *Die Dame*, Nov. 1929, no. 3, 22–23.

[63] See Stephanie Kaul, "Die individuelle Mode," *Die Dame*, Sept. 1930, no. 26, 14–15, and "Beschwingte Sommer-Mode," *Die Dame*, Mar. 1930, no. 13, 16–17; and Johanna Thal, "Empire und 1905," *Die Dame*, Oct. 1929, no. 1, 84.

[64] "Die mondäne Frau, wie sie sich bis vor kurzem in der Phantasie der Umwelt spiegelte, war eine märchenhafte Erscheinung. . . . Mondän ist nicht mehr modern. . . . Die moderne Frau letzter Ausgabe ist eine Art Weltwunder. Sie kann alles. . . . Sie will gar nicht repräsentieren, sie will sich ausleben. Wie sie es tut, ist ihre ganz private Angelegenheit. Es gibt keine mondänen Frauen mehr, nur noch moderne Frauen." See Anita, "Mondän ist nicht mehr modern," *Die Dame*, Jul. 1928, no. 21, 44–46.

3: In the Waiting Room of Literature: Helen Grund and the Practice of Fashion and Travel Writing

ONE OF THE ESSAYS in Franz Hessel's 1929 collection *Spazieren in Berlin* includes a kaleidoscopic image of Berlin's press district (Zeitungsviertel) and introduces the *flâneur* in one of his quintessential roles: as a free-lance contributor to some of Germany's popular illustrated magazines and daily newspapers. The *flâneur* as author spends hours waiting in the reception areas of the publishing conglomerates in the hope of drawing the attention of the editors to his "charming short pieces" (reizende kleine Sachen). Here is how Hessel characterized this group of aspiring writers who shared the same fate in the waiting rooms of the press:

> Imposing and friendly doormen let us in with all our manuscripts and requests. . . . And there is the reception hall with many young employees. They know us, although we don't work in the building. Oh, we don't want to go to the serious departments of the newspapers where they talk politics and business. We belong in the commentary section and in the entertainment supplements . . . There are many women among us; some of them are rather shy and anxious, and they are the very ones who write the cheeky reports on the latest fashions.[1]

Two points in this short paragraph prompt a closer look. First, in a self-ironic gesture Hessel draws our attention to a seemingly marginal genre (unter dem Strich), namely the feuilleton, the short prose form (die kleine Form) that gained extreme popularity in the Weimar years.[2] As many scholars of the period have noticed, the feuilleton became the "ideal form for recounting the pointillist splendor" of the modern city, because feuilleton writers observed rather than explained, and they produced a large number of sketches, snapshots, and vignettes that captured the endless variety of the city experience.[3] In addition, as Hessel points out, many aspiring women writers at the beginning of the century ventured to use feuilleton and fashion writing as a springboard to a literary career. In fact Hessel's wife, Helen Grund, is an excellent example of this connection between the medium of fashion writing and the transformation of modern literary forms. Her presence on the German literary and artistic scene from the early 1920s until the mid-1930s demonstrated how professional writing on fashion could be transformed into an idiosyncratic sphere of creativity where female *flânerie*, modernism, and surrealist experimentation crossed paths.

Helen Grund was one of Weimar Germany's most intriguing authors of fashion journalism and short prose. In addition to being an expert on fabrics, fashions, hats, furs, and other fashionable accessories, she was a fascinating public personality whose writings for the *Frankfurter Zeitung* and *Die Dame* were followed with interest by a large middle-class female audience. These long-forgotten essays on the minute twists and turns of fashion in the decade between 1925 and 1935 enriched in many specific ways the generic spectrum of the feuilleton and the travelogue and represent a form frequently preferred by women writers and reporters of the time. A close reading of her texts can also remedy an omission in numerous recent studies of the Weimar feuilleton, which focus mainly on the writings of Siegfried Kracauer, Joseph Roth, and Bernard von Brentano and the features of the male *flâneur*.[4] In the narrators in Helen Grund's essays we recognize the German *flâneuse*, the female counterpart of the *flâneur* in the Weimar cultural and literary scene.

Written as reflective accounts of enchanting strolls and encounters in Paris, Grund's short prose provides an example of specifically feminine experience in the modern metropolis and demonstrates her contribution both to the representation of women's modernity in the mass press and to the creation of a women's public sphere in the 1920s. She often reached beyond the topic under immediate discussion, namely the season's fashions, and offered a highly informative and even critical perspective on a variety of social and cultural aspects of the fashion industry. Grund reported exclusively on and for the constantly growing number of women who designed, sewed, exhibited, and consumed the new fashions, largely ignoring the well-known male designers, and thus demonstrating that fashion constituted a public sphere dominated by women's aesthetic vision and creative practices. Within this public sphere a notion of modernity emerged that veered away from the traditional fixation on technology, architecture, and youth culture. Grund, in fact, was one of several middle-aged and middle-class female fashion writers for the popular press at that time who attempted to offer their own original definition of modernity on the basis of their direct involvement in the *everyday* culture and practices of fashion.

Who Was Helen Grund?[5]

Throughout the decades of scholarly studies of Weimar culture, Helen Grund herself remained "under the line," appearing usually as a mere biographical detail in a footnote to essays on Franz Hessel.[6] She is perhaps best known as the inspiration for the Jeanne Moreau character, Kathe, in François Truffaut's film *Jules and Jim* (1962), the other real-life prototypes in the film being her husband Franz Hessel (Jules) and his best friend in Paris, Henri-Pierre Roché (Jim).[7] Numerous references to Helen Grund as the professional fashion reporter from Paris and expert on fashion appear in reviews of Franz Hessel's books by Kurt Tucholsky, who goes as far as to hint at Grund's influence on her husband's writing. His assertion that there was something of a "female quality," not "masculine enough," and "too coquettish" in Hessel's prose could be best explained by the fact that in reality Helen did — at her husband's request — write or revise passages that described with some sophistication clothes, appearances, designer stores, and fashion shows.[8] Helen Grund served as the prototype for the first-person narrator in Franz Hessel's short story "Das Lederetui" (The Leather Case, 1934) and for the character Lella in his unfinished novel *Alter Mann* (Old Man), a hard-working journalist and fashion expert reporting from Paris for a German newspaper, who was characterized in the following manner: "She delved with a researcher's intensity into the philosophical and even the national-economic laws of fashion and wrote about the regular 'three-month jolt' that they gave every ideal model, about politics among the dressmakers of reactionary and progressive temperament . . . She joined a circle of male and female artists who created fabric and fashions in the spirit of the most modern paintings."[9]

Walter Benjamin's collection of quotations and notes for his unfinished *Arcade Project* (*Passagen-Werk*) also acknowledges Helen Grund as an author in her own right. Her 1935 essay "Vom Wesen der Mode" (The Nature of Fashion) is among the works most frequently cited by Benjamin in the section titled "Mode" (Fashion), along with texts by philosophers, sociologists, and writers such as Friedrich Theodor Vischer, Georg Simmel, and Paul Valéry.[10] Benjamin and Adorno were regular readers and ardent admirers of Helen Grund's fashion reviews for the *Frankfurter Zeitung* (*FZ*) between 1925 and 1935, not only because she was the wife of Benjamin's close friend, but also because her writings revealed some of fashion's hidden implications for an understanding of modernity and mass culture. After reading an exposé of the *The Arcade Project*, especially the section on fashion, Adorno offered Benjamin some criticism and advised him to discuss the issue further with "Mrs. Hessel":

> When I read your passage on fashion — which I think is very important, though your argument should have less to do with the "organic" and more to do with "life" — I found myself thinking about that shimmering French fabric called "changeant" that was so expressive of the nineteenth century and was presumably also a result of new industrial processes. You might pursue that idea. Mrs. Hessel, whose reports in the *FZ* we always read with great interest, will certainly know more about it.[11]

Precisely these seemingly unpretentious but highly evocative texts in the press on contemporary fashions demonstrate how Helen Grund transformed the genre of the feuilleton and contributed to the modernist tradition of the Weimar period.

Born on April 30, 1886, in Berlin, Helen Grund moved to Paris in 1912 to study art. As a student of Fernand Léger and Le Fauconnier she moved in artistic circles, frequently visiting the famous Café du Dôme, where another Berlin bohemian, Franz Hessel, was introduced to her by his friend Henry-Pierre Roché, and in 1913 the dynamic, vital, adventurous Helen married the mild-mannered, rather phlegmatic and dreamy Franz.[12] The most productive, independent, and professionally fulfilling part of Grund's life began in 1925, when she moved with her children from Berlin to Paris to assume the newly created position of foreign fashion correspondent for the national edition of the prominent, liberal *Frankfurter Zeitung* (*FZ*). Initially she contributed only to the feuilleton section of the newspaper, but soon she became responsible for the fashion section in the monthly supplement *Für die Frau: Monatliche Beilage für Mode und Gesellschaft* (For Women: A Monthly Supplement on Fashion and Society), which was launched in 1926 and aggressively advertised in the pages of the *FZ*. Grund remained the chief fashion reporter for the *FZ* until 1935, by which time she had published over sixty essays, not to mention some short, topical commentaries. She became well-known to avid readers of the feuilleton section of the *FZ* among other frequent contributors such as Siegfried Kracauer, Walter Benjamin, Robert Walser, Joseph Roth, Bertolt Brecht, Kasimir Edschmid, and Else Lasker-Schüler.

After 1933 Helen Grund became very close to the community of German writers in France, later settling in the little coastal town Sanary-sur-Mer, one of the major centers of literary exile. After the end of the Second World War and until her death in 1982, Grund lived in Paris in the house of the painter Ann-Marie Uhde. Her most remarkable literary activity of the late 1950s was the first German translation of Vladimir Nabokov's *Lolita*.[13] In the early 1970s the life and work of her husband, Franz Hessel, were enthusiastically rediscovered and examined by German literary historians while Grund's own achievements, in contrast, still remain obscure.

Early Publications

Before assuming the position of chief fashion editor for the *FZ*, Grund had published sporadically in the literary press.[14] Her breakthrough in feuilleton writing came around 1924. Among her best-known essays from this period are impressions of Paris, which she wrote in the style of the *flâneur*: "Pariser Bilderbogen" (Picturebook of Paris) and "Aufatmen in Paris" (Breathing in Paris) were published in the journal *Das Tage-Buch* in 1924, and "Musikalische Magier" (Musical Magicians) appeared in the *FZ* in 1925.

Her first essay on fashion, based on her observations in the French capital, "Im Klima der Mode" (In the Climate of Fashion), appeared in the magazine *Der Querschnitt*, Ullstein's "journal for the exacting taste" (Zeitschrift für die Anspruchsvollen), which prided itself on "reflecting the intellectual and artistic activity of modern life" and "having no room for cheap sensations."[15] It testifies to Grund's intention to appeal as a fashion expert to a broader women's public as well as to more "intellectual" readers.

Between 1924 and 1925 Grund wrote mostly travel narratives about distant, fascinating locales. They fit well into a long-established German literary tradition of travel accounts from Paris, which stretched from the early nineteenth century — the Paris letters by Heinrich von Kleist, Heinrich Heine, and Ludwig Börne, for instance — to the 1920s journalistic reports by Siegfried Kracauer, Joseph Roth, and Franz Hessel.[16] A major characteristic of this tradition was that it linked the experience of modernity with the experience of Paris in the German literary imagination.

In the nineteenth century Ludwig Börne had hinted at an important gender differentiation in perceptions and observations of the French metropolis. He maintained that for women it was the encounter with the new fashions and the prospect of bragging about it when they returned home that constituted the quintessential experience of Paris: "While men find it pleasant to be in Paris, for women it is a far greater pleasure to have been there and to be reporting about their experience."[17] This quote acquired renewed actuality in the mid-1920s when, after several postwar years of severe economic restrictions, rigid protectionist trade policies, and loud nationalistic attacks in the German press, Paris reappeared in German magazines and newspapers as the most attractive and accessible destination for travel, especially for female journalists contributing to the fashion sections of magazines and newspapers. Börne's Paris impressions, indeed, were rediscovered and quoted in the fashion magazine *Styl* by Julie Elias, an active contributor to this and other illustrated women's periodicals such as *Die Dame*, and linked to the renewed obsession of German women with Paris and Paris fashions.[18]

Written as travel accounts from Paris, Helen Grund's essays from the early 1920s offer intriguing glimpses into a barely studied aspect of the genre.[19] They demonstrate how women authors in the Weimar period used the travelogue to convey a notion of female experience of and female sensitivity to the modern metropolis. Her essays "Aufatmen in Paris" and "Pariser Bilderbogen" are exemplary in that respect. Each represents a loose travel narrative consisting of more than a dozen short episodes located in places that constitute the conventional topoi of the genre: the train ride from Cologne to Paris, the Paris Metro, the atelier of a French sculptor, the luxurious restaurant, the bistro, the nightclub, the hotel, the circus, the fashion show, the street, the old landlady. The tone of the account is aloof, almost impartial.

At first glance, both essays exhibit most of the typical elements of the *flâneur*'s account of a big city. The narrator takes immense pleasure in her immersion in the colorful city crowds, and as she wanders around Paris, she seems to have no particular goal in mind, no clear destination. It seems that the street, to use Benjamin's classical formulation, has truly become her living room. Like the *flâneur*, she is attracted by surface phenomena and external appearances; she is constantly engaged in the incessant and conscious process of "reading" the street and deciphering the signs of electric city lights, old façades, and display windows.

Yet there are some subtle differences that distinguish these Paris essays from the many written by male writers and journalists. It strikes the reader that the narrator uses mostly the first-person plural to refer to the subject of experience: a timid "wir" instead of an independent "ich." "In a side street off the Boulevard Haussmann we find the inconspicuous entrance to a restaurant where the salespeople from the nearby department stores spend a cheerful lunch break," writes the author, and "We slow down: for a moment we pause amidst the busy traffic."[20] "We" refers to the narrator herself, as well as her un-named male companion ("mein Begleiter"), who is obviously more knowledgeable about the city, the people, and the history of Paris, and who leads her firmly and confidently on her journey. "My companion has a story to tell about most of these people," she comments (153).[21]

Although almost every thematic section of the travel narrative starts with one of those sentences in which "we" is the subject, a clear pattern also emerges as to when an "I" appears and whence it draws its poise. The self-awareness of the "I" is often highlighted in relation to her external appearance, to her clothes. Surrounded by the symbols of a painful artistic process of creation for eternity ("blocks of marble, wood, plaster, columns, pedestals") in the atelier of a sculptor, the narrator suddenly becomes self-conscious about her appearance: "I am alone and I don't move. I am afraid that I am disturbing the peace of this studio with the bold colors of my clothes."[22]

The narrator again confidently adopts the first-person-singular point of view in "Amélie rue Castiglione," describing a visit to the regular afternoon fashion show in a big department store, Trois Quartiers. Although her knowledgeable companion is still present, this episode is rendered entirely in the "I" form, and the dazzling multitude of impressions emblematic of the modern metropolitan street and big-city traffic are now associated with the display of fashionable attire, with the trying-on of clothes, and with the numerous possibilities of adopting a new and more attractive appearance:

> What would you like, Madam? Fabrics unroll, folds and creases surround me, chairs are moved, people sit down and get up, dull light and

thundering noise come through the windows — out on the street the flow of cars is rushing in circles and small clouds of exhaust caress the pavement. . . . And all of a sudden four girls are busy around me, sliding one shirt after the other over my head. The tall, thin one seduces me with the latest models from her department, finely pleated or loosely gathered little silk dresses, multicolored and black. . . . I see myself transformed multiple times in the generous, wide mirror, and the sisterly hands of the girls work confidentially. Their deft fingers touch me like a gentle rain.[23]

As narrator, then, Grund articulates two views of creativity and artistic self-expression. The one associated with the male artistic sphere she perceives as permeated with coldness (eisig, arktisch), "a field of ruins" (ein Trümmerfeld). Walking around the artist's studio, she touches the various sculptures "with fear, even horror" (139), and when she comments on some male dancers and their female partners, the contrast between coldness and warmth, lifelessness and vitality again comes to the fore: "Ah, these men, pale and unseeing, hold in their arms the warm bodies of their partners — a frightening image, as if life has withdrawn from their faces and pulses to some other place, hidden from view."[24] The other view of creativity is associated with the female playground of fashion, which the narrator considers one of the most enchanting spectacles of Paris: "This city is brimming with women! And all these sisters — how naturally they play the game of seduction! I don't see them sizing each other up; I don't detect a gesture or a posture that aims at anything but to enjoy themselves and help each other do the same."[25] In this sphere of public life, the sense of fear and dependence disappears and the *flâneuse* envisions herself as a respected participant, both an understanding viewer and an active performer, or, as she puts it, "a participant in the celebration of beauty" (Mitspieler des feierlichen Hübschen) (145).[26] And it was a very fortunate development in Grund's life that her sincere admiration for the "modern" personified by Paris women — by their sense of fashion, elegance, and playfulness — coupled with her own passion for writing could be transformed into a steady professional engagement when she became a fashion journalist for the *Frankfurter Zeitung*.

Helen Grund and the *Frankfurter Zeitung*

When Joseph Roth, a well-known contributor to the cultural section of the *FZ*, published in the pages of the newspaper a series of short, humorous character studies devoted to fellow journalists in 1929, one of the essays, "Fräulein Larissa, der Modereporter" (Miss Larissa, the fashion reporter), drew a mild caricature of the fashion journalist as he remembered her from before the First World War:

> Mademoiselle Larissa had a pen name but apparently no last name.... She had been a loyal contributor to the paper from time immemorial.... She was a fashion reporter; however, since writing on fashion alone did not pay enough, Larissa covered all topics of public interest that, according to widespread opinion, were "nearer and dearer" to women than to men: protection of mothers, for example, orphans, benefit events, lotteries, divorce cases, flower shows, and housing for the homeless.... Being well connected, she was dressed not in the "latest fashion," but in the one that was yet to come.... That was the highest level of journalistic perfection: she transformed herself into her articles, and the lines that she wrote — or that were edited out — were awkward only because her appearance had created certain assumptions about her skills as a journalist.[27]

Roth's portrait of his colleague Larissa reveals the ambiguous and subtly disparaging attitude toward female fashion journalism prevalent during the rise of the mass press in the pre-Weimar period. On the one hand, the fashion reporter had some of the aura of the actress or the movie star: she adopted an artistic alias, became the woman she wrote about in the public mind, and transformed herself into a model whose external appearance would be admired and imitated on a mass scale. On the other hand, however, the fact that her family name was not only missing but long forgotten showed an illegitimate and unacknowledged authorship. The author of fashion reviews dissolved and disappeared into the subject matter. But at the end of his essay, Roth wrote about Larissa's death of typhus as a nurse during the First World War and gave her family name for the first and last time in the paper, and he suggested that with her a chapter in German fashion journalism had ended and that soon, namely from the mid-1920s on, a new type of *Modereporterin* would emerge.

Indeed, Larissa's successor at the *FZ*, Helen Grund, had quite a different public presence and professional reputation. From the very beginning of her career as a reporter for the *FZ* in 1925, her regularly appearing fashion vignettes were always signed with her maiden name, Grund, and when she tried to reach beyond the narrow limits of fashion journalism, she did not accept just any topic that appeared "suited to the female nature," but ventured quite self-confidently into the domain of short literary prose.[28] In a way Grund was a pioneer in the mass press because her contributions to the pages of the *FZ* transformed entrenched notions about the role of women intellectuals in the expanding sphere of Weimar's mass culture.

Still, despite her tremendous success with the newspaper's reading public for nearly a decade, she was completely ignored by the "official" chroniclers of the *FZ*. One explanation could be that women were simply not admitted to the editorial board or other decision-making positions, though many of them contributed to the newspaper on a regular basis.

Karl Apfel, an editor and long-time correspondent for the newspaper, from 1925 to 1942, wrote in his memoirs that women were not accepted on the editorial board as a matter of principle.[29] For this reason, the narrated and documented history of that prominent institution of liberal democratic consciousness in Germany almost completely lacks the names of women. Indeed, more recent studies of the *FZ* and the feuilleton genre also regard essays on fashion as unworthy of analysis — a gesture very similar to the condescending attitudes toward fashion journalism in the early 1920s.[30]

In the course of her successful career as a fashion reporter in Paris, Helen Grund published texts that continued to tap into the tradition of the travelogue, but at the same time she leaned towards that other genre of short prose writing, the feuilleton, and contributed considerably to its development. The feuilleton was extraordinarily popular in Weimar Germany for a number of socio-historical reasons. With the rise and expansion of the modern metropolis, both short forms, feuilleton and travelogue, focused thematically on the experience of the big city or even attempted to emulate its dynamism in their form.[31] The press emerged as the primary public forum for vigorous disputes on issues of modernization, and within the institution of the mass press, the feuilleton assumed the function of mediating and explaining the new cultural practices to the public. Feuilletons were not only highly informative on non-political issues such as literature, art, everyday life, health, theater, and fashion; they also served as a vehicle of mass entertainment. In other words, both feuilleton and travelogue were transformed as a result of the rhetorical interaction of pragmatic and aesthetic intentions. They embraced the metropolis as a paradigm of modernity and became symptomatic of changes in the public sphere as traditional literary hierarchies became unsettled and non-canonical forms of aesthetic reflection came to the fore.

An inquiry into the modernist form of feuilleton used by women writers for predominantly female audiences offers glimpses into an intensely politicized debate on the appeal of a particular literary form to particular groups of authors and readers. While admirers of the feuilleton in France and Germany from the 1870s on, and especially after the First World War, saw it as a "daily corrector of opinions and conceptions that were becoming instantly obsolete," the conservative critics of the genre considered it merely a dangerous symptom of the trivialization of literature. If proponents of modernism considered it the "only means for modern man to keep abreast of the spirit of his own time," others disliked the high entertainment value of the feuilleton and blamed its superficiality on the poor taste of women readers.[32] Theories emerged that explained the general popularity of short prose with the female public by allusions to women's supposedly shorter attention span. Other critics attributed the rise of the feuilleton to the economic success of the newspaper as a vehicle of mass entertainment. In Karl Bücher's opinion of 1919, it was due to the feuilleton, which combined serious political and economic content with a light, entertaining element, that newspapers became popular with large sections of the population, especially women.[33]

The study of the feuilleton as an aesthetic form able to mediate the mass experience of modernization and metropolitan life started as early as the late 1920s with a groundbreaking work by Hermann Hausler, *Kunstformen des feuilletonistischen Stils: Beiträge zur Ästhetik und Psychologie des modernen Zeitungsfeuilletonismus* (The Forms of Feuilleton Style: On the Aesthetics and Psychology of the Contemporary Feuilleton in the Newspapers; 1928). Hausler defined the feuilleton as the medium for impressions, subjective experiences, and observations, and focused on one of its variations, the *Plauderei* (informal commentary), which he characterized as an illuminating and lively account (lebendig, veranschaulichend) of phenomena that attract particular interest, as well as of contemporary events and trends.[34] He described the genre further as employing vivid descriptions through the eyes of an expert (Anschaulichkeit des Speziellsehens), including much concrete detail (Bevorzugung des Konkreten) and more sensory images (sinnliches Bild), especially in describing clothes, textures, and colors. Generally, the *Plauderei* should be "topical, pointed, interesting, entertaining, and stimulating."[35] Considering such stylistic premises, it comes as a surprise that Hausler's elaborate discussion never refers to fashion as a possible topic for a feuilleton essay, nor does it mention a single female journalist as a feuilleton writer.

In the pages of the press, however, the very term "Plauderei" appeared quite often in the rubric *Modeplauderei*, which in turn had become an indispensable element in virtually every daily newspaper and weekly illustrated supplement and magazine by the 1920s. Because it was ubiquitous, the genre was often looked down upon as a routine and unsophisticated mode of writing. Even fashion journalists themselves distinguished between the *Modeplauderei* as a mundane, superficial, merely descriptive piece of prose and a more philosophical, sociologically inflected essay on the phenomenon of fashion. In the introduction to her talk *Vom Wesen der Mode*, which she gave repeatedly between 1935 and 1937 to young women venturing into the career of fashion design in the Meisterschule für Mode in Munich, Helen Grund emphasized with an obvious defensiveness in her tone that this time she intended to offer her audience not a mere *Modeplauderei*, but something more serious: "It doesn't seem appropriate to present you with mere fashion chit-chat (Modeplauderei); it doesn't seem appropriate for us to content ourselves with entertaining yet superficial descriptions. At the risk of disappointing some, I have decided to treat the topic with all the seriousness due to it."[36] It was Grund's ambition and constant effort throughout her journalistic career in fashion to transcend the narrowness and "superficiality" of the popular genre *Modeplauderei* and to aspire to the more distinguished tradition of the feuilleton.

We can see the specific ways in which fashion journalism conformed to as well as modified the generic conventions of the feuilleton if we take a closer look at the texts Grund published in *Für die Frau*, the women's supplement to the *FZ*. On the surface these texts appear to be dominated by a nonchalant tone and a perhaps overly playful approach. Saturated with sartorial details, they focus on the fragmentary experiences of everyday life, on the apparently ephemeral, the trivial, and the deeply inauthentic. The fashionable details themselves seem to evolve from experience, "which appears sensuous, ornamental, and superfluous."[37] At the same time, however, the inclusion of myriad fashion details into the narrative mirrored the inscription of Weimar fashion practices into women's everyday lives. It would not be an exaggeration to say that Grund's collection of sartorial minutiae resembles in some ways Benjamin's archival project: she retrieved microscopic pieces of the present in order to read them as symptomatic of various sociological trends.

Many of these essays, for example, offer a provocative and rare inside look into fashion as the field of professional fulfillment for many lower- and middle-class women. In a 1928 essay Grund introduced her readers to one of the numerous behind-the-scenes actors on the glamorous stage of the fashion industry. In the course of her first-person account she praises, for instance, the intelligence and taste of Renée, a public-relations person for a Paris designer house, whose duties include keeping the journalists up-to-date on the newest productions.[38] Other reports and interviews she dedicated to the work of less famous self-made female fashion designers who had successfully established themselves in Paris in rigid competition with the undisputed great names in the profession such as Patou and Worth. One of them was Renate Green, a former disciple of the Bauhaus school and a creator of clothes "designed according to completely new social principles." In interviewing the designer Grund took the opportunity to describe the atmosphere of the profession in which Green was known for her simpler and more affordable designs: "What I saw was an enormous work effort in which both snobbism and the desire for high profits played a large role. No one, however, had the goal of giving women of all classes the opportunity to dress well and beautifully at the lowest possible cost."[39] Here as in many of her reports and interviews, Grund took the opportunity to promote her own notion of the ideal fashion for modern times, embodied in "dresses that all women can wear regardless of their social class — the banker's wife as well as the young shop assistant, the aristocrat as well as the maid."[40]

In her provocative inquiries into the often invisible life and work of many women professionally engaged with fashion, Helen Grund also paid tribute to the mannequins, a highly visible group of women whose dreary professional duties were generally hidden from the public. The journalist saw it as her task to disperse the romantic aura surrounding the mannequin

Für die Frau

VORZEITIGER ABSCHIEDS-GRUSS

VON HELEN GRUND

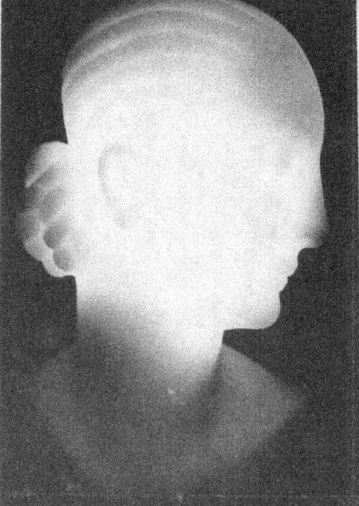

Die Sarode

Von innen erleuchtete Wachsmannequin

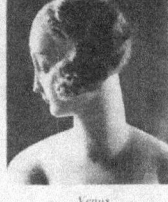

Venus

Aufnahme Germaine Krull
Sommerliches Mantel-
kleid aus beige Rips
Model Drecoll, Mannequin Siegel, Paris

Als ich zum ersten Male einer Pariser Modevorführung beiwohnte, war es mir fast unmöglich, etwas anderes zu beobachten als die Mannequins. Ihre Nonchalance, das Heben und Senken der roten Arme, die kurze Wendung ihres vom Zuschauer immer dritten Kleides wie abgehetzten Schritte, alles das schien mir in geheimnisvoller Weise mehr und tieferes über den Begriff „Mode" auszusagen als die Kleider, die sie vorführten, Musterexemplare einer für ihre Unzahl berühmten Rasse — wie teilhaft waren sie geschminkt, wie rührend die schmalen Hüften und die Lächeln, verwöhnt, zerstreut oder melancholisch?

Inzwischen hatte ich mit vielen von ihnen eine nähere Bekanntschaft gemacht. In der Mittagspause saßen auch sie in ihren kurzen Peignoirs, herumlungernd neben, vor und nach dem Diwaner, das ihnen im Hause serviert wird, ein ausgewähltes Menü, nichts, was dick macht oder den Teint gefährdet. Dennoch geschwätzig durch ihren Standesinstinkt ließen ihr Lachen, Plaudern, Schimpfen, Neigung, wie es sich für alle gehört, die auf der Mode so und haben flüstern sie auf und gruppierten sich wie eine Vogelschar um die neue Nummer der „Frau", zankten sich wie um Buketts künstlicher Blumen um die Photographie ihrer Kolleginn oder ihrer selbst. Ihre Kommentare sind naiv und manchmal nicht immer wohlwollend. Es gibt viel Eifersucht unter ihnen, die Neue hat es nicht leicht, bis sie eine Freundin gewinnt. Dann wird auch das Bateaste zum „Thema".

Von der Leistung dieser hübschen und unkomplizierten Geschöpfe habe ich noch immer den größten Respekt. Im Zeitraum von zwei Stunden und zweimal am Tage dreißig und mehr Kleider über- und auszuziehen mit ihrem Zubehör an Gürteln, Knöpfen, Schärpen und Schleifen, ohne Frisur und Laune zu verderben, sie vorzuführen, als sei jedes das „erste", sich in den Ateliers von der Modellistin drehen, wenden und kritisieren zu lassen, als sei man ein totes Ding, gehör- und gefühllos! „Des Abends ist man müde," erzählen sie, „man geht zeitig zu Bett. Unsere Existenz ist nicht sehr romantisch. Eine aufregende Liebe, die uns nicht endgültig diesem Milieu entzieht ist gefährlich, man wird blaß und unlustig, eines Tages gefällt man nicht mehr." Diese bedrückende Perspektive wird immer wieder erwogen.

Im Kosmos des Hauses spielt das Mannequin eine besondere Rolle. Der Chef legt ihr den Arm um die Hüfte, während er mit einer Kundin plaudert, er duzt sie und nennt sie „mon petit". Die Direktrice kritisiert wie eine strenge Pensionsmutter, in einem Blick sieht sie jede Versäumnis, eine Falte im zu eilig übergestreiften Unterkleid, ein Zuviel an Puder, den ein wenig verwischten Lippenbogen, den offengebliebenen Knopf der Manschette. Mit der Verkäuferin ist es anders, mehr als einmal ist sie auf den guten Willen des Mannequins angewiesen. Ob wirr, beige oder grau uniformiert, neben der hundifts und sauer auf Zeichen der Kauflust. „Simone", ruft sie noch einmal hinüber! aber Simone ist schon im Neben-
(Fortsetzung auf Seite 14)

Fig. 10: Page from *Für die Frau*, 1928, no. 5, 11. Staatsbibliothek Berlin.

Fig. 11: Page from *Für die Frau*, 1929, no. 6, 8. Text by Helen Grund and illustrations by Marietta Riederer. Staatsbibliothek Berlin.

and remove the veil of glamour that made that profession so attractive to many young women during the Weimar period. In her 1928 essay "Vorzeitiger Abschiedsgruß" (An Early Goodbye), Grund painted a negative picture of the tedious and senseless work of the mannequin in a typical medium-sized designer house in Paris:

> Twice a day for two hours [the mannequin] puts on and takes off thirty or more dresses and all the attendant accessories — belts, buttons, sashes, and ribbons. She is expected to keep her hairdo and her mood intact and to present every dress as "unique." She turns around in the studio of the designer [Modistin] and endures all kinds of looks and criticism as if she were a dead object, deaf and numb. While talking to a customer, the boss might swing an arm around her hips and and call her "mon petit"; the chief dressmaker [die Direktrice] might scold her as if she were a schoolchild, spotting with a single glance every defect, every crease . . ., any excess of powder or smudged lipstick line.[41]

With a few powerful brushstrokes the author depicts the humanity concealed under the mask of perfect beauty and elegance: the fatigue, the indignity, the variety of personal opinions and feelings. Grund interviewed many of these mannequins and quoted their not always flattering views of the fashion trade. In these statements, as well as in Grund's own observations, the reader discovers the darker side of the 1920s obsession with glamorous fashion, namely the pervasive objectification of women. The body of the mannequin was transformed into a lifeless platform for parading attractive clothing in front of potential buyers. At the end of the essay Grund offered a solution that would put an end to the humiliation at least of the living female body: she suggested that clothes be displayed only on artificial mannequins in order to save the live women's bodies from the pressures of continuous objectification.

The acuteness of Helen Grund's comments on the fate of the female mannequins in the Weimar age is not surprising given the fact that in her writing she was always extremely conscious of her own professional status. Not without self-irony and criticism, she remarked that in modern times fashion reporters were often placed in the peculiar position between a "mere" mannequin and a "real" writer, being both avid observers and mediators of aesthetic judgment and, at the same time, objects of intense observation and critical assessment by the public. In her 1930 essay "Premiere der Wintermode" (The Premier of Winter Fashions), Grund introduced the reader to one of "the most demanding and attractive shows that Paris [could] offer" as she analysed not only the new models but also the modes of self-presentation of her fellow fashion journalists:

> While we laugh, the fat lady with the turquoise cape is too busy taking notes to be distracted. She represents one of the most important New York newspapers and has to write a column every day. Particularly beautiful

is the Creole woman in the white evening dress with her shining black head. She writes for a Hollywood studio and is interested only in photogenic clothes, mostly tea gowns. Two blond Swedes are chatting, smoking, and drinking. If you have been around a while, you can tell by the position of the correspondents in the room how their respective paper is ranked and what its circulation is. In the main room are the reporters for *Vogue* and *Fémina*, *Harper's Bazaar* and *Jardin des Modes*; they are escorted by men in impeccable tailcoats, and their place is next to the artists and fashion photographers, the textile manufacturers, the jewel designers, and the friends of the house.[42]

Grund's essays disclose the real responsibilities and daily tasks involved in the glamorized profession of the fashion reporter. In many respects it was a show within a show, in which the journalists themselves were expected to perform as promoters of certain fashion trends, to embody the status and prestige of various mass-media institutions. At the same time, there was ample and wearisome work to be done, a fact that often remained hidden from the many readers of the fashion magazines:

> In the course of two weeks the conscientious fashion journalists look at two to three collections per day, in the morning, in the afternoon, and at night, and that makes a total of some 3,500 models. These numbers give you an idea of the sifting process that takes place before the slogans are coined and the "big hits" determine the future course of fashion.[43]

Grund was the only fashion reporter of her time to convey to readers the essence of her work and to demystify the daily routine performed by the fashion reporter of the Weimar era. As she explained to the public, the field of fashion meant not only glamour and glitz, but also time-consuming, diligent work on the part of numerous women.

Work outside the home and the constant exposure to public attention constituted just one aspect of the life of the modern, professionally engaged female intellectual of the 1920s and early 1930s. In her publications for the *FZ*, Helen Grund also ventured to describe the modern woman's experience of leisure, as in her 1931 essay "Zwischen Abreise und Ankunft" (Between Departure and Arrival), which succinctly conveys the author's perceptions and thoughts on driving a car out of Paris into the French countryside for a weekend.[44] At first glance it seems that this text feeds into the Weimar mythology, which included the image of the woman driver as a symbol of modernity (although in fact the number of women who could afford a car was very low). But upon a closer look, the essay offers rare insight into the actual experience of this "modernity" from the standpoint of the woman. It differs tremendously from other texts published in *Für die Frau*, such as Heinrich Hauser's "Auto und Frau" (The Car and the Woman), which presents a quasi-sociological approach to the phenomenon of women driving cars and focuses on the importance of cars to women as just another fashion accessory.[45] Grund's essay, in contrast, reveals the purely subjective experience of driving alone and translates it into a statement of independence and freedom: "Off I go . . . today! No, now! 'Au revoir, my dear. Be happy.' My coat is on the passenger seat and the maps are in the pocket. Farewell!"[46] The guided tour of Paris that started more than a decade ago with the knowledgeable *flâneur* at her side and that was reflected in her early essays has now been transformed into a race for independence and self-assertion. The initial timidity of the "I" in the first essays of the *flâneuse* has given way to the sovereign "I" of the unstoppable traveler:

> The cool air is pleasant and covers my face with a gentle mask; the slate-gray highway stretches away smoothly and shimmers enticingly. And then, suddenly, the real thing happens. Departure and arrival evaporate and become empty shells between which stretches sheer happiness: I'm on the road! In this moment there is no more promise for tomorrow, no sense of relief about yesterday. This is pure, unfettered happiness that stands on its own. . . . How lovely to be by myself![47]

The outwardly directed gaze of the classical *flâneur* who feels at home in the big-city street is replaced here by a much more introverted *flâneuse*. She is equipped with one of the latest technological achievements of the modern age — the automobile — and is determined to make up for something that has been denied her for many centuries: the opportunity to explore her freedom and independence.

Grund's essay resonates, too, with the emancipatory notes that permeate the writings of a contemporary woman writer from another, younger, generation, Erika Mann, who also published frequently in *Für die Frau* and who also drove a car alone around Europe. Perhaps not coincidentally, Mann provided the best indirect characterization of Grund's contribution to German literature and culture during the Weimar period. As a young aspiring actress, Mann started a career in occasional journalism in 1928 with travelogues and feuilletons that appeared in most of Ullstein's publications.[48] She displayed an acute understanding of the new type of female intellectual who established herself in the 1920s and of whom Helen Grund was an eminent representative. Her 1931 essay "Frau und Buch" (Women and Books) provides a succinct summary of both the general phenomenon and the specific case of Helen Grund:

> Recently a new type of woman writer has emerged, and I think that she has excellent prospects: the woman who covers day-to-day events in essays, plays and novels. She doesn't pour her heart out, nor does she scream her head off; her own life is set quietly aside and she practices reporting rather than confessing. She knows the world, she knows the score, she is clever and has a good sense of humor and the power of detachment. It is almost as if she were translating life into literature, into

a literature that does not occupy celestial heights and yet is a decent, useful, and often charming type of literature.

Yesterday as I was driving on the Hohenzollerndamm, I met a middle-aged gentleman. He was a dreamer, looking at the sky, and I almost ran him over. He expostulated, "Damn women, why don't you stay in the kitchen!" This essay is dedicated to this gentleman.[49]

Coda

Grund was one of the few fashion journalists of the 1920s whose career was not interrupted in the wake of the Nazis' coming to power in 1933, although it experienced some critical changes. She remained on the staff of the *Frankfurter Zeitung* until 1935 and then started working for *Die Dame*, which even after 1933 was still determined to publish regular fashion reports from Paris.[50] This situation remained basically unchanged until late 1936. Her career as a fashion journalist ended officially in 1938 after *Kristallnacht*, which she experienced in Berlin.[51] Most fashion periodicals after 1933 were involved in persistent attempts to formulate a notion of "German fashion" as part of the pervasive nationalistic ideology.[52] Even the word *Mode* itself was resented as an expression of a phenomenon too much tainted by French and/or Jewish influences. A newly-coined term — *Kleidkultur* (clothing culture) — was meant to signify adequately the national spirit of fashion.

In strong contrast to the pompous editorial rhetoric about traditional German *Kleidkultur* that filled other magazines, the issues of *Die Dame* from 1935 and 1936 continued to publish French designs and articles sent directly from their Paris correspondent.[53] It was Helen Grund, in fact, who sent detailed reports from the French capital. Her later texts do not strike the reader as radically different in tone from what she wrote before 1933, nor is there any reference to the new political mission of fashion in her essays. Even their form became controversial, because she sent them as "letters" on Parisian hotel letterhead, and she defiantly continued to use French terms in her reports. Her highly individualized and uncompromising style in *Die Dame* prompted the SS newspaper *Das Schwarze Korps* to launch a fierce attack against her:

> *Die Dame*'s foreign correspondent writes from Paris. Yes, "from Paris," and the reports are signed with the beautiful name Helen.... We think it is very important to inform our readers about this latest fad concerning western-created femininity.... If Mademoiselle Helen were not able to escape from us abroad, we would force her to produce a fair copy of her reports with goose-quills by the light of a gas lamp.... We would then expose her writings for what they really are: totally foreign despite all our aryanization![54]

Despite the fiery rhetoric of this anonymous editorial, the writer had clearly grasped a trend in Grund's recent publications: her ambition to link fashion to the more general issues of modern femininity. Again her public lecture "Die Beziehung der Frau zu ihrer eigenen Erscheinung" (Woman's Relation to her Own Appearance), which she published in 1935 under the title *Vom Wesen der Mode* (The Nature of Fashion), testified to the increased sophistication of her writing on fashion in the last years of her career, but at the same time it seemed designed to infuriate the authorities. After stating that her approach to fashion was serious and grounded in professionalism, she declared that she would talk about a topic she knew inside and out, a topic that deserved wide public and critical attention: the "Pariser Modeschaffen" (Fashion-Making in Paris), and this justification of her choice of topic was like a slap in the face of nationalist propaganda:

> All attempts to create a national fashion — and there have been such in England, America, and Germany — have failed so far. Only Vienna has been able to create and maintain a fashion of its own that is strong enough to influence neighboring lands and flexible enough to open itself up fearlessly to Paris fashions. This sole exception is very interesting. For me it confirms the validity of theories that we will address in a moment.[55]

The anti-nationalistic line of her argument had an anti-paternalistic underpinning. According to Grund, it was mostly German men who misinterpreted the function and meaning of fashion for women and spread hostility toward Parisian styles. In a gesture of seeming appeasement toward the regime, she actually ridiculed male writers who dictated current fashion to women:

> In France you would rarely find a man who would make fun of new fashions or stop his wife from following them. To the same extent that a German woman would not even think of laughing at the heroic essence of a man, French and Viennese men would never feel called upon to despise a woman's instinct for beauty, regardless of the form that it might take, and would never make a scandal about red nail polish, a powdered face, a fancy hairdo, or painted lips. Whether he is aware of it or not, he respects the driving force behind these phenomena.[56]

This insistence on the autonomy of women's opinions and decision-making in matters of fashion allowed Grund to sneak into her presentation more general observations about fashion as a sphere of self-reflective and self-assertive practices. "Fashion teaches women to be constantly aware of their physicality" (ein fortwährendes Bewußtsein ihrer Körperlichkeit), she wrote, and she argued ardently against the usual assumption that women are predisposed to be obsessed with changing clothing styles because fashion in itself is something "unreasonable" and "superficial" (5). To such clichés Grund offered convincing explanations as to why fashion is only "*seemingly* irrational" ("das *scheinbar* Unvernünftige"; 6). At the same time, however, it would be inaccurate to interpret her lecture as a daring feminist statement, because she has often spoken in favor of such traditional functions of fashion as facilitating the natural purpose of women: to seduce men to love (8).

Helen Grund was forced to give up her career after a renewed series of attacks against her in the Nazi press in 1937/38. In an inflammatory article, "Die Sorgen einer Meisterschule" (The Concerns of One Professional School), *Das Schwarze Korps* wrote: "We can't tolerate this. . . . Even in Munich *Gemütlichkeit* ends where Helen Grund, of all people, proposes to lecture on the culture of German women."[57] The former correspondent of the "most Jewish newspaper of all" was threatened with sanctions if she did not discontinue her anti-German propaganda. As a result she retreated into silence and, subsequently, into an oblivion which lasted for many decades. Yet despite literary history's neglect of Helen Grund, her writings on fashion from the 1920s and 1930s remain exemplary for the ways in which a talented fashion journalist in Weimar Germany not only participated in the debates on modernity but also made a lasting contribution to the development of the modernist genres of the feuilleton and the travelogue.

Notes

An abridged version of this chapter was published in the *Women in German Yearbook* 19 (2003): 117–40

[1] "Wir mit unseren Anliegen werden freundlich hereingelassen von stattlichen Pförtnern . . . Und da ist nun der Anmelderaum mit vielen kleinen Boys. Die kennen schon so manchen von uns, obwohl wir nicht zum Hause gehören. Ach, wir wollen nicht in die ernsthaften Bereiche, wo Politik, Handel und das Lokale gemacht wird. Wir gehören unter den Strich und in die Unterhaltungsbeilagen . . . Viele Frauen sind darunter, manche etwas schüchtern und bekümmert, das sind die, welche die kecken mondänen Plaudereien schreiben." See Hessel, *Ein Flaneur in Berlin* (Berlin: Arsenal, 1984), 258. Reprint of *Spazieren in Berlin* (Wien und Leipzig, Epstein, 1929).

[2] The expression "unter dem Strich" carries a double meaning. Idiomatically it means "of lower quality," "below par," and refers to the way the genre of the feuilleton is looked upon by literary and journalistic establishments. For writers of literary fiction, it is too journalistic, and for journalists, it deals with issues less serious than politics and economy. At the same time, however, the phrase "unter dem Strich" depicts literally the location of cultural discussions, short essays, and book reviews on the page of most German daily newspapers during the twenties, namely in the bottom part, separated from the other news articles by a thick line.

[3] See Fritzsche, *Reading Berlin, 1900* (Cambridge, MA: Harvard UP, 1996), 106–7.

[4] A notable exception is Anke Gleber's book *The Art of Taking a Walk: Flanerie, Literature, and Film in Weimar Culture* (Princeton, NJ: Princeton UP, 1999); see esp. 171–213.

⁵ Although she always signed her published texts with her maiden name "Grund," in secondary literature she is often referred to as Helen Hessel or Mrs. Hessel. Throughout the chapter I will refer to her as (Helen) Grund.

⁶ See Hartmut Vollmer, "Der Flaneur in einer 'quälenden Doppelwelt': Über den wiederentdeckten Dichter Franz Hessel," *Neue Deutsche Hefte* 34 (1987): 734–35. For other references to Helen Hessel, see Hans Puttnies and Gary Smith, *Benjaminiana: Eine biographische Recherche* (Giessen: Anabas, 1991), 214–15. Puttnies and Smith quote from her correspondence with Walter Benjamin and draw parallels between the two couples — the Hessels and the Benjamins — in which both women, Helen Grund and Dora Sophie Kellner, stand out as independent, ambitious, and practical personalities with successful journalistic careers of their own. Benjamin's wife, Dora (known both as Dora Benjamin or Dora Sophie Kellner), wrote for Ullstein's illustrated periodicals, primarily *Die Dame*, and after 1926 became an editor for the fashion magazine *Die praktische Berlinerin*.

⁷ In 1953 Herni-Pierre Roché, a French art dealer and Grund's lover for over ten years, published a novel based on his journal entries. In 1955, François Truffaut ran into Roché's novel and immediately decided to use it as a script for a film. He discussed his plans with the author, and after looking at some of Jeanne Moreau's photographs that Truffaut had sent him, Roché agreed that she was probably the best choice for Kathe's role. Roché died in 1959, before the premier of the film in 1962. According to Truffaut, Grund was in the audience during the premiere and she later wrote in a letter to him: "But what disposition in you, what affinity could have enlightened you to the point of recreating — in spite of the odd inevitable deviation and compromise — the essential quality of our intimate emotions? On that level, I am the only authentic judge because the other two witnesses are no longer here to tell you 'yes.'" See François Truffaut, introduction to *Jules et Jim*, by Henri-Pierre Roché, trans. Patrick Evans (New York: Marion Boyars, 1993), n.p. For more on the "real story" behind the film, see Dudley Andrew, "Jules, Jim, and Walter Benjamin," in *The Image in Dispute: Art and Cinema in the Age of Photography*, ed. D. Andrew (Austin: U of Texas P, 1997), 33–54, and Manfred Flügge, *Gesprungene Liebe: Die wahre Geschichte zu "Jules und Jim"* (Berlin: Aufbau, 1993).

⁸ For example, in a review of Franz Hessel's book *Teigwaren, leicht gefärbt* (1926) Tucholsky wrote: "Ganz abgesehen davon, daß ich neidisch auf den Titel bin: es stehen so bezaubernd leichte Dingelchen in dem Buch, so hingehaucht, wirkliche 'soufflés' — zum Beispiel . . . das geradezu echte Gespräch im Modesalon —, es ist unfaßbar, wie ein Mann so etwas schreiben kann. . . . Die stärksten Stücke reichen an Robert Walser heran, und es ist eine Freude, immer wieder darin zu blättern." And, three years later, in 1929, after Hessel's collection *Nachfeier* had appeared, Tucholsky touched again on the same theme: "Es ist eine Art Mannesschwäche in diesem Mann, etwas ganz Weibliches (nicht: Weibisches) — schon in dem reizenden Bändchen *Teigwaren, leicht gefärbt* sind Stellen, die fast von einer Frau geschrieben sein könnten — es ist etwas Lebensuntüchtiges, oh, wie soll ich dies Wort hinmalen, damit es nicht nach Bart und Hornbrille schmeckt? Und das weiß Hessel." See Kurt Tucholsky, *Gesammelte Werke: 1925–1928*, ed. Mary Gerold-Tucholsky and Fritz J. Raddatz (Reinbek bei Hamburg: Rowohlt, 1960), 2:1128 and 3:217. See also Flügge, *Gesprungene Liebe*, 193–94.

⁹ "Sie vertiefte sich mit forscherischer Intensität in die philosophischen und sogar die nationalökonomischen Gesetze der Mode und schrieb von dem 'dreimonatlichen Ruck, dem man einem Idealmannequin gibt,' von der Politik der reaktionären und fortschrittlichen Temperamente unter den großen Schneidern . . . Sie kam in einen Kreis von Künstlern und Künstlerinnen, die aus dem geiste der modernsten Malerei Stoffe und Modelle schufen." See Franz Hessel, *Alter Mann: Romanfragment*, ed. Bernd Witte (Frankfurt am Main: Suhrkamp, 1987), 55, and "Das Lederetui," *Die Dame*, Sept. 1934, no. 22, 17–18. Additional indirect reference to Helen Grund's professional involvement in the field of fashion and admiration for her expertise is found in Hessel's "Mitgenommen in eine Modeschau," *Für die Frau* 5, May 1930, 8.

¹⁰ See Benjamin, *Gesammelte Schriften*, ed. Rolf Tiedemann (Frankfurt am Main: Suhrkamp taschenbuch, 1991), 5/1:110–32.

¹¹ "Mir ist zu der Stelle über Mode, die mir sehr bedeutend scheint, aber in ihrer Konstruktion vom Begriff des Organischen wohl abgelöst und aufs Lebendige bezogen werden müßte, . . . wohl noch eingefallen der Begriff des Changeant, des schillernden Stoffes, der wohl für das 19. Jahrhundert Ausdrucksbedeutung hat, wohl auch an industrielle Verfahren gebunden ist. Vielleicht gehen Sie dem einmal nach, sicherlich weiß Frau Hessel, deren Berichte in der FZ wir stets mit großem Interesse verfolgen, damit Bescheid." See Adorno's letter to Benjamin from August 2, 1935 in Benjamin's *Gesammelte Schriften*, 5/2:1133.

¹² For more biographical data on Helen Grund, see Anna Rheinsberg, " 'Alle Risiken auf sich nehmen und für alles bezahlen': Helen Grund," in *Zwischen Aufbruch und Verfolgung: Künstlerinnen der 20er und 30er Jahre*, ed. Denny Hirschbach and Sonia Nowoselsky (Bremen: Zeichen + Spuren, 1993), 158–64; Barbara Ungeheuer, "Helen Hessel," in *Femmes Fatales: 13 Annäherungen*, ed. Ines Böhner (Mannheim: Bollmann, 1996), 71–80; Claudia Becker, "Helen Grund," in *"Genieße froh, was du nicht hast": Der Flaneur Franz Hessel*, ed. Michael Opitz and Jörg Plath (Würzburg: Königshausen & Neumann, 1997), 191–209; and Birgit Haußstedt, *Die wilden Jahre in Berlin: Eine Klatsch- und Kulturgeschichte der Frauen* (Berlin: edition ebersbach, 2002), 81–116. I am indebted to Manfred Flügge for giving me a most precise and comprehensive account of the life and career of Helen Grund. See also his *Letzte Heimkehr nach Paris: Franz Hessel und die Seinen im Exil* (Berlin: Arsenal, 1989) and *Wider Willen im Paradies: Deutsche Schriftsteller im Exil in Sanary-sur-Mer* (Berlin: Aufbau, 1996), 100–104.

¹³ See Helmut Winter, "Pockennarbig von Fallen: Eine kleine Geschichte der Übersetzungen von Nabokovs 'Lolita,' " *Frankfurter Allgemeine Zeitung*, 27 Jan. 1990, 28.

¹⁴ Grund's earliest publications date from 1921 in *Das Tage-Buch*. These are epigrams, aphorisms, and a longer essay titled "Kriegsgewinnler" (War Profiteers).

¹⁵ *Der Verlag Ullstein zum Weltreklamekongress: Berlin, 1929* (Berlin: Ullstein, 1929), 11. See Helen Grund, "Im Klima der Mode," *Der Querschnitt* 5.6 (1925): 515.

¹⁶ In his essay "Vorschule des Journalismus: Ein Pariser Tagebuch," Franz Hessel called these texts Paris's "most desirable export goods for the German newspaper." See Franz Hessel, *Nachfeier* (Berlin: Rowohlt, 1929), 160.

[17] "Wenn es für Männer angenehm ist, in Paris zu sein, so ist es für Frauen noch angenehmer, dort gewesen zu sein und davon zu berichten." See Ludwig Börne, *Sämtliche Schriften*, ed. Inge und Peter Rippmann (Düsseldorf: Melzer, 1962), 2:33.

[18] Julie Elias, "Die Dame im Sommer," *Styl* 2 (1924): 33–34.

[19] Substantial research has been done within the field of German Studies on women and journalistic travel-writing in the eighteenth and nineteenth centuries, with a focus on Sophie von La Roche, Fanny Lewald, Ottilie Assing, Ida Pfeiffer, Ida Hahn-Hahn, and Johanna Schopenhauer. For a comprehensive examination of paradigms of feminine travel experience and the ensuing transformation of the travelogue genre, see Elke Frederiksen, "Blick in die Ferne: Zur Reiseliteratur von Frauen," in *Frauen — Literatur — Geschichte: Schreibende Frauen vom Mittelalter bis zur Gegenwart*, ed. Hiltrud Gnüg and Renate Mohrmann (Stuttgart: Metzler, 1985), 104–22, and Tamara Felden, *Frauen reisen: Zur literarischen Repräsentation weiblicher Geschlechterrollenerfahrung im 19. Jahrhundert* (New York: Peter Lang, 1993).

[20] See Helen Grund, "Aufatmen in Paris," *Das Tage-Buch*, 5, 1924, 958–63; repr. in *Bubikopf: Aufbruch in den Zwanzigern: Texte von Frauen*, ed. Anna Rheinsberg (Darmstadt: Luchterhand, 1988) 147–55. All quotations are from the latter edition. "In einer Seitenstraße des Boulevard Haußmann finden wir den unscheinbaren Eingang zu einem Restaurant, in dem die Angestellten der umliegenden Warenhäuser ihre muntere Mittagsstunde verleben . . . Unser Tempo ebbt ab, wir stehen einen Augenblick im Gedränge der vielen Gefährte" (147, 149).

[21] "Zu vielen dieser Physiognomien weiß mein Begleiter eine Geschichte zu erzählen" (153).

[22] "Ich bin allein, lange ohne mich zu rühren. Mich bedrückt das Farbige meiner Kleidung wie eine Indiskretion" (139).

[23] "Madame wünscht? Stoffe rollen, Falten stehen, drehen, sinken, Stühle wechseln, leer und beschwert, durch die Scheiben dringt mattes Licht, rollendes Gesause — draußen eilt der Kreislauf der Autos, Benzingewölk streichelt geleertes Pflaster . . . Und dann sind plözlich vier Mädchen um mich beschäftigt, Blusen gleiten über meinen Kopf . . . Die Große, Schlanke lockt mit den letzten Neuheiten ihres "rayons," schmalplissierten und lose gerafften Seidenkleidchen, bunten und schwarzen . . . In der generösen Weite des Spiegels sehe ich mich in schneller Folge vielfach verwandelt, die Hände der Probierenden sind vertraulich, schwesterlich. Ihre flinken Finger berühren mich wie sanft rieselnder Regen" (146, 149).

[24] "Ja, diese Männer: bleich und blicklos drehen sie das Warme, das ihre Arme halten — erschreckend, fast als sei das Leben aus diesen Gesichtern verzogen, anderswohin, und tobte nur dort, den Blicken verborgen" (144).

[25] "Wie voll von Frauen ist diese Stadt, wie natürlich scheint es diesen Schwestern, verführerisch zu sein. Ich sehe keinen kritisch abschätzenden Blick von einer zur anderen, keine Geste, keine Haltung, die anderes bezweckte, als zu gefallen und zu genießen. Lust und Mitlust" (145).

[26] My understanding of the emerging notion of female subjectivity tied to the experience of fashion corresponds to Birgit Tautz's observations in her illuminating

essay on the fashion discourse in an eighteenth-century travel narrative. Tautz demonstrates how for the male writer/traveler, the latest female fashions signal instability, fear, and insecurity, while "women become the *media* of fashion in the narrative." See Birgit Tautz, "Fashionable Details: Narration in an Eighteenth-Century Travel Account," *Germanic Review* 72. 3 (Summer 1997): 201–12; emphasis in the original.

²⁷ "Fräulein Larissa verfügte zwar über ein Pseudonym, aber anscheinend nicht über ein Familiennamen . . . Sie war Berichterstatterin über Modeangelegenheiten. Da aber die Mode allein nicht genug Erträgnisse einbrachte, kümmerte sich Larissa auch um alle jene öffentlichen Dinge, die nach einer weitverbreiteten Meinung der weiblichen Natur 'näher liegen' als der männlichen. Zum Beispiel um Mutterschutz, Waisenkinder, Wohltätigkeitsfeste, Lotterien und Scheidungsprozesse, Blumenausstellungen und Obdachlosenasyle . . . Sie ging, weil sie die besten beruflichen Verbindungen . . . hatte, nicht etwa nach der 'letzten Mode' gekleidet, sondern bereits nach der nächsten . . . Es gibt keine größere journalistische Vollkommenheit. Sie verwandelte sich selbst in ihre Artikel — und die Zeilen, die sie schrieb und die man ihr strich, waren vielleicht nur deshalb so unbeholfen, weil ihre äußerliche Erscheinung ihre journalistischen Fähigkeiten vorweggenommen hatte." See Joseph Roth, "Fräulein Larissa, der Modereporter," *Frankfurter Zeitung* 12 May 1929; reprinted in Joseph Roth, *Panoptikum: Gestalten und Kulissen* (Cologne: Kiepenheuer & Witsch, 1983), 25–28. The quotation here is from Roth, *Panoptikum*, 25.

²⁸ Roth, *Panoptikum*, 25.

²⁹ See Karl Apfel, "In den zwanziger Jahren: Erinnerungen an die Frankfurter Zeitung," *Archiv für Frankfurts Geschichte und Kunst* 55 (1976): 235–53; here, 236. Other regular contributors to the *Frankfurter Zeitung* included Irene Seligo and Heddy Neumeister. On discrimination against female journalists, especially those who aspired to be political commentators and foreign correspondents, see Margret Boveri, *Verzweigungen: Eine Autobiographie* (Frankfurt am Main: Suhrkamp, 1996), 157, 218, and 222.

³⁰ See Almut Todorow, *Das Feuilleton der "Frankfurter Zeitung" in der Weimarer Republik: Zur Grundlegung einer rhetorischen Medien Forschung* (Tübingen: Max Niemeyer, 1996), and "'Wollten die Eintagsfliegen in den Rang höherer Insekten aufsteigen?' Die Feuilletonkonzeption der *Frankfurter Zeitung* während der Weimarer Republik im redaktionellen Selbstverständnis," *Deutsche Vierteljahrsschrift für Literaturwissenschaft und Geistesgeschichte* 62 (1988): 697–740. See also Wolfgang Schivelbusch, *Intellektuellendämmerung: Zur Lage der Frankfurter Intelligenz in den zwanziger Jahren* (Frankfurt am Main: Insel, 1983), 42–62.

³¹ For an elaborate discussion of these theses, see Eckhardt Köhn, *Strassenrausch: Flanerie und die kleine Form: Versuch zur Literaturgeschichte des Flaneurs bis 1933* (Berlin: Das Arsenal, 1989), 7–15, and Anke Gleber, "Die Erfahrung der Moderne in der Stadt: Reiseliteratur in der Weimarer Republik," in *Der Reisebericht: Die Entwicklung einer Gattung in der deutschen Literatur*, ed. Peter J. Brenner (Frankfurt am Main: Suhrkamp, 1989), 463–89.

³² See Wilmont Haacke, *Handbuch des Feuilletons*, 2 vols. (Emsdetten: Lechte, 1951), 2:224–25 and 1:294–95.

33 See Haacke, *Handbuch*, 1:295.

34 See Hermann Hausler, *Kunstformen des feuilletonistischen Stils: Beiträge zur Ästhetik und Psychologie des modernen Zeitungsfeuilletonismus* (Stuttgart: Württemberger Zeitungsverlag, 1928), 27–28.

35 Hausler, *Kunstformen*, 29.

36 "Es ziehmt sich also nicht, daß ich Ihnen nur so etwas wie eine Modeplauderei bieten sollte, es ziehmt sich nicht, uns mit einer oberflächlichen Schilderung zu beschäftigen, die vergnüglich sein könnte. Auf die Gefahr hin, einige zu enttäuschen, bin ich entschlossen, das Thema mit allem Ernst zu behandeln, den es verdient." See Helen Grund, *Vom Wesen der Mode* (Munich: Meisterschule für Deutschlands Buchdruck, 1935), 3.

37 See Tautz, "Fashionable Details," 201.

38 See Helen Grund, "Für die erste Reise 1928," *Für die Frau*, Jan. 1928, 10–11.

39 "Eine enorme Arbeitsleistung sah ich, in der Snobismus und Prestigefrage neben dem Verlangen, möglichst große Summen zu verdienen, eine große Rolle spielten. Nirgends aber erstrebte man das Ziel, den Frauen aller Ständen so billig wie möglich die Gelegenheit zu verschaffen, sich hübsch und gut anzuziehen." See Helen Grund, "Deutsche Mode in Paris: Ein Gespräch mit Renate Green," *Für die Frau*, Jan. 1932, 2. Renate Green (born Erna Niemeyer), who signed her work also as "Renee" or "Ré," lived in Paris from 1925 on, had her own fashion studio, and submitted regular contributions on fashion — sketches and articles — to *Sport im Bild* and *Für die Frau* for almost a decade. Later she made herself a name as a photographer and was known as Ré Soupault. See Ursula März, *"Du lebst wie im Hotel": Die Welt der Ré Soupault* (Heidelberg: Wunderhorn, 1999); Manfred Metzner, "Ré Soupault, Neues Sehen, Neues Denken: Vom Bauhaus in die Welt," in *Ré Soupault: Die Fotografin der magischen Sekunde*, ed. Manfred Metzner (Heidelberg: Wunderhorn, 2007), 7–18.

40 Grund, "Deutsche Mode in Paris," 3.

41 "Im Zeitraum von zwei Stunden und zweimal am tage dreißig und mehr Kleider über- und ausziehen mit ihrem Zubehör an Gürteln, Knöpfen, Schärpen und Schleifen, ohne Frisur und Laune zu verderben, sie vorzuführen, als sei jedes das 'eine,' sich in den Ateliers von der Modelistin zu drehen, wenden und kritisieren lassen, als sei man ein totes Ding, gehör- und gefühllos . . . Der Chef legt ihr den Arm um die Hüfte, während er mit einer Kundin plaudert, er dutzt sie und nennt sie 'mon petit,' die Direktice kritisiert wie eine strenge Pensionsmutter, in einem Blick sieht sie jede Versäumnis, jede Falte, . . . ein Zuviel an Puder, den ein wenig verwischten Lippenbogen." See Helen Grund, "Vorzeitiger Abschiedsgruß," *Für die Frau*, May 1928, 9.

42 "Wir Umsitzenden lachen . . . die dicke Dame mit türkisfarbenen Cape aber notiert viel zu eifrig, um sich zerstreuen zu lassen. Sie ist eine Vertreterin eines der wichtigsten New York Blätter und muß jeden Tag eine Spalte schreiben. Hübsch ist die kreolisch Matte im weißen Abendkleid, ihre schwarze Scheitel glänzend. Schreibt für ein Hollywood-Syndikat und hat nur für photogenische Kleider Interesse, vor allem für Teagowns. Zwei blonde Schwedinnen plaudern, rauchen, trinken. Ist man ein wenig eingeweiht, so kann man aus der Placierung der

Korrespondentinnen den Rang und die Auflageziffer ihrer Zeitungen erkennen. Im Hauptsalon Linden, eskortiert von tadellos Befrackten die Mitarbeiterinnen von *Vogue* und *Fémina*, von *Harper's Bazar* und *Jardin des Modes*, ihren Platz neben den Zeichnern und Modephotographen, neben Stofffabrikanten, Juwelieren, Freunden des Hauses." See Helen Grund, "Premiere der Wintermode" *Für die Frau*, Sept. 1930, 8.

[43] "Etwa 14 Tage hindurch sehen die gewissenhaften Modeberichterstatterinnen täglich zwei bis drei Kollektionen, vormittags, nachmittags und abends, zusammen etwa 3500 Modelle. Diese Zahlen geben Ihnen eine Vorstellung von der Filtrierung, die vor sich geht, ehe die 'Schlagworte' zustande kommen und ehe die 'großen Erfolgsnummern' die Richtung der Mode festlegen." See Grund, *Vom Wesen der Mode* (Munich: Meisterschule für Deutschlands Buchdruck, 1935), 21.

[44] For more on Grund's own inexhaustible passion for travel, see Charlotte Wolff, *Hindsight* (London: Quartet Books, 1980). Wolff, a psychiatrist who was forced to leave Germany in 1933, found shelter in Helen Grund's apartment in Paris, and accompanied her on many trips, wrote: "Off we went in Helen's old Ford, on a tour through riveting landscapes and arresting towns" (112).

[45] See Heinrich Hauser, "Auto und Frau," *Für die Frau*, Jul. 1927, 11–12.

[46] "Fort also, heute schon, jetzt gleich. — 'Au revoir, mein Lieber. Sei froh.' Den Mantel neben mich, die Karten rechts in die Seitentasche. Leb wohl." See Helen Grund, "Zwischen Abreise und Ankunft," *Für die Frau*, Aug. 1931, 10.

[47] "Die Kühle tut wohl, die andrängende Luft faßt das Gesicht in eine weiche Maske, das schieferblaue Band der Straße liegt glatt und glänzend in unablässiger Lockung. Und dann geschieht es plötzlich, das Eigentliche. Abreise und Ankunft werden zu nichts, zu Hülsen, die den Bogen des Glücks halten: ich reise! Kein Versprechen für morgen liegt darin, kein Entlastetsein für gestern hat teil daran. Es ist ein reines, ein herausgeschältes, ein selbständiges Glück . . . wie schön ist es so allein." Grund, "Zwischen Abreise und Ankunft," 10.

[48] Between 1928 and January 1933 Erika Mann published more than 100 articles, essays, and travelogues, the majority of them in Ullstein's newly founded daily paper *Tempo*. For more on her journalistic writings, see Irmela von der Lühe, *Erika Mann: Eine Biographie* (Frankfurt am Main: Campus, 1993), especially the chapter "Bühne-Schreibtisch-Automobil," 44–47.

[49] "Seit kurzem gibt es einen neuen Typ Schriftstellerin, der mir für den Augenblick der aussichtsreichste scheint: Die Frau, die Reportage macht, in Aufsätzen, Theaterstücken, Romanen. Sie bekennt nicht, sie schreibt sich nicht die Seele aus dem Leib, ihr eigenes Schicksal steht still beiseite, die Frau berichtet, anstatt zu beichten. Sie kennt die Welt, sie weiß Bescheid, sie hat Humor und Klugheit, und sie hat die Kraft, sich auszuschalten. Fast ist es, als übersetzte sie: das Leben in die Literatur, in keine ungemein hohe Literatur, aber doch in eine brauchbare, anständige, oftmals liebenswerte.

Gestern habe ich auf dem Hohenzollerndamm einen Herrn getroffen, mittelalt. Der Herr war ein Träumer, er schaute in den Himmel, und ich hätte ihn mit dem Auto beinahe überfahren. Er sagte zu mir: 'Weibervolk, verdammtes, schert euch in die Küche.' Diesem Herrn widme ich diesen Aufsatz." See Erika Mann, "Frau und Buch," *Tempo*, 21 Mar. 1931, repr. in and quoted from Rheinsberg, *Bubikopf*, 11–12.

⁵⁰ An important collaborator in that period was Marietta Riederer, a promising graphic designer and fashion writer who started her journalistic career at the *Frankfurter Zeitung* with Helen Grund's generous support and continued to work with her throughout the 1930s. See Appendix I for more detail.

⁵¹ Grund's first-person account of the events includes an episode on the attacks on Jewish-owned fashion businesses. See Helen Hessel, "Berlin in November 1938," in *Letzte Heimkehr in Paris: Franz Hessel und die Seinen im Exil*, ed. Manfred Flügge (Berlin: Arsenal, 1989), 43–66.

⁵² The discourse on fashion after 1933 and the institutional reorganization of the German fashion industry constitute a huge topic that cannot be adequately covered here. For some excellent historical studies, see Guenther, *Nazi Chic? Fashioning Women in the Third Reich* (Oxford: Berg, 2004); Andreas Ley, *Mode für Deutschland: Fünfzig Jahre Meisterschule für Mode* (Munich: Stadtmuseum, 1979), 8–22; and Sigrid Jacobeit, "Aspekte der Kleidungsgeschichte im faschistischen Deutschland," in *Sich kleiden*, ed. Gitta Böth and Gaby Mentges, Hessische Blätter für Volks- und Kulturforschung 25 (Marburg: Jonas Verlag, 1989), 153–70.

⁵³ For an analysis of how little the journalists of *Die Dame* and popular Berlin fashion designers complied with the official appeals to "liberate the German woman from the tyranny of French fashions," see Brigitte Stamm, "Berliner Modemacher der 30er Jahre," *Der Bär: Jahrbuch des Vereins für die Geschichte Berlins* vol. 38–39, 1989/90: 189–203. For more on fashion journalism in the 1930s, see Julia Bertschik, "Zopf mit Bubikopf: Modejournalismus im Dritten Reich am Beispiel der Zeitschrift *Die Mode* (1941-1943)," in *Reflexe und Reflexionen von Modernität, 1933–1945*, ed. Erhard Schütz and Georg Streim (Bern: Peter Lang, 2002), 273–92.

⁵⁴ "Die Frontberichterstatterin der 'Dame' schreibt von Paris. Jawohl, 'schreibt aus Paris' unterzeichnet mit dem schönen Namen Helen. . . . Wir können es uns nicht vorbehalten, diesen letzten Schrei westlich geformter Weiblichkeit hier unseren Lesern wiederzugeben. . . . Wenn Fräulein Helen sich nicht jenseits der Reichsgrenzen unserem Zugriff entziehen könnte, wir würden sie zwingen, ihre Berichte mit Gänsekielen bei Petroleumlicht in Reinschrift zu übertragen . . . Wir werden auch dieses Bekenntnis als das entlarven, was es tatsächlich ist: artfremd trotz aller Arisierung!" See *Das Schwarze Korps*, 29 Sept. 1938, 31.

⁵⁵ "Alle Versuche, die bisher unternommen sind, nationale Moden zu schaffen — es gab solche in England, in Amerika und in Deutschland, sind bisher gescheitert. Nur in Wien hat sich eine eigene Mode gebildet und erhalten, kräftig genug, um auf die Nachbarländer zu wirken, geschmeidig genug, um sich dem Einfluß der Pariser Mode furchtlos zu öffnen. Diese einzigartige Ausnahme ist sehr interessant. Sie bestätigt mir die Richtigkeit der Theorien, auf die wir gleich eingehen werden." Grund, *Vom Wesen der Mode*, 4. The page numbers for subsequent quotations from this text are given in parentheses.

⁵⁶ "Selten werden Sie in Frankreich einen Mann finden, der sich über neue Modeerscheinungen lustig macht, oder seiner Frau verbietet sie mitzumachen. So wie eine deutsche Frau es sich nicht einfallen ließe, das Heldische im Manne zu verlachen, so wenig fühlt sich der Franzose, der Wiener berufen, den Schönheitstrieb der Frau, in welcher Form er sich auch äußert, verächtlich zu machen und sie etwa

für rotlackierte Nägel, ein gepudertes Gesicht, eine kunstvolle Frisur oder geschminkte Lippen zu schelten. Ob es ihm bewußt ist oder nicht, respektiert er den Hintergrund dieser Erscheinungen" (9).

[57] "Aber auch in München hört die Gemütlichkeit auf, wenn man ausgerechnet von Helen Grund über deutsche Frauenkultur belehrt werden soll." See "Die Sorgen einer Meisterschule," *Das Schwarze Korps*, 21 Jan. 1937. For a more detailed analysis of Helen Grund's writings after 1933 in the context of fashion journalism in the Nazi media, see Bertschik, *Mode und Moderne: Kleidung als Spiegel des Zeitgeistes in der deutschsprachigen Literatur (1770–1945)* (Cologne: Böhlau, 2005), 274–82.

Displays of Fashion

4: Weimar Film as Fashion Show

> The film star as model: On Thursday afternoon, Lya de Putti will present the latest fur fashions from Alexander Baum & Co. at the Hotel Adlon.
> — *Film-Kurier*, 26 November 1924[1]

> A fashion show in the Zoo film studios: A magnificent fashion salon was set up, and for a few hours we could admire the most recent creations of Paris fashion presented by the Drecoll company of Paris. We could also witness the brilliant performance of Asta Nielsen . . . she is one of the leads in the film *Joyless Street*, which is currently being shot in the Zoo studios of Sofar-Film.
> — *Reichsfilmblatt*, 21 February 1925[2]

> No one who wants to learn about modern costumes and fashions should miss a film with Brigitte Helm.
> — Dr. Koch, review of *Manolescu* (1929),
> *Die Filmwoche*, 4 September 1929

CINEMA PRESENTED THE MOST SPECTACULAR SITE for the display of Weimar fashion. Film and fashion, in tandem, not only satisfied the audiences' desire for entertainment and visual pleasure but also managed to seduce female viewers into believing that their own fantastic transformations were somehow possible. The main agents of that seduction were, of course, the actresses of the 1920s, who in effect doubled as models, presenting the new fashions on-screen as well as on the pages of illustrated magazines. In a 1919 interview for *Elegante Welt*, Danish star Asta Nielsen, who had just resumed filmmaking in Germany after the war, declared publicly her conscious involvement in the promotion of clothes and trendy appearances from the movie screen: "I read lately that a well-made film must, at any moment, have the effect of a good fashion magazine. This fact was quickly appreciated in countries where fashion is taken seriously. Today's actresses pay special attention to this aspect of film."[3] Indeed, Nielsen was extremely effective in launching new worldwide fashions throughout her prolific career. The distinctive hair style, the shawls, tight dresses, and hats in which she appeared in her films made many women in her audience aspire to reinvent themselves "à la Asta Nielsen."[4] According to director Rudolf Meinert, she also had an acute sense of how colors, lines, and fabrics appear on-screen and "often was much better than camera people in understanding how these visual effects work."[5] Thus she frequently determined for herself what clothes and accessories to wear for a film and how exactly to present them, and that was important, because in many cases it was the costumes and not so much the plot that the viewers noticed and remembered.

Of course what the public saw when it observed the fashions on the screen was very much determined by gender. For men in the audience, as contemporary commentator Curt Moreck noted, the actress's fancy clothes, fine stockings, and beautiful shoes blended into an undifferentiated "erotic fantasy image" (erotisches Wunschbild), while female spectators never failed to notice the exact details of cut, ornament, and accessories in the performers' costumes. Women viewers often regarded the lead actress as "a live fashion magazine" (ein lebendiger Modejournal) from which they took advice for their own everyday practices of fashion.[6] Not long after her statement about the role of fashion in film, Asta Nielsen starred in one such film, Felix Basch's *Die Geliebte Roswolskys* (Roswolsky's Mistress, 1921), in which she played an ordinary girl who is mistakenly believed to have become the mistress of a billionaire, and as part of her role, Nielsen paraded, according to one contemporary critic who kept a close count, in thirty-six different outfits.[7]

Cinema was also the most affordable form of fashion consumption. The interest in fashion on the silver screen was particularly high in times of deep economic crisis, fabric shortage, and inflation, when film could easily satisfy the consumerist desires of its lower- and middle-class audiences by *showing* them otherwise unattainable products. In 1921 it was reported in the popular society magazine *Elegante Welt* that the price of fur had risen to a quarter of a million marks, so that even a small movie star could not afford one. Yet ordinary Germans found a way to enjoy elegance and luxury; as the magazine wrote, the Berlin woman, instead of buying chinchilla, now bought a ticket to the movies to take a closer look at the fashionable outfits in Fritz Lang's film *Dr. Mabuse, der Spieler* (Dr. Mabuse, the Gambler, 1921).[8]

Despite the abundance of references in the Weimar press to film as an indispensable commentator, trend-setter, and promoter of stylish appearance, and despite the ubiquitous display of fashion in film, the relationship between the two media garnered little scholarly notice. The multiple intermedial and intertextual connections between the institutions of cinema and fashion can be examined in two central case studies: first, the development of the fashion farce (*Konfektionkomödie*) from its beginnings before the First World War to the end of the 1920s, and second, Brigitte Helm's star status within German culture and aspects of her on-screen presence that relate to the explicit depiction of and commentary on Weimar's aesthetic practices in the world of clothes and fashion. This chapter documents some of the lost, forgotten, and recently discovered works that are part of the sub-genre of the fashion farce and proposes a reevaluation of the role of fashion in film and of the context of modernity in

Fig. 12: Asta Nielsen in *Die Geliebte Roswolskys* (Roswolsky's Mistress, 1921). Deutsche Kinemathek.

which both German cinema and German *Konfektion* came to thrive. Both studies — of *Konfektionskomödie* and Brigitte Helm as a fashion model — demonstrate on the one hand how fashion and film together guided the audience from the screen to see and experience modern life. At the same time, the visual style of the films discussed here was often influenced by popular forms of live entertainment in Weimar such as the fashion show (*Modenschau*) and the numerous fashion pageants (*Modekonkurrenzen*), in which mannequins competed to become fashion queens (*Modeköniginnen*). As it addresses questions of cinematic tradition, visual pleasure, female audience, and genre, this discussion of film and fashion offers a better and more nuanced understanding of how both media engaged the senses, molded the tastes, influenced everyday practices, and ultimately determined the experience of modernity for the mass viewer.

Film, Fashion, and Modernity

The impetus for both critique and theoretical reevaluation of the role of fashion in film can be traced back to Siegfried Kracauer's film essays from the 1920s. Basically disparaging, Kracauer saw fashionable images in film primarily as an empty vehicle for entertainment — escapist, conformist, and unrealistic. In "Film 1928" he characterized contemporary films as "the most daring *escape attempts*," in which "social reality is evaporated, petrified, and distorted": "[The protagonists] chauffeur themselves, live in Berlin, in Paris, and on the Riviera, dress almost exclusively in sports clothes or in full evening attire, and fall on hard times only once (at most) in order to marry into money immediately afterward."[9] Yet in Weimar the enormous appeal of cinema to contemporary audiences — an appeal documented in numerous reviews including in Kracauer's own writing — was compelling enough to demand a closer look at how exactly the pleasurable visual experience was constructed through the theme of fashion. A critical revisiting of numerous popular films featuring ostentatious displays of fashionable styles, sensual glamour, and cosmopolitan flair would be in the spirit of Kracauer's initial interest in "stupid and unrealistic film fantasies" precisely because they are, in his own words, "*daydreams of society* in which its actual reality comes to the fore and its otherwise repressed wishes take on form."[10]

Kracauer believed that despite its strong roots in capitalism and consumer culture, cinema as a mass medium could be instrumental in the process of democratizing culture. In his 1926 essay "Cult of Distraction," as well as in other critical writings around that time, he suggested that the film experience was predicated upon a pervasive form of distracted consumption that replaced the contemplative fascination associated with highbrow, bourgeois art. Although Kracauer focused primarily on the "elegant surface splendor" of Berlin's movie theaters, the representation of glamour and fashion on the screen, too, offered pleasurable distraction and shaped cosmopolitan urban audiences. In his early writings Kracauer still saw this "distraction," this mass experience of visual pleasure, as a redeeming and socially useful phenomenon, because cinema offered the possibility of "self-representation of the masses subject to the process of mechanization."[11] He read the entertaining and popular features of film as subtle signs of resistance to the pressures of a depersonalized capitalist society. By engaging a heterogeneous public on the most immediate level, the level of the senses, as Kracauer scholar Miriam Hansen argues, film introduced its mass audience to new forms of perception, awareness, and attention and, as a result, helped it navigate an increasingly complex modern environment. Thus if cinema presents, as Hansen proposes, an incarnation of a "vernacular modernism," a modernist aesthetic that articulates and mediates a wide array of quotidian cultural practices, then fashion (within film), given its distinct visuality and its obvious connections to everyday usage, can be considered one of the most pronounced forces shaping the experience of modernity for the masses.[12]

Admittedly, both industries, fashion and film, nourished fantasies of unattainable glamour. What Jeanne Allen emphasizes in her study of American film and consumerism in the 1930s and 1940s applies to the earlier context of Weimar popular films as well: they offered access — "ownership by viewing" — to an often inaccessible material environment, to a way of dressing and living that consumerism "promised to the viewer ideologically, but awarded only to the eye."[13] Sabine Hake, however, complicates our understanding of the close collaboration between the world of commerce and the visual arts in modernity by pointing out that their synergy is predicated upon two parallel processes — "spectacularization of the commodity" and "narrativization of consumption."[14] Within a modernist, Fordist culture that validated mass production and mass consumption as forms of democratization, film transferred these ideas into the sphere of fantasy production, into the world of images and stories. In other words, as Hake claims, because of the role of film and other visual arts in the presentation and promotion of products, consumer culture became both a spectacle and a narrative. Particularly productive is Hake's statement about the affinity between product advertisement and film within modernity, since this statement is applicable to the relationship between fashion and film as well. One could claim that both media — Weimar cinema and Berlin *Konfektion* — employed display practices that expanded the horizon of visual experience for the mass audience, addressed real human needs and desires by cultivating an imaginary relationship to the material world, and used images, text, and sound to spin out a variety of individual identification scenarios that were part of larger processes of social, ethnic, gender, and national identity formation.[15]

So fashion in film played a role in shaping notions of modernity, especially for the audience of increasingly mobile and often working lower- and middle-class women. As a peculiar mix of narrative and spectacle, films that featured lavish fashion displays guided the viewers through sartorial practices that could be relevant, with some adaptation and modification, in their own everyday lives. After all, the New Woman of the 1920s, as recent studies have pointed out, was not only a projection of the mass media, a passive or imaginary product, but also a "real" subject, actively involved in the creation of her own modern image. She was employed outside the home and had some — albeit limited — leisure time and money to spend. Weimar women, working office jobs and present in the public realm, were particularly interested in knowing what the up-to-date fabrics, designs, and haircuts were, how makeup and lipstick were applied, and what clothes were appropriate on what occasions. And by going to the movies female viewers were able satisfy this curiosity in the cheapest and most immediate way. In other words, the *Konfektionskomödie* and other Weimar films functioned as a compendium of suggestions, tips, and updates disseminated to a mass audience at no extra charge. In short, films offered fantasies beyond reach, but they were also a source of practical, usable advice.

The Fashion Show: Origins and Appropriations

It was the Parisian couturier Charles Frederick Worth who introduced the live mannequin and invented the fashion show. Early in his career, when he was working as a salesman for a Parisian mercer, Worth observed specially hired young women who would walk around the premises modeling shawls while a sales pitch was made to a client.[16] He was then convinced that clothing worn in movement (as opposed to the static display on a dummy) enhanced his clients' visual and tactile experience of fashion and that this spectacle did, indeed, affect sales. When his own *maison de couture* opened in 1858, Worth hired several mannequins and made sure that they were always available to put on a dress for the inspection of a client. This novel practice established a firm connection between certain forms of exhibition and the volume of sales, between aesthetics and commerce, and was adopted by all upscale fashion salons throughout Europe in the later decades of the nineteenth century.[17]

The spectacular presentation of clothes took place not only in professional couture houses but also in a variety of other public spaces, such as at the races. There, as a visitor in Paris reported, "you will find all the leaders of fashion displaying the latest creations . . . the most striking and audacious gowns are worn by 'mannequins' or dressmakers' models who are paid to be stared at."[18] In late nineteenth-century Paris, the racecourse at Longchamp and the Bois de Boulogne became the most fashionable parading grounds for dress. In Berlin it was the horse track in Grunewald and various private boating and yacht clubs on the lakes in the city's southwest outskirts that became the trendy spots for the presentation of the latest models.[19] During the 1920s, horse races at Grunewald, for example, became inseparable from the so-called "fashion races" (Moderennen): at regular intervals, a contemporary observer writes, "the poor horses are given half-an-hour break so that girls in furs, coats, and hats can perform a little trot on the glorious lawn."[20] Along with other public settings that attracted big crowds of fashion-conscious and relatively affluent people, such as parks, beaches, up-scale resorts, and hotels, racetracks remained important venues for the display of designers' most recent creations everywhere in Europe, including Berlin, in the first three decades of the twentieth century and reinforced the trend toward the increased public visibility of fashions.

When turn-of-the-century stage productions started discovering the dramatic potential inherent in varying costumes, theater became another space for sartorial display. Realizing the increased importance and accessibility of fashion to the middle classes and in order to attract a wider female audience, dramatic productions began to mimic the presentational practices (die Vorführungen) common in the *haute couture* salons. The distinction between actresses and mannequins collapsed as fashion and theatre merged into the new genre of the "fashion play," a form of musical comedy that stormed the stages of London, Paris, Berlin, and Vienna from the 1890s up to 1914.[21] Similarly, the revue — specifically the *Ausstattungsrevue*, or "production-number revue" — modeled after the "grand spectacles" of the French Folies-Bergère and dominated by an abundance of sensual visual effects, also included a large number of fashion tableaux.[22] Both the fashion plays and the revues presented a series of dramatized fashion plates: the primary focus was on the performative aspect of wearing clothes, and the meager plots were usually secondary to the goal of featuring the lead actresses in as many different outfits as possible.

In the two decades preceding the First World War, German audiences were entertained by dozens of burlesques, operettas, and light farces with plots steeped in the milieu of Berlin's flourishing garment industry and costumes provided by its premiere companies. These plays formed a subgenre of low-brow popular comedy called "Konfektionspossen," and their titles were indicative of the genre's primary interest in the presentation of fashions on stage: *Das Warenhausmädchen* (The Department Store Girl, by Otto Reinhard Popper, 1908), *Ein Kostüm* (Costume, by Alois Berla, 1909), *Gelbstern* (Mannequin, by Jacques Burg and Walter Turszinsky, 1907), *Der Damenschneider* (The Ladies' Tailor, by Carl Lindau, 1904), and *Die Unschuld im Tailor-made* (Innocence in Tailor-Made Clothes, by Carl Rössler and Ludwig Heller, 1910), to name just a few.[23] In many cases, for example in the five-act play *Modenschau um Mitternacht* (Fashion Show at Midnight, 1913) or the pantomime *Die östliche Göttin* (The Eastern Goddess, 1914), these works were directly commissioned by one or more *Konfektion* businesses. The plays would be reviewed as fashion shows in the fashion trade journals and women's magazines such as *Der Konfektionär* and the *Illustrierte Frauenzeitung*, and the costumes would be described in detail for those readers who could not see the play but would like to be informed of the latest trends.

With the widespread popularity of such plays, the distinction between fashion and performing arts, promotion and entertainment, began to disappear. This new trend manifested itself often in the timing of the premieres: usually the "Konfektionspossen" were launched during the semi-annual *Konfektion* trade fair, the *Durchreise*, and targeted the hundreds of wholesale buyers from all over Germany who descended on Berlin, not only to catch up on the most recent styles and place orders with the capitals' fine fashion salons, but also to enjoy the sumptuous and unfettered metropolitan night life. Even if the plays in a theater's repertoire were not related thematically to fashion, the fashion industry still used the stage as a venue for advertising: for the two-week period of the *Durchreise*, fashion parades (Modellschauen) were scheduled to take place during the intermissions of most theatrical performances.[24]

Since turn-of-the-century actresses were expected to supply their own costumes for plays set in contemporary times, the clothes that they wore in their roles almost always came from their personal wardrobe. This tradition may have contributed to the proliferation of designer fashion in plays and, later on, in early films. Couturiers saw an opportunity to advance their brands by luring the most popular among the actresses with discounts into becoming their exclusive customers. It was on the stage of the popular theater, operetta, and revues — with performers such as Fritzi Massary, Lori Leux, and Tilla Durieux — that the prototype of the future film star was born and the image of stardom became inseparably connected with the task of modeling or directly promoting the latest, most glamorous fashion styles of the designer houses.[25] Commenting adoringly on the costumes of Fritzi Massary, one of the best-dressed actresses in Berlin, fashion journalist Elsa Herzog proclaimed that both "the German stage and the German fashion industry could only profit" if there were more performers with Massary's "talent for clothes."[26] Other critics who were less enthusiastic about ostentations sartorial display during performances noted how the nation's theaters had turned into "pure fashion shows" marketing images of products (Warenbilder) directly to the consumer.[27]

Owing much to the repertoire of theatrical display, the formal fashion show was launched in Europe between 1908 and 1910. It not only targeted the individual female clients entering the premises, but was specially organized for a select audience of consumers and connoisseurs, female as well as male. However, while turn-of-the-century theater embraced fashion display as a way to escape its elitist aura and broaden its popular appeal, the fashion show borrowed from theater pomp and exclusivity in an effort to legitimize its own high cultural status. Parisian fashion reformer Paul Poiret and London-based couturier Lucile (Lady Duff Gordon), fierce competitors, both claimed to have invented the fashion show after being inspired by contemporary theatrical performances. They consciously styled their mannequin parades as dramatic plays and even went on international "tours" with their troupes of mannequins. It was in those early fashion shows that the "theatricalization" of fashion marketing reached a peak.[28]

Between 1910 and 1913 Poiret "performed" in a dozen European cities, and one of his first stops, in 1911, was Berlin, where he was invited by the capital's premier *Konfektion* company, Herrmann Gerson.[29] Keenly aware of current international trends and oblivious to local, often nationalistically flavored calls to liberate Germans from the domination of French fashions, the co-owner of the Gerson store from 1889 till 1919, Philipp Freundenberg, struck a personal friendship with Poiret, invited him repeatedly to Berlin for shows and lectures, and actively supported reforms in the design, production, and public presentation of fashion that would make it part of German women's everyday lives.[30] As it turned out, Berlin's metropolitan public, too, was eager for fashion as public entertainment. On its initial visit in Germany, Poiret's show became the object of mass fascination and intense scrutiny. It was not so much the dresses themselves but the novel form of their public presentation that thrilled the observers. As one magazine reported, Poiret's creations were demonstrated not on wax dummies but by live mannequins, specially trained, who appeared almost as actresses (Interpreterinnen, Schauspielerinnen).[31] While only a select few people could attend the show, the public at large enthusiastically followed the Parisian mannequins' every step in the city, reading reports in the press about their diet, their street clothes, and the exact measurements of their bodies.[32]

By hosting Poiret's first show in Berlin, the Herrmann Gerson store enhanced its reputation, not only as a leader in the sale and export of mass-produced clothes, but also as a trendsetter in the public display of fashion in Germany. From around 1910 on, Gerson, as well as numerous other designers' salons and department stores in Berlin, held formal fashion shows with living mannequins at a fixed time in the afternoon a few times each week on a regular basis, in specially designed salons that resembled theaters, including an elevated stage or a dramatic staircase, curtains, and seats for the members of the audience, be they invited or paying guests. While some shows were mere walkabouts, during which an orchestra played and tea was served to the clientele — the popular "Modentee," which persisted well into the 1920s as is evident from scenes in Walter Ruttmann's film *Berlin: Symphony of a Grerat City* — many other shows, in an attempt to gain a competitive edge, employed simpler scenarios and models who had already had some stage coaching.[33] During the more prosperous stabilization years of the Weimar Republic, the fashion show turned into an elaborate spectacle, often complete with lectures, dances, poetry, and concerts; the audience was treated to tea and cookies, and well-known actors were hired to announce the prices during the mannequin parade.[34]

Konfektionskomödien: Fashion Farces from Lubitsch to the End of the Silent Era

When it came out in 1927, Richard Eichberg's film *Fürst von Pappenheim* (The Prince of Pappenheim) offered the type of entertainment that the mass audience at the time craved. It features a runaway princess (Mona Maris) who works incognito as a top fashion model in an upscale Berlin designer house, as well as a former mannequin (Dina Gralla) who has married a count and can now afford all the fashionable clothes that her heart desires. The comic entanglements culminate in a hilarious cross-dressing scene in which the male shop assistant (Curt Bois) parades in front of an admiring audience as a masked mannequin in a dazzling evening gown. In addition to the ostentatious fashion show in an expensive hotel — perhaps one of the longest and most lavish fashion-show scenes in Weimar cinema — the film also contains several routine in-house presentations of clothes for individual clients and, to lure an even bigger audience, the program for the film's premiere boasted that all the costumes were provided by Berlin's distinguished designer house Herrmann Gerson.

Although contemporary critics sneered at the predictability of the story, the film's escapism, and the director's limited ambition, *Der Fürst von Pappenheim* was a crowd-pleaser.[35] Its success with contemporary audiences is a reminder that film production between 1918 and 1933 consisted of more than a just the few dozen serious art films that make up what is now considered the Weimar canon. In fact for the most part, cinema of that period was genre cinema. Of all feature-film productions — an average of 300 films per year during the Weimar Republic — one third were popular comedies, a genre still in need of systematic scholarly exploration within German Studies.

As one of the most popular comedies of its time, *Der Fürst von Pappenheim* is also a prime example of the complex relationship between film and fashion. It belongs to a group of works from the Weimar era in which fashion not only was part of a spectacular *mise-en-scène* but also served as the raw material for the narrative. The fashion theme shaped distinct cinematic conventions, with the result that a sub-genre emerged that became known as the *Konfektionskomödie*, or "fashion farce," whose rise coincided with the flourishing of Berlin's garment industry, *Konfektion*, from the turn of the century to the late 1920s. Fashion farces were among the first longer and commercially successful feature movies shortly after 1910, including the first productions featuring Ernst Lubitsch, initially as the leading actor and later as both actor and director. These films linked the notion of the early German comedy to specific situations — masquerades, cross-dressing, infatuation with appearances, mix-ups, and the transformative potential of clothes — with the milieu of the big-city clothing stores, and with Jewish humor and Jewish characters.[36]

Fig. 13: The fashion salon in *Der Fürst von Pappenheim* (Prince of Pappenheim, 1927). Deutsche Kinemathek.

Throughout the 1920s and early 1930s, fashion comedies continued to proliferate. They showed alluring locations, events, and products associated with the modern lifestyle of the German metropolis — designer salons, upscale department stores, fashion parades, and stylish clothes. Moreover, the sites and fashion practices displayed there were quite familiar to even lower- and middle-class women, who were drawn to them, if not as customers, then at least as avid window-shoppers and consumers of visual delights. The protagonists in these films also appealed to the mass public: there was always the shrewd male shop assistant who knew how to cater to capricious and vain customers, and the ambitious, smart, indispensable female mannequin (Konfektionsmädel, Probiermamsell, Gelbstern, or Konfektioneuse) who hoped to acquire middle-class status, to become a "fashion queen" (Modekönigin), an actress, a film star, or the owner of a designer salon. As the mostly Jewish-owned fashion industry in Germany was "aryanized" in the course of the 1930s, Weimar's fashion farce with its slapstick humor and subversive laughter disappeared. Since National Socialist rhetoric associated the fashion industry with corrupt Jewish influences, and the male lead was played by the Jewish actor Curt

Bois, the comic scenes of cross-dressing at the fashion show in *Der Fürst von Pappenheim* were seen as "decadent," "perverse," and "poisonous."[37]

The collaboration between film and fashion dates back to the emergence of film as a new mass medium early in the twentieth century, when the fashion business quickly realized its potential for distributing fashionable images to ever larger audiences. Paul Poiret is reported to have been the first couturier, in 1911, to film his mannequins in motion and thus take the fashion show on the road even when he could not afford to have the whole "troupe" travel with him.[38] At the same time, newsreel companies such as Pathé and Gaumont, which dominated the European market in the second decade of the twentieth century, began to integrate footage of Paris fashions in their newsreels.[39] From 1920 on, fashion shows from all over the world were regularly featured on the German newsreels "Messter-Woche," "Deulig-Wochenschau," and "Emelka-Woche." And it was in the same period, the 1920s, that numerous short films advertising fashion products (furs, hats, clothes, and fabrics), clothing stores, and department stores were produced and added to the newsreels.[40]

The merger of the *Konfektion*'s business interests with the audience's growing appetite for new forms of entertainment was most evident in the rise of early film comedy. The success of the "Konfektionspossen" or "Konfektionsgrotesken" on the theater stage prompted subsequent film adaptations as well as the emergence of a similar film genre. Walter Turszinsky and Jacques Burg's popular play *Gelbstern* (1908), for example, took on a second life as a two-reeler, *Gelbstern* (Mannequin, 1913). No copies remain, but contemporary reviews pointed out that it was the first German film in which the audience was delighted to see "a fashion show with flesh-and-blood mannequins."[41] Encouraged by *Gelbstern*'s sensational popularity and convinced that contemporary mass audiences were ready to watch longer films (Ein-Stunden-Filme), especially if the basis of the films' "fascination ois concrete and physical" (in der Werkstatt des Konkreten, Körperlichen) rather than itellectual, Turzinsky went on to write over a dozen more screenplays for comic films.[42] Not surprisingly, many of his stories revolved around garment stores, mannequins, and fashion shows, a milieu that he expected to offer all the visual attraction and sensual pleasure that one could hope for in a longer film. Most successful among these films — and incidentally also the first ones in which Ernst Lubitsch appeared in major roles, always as the sales apprentice (*Kommis*, or *Konfektionslehrling*) — were *Die Firma heiratet: Drei Kapitel aus dem Leben einer Probiermamsell* (Marriage in the Company: Three Chapters from the Life of a Mannequin, 1914) and *Der Stolz der Firma: Die Geschichte eines Lehrlings* (The Pride of the Company: The Story of an Apprentice, 1914). These were followed by some of the first films that Lubitsch himself directed, the enormously popular three-reeler *Schuhpalast Pinkus* (Shoe Palace Pinkus, 1916) and *Der Blusenkönig* (The Blouse King, 1917).[43]

These pre-First World War slapstick and situation comedies are set in a social and geographical milieu that was immediately recognizable to the contemporary audience — Berlin's *Konfektion* district — and directly address themes of modern female consumerist desires and infatuation with fashion. In *Die Firma heiratet* and *Schuhpalast Pinkus*, for example, in order to increase sales, salesmen deceive their female customers by selling larger shoe and clothing sizes as smaller ones, since smaller feet and slimmer figures are considered more attractive. Contemporary reviews attributed the enormous success of these early comedies to Lubitsch's convincing performance as an ambitious, arrogant, shrewd, opportunistic, and yet likable apprentice in the "rag business," appearing under the names of Moritz Abramowsky, Siegmund Lachmann, Sally Katz, or Sally Pinkus. Critics have repeatedly emphasized the affinity between Lubitsch's petty-bourgeois characters in these early comedies and his own social background. As a Berliner who grew up among poor Eastern European Jews, Lubitsch strove to overcome the financial and social limitations of his environment, but at the same time he was very familiar with the Jewish *Konfektion* milieu. In fact, before joining Max Reinhardt's theater he had followed his clothing-store-owner father's wishes and worked as an apprentice in a clothing store in Berlin.[44]

To the extent that these films have been studied by scholars of early cinema at all, the attention has been primarily on Lubitsch's screen persona: his performance style, his indebtedness to popular forms of entertainment — vaudeville, circus, pantomime — his Jewish humor, and his affinity for themes from the retail fashion and garment industries. Elsaesser, Hake, and others have also pointed out that his early films show how connected cinema is to commerce, marketing, consumer goods, and fashion, and how the *Konfektion* milieu as a world of make-believe "effectively mirrors or parodies cinema itself."[45] However, these early *Konfektionskomödien* are also remarkable for combining a focus on gender and class issues with visual pleasure and a genuinely democratic perspective. The female characters are endowed with a degree of erotic and social freedom that hardly existed in real life in any class at the time. The stories often center on a star mannequin, a young woman of lower-class background, who at first appears to be easy prey for the men in the company — from the owner down to the sales clerks, who all plot to become her lover. In fact, she very quickly asserts her own will, primarily because she is smarter, more ambitious, independent, and liberated than anyone had expected. According to film reviews and judging from the surviving screenplay, Fränze (Thea Sandten), the mannequin in Otto Rippert's 1913 film *Gelbstern*, is seen smoking cigarettes, taking acting lessons, helping out the poor whenever she has extra money, and planning to travel on her own to Paris. Her character embodies erotic initiative and social ambition of almost utopian proportions, which helps her resist effectively the intentions of the men around her.⁴⁶ Still, a conservative streak in these grotesque farces prevails, as the happy ending is always associated with marriage. Typically, as in *Gelbstern* and *Der Blusenkönig*, the marriage at the end is between members of the same class: after a series of complicated escapades the mannequin ends up united with her sweetheart, a fellow employee at the fashion salon, rather than the wealthy boss. On rare occasions, as in *Die Firma heiratet*, the mannequin, Trude Hoppe (Resl Orla), does cross class lines. She marries the owner of the salon, but not until she proves herself indispensable to the business and imposes her own terms on the marital union.

On a purely visual level it was the spectacle of fashion presentation in these films that fascinated the public. For one, the *Konfektion* comedies foregrounded fashionable products and the uninhibited pleasure of their consumption. As contemporary critics observed, the audience was entertained not only by the comic situations in the film (das ganze Parkett hat gelächelt, gelacht, gewiehert und gebrüllt), but also by the constant parade of fashionable clothes, shoes, and accessories in which not only the female mannequins but also Lubitsch's characters were involved (in both *Der Stolz der Firma* and *Schuhpalast Pinkus*, before taking on the job in the fancy fashion store the male apprentice buys an elegant suit and swirls around as a mannequin in a fashion show).⁴⁷ Since the fashion shows were cast as a form of exclusive entertainment, accessible only to small, elite audiences, film suddenly provided the ideal opportunity for the masses to partake in the same visual attractions that only the select few could enjoy in the fashion salons. And the sense that the cinema audience was part of an elite fashion-show audience was reinforced by explicit announcements in the intertitles: the public was informed that the costumes and the hats for *Die Firma heiratet*, *Der Stolz der Firma*, and *Der Blusenkönig* came from the salons Glaser & Goetz and/or Auguste Muenzer; the shoes and boots in *Schuhpalast Pinkus* were provided by the designer house Emil Jacobi in Berlin.

The fashion-show sequences in the two surviving films from that period reproduce with almost documentary precision the rituals and conventions of successful product marketing. As Siegmund Lachmann, Lubitsch's character in *Der Stolz der Firma*, arrives for an interview in the Berlin store of J. C. Berg, a spring fashion parade happens to be under way. About a dozen mannequins are lined up in identical poses, and as the camera zooms in they step up and turn around slowly for their dresses to be inspected by the chief *directrice* (a former star mannequin) and the store owner. In *Schuhpalast Pinkus*, after a disappointing drop in sales, Sally Pinkus, the nouveau-riche store owner, invents a strategy for success: first, during the applause after a dancer's performance at the theater, Pinkus presents the actress (Melitta Hervé) with a pair of shoes and announces to the audience: "These charming shoes can be found only in Shoe Palace

Pinkus"; then, as the public is leaving the theatre, he hands out cards to everyone inviting them to a shoe show to take place on the following day. During the shoe parade about a dozen mannequins walk down a staircase and onto an elevated platform where they pause in the middle, slightly raising their skirts to expose the shoes, and in the next few seconds the camera closes up on their feet while Pinkus explains the design of each shoe model. At the end the of the show, the mannequins assemble again at the stairs as if for a group picture, but the camera quickly moves downward, zooms in on their feet and lower legs, and slowly pans around. In both films the fashion-show sequences disrupt the flow of the narrative and culminate in a series of close-ups of products (dresses, shoes) intended to entice the spectator/prospective buyer.

At the same time, the focus in these early Lubitsch films was also on the star mannequins, who embodied, despite their humble background, a mixture of professional confidence and impeccable elegance, emancipated independence, and irresistible eroticism. Moreover, they could be considered female doubles of sorts to the ambitious Jewish apprentices, recent arrivals from the provinces, since both groups were "social climbers" and "adventurous hedonists" who mastered perfectly the tasks of advancement, assimilation, and maximum success in life.[48] Moreover, on-screen, unlike in real life, the mannequins who paraded the fashionable outfits were allowed to display temperament, opinions, and ambition of their own, thus inviting the audience to identify with them on several levels. As part of her job, the model presented clothes that she possessed only temporarily, only during the show, and in reality could never buy. Nevertheless, the fashionable attire and the experience of wearing it seemed to embody her dreams of future fame and prosperity. She liked to think that her involvement with fashion and all its fleeting fascination was just the first step toward her imagined future realization as "a real actress."[49] Similarly, for the women in the audience, the spectacular display of fashion on the screen could easily serve as a reminder of what they neither owned nor could afford. Nevertheless, the viewers preferred to indulge, at least for the duration of the film, in the visual pleasure of such fashions and in the fantasy of one day becoming one of these images. It is in this act of doubling powerful on- and off-screen illusions that the mannequins in the farces emerged in the peculiar function of role models for an upwardly mobile yet still very constrained female audience.

Comedies featuring mannequins, designer salons, and fashion shows from the subsequent Weimar years, although different in length and comic style, rehearsed the same narrative tropes established in the early films. In *Die Dame, der Teufel und die Probiermamsell* (The Lady, the Devil, and the Mannequin, 1919), Henny Porten created what the press then called "a new type: the German mannequin" (das deutsche Konfektionsmädel).[50] In fact, she reenacted for postwar audiences a persona already familiar from the prewar "Konfektionspossen." This film, like several of the comedies that Robert Wiene wrote and/or directed between 1914 and 1919, shows throughout the powerful influence of his first mentor and collaborator, Berlin fashion-milieu expert Walter Turszinsky, and explores classical comic situations involving mistaken identity, masquerades, and disguises.[51] Porten's character in *Die Dame, der Teufel und die Probiermamsell*, "a natural, healthy Berlin girl," works as a model in a fashion shop and falls in love with an ermine coat that she displays during a fashion show and that a wealthy customer later buys for his mistress, a baroness. After the mannequin has a dream in which the gentleman appears as the devil and tries to seduce her with the same coat, she is awakened by the baroness knocking on the door and suggesting that they trade identities. As a result, for a week the model can wear the ermine coat and enjoy the pleasures of a luxurious life with the wealthy gentleman, while the baroness meets and captivates the model's fiancé, Fritz, at his humble quarters. Of course, after a week the Berlin mannequin realizes that she is much happier as a model in her fashion salon than as a pampered aristocrat. The happy ending materializes when the couples are realigned and the model is "cured" of her passion for the coat. She returns to her not-so-rich boyfriend and to the routine of indulging in fashionable clothes at work only, during the fleeting moments of the fashion show. Thus the meaning of fashion established through the plot on-screen — namely that it has to be "consumed," enjoyed, and felt in all its ephemerality, rather than truly possessed — seems to double the meaning of cinematic entertainment per se: the film audience is invited to take pleasure in the spectacle of glamour (particularly in the several scenes of a fashion show) and to indulge fantasies about social transformation through clothes, but only for the duration of the show; as soon as the film is over, the viewers must abandon such dreams, exit the theatre, and resume ordinary life.

The popularity of the comedies set in a city fashion store — films of often questionable artistic value but very attractive to audiences — continued throughout the 1920s.[52] A new generation of screenwriters, too, demonstrated exceptional familiarity with the Berlin fashion trade and brought its ambience, rituals, and characters into the stories. For example, one of the most prolific screenwriters in post-First World War silent cinema, Ruth Goetz, with more than sixty films to her credit, was known also as a freelance fashion journalist who published regularly in *Die Dame*, *Elegante Welt*, and *Der Modenspiegel* in the 1920s and 1930s. Goetz wrote the script for *Die Kleine aus der Konfektion* (The Little Mannequin, 1922), a comedy of errors and mix-ups that starts as a melodrama but continues with a spectacular series of fashion shows. Poor Trude Schneider (Evi Eva) is thrown out of her home, rejected by her lover (Reinhold Schünzel), and saved by noble industrialist Köllner (Karl Beckersachs) when she is desperate and nearly jumps into the cold River Spree. But before the deprived working-class girl and the rich factory owner are finally united in a happy marriage, the film traces Trude's successful career as a mannequin for a distinguished Berlin fashion store.

These scenes portraying the everyday life of the mannequin with a mixture of realism and fantasy were characteristic of many of the fashion farces, and it was in these scenes that the expertise and craftsmanship of the fashion journalist as a script writer were crucial. Film critics characterized the film *Die Kleine aus der Konfektion* repeatedly as a credible study of Berlin's fashion milieu because it offers glimpses of the life of a typical mannequin who parades fashionable dresses for upper-class customers. The job was less glamorous than it appeared: for minimal pay, Trude is required to change into and out of dozens of outfits per day, yet she is not allowed to talk to the customers or to collect any commission from sales.[53] At the same time, setting substantial parts of the film in a clothing store was used as an excuse to stage several fashion shows — pure visual extravaganzas that contributed little to the development of the plot but fulfilled other functions. To begin with, fashion shows within the film served as effective advertisement for the Berlin designer houses that provided the costumes and were often mentioned by name in the credits. Moreover, while in reality the seasonal fashion shows in department stores and designer salons charged high prices for attendance (as if one were going to the theater), the fashion show within the film, as mentioned earlier, could be enjoyed with no extra fee and thus constituted a significant draw for the mass audience.

Not unlike other works in the genre, *Die Kleine aus der Konfektion* made up in attractiveness to a large audience what it lacked in artistic value. Or as the reviewer for *Film-Kurier* summed up its merits despite its weaknesses: "Nevertheless, the director has an instinct for what will lure a big audience and so he created a film that, for sure, will make a good profit."[54] And it is this spectacle of fashionable display that constituted the primary draw of such films, especially for female viewers: "Ah, the female viewers [Zuschauerinnen] will be thrilled to see much more than they paid for when they watch the long parades of mannequins!"[55]

This tendency to favor the exhibition at the expense of the story or artistic sophistication was strong in the film *Luxusweibchen* (1925), scripted by another expert in the workings of the fashion world, journalist Ola Alsen. The title character, Harriet von Randow (Lee Parry), presents a second type of mannequin in the 1920s fashion farces — not a working-class girl who rises to the ranks of high society through her employment in a *Konfektionshaus*, but a spoiled upper-class woman who is abandoned by her wealthy husband and, in order to support herself, must take a job as a mannequin in a fashion salon (Modehaus Rainer). Not only is she successful in her professional career as a mannequin, but her talents and skills also help the owner of the salon overcome a difficult financial situation.

Needless to say, the two of them fall in love, and after a series of comical complications they marry. And as in the other fashion farces, here too the predictable scenario is subordinated to the spectacle of the fashion show: "The film becomes so-to-speak a 'Bädecker' of the world of elegance: nightclubs and fashion salons with their regular fashion shows. . . . The plot serves as a pretext for the display of diverse shows. . . . It is altogether a tasteful picture album that every audience would like to browse in."[56]

Overall, the message of the film was as mixed as its aesthetics. It was reminiscent of the fashion advice that journalist Ola Alsen gave regularly to the readers of her columns in *Elegante Welt*: on the one hand, when it comes to the consumption of luxury items, moderation is better, because an obsession with appearances could bring about both break-ups and bankruptcies within the family; on the other hand, the film as well as the career of the script writer herself suggested that fashion, especially in times of financial and marital crisis, could be a viable field for the professional realization of women. This narrative twist was then used as a pretext to offer even more lavish scenes of fashion parades, prompting the audience to indulge in the fantasies presented on the screen.

Judging from the reviews in the press and the descriptions filed with the film censorship office — the films themselves have in most cases been lost — these comedies perfected a clichéd scenario: Berlin mannequins were not only chic but shrewd, and fashion salons functioned primarily as the set for flirting and intricate love affairs, often across class lines, before all the action is finally channeled into the "secure harbor of marriage."[57] Such films came to be called "Boulevardfilme," a popular counterpart to the "art film" and, as a reviewer of *Drei Mannequins* pointed out, by including numerous fashion shows (Modenball- und Modeschauszenen) in their plot lines, they played directly to the visual desires of the mass audience.[58]

For today's scholars of Weimar film, the rediscovery of the fashion farces of the 1920s not only fills a gap in German film history but also reveals the mechanisms by which popular culture shaped and manipulated the experience of modernity for the masses. And the emerging film star played a central role in enacting modernity for a mass audience. As a discussion of famous actress Brigitte Helm will show, star status was inseparable from the fashion icon.

Brigitte Helm as Star Actress and Mannequin

Brigitte Helm's ascendance to stardom began in 1925 when the twenty-year-old with no previous acting experience was chosen by Fritz Lang to star in *Metropolis* (1927). Following her spectacular performance in the double role of the good and the evil Maria in that film, Helm signed a contract with the German film studio UFA (Universum Film-Aktiengesellschaft), where she worked for about ten years. During this period she starred in about thirty films (ten silent films, nineteen talkies, and a few British and French versions of the original German productions).[59] Contemporary as well as later audiences associated Helm's star status primarily with her impersonations of *femmes fatales*, vamps, and modern monsters. She played the demonic artificial creation of a scientist in Henrik Galeen's *Alraune* (1928), the fatally attractive woman in Viktor Tourjansky's *Manolescu* (1929), and numerous other roles as dangerous spies, seductresses, and actresses, prompting critics to declare that she had achieved the status of "European Super-Vamp" (europäische Übervamp).[60] Borrowing a metaphor from the mass-produced clothing industry, one critic suggested somewhat dismissively that her performance lacked the allure of a real star because she "always wears her demonic look as if it were a ready-to-wear outfit" (Brigitte Helm ist nun ganz mit Dämonie konfektioniert).[61]

There was, however, more to her celebrity allure than the hallmark vampish appeal. By the end of her short career, in 1935, when she decided not to renew her contract with UFA, Brigitte Helm had not only become the biggest female star of Weimar cinema but had also established herself as a unique fashion icon, famous for her presentation of contemporary clothing on and off the movie screen. At first the destructive, evil, inhuman *femmes fatales* that she so often played seem incongruent with the role of promoting contemporary fashion to the masses. However, during her presence in German cinema, which lasted for ten years, Helm's screen persona resonated, especially with her female audience, in part because she was always attuned to the attractive clothing styles and customary presentation practices of the current moment. On the one hand Helm was known as a loyal client of the Berlin *Konfektion* firm Mahrenholz, which provided the contemporary clothes for most of her films, and she often wore Mahrenholz outfits at the premieres of her films, as well as in photographs taken specially for fashion magazines such as *Elegante Welt*, *Vogue* (the German edition), and *Die Dame*.[62]

On the other hand, as many critics acknowledged, Brigitte Helm transformed the films in which she appeared, especially G. W. Pabst's *Abwege* (Crisis, 1928), Hanns Schwarz's *Die wunderbare Lüge der Nina Petrowna* (The Wonderful Lie of Nina Petrovna, 1929), and Johannes Meyer's *Eine von uns* (One of Us, 1932), into fascinating "costume tales" (Kleidergeschichten) in which middle-class women could assert themselves as modern bourgeois subjects, independent, sensuous, and desirable.[63] Despite all their criticisms, contemporary commentators agreed that Helm had mastered the indisputable art "of moving through space displaying dresses in a uniquely attractive way."[64] Moreover, regardless of the theme and genre of the films in which Helm starred (ranging from science fiction to musicals, dramas, and melodramas), her protagonists consistently managed to put on a fascinating fashion show within the film — a show that

Fig. 14: Brigitte Helm featured in *Vogue* (German edition), 27 Mar. 1929, 37. Kunstbibliothek, Staatliche Museen zu Berlin.

Fig. 15: Brigitte Helm in *Die Yacht der sieben Sünden* (The Yacht of Seven Sins, 1928). Deutsche Kinemathek.

temporarily suspended the diagetic world of characters and actions and ushers and audience into a realm of pure spectacle and sensual pleasure. And the style of her performance in those scenes was consistently influenced by the popular fashion shows and mannequin competitions, thus expanding the audiences for these spectacles from wealthy consumers to the heterogeneous mass public of the movies.

Brigitte Helm began her spectacular career in the science-fiction classic *Metropolis*. One particular sequence in it, overloaded with excess, combines with remarkable fluidity the phantasmagoric show with the realistic details and the ambience of the contemporary entertainment scene — the robot's appearance on the round cabaret stage of the nightclub Yoshiwara and her orgiastic striptease dance in front of an all-male audience in evening wear. Rotwang, the creator of the automaton, and his master, John Frederson, organize a soirée in order to introduce the robotic Maria to male high society and to test the believability of her fleshly incarnation. This sequence has been given numerous insightful analyses, all of them focusing on the complicated visual relationship between the robot and her audience. Tom Gunning has detected Lang's systematic employment of parallel editing, shot/reverse shot, and jump-cutting in order to create a visionary scene of remarkable spatial ambiguity. The image of the dancing Maria enraptures not only the men in the soirée, whose unblinking eyes merge into one single staring eye filling the screen; she also mesmerizes young Freder, who is lying in bed, witnessing the dance through clairvoyance, hallucination, or pure sexual fantasy.[65] In his seminal essay on *Metropolis*, Andreas Huyssen points out the radical ways in which this scene lays open a fundamental filmic convention, namely that the woman's body is treated by cinema as a projection of male vision. Moreover, Huyssen argues, whenever women internalize technology and power (created by men) and desert their nurturing, motherly roles, they and their looks become manipulative, threatening, and destructive.[66]

The demonization of the feminine under the male gaze takes place also in a later film with Helm, *Alraune* (1928). In a dramatic scene in which Alraune seduces her "father," the scientist who created her, Helm's character, dressed in a spectacular nightgown, swirls around in her shiny white dress, drops her cape on the floor, and reclines on a bed. The camera, aligned with the stare of the mesmerized man, follows her closely and then repeatedly zooms in on her lower legs and feet clad in shimmering silk stockings and elegant shoes.[67] Again, as in *Metropolis*, irresistible sexual attraction is supposed to serve as the ultimate proof of authentic womanhood embodied even by an artificial creation. More importantly, in both cases — *Metropolis* and *Alraune* — as Laura Mulvey argues, sexual attraction is associated primarily with the act of looking, which involves an enthralled male spectator projecting a fantasy onto a narcissistically indulging female performer.[68]

While analyses along the lines of Mulvey's and Huyssen's are thoroughly convincing, I believe that our understanding of these scenes will be richer and more nuanced if we revisit them in relation to some non-cinematic domains, such as Germany's contemporary entertainment and fashion industries, to whose excesses Helm's performance undoubtedly contains numerous references. In his monograph on the film, Thomas Elsaesser emphasizes that "in its slant on the present [*Metropolis*] does have documentary value. Its story can be read as a compendium text of topical material."[69] He notes also that "in its iconography, too, *Metropolis* is a subtly knowing film, as *Zeitgeist*-conscious as *haute couture* and bestseller *belles-lettres*," and that "its wealth of direct reference to the visual arts, paintings, graphics, sculpture, museum pieces, fashion accessories, book-design, and commercial art is astonishing."[70] At the same time, Elsaesser does not comment extensively on the connections between contemporary fashion and film aesthetics beyond mentioning that some of designer Aenne Willkomm's costumes for the ladies of the night are taken from a Bauhaus collection by Oscar Schlemmer.[71] More concretely, I suggest that the dance sequence, particularly its costumes, presentational style, and spatial organization, can be read partly in contrast, partly parallel to a rising spectacle of the mid-1920s, namely the fashion show. Some of the unofficial venues for high-fashion presentations were the nightclubs, the variety show (*Ausstattungsrevue*) of the 1920s, where a large portion of the program would be taken up by the so-called fashion tableaux: in their dazzling contemporary costumes and glittering jewelry the stars of the show would appear in a dramatic setting — walking slowly down a staircase, materializing mysteriously from the dark center of the stage or brought out, literally, on an elevated platform held by several male performers. The number would often combine contrasting elements: both dressing and undressing, demonstration of dazzling fabrics and a strip-tease, static postures and seductive gyrations.[72]

These elements of the variety performance, as well as the more moderate presentation routines of the fashion parades, are certainly visible in the nightclub scene in *Metropolis*. The "robot's" figure emerges perfectly still, with eyes cast down, from the darkness of an urn, and discernible in the silhouette are a glitzy crescent-shaped headdress and translucent cape. In a classic, even if exaggerated, move known from the 1920s live and filmed fashion shows, Brigitte Helm's character starts slowly turning around in a full circle as she spreads her arms and opens up the cape around her as if giving the audience an opportunity to appreciate the astounding qualities of the cape before she ultimately sheds it entirely, revealing her nearly naked body. Later on in the sequence, the camera zooms out to reveal the woman in a triumphant pose: her torso bends backwards as she is perched on top of a mythical creature, itself supported on the backs of other mythical creatures, with dozens of men's hands stretched up to her.

For the contemporary audience in 1927, the scene of Helm's extravagant dance and lascivious poses would have resonated with impressions from another ostentatious spectacle that was rapidly gaining popularity: the annual contests (Modekonkurrenzen) to elect a fashion queen (Modekönigin). These contests constituted perhaps the most spectacular fashion display in Weimar Germany. The fashion queen was supposed to be the most graceful model among those employed in Berlin's designer salons, hence the "ideal fashionable woman for our times: not too thin and not too sumptuous, partly gamin and partly lady, refined and natural at once."[73] In December 1925, the German fashion industry's professional association ("Verband der deutschen Modenindustrie") organized the first competition during its first ball (Modenball) in Berlin.[74] Widely covered in the media, this event combined elements of the beauty pageant, the upscale fashion show, and the revue kickline. The first fashion queen was nineteen-year-old Sonja Jovanowitsch, a mannequin at the salon Heß, who was proclaimed "Sonja I."[75] She was followed the next year by sixteen-year-old Hilde Zimmermann, employed by the salon Gerson, and then by Asta Offermann

Fig. 16: Hilde Zimmermann as a fashion queen. *Elegante Welt*, 12 Jan. 1927, 36. Kunstbibliothek, Staatliche Museen zu Berlin.

in 1929.[76] Both Jovanowitsch and Zimmermann were featured in traditional royal vestments — a crown and a velvet ruby-colored cape over their typical mid-1920s outfits — on the cover pages of the respective January 1926 and January 1927 issues of *Elegante Welt*.[77] By the end of the decade, fashion shows and contests of all kinds had become so ubiquitous and frequent in the German capital, and the occasions to observe fashion so numerous, that the press gave up its efforts to cover them all. "The Berlin fashion season has gone mad; it is not a season anymore, it is a permanent wave," admitted the German edition of *Vogue* in 1928.[78]

The newsreels as well as the print media had covered these first two competitions extensively. A segment from the 1926 "Deulig-Wochenschau" newsreel that featured a three-minute-long story on "Germany's first fashion competition," for example, opens with an extreme close-up above the crown-covered head of Sonja I, Berlin's first fashion queen, with the camera slowly moving down to her face — her eyes slightly cast down, her head framed in a high, shiny, Elizabethan collar. The close-up is then repeated, this time with the camera focusing on the back of her head. As the camera gradually pulls away, the model turns slowly, revealing her face and stretching her arms to show the inside drape of her mantle; then she spins around, takes off the cape, and ends her performance in a pose that seems to have been the staple of the beautiful woman's ultimate reign over an ecstatic audience of admirers: her upper body bent backwards, her hips thrust forward. We see the same pose featured on the poster for Richard Eichberg's *Der Fürst von Pappenheim* (see book cover), mentioned earlier, which is set in a fashion store and contains numerous scenes from a fashion show.[79] And then again the same pose is found in a drawing on the pages of the journal *Der Querschnitt* from the same year, where the caption reads: "The Award Ceremony for the Fashion Queen Hilde Zimmermann" (Prämierung der Modekönigin Hilde Zimmermann). Both depictions of the final stage in the competition are choreographed in a similar style: the fashion queen is perched on an elevated stage above an excited crowd of observers, mostly men; her slim body is bowed backwards and her torso appears to be almost nude, as it is hard to tell where her gown ends and her bare skin begins.

This triumphant fashion-queen pose, combined with the spectacle of the mini-fashion show, found its way into almost every film in which Brigitte Helm played during the 1920s. One brief scene in the dark, fantastic tale of *Alraune* stands out as a particularly realistic comment on the contemporary infatuation with modern fashions. The central female character, Alraune, played by Helm, is brought up in a convent. One night, as the giggly young women, all dressed in fashionable, short-hemmed white nightgowns, are getting ready for bed, she decides to entertain them with a little fashion show. She takes out a new camisole from her locker, climbs on top of her bed and demonstrates to the other girls her stylish, soft, shiny underwear, letting them touch and admire the quality of the fabric. Then, almost parodying the nightclub performance of the robot Maria in *Metropolis*, Alraune breaks out in a dance while her spectators, now only women, stretch their arms toward her in excitement. An episode set in a different context but with a similar structure and similarly unconnected to the main narrative line appears in Helm's later film *Eine von uns* (One of

Fig. 17: The Award Ceremony for the Fashion Queen Hilde Zimmermann. *Der Querschnitt* 1 (Jan. 1927): 71. Staatsbibliothek Berlin.

Us, 1932), based on Irmgard Keun's popular novel *Gilgi* (1931; see chapter 6 in this book). This time the impromptu fashion show takes place in an office space, where about a dozen young women, Gilgi's colleagues, uniformly dressed in white smocks (very much like the light satin coats that mannequins in fashion stores would wear between presentations) are diligently at work behind their typewriters. All of a sudden, without any apparent reason and without any further consequences for the plot, one of the typists gets up, walks to the front of the room, opens up the white smock, and for a few seconds shows her fine, silky underwear to the admiring audience of co-workers.

Watching each of these films — *Alraune*, from 1928, where she is cast as the title character, a demonic, artificially created woman, or the more realistic bourgeois drama *Abwege* (Crisis, 1929), where she plays a bored wife trapped in an emotionally sterile marriage, or less-known productions such as Jakob and Luise Fleck's *Die Yacht der sieben Sünden* (The Yacht of Seven Sins, 1928), *Manolescu* (1929), and *Die wunderbare Lüge der Nina Petrowna* — is indeed like browsing through a fashion magazine. Helm displays a complete array of contemporary attire for different parts of the day and for a variety of social occasions, from silk pajamas and fine underwear to sports outfits for morning gymnastics and tennis, and from afternoon dresses and travel suits and to glitzy evening gowns. The fashion shows within these films of various genres — from the fantastic to the comedy and melodrama — seem not to be called for by any developments in the plot; they are brief intrusions into the flow of the narrative, often taking less than a minute of screen time. The camera frequently zooms in on details of the external appearance — stockings, shoes, the neckline of a dress, or silk pajama bottoms — as if inserting within the film the fashion photographs that were ubiquitous in the contemporary magazines such as *Elegante Welt* and *Die Dame*. As in the case of fashion photography (most prominently in the work of Helm's contemporary, photographer Yva), one can argue that the heightened attention to fashion display seems to address primarily the female audience. Either women viewers are invited to reflect critically upon the prevalent fetishization or, more likely, their attention is directed to the texture, quality, and attractiveness of the fashionable items as opposed to what was provided by nature — the body.[80]

Halfway into her ten-year career in the movies, it became increasingly apparent that Brigitte Helm disliked being typecast as a "vamp." This resentment gave rise to the lawsuit she launched against UFA, but at the same time Helm worked incessantly through her acting, and especially through her distinct presence as an icon of fashion in all of her films, to undermine her staple appearance as a *femme fatale*.[81] Not unlike Asta Nielsen a decade earlier, Helm began to publicize her active engagement in selecting and designing the contemporary attire that she wore in her movies and that would have an appeal to a broad female audience. In an extensive 1933 interview for the magazine *Die junge Dame*, Helm described her involvement in film fashions and revealed her awareness of the fact that she served as a fashion model for the masses: "I never go for the most extravagant costumes. That is something to avoid at any cost, because extraordinary fashions go by quickly and are soon 'passé.' I have to choose clothes that in half a year — when the film appears on screen —

Fig. 18: Brigitte Helm on the second cover in *Elegante Welt*, 16 Sept. 1929. Kunstbibliothek, Staatliche Museen zu Berlin.

are still fashionable."[82] The audience and the film critics, too, noticed that Helm had developed a unique way of displaying contemporary costume on- and off-screen that served as a counterweight to the stereotype of cold, machine-like, frightening beauty that she was supposed to represent. After the premiere of the contemporary melodrama *Eine von uns* in 1932, the media acknowledged with some satisfaction that Brigitte Helm was finally set free from her vampish appeal. The mise-en-scène, steeped in the everyday life of the big-city lower-middle classes, and particularly Brigitte Helm's performance, were praised for their realism and for possessing a different kind of attractiveness, one that played primarily to the "visual needs" (Schaubedürfnis) of the contemporary mass audience.[83]

The focus on selected scenes that are choreographed in the style of a fashion show confirm that fashion constituted not only an important subtext in many Weimar films but also a spectacle within the spectacle of cinema, a brief, interruptive moment of pure visual pleasure within the narrative. And looking more closely at the career of Brigitte Helm demonstrates again that involvement in fashions — on and off the screen — was inseparable from the making of female stars in German cinema of the 1920s. As cultural critic Curt Moreck remarked in 1926, the film actress is and should be constantly aware that she serves as an ideal for the masses who adore her, and that she is the object of a certain cult of beauty (Schönheitskult): "For the women, she provides a model that they follow when they dress and move, when they smile and turn their eyes."[84]

Explicit and implicit fashion shows incorporated into Weimar popular films fulfilled multiple overlapping functions, some direct and understandable, others more subtle and elusive. Most obviously they provided an occasion for direct product placement and, needless to say, German designer houses such as Gerson and Wolff frequently took advantage of this opportunity. The fashion shows also became one of the paradigmatic cinematic moments in which the female body was transformed literally into a spectacle, with the camera zooming in on the new, fetishized forms — slender torsos and exposed legs. At the same time, the fashion shows within the films constituted significant breaks in the narrative flow, during which the spectators were offered glimpses of the earlier cinema of attraction preserved fragmentarily in the fabric of Weimar's popular story-based cinema. This disruption associated with the fashion show in early Weimar cinema reflected — even in the most straightforward and trivial narratives — the experience of modernity, which was in essence the experience of an environment becoming increasingly distracting, disjunctive, and fragmented.

Notes

A much shorter version of this chapter was published in *German Studies Review*, 30.2 (May 2007): 288–310.

[1] "Der Filmstar als Mannequin: Lya de Putti wird am Donnerstag nachmittag im Hotel Adlon in der dort stattfindenden Pelzausstellung von Alexander Baum & Co. die neuesten Pelzmodelle vorführen."

² "Eine Modenschau im Zoo-Atelier: . . . Ein pompöser Modesalon war für ein paar Stunden im Zoo-Atelier eröffnet, dort konnten wir die letzten Schöpfungen der Pariser Mode, die die Pariser Firma Drecoll vorführte, bewundern. Dort konnten wir wiederum das geniale Spiel von Asta Nielsen sehen. . . . Sie spielt eine der tragenden Rollen im Film *Die freudlose Gasse*, der augenblicklich im Zoo-Atelier von der 'Sofar-Film' gedreht wird."

³ "Ich las neulich einmal, ein gutgemachter Film muß jederzeit wie ein tadelloses Modejournal wirken. In Ländern, in denen Modefragen erhebliche Geltung haben, wurde dies rechtzeitig erkannt. Heute wenden unsere schönen Filmfrauen dieser wichtigen Frage ihr besonderes Augenmerk zu." See "Asta Nielsen wieder in Berlin," *Elegante Welt*, 18 June 1919, 7.

⁴ See Katja Aschke, "Die geliehene Identität: Film und Mode in Berlin, 1900–1990," in *Berlin en vogue: Berliner Mode in der Photographie*, ed. F. C. Gundlach and Uli Richter (Berlin: Wasmuth, 1993), 244–45. In her groundbreaking 1913 study *Zur Soziologie des Kinos* (A Sociology of the Cinema), Emilie Altenloh singled out Asta Nielsen's unrivaled fame, especially among female office workers interested in films depicting "the glamour of modern cosmopolitan circles." No other film star is mentioned by Altenloh, and of Nielsen she writes: "It . . . goes without saying that Asta Nielsen enjoys huge popularity and arouses great admiration." See Emilie Altenloh, "A Sociology of the Cinema: the Audience," *Screen* 42.3 (2001): 283.

⁵ Quoted in Ernst Moritz Mungenast, *Asta Nielsen* (Stuttgart: W. Hädecke, 1928), 116.

⁶ See Curt Moreck, *Sittengeschichte des Kinos* (Dresden: Paul Aretz, 1926), 240.

⁷ See Hans Siemsen, "Die Geliebte Roswolskys," *Die Weltbühne* 47 (1921): 530. For more on Nielsen's fashions, see also Renate Seydel and Allan Hagedorff, eds., *Asta Nielsen: Ihr Leben in Fotodokumenten, Selbstzeugnissen und zeitgenössischen Betrachtungen* (Munich: Universitas, 1981), 168.

⁸ Quoted in Barbara Mundt, "Entwicklung der Mode von 1919–1930," in *Metropolen machen Mode: Haute Couture der Zwanziger Jahre*, ed. B. Mundt (Berlin: Dietrich Reimer, 1977), 52. The costumes for the female lead in *Dr. Mabuse, der Spieler* were designed by Vally Reinecke, who was also an influential fashion editor at *Die Dame* and reported frequently from Paris. See Appendix I.

⁹ See Kracauer, "Film 1928," in *The Mass Ornament*, 308 and 310.

¹⁰ See Kracauer, "The Little Shopgirls Go to the Movies," in *The Mass Ornament*, 292.

¹¹ See Kracauer, "Berliner Nebeneinander: Kara-Iki — Scala-Ball im Savoy — Menschen im Hotel," *Frankfurter Zeitung*, 17 Feb. 1933; reprinted in Kracauer, *Kleine Schriften zum Film*, ed. Inka Mülder-Bach (Frankfurt am Main: Suhrkamp, 2004), 6/1:418.

¹² See Miriam Bratu Hansen, "The Mass Production of the Senses: Classical Cinema as Vernacular Modernism," in *Reinventing Film Studies*, ed. Christine Gledhill and Linda Williams (London: Arnold, 2000), 332–50.

¹³ See Jeanne Allen, "The Film Viewer as Consumer," *Quarterly Review of Film Studies* 5 (Fall 1980): 481–99. For more on the connection between films and

consumer culture, see Jane Gaines, "The Queen-Christina Tie-Ups: Convergence of Shop Window and Screen," *Quarterly Review of Film and Video* 11 (1989): 11–35. For case studies of the relationship between costume and stardom in Hollywood cinema of the 1930s, see Charlotte Herzog, "Powder Puff Promotion: The Fashion Show-in-the-Film," in *Fabrications: Costume and the Female Body*, ed. Jane Gaines and Charlotte Herzog (New York: Routledge, 1990), 134–59, and Charlotte Cornelia Herzog and Jane Marie Gaines, "Puffed Sleeves before Tea-Time: Joan Crawford, Adrian, and Women Audiences," in *Stardom: Industry of Desire*, ed. Christine Gledhill (New York: Routledge, 1991), 74–91.

[14] Sabine Hake, "Das Kino, die Werbung und die Avantgarde," in *Die Spur durch den Spiegel: Der Film in der Kultur der Moderne*, ed. Michael Wedel, Johann N. Schmidt, and Malte Hagener (Berlin: Bertz, 2004), 193.

[15] See Hake, "Das Kino" 193–94.

[16] See Diana De Marly, *Worth: Father of Haute Couture* (London: Elm Tree Books, 1980), 103–4.

[17] In addition to employing flesh-and-blood mannequins, Worth also started presenting two collections a year on living models at his *haute couture* salon, but there were no fixed dates for collections as there are now, and no organized fashion shows. See Caroline Evans, "The Enchanted Spectacle," *Fashion Theory* 5.3 (2001): 271–310.

[18] See Alice Ivimy, *A Woman's Guide to Paris* (London: J. Nisbet, 1909), cited in Valerie Steele, *Paris Fashion: A Cultural History*, 2nd revised ed. (Oxford: Berg, 1998), 170. This promotional tactic was again pioneered by Worth. His wife and business collaborator, Marie Vernet, not only worked as a mannequin, trainer of models, and chief *vendeuse* but also went out to wear his creations in public and mingle socially with the clientele. Later, couturiers such as Poiret, Paquin, and Chanel also hired women regularly to wear their clothes and go out into some fashionable milieu. See Evans, "The Enchanted Spectacle," 273–74.

[19] See "Der Modentee am Strande von Gatow: Ein Ereignis im sommerlichen Gesellschaftsleben Berlins," *Elegante Welt*, 24 Jun. 1929, 26–27.

[20] See Axel Eggebrecht, "Konfektion," *Die Weltbühne* 28.19 (1932): 717.

[21] See Erika Diane Rappaport, *Shopping for Pleasure: Women and the Making of London's West End* (Princeton: Princeton UP, 2000). The development of the fashion play in Paris is extensively studied by Nancy J. Troy, *Couture Culture: A Study of Modern Art and Fashion* (Cambridge, MA: MIT Press, 2002). For a detailed account of the fashion play in London, see Joel Kaplan and Sheila Stowell, *Theatre and Fashion: Oscar Wilde to the Suffragettes* (Cambridge, UK: Cambridge UP, 1994).

[22] For more on fashion display in revues, see Peter Jelavich, *Berlin Cabaret* (Cambridge, MA: Harvard UP, 1993), 104–17. See also Franz-Peter Kothes, *Die theatralische Revue in Berlin und Wien, 1900–1938* (Wilhelmshaven: Heinrichshofen Verlag, 1977), and Reinhard Klooss and Thomas Reuter, *Körperbilder: Menschenornamente in Revuetheater und Revuefilm* (Frankfurt am Main: Syndikat, 1980).

[23] For more on the "Konfektionsposse" as a theatrical genre, see Julia Bertschik, *Mode und Moderne: Kleidung als Spiegel des Zeitgeistes in der deutschsprachigen*

Literatur (Cologne: Böhlau, 2005), 168–78. See also Brunhilde Dähn, *Berlin, Hausvogteiplatz: Über 100 Jahre am Laufsteg der Mode* (Göttingen: Musterschmidt-Verlag, 1968), 203–5.

[24] See Dähn, *Berlin, Hausvogteiplatz*, 206–7. For more on the importance of the *Durchreise*, see Moritz Loeb, *Berliner Konfektion* (Berlin: Hermann Seemann, 1906), 30–39.

[25] Massary was a client of Berlin designer Clara Schultz and French couturier Drecoll, and she promoted their creations, fiercely competing with other actresses. Her stage presence is credited for transforming the revue at the Metropol Theater into the most spectacular fashion show. For more on her involvement with fashion, see Carola Stern, *Die Sache, die man Liebe nennt: Das Leben der Fritzi Massary* (Berlin: Rowohlt, 1998), 77–103.

[26] See Elsa Herzog, "Mode und Bühne," *Jahrbuch der Berliner Bühnen* 1.1 (1925): 119–23.

[27] Theater critic Herbert Ihering, quoted in Klooss and Reuter, *Körperbilder*, 53.

[28] See Kaplan and Stowell, *Theatre and Fashion*, 117.

[29] The company was founded in 1835 by Herrmann Gerson, a Jew from East Prussia who had only recently arrived in Berlin. In 1848 he acquired a spacious three-story building on Werderscher Markt in Berlin that housed both presentation rooms (Vorführräume) and a department store for clothes. It was the main supplier of fashionable clothes to both the royal court and the international mass market. Most important, Gerson was seen as a powerhouse of innovation as far as presentational practices were concerned. It was the first fashion store in Berlin in the second half of the nineteenth century to employ numerous "living models," including one that had the exact proportions of the empress Augusta Victoria: Charlotte Krüger, a humble Berlin woman, was specially selected to model clothes whenever the company gave a presentation at the royal court. Herrmann Gerson died in 1861, and the business was then run by his brothers until 1888, when they sold it to the Freudenberg family. Philipp Freudenberg presided over its most glamorous period, from 1888 to 1919, during which the salon Gerson was the biggest and best known company in Germany's fashion industry. See Westphal, *Berliner Konfektion und Mode, 1836–1939: Die Zerstörung einer Tradition*, 2nd ed. (Berlin: Edition Hentrick, 1992), 207; Christine Waidenschlager, "Aus den Anfängen der Berliner Konfektion," in *Berliner Chic: Mode von 1820 bis 1990*, ed. C. Waidenschlager (Berlin: Stiftung Stadtmuseum Berlin, 2001), 11–24; and Frieda Vallentin, "Ich muß zu Gerson: Erinnerungen an das Modehaus," *Gerson-Brevier* 2.3 (1929): 44–49. A sumptuously illustrated article on Gerson in the magazine *Moderne Kunst* contains numerous lithographs of the interior and exterior of the salon. See Paul Dobert, "Im Reiche der Mode," *Moderne Kunst* 7.11 (1892/93), 137–40.

[30] In his autobiography Poiret wrote extensively of his travels to Germany before the First World War and of his visits with the Freudenberg family, where he felt particularly welcomed and appreciated. See Paul Poiret, *Kings of Fashion: The Autobiography of Paul Poiret*, trans. Stephen Haden Guest (Philadelphia, PA: J. B. Lippincott, 1931), 155–59.

[31] M. von Suttner, "Berliner Moderevüen: Sechs Poiret-Kleider von der Modenschau bei Herrmann Gerson" *Illustrierte Frauenzeitung* 38.5, 1 Dec. 1911, 42.

[32] See Dähn, *Berlin: Hausvogteiplatz*, 144–45. After the first day of presentations in Berlin, Poiret wrote to his wife: "You could have counted the people who came this morning only by the thousands, and a few minutes ago, when the afternoon show was over, an entire crowd, delirious with joy, acclaimed your little sweetheart with an enthusiasm unprecedented in Berlin." This letter is quoted in Palmer White, *Poiret* (New York: Clarkson N. Potter, 1973), 72.

[33] For an extensive overview of London's premier couturier Lucile (Lady Duff Gordon) and her mannequin parades, see Caroline Evans, "The Enchanted Spectacle," 274–97.

[34] On how it became impossible for many of the smaller *Konfektion* companies to keep up the cost of such lavish spectacle, see Martin Ledermann, "Die Modenschau — ein erledigtes Kapitel? Führende westdeutsche Konfektionshäuser gründen eine 'Anti-Modenschau-Liga,'" *Der Konfektionär*, 19 Oct. 1927. These companies founded an "Anti-Fashion-Show League" and organized a boycott of all fashion shows during the fall *Durchreise* in protest against practices that had gotten out of hand.

[35] For critics' reactions, see Siegfried Kracauer, "Der Fürst von Pappenheim," in *Kleine Schriften zum Film*, ed. Inka Mülder-Bach (Frankfurt am Main: Suhrkamp, 2004), 6/1:418. See also Hans Feld, "Der Fürst von Pappenheim," *Film-Kurier*, 8 Sept. 1927; repr. in *Die deutsche Filmkomödie vor 1945: Kaiserreich, Weimarer Republik und Nationalsozialismus*, ed. Jörg Schöning (Hamburg: Cinegraph, 2005), 86–87; Erich Kästner, "Bois de Berlin," *Neue Leipziger Zeitung*, 25 May 1929; repr. in Kästner, *Gemischte Gefühle* (Zurich: Atrium, 1991), 2:193–95.

[36] For a discussion of early German film comedy, see Jürgen Kasten, "Verweigerung der korrekten Assimilation: Jüdische Typen, Milieus und Stereotype in Komödien Ernst Lubitschs und Reinhold Schünzels," in *Spaß beiseite, Film ab: Jüdischer Humor und verdrängendes Lachen in Filmkomödie bis 1945*, ed. Jan Distelmeyer (Hamburg: edition text + kritik, 2006), 33–47.

[37] Nazi propaganda singled out Curt Bois's performance in the cross-dressing scene in *Der Fürst von Pappenheim* as an example of Jewish decadence. See Carl Neumann, Curt Belling, Hans-Walther Betz, *Film-"Kunst," Film-Kohn, Film-Korruption: Ein Streifzug durch vier Filmjahrzehnte* (Berlin: Hermann Scherping, 1937), and Fritz Hippler's "documentary" *Der ewige Jude* (The Eternal Jew, 1940), which includes the fashion-show sequence from the film. See Thomas Brandlmeier, "Mit Grazie, Charme und Chuzpe," in *Ich mache alles mit den Beinen . . . : Der Schauspieler Curt Bois*, ed. Sabine Zolchow und Johanna Muschelknautz (Berlin: Vorwerk 8, 2001), 102–33.

[38] According to Nancy Troy, this 1911 film version of a fashion show as well as subsequent fashion films by Poiret are now lost. There is, however, a surviving American film of a fashion tour from 1915, featuring American and French designers, including Worth and Paquin. See Troy, *Couture Culture*, 99, and Evans, "The Enchanted Spectacle," 285.

[39] The popularity of the fashion parades in the newsreels of 1911, especially with the "thousands of feminine viewers," gave a real boost to some of the first color experiments. Pathé's fashion shows in the newsreels were illustrated with stencil color. See Elizabeth Leese, *Costume Design in the Movies* (Bembridge: BCW Publishing, 1976), 9.

⁴⁰ The Film Museum in Berlin owns one of the first fashion shows filmed: "Dresdener Modenschau" (1912). The Bundesarchiv/Filmarchiv in Berlin has preserved about 30 newsreels containing fashion shows and promotional films under headings such as "Modelaunen in den Bädern der großen Welt" (Fashion Trends in the Great World Spas, 1926), "Wie fessele ich meinen Mann? Damenmodenschau im Modehaus Goldmann, Dresden" (How to Captivate Your Man — Women's Fashions at Salon Goldmann in Dresden, 1926), "Vorführungen des Modehauses Hess" (Fashion Shows at Salon Hess, 1925), "Was die Dame trägt: neue Pariser Modelle" (What Women Are Wearing: The Newest Styles from Paris, 1927), "Modenschau mit Pelzen der Firma Wolff in Berlin" (Fashion Show with Furs by Wolff in Berlin, 1928), "Modelaunen in Berlin" (Fashion Trends in Berlin, 1929) and many others. To see enlarged frames of a fashion show from a 1910 Gaumont newsreel and for a fascinating overview of fashion in the newsreels shown in London and the USA, see Leese, *Costume Design in the Movies*, 10.

⁴¹ See Dietmar Jazbinsek, "Vom Sittenspiel der Grosstadt zum Sittenfilm: Über die populärkulturellen Zusammenhänge der frühen deutschen Filmproduktion," in *Geschlecht in Fesseln: Sexualität zwischen Aufklärung und Ausbeutung im Weimarer Kino, 1918–1933*, ed. Malte Hagener (Munich: edition text + kritik, 2000), 80–101; here, 84.

⁴² See Walter Turszinsky, "Der Ein-Stunden-Film" (1912), in *Kinometerdichter: Karrierepfade im Kaiserreich zwischen Stadtforschung und Stummfilm*, ed. Dietmar Jazbinsek, http://bibliothek.wz-berlin.de/pdf/2000/ii00-505.pdf.

⁴³ The earliest film in which Lubitsch played a small role was *Die ideale Gattin* (1913), recently rediscovered in fragments. See Helmut Asper, "Neues vom Stummfilm," *Film-Dienst* 53.6 (March 2000): 61. For a detailed filmography of Lubitsch, see Herta-Elisabeth Renk, *Ernst Lubitsch* (Reinbeck: Rowohlt, 1992), 146–54. Of the early films with and/or by Lubitsch listed above, only two have survived, *Der Stolz der Firma* and *Schulpalast Pinkus*.

According to advertisement posters and numerous reviews in the press, the first one, *Die Firma heiratet*, was tremendously successful. The film premiered on January 21, 1914 and in the two months after that it played over 500 times in Berlin. Resl Orla played Trude Hoppe, the mannequin, Victor Arnold played the owner of salon "Mayer," and Ernst Lubitsch played Moritz Abramowski, the apprentice. See Michael Hanisch, *Auf den Spuren der Filmgeschichte: Berliner Schauplätze* (Berlin: Henschel, 1991), 284.

Der Stolz der Firma was conceived as a sequel to *Die Firma heiratet*. It premiered on July 30, 1914 and featured Martha Kriwitz in the role of Lilly Maass the mannequin, Victor Arnold and Ernst Lubitsch, again, respectively in the roles of the owner J. C. Berg and the apprentice Siegmund Lachmann.

Lubitsch appeared also in *Arme Maria: Eine Warenhaus-Geschichte* (1915), cowritten with Robert Wiene and directed by Max Mack. *Arme Maria* was a melodrama, in which Maria's marriage to the shop owner does not protect her from the revenge of her former superior, who drives her to suicide. It premiered on May 7, 1915; Hanni Weisse played the role of the sales girl, and Lubitsch played the apprentice, Moritz Rosenthal.

Der Blusenkönig is preserved only as a fragment. For a plot summary and review, see "Der Blusenkönig," *Der Kinematograph*, 568, 7 Nov. 1917.

Photographs and short biographies of the popular actresses Orla and Weisse can be found in Vittorio Martinelli, "Kino-Lieblinge," *Giffithiana*, 38/39 (Oct. 1990) 25: 39.

[44] See Hanisch, *Auf den Spuren der Filmgeschichte: Berliner Schauplätze* (Berlin: Henschel, 1991), 270–73.

[45] See Thomas Elsaesser, "Early German Cinema: A Second Life?" in *A Second Life: German Cinema's First Decades*, ed. T. Elsaesser and Michael Wedel (Amsterdam: Amsterdam UP, 1996), 9–37; here, 25. For further analyses, see also Sabine Hake, *Passions and Deceptions: The Early Films of Ernst Lubitsch* (Princeton: Princeton UP, 1992), 25–36.

[46] Georg Seeßlen claims that the utopian moment in Wilheminian as well as later Weimar comedy is tied to the image of the emancipated, proactive, and socially mobile woman. See Georg Seeßlen, "Das Unterhaltungskino II: Das Spiel mit der Liebe: Aspekte der deutschen Stummfilmkomödie," in *Die Perfektionierung des Scheins: Das Kino der Weimarer Republik im Kontext der Künste*, ed. Harro Segeberg (Munich: Wilhelm Fink Verlag, 2000), 95–110; here, 99–102. For an extended and incisive discussion of early Weimar popular cinema, especially the importance of visual pleasure, see Christian Rogowski, "From Ernst Lubitsch to Joe May: Challenging Kracauer's Demonology with Weimar Popular Film," in *Light Motives: German Popular Film in Perspective*, ed. Randall Halle and Margaret McCarthy (Detroit, MI: Wayne State UP, 2003), 1–23.

[47] See the review of *Die Firma heiratet* in *Lichtbild-Bühne*, 24 Jan. 1914.

[48] See Jürgen Kasten, "Der Stolz der deutschen Filmkomödie: Die frühen Filme von Ernst Lubitsch, 1914–1918," in *Die Modellierung des Kinofilms: Zur Geschichte des Kinoprogramms zwischen Kurzfilm und Langfilm, 1905/06–1918*, ed. Corinna Müller and Harro Segeberg (Munich: Wilhelm Fink Verlag, 1998), 301–32; here, 308.

[49] For a sociological portrait of mannequins during the 1920s and their presence in the Weimar fashion discourse, see chapter 5.

[50] See C. B., "Die Dame, der Teufel und die Probiermamsell," *Der Film*, 25 Jan. 1919, 36.

[51] At the beginning of his career Wiene coauthored five film scripts with Turszinsky. Their collaboration was terminated by Turszinsky's untimely death in 1915 at the age of forty-one. See Uli Jung and Walter Schatzberg, *Beyond "Caligari": The Films of Robert Wiene* (New York: Berghahn, 1999), 10–23. For a discussion of Wiene's early comedies, see also Uli Jung and Walter Schatzberg, "Robert Wiene's Film Career before 'Caligari,'" in *Before Caligari: German Cinema, 1895–1920*, ed. Paolo Cherchi Usai and Lorenzo Codelli (Pordenone: Edizioni Biblioteca dell'Immagine, 1990), 292–311; here, 298.

[52] For a list of 1920s films with a thematic focus on fashion, see Appendix II.

[53] On the mannequin as a social type, see Mila Ganeva, "The Beautiful Body of the Mannequin: Display Practices in Weimar Germany," in *Leibhaftige Moderne: Körper in Kunst und Massenmedien, 1918–1933*, ed. Michael Cowan and Kai Sicks (Bielefeld: transcript, 2005), 152–68.

[54] Review of *Die Kleine aus der Konfektion* in *Film-Kurier*, 16 Apr. 1924.

⁵⁵ Review of *Gelbstern* in *Film-Kurier*, 28 Jan. 1922.
⁵⁶ Review of *Luxusweibchen*, *Film-Kurier*, 21 Apr. 1925.
⁵⁷ Siegfried Kracauer, "Phantasien aus einem Modehaus" (review of *Jennys Bummel durch die Männer*), *Frankfurter Zeitung*, 8 Feb. 1930.
⁵⁸ "Drei Mannequins," *Film-Kurier*, 9 Aug. 1926.
⁵⁹ A complete filmography can be found in MS, "Brigitte Helm," *Film dope* 24 (Mar. 1982): 15–16. For general overviews of Brigitte Helm's film career, see Robert Ramin, *Brigitte Helm: Geschichte einer glücklichen Karriere* (Berlin: Scherl, 1933); Peter Herzog and Gene Vazzana, *Brigitte Helm: From Metropolis to Gold: Portrait of a Goddess* (New York: Corvin, 1994); Andrea Böhm, "Brigitte Helm: Heilige und Vamp," in *Grenzgänger zwischen Theater und Kino: Schauspielerporträts aus dem Berlin der zwanziger Jahre*, ed. Knut Hickethier (Berlin: Ästhetik & Kommunikation, 1986), 194–212; and Robert Müller, "Die Frau aus Marmor: Brigitte Helm — ein deutscher Vamp," in *Schauspielen und Montage: Schauspielkunst im Film*, ed. Knut Hickethier (St. Augustin, Germany: Gardez!-Verlag, 1999), 15–30.
⁶⁰ See Hans Feld, "Manolescu," *Film-Kurier*, 23 Aug. 1929, 2.
⁶¹ See Paul E. Marcus, "Manolescu," *LichtBild-Bühne*, 23 Aug. 1929.
⁶² See Aschke, "Die geliehene Identität," 250. UFA considered costumes an essential element of the advertising for an upcoming film premiere. The brochures for the films with Brigitte Helm always listed the designer who provided the costumes for her role although, given the heightened viewer interest in her outfits, UFA kept the details about her costumes secret until the night of the premiere. See Michael Töteberg, "Reklame! Reklame! Reklame!" in *Das Ufa-Plakat: Filmpremieren 1918 bis 1943*, ed. Peter Mänz and Christian Maryska (Heidelberg: Edition Braus, 1998), 15. In addition to Mahrenholz, Helm was also dressed by the designer houses Max Becker, Wolff, and René Hubert.
⁶³ On the term "costume tales" (Kleidergeschichten), especially in the context of films directed by G. W. Pabst, see Klaus Kreimeier, "Trennungen: G. W. Pabst und seine Filme," in *G. W. Pabst*, ed. Wolfgang Jacobsen (Berlin: Argon, 1997), 11–124; here, 27.
⁶⁴ See Hanns G. Lustig, "Die wunderbaren Lügen der Nina Petrowna," *Tempo*, 16 Apr. 1929, 20.
⁶⁵ For an extended, multi-faceted analysis of this scene, see Tom Gunning, *The Films of Fritz Lang: Allegories of Vision and Modernity* (London: British Film Institute, 2000).
⁶⁶ See Andreas Huyssen, "The Vamp and the Machine: Fritz Lang's 'Metropolis,'" in *After the Great Divide: Modernism, Mass Culture, Postmodernism* (Bloomington: Indiana UP, 1986), 65–81.
⁶⁷ In his review of the film, Siegfried Kracauer has singled out this scene — "ausgezeichnete Szene im Gesellschaftskleid, in der sie den Pseudovater versucht" — as the one in which Helm achieves her most effective performance, combining "involuntary naiveté and vampish allure." See Siegfried Kracauer, "Alraune," *Frankfurter Zeitung*, 12 Feb. 1928; reprinted in Siegfried Kracauer, *Kleine Schriften zum Film*, ed. Inka Mülder-Bach (Frankfurt am Main: Suhrkamp 2004), 6/2:31–32.

[68] See Laura Mulvey, "Visual Pleasure and Narrative Cinema," *Screen* 16.3 (1975): 6–18.

[69] See Thomas Elsaesser, *Metropolis* (London: bfi Publishing, 2000), 16.

[70] Elsaesser, *Metropolis*, 20.

[71] Elsaesser, *Metropolis*, 21. Similarly, other scholars have made only brief comments on the references to contemporary visual culture. See Heide Schönemann, *Fritz Lang: Filmbilder Vorbilder* (Berlin: Hentrich, 1992), 58–59, and Anton Kaes, "Cinema and Modernity: On Fritz Lang's 'Metropolis,'" in *High and Low: German Attempts at Mediation*, ed. Reinhold Grimm and Jost Hermand (Madison: U of Wisconsin P, 1994), 19–33. Lucy Fischer argues that Brigitte Helm's screen protagonist in *Metropolis* in its evil incarnation embodies an "Art Deco fantasy female" and interprets the film as "a monument to Art Deco design"; see Lucy Fischer, *Designing Women: Cinema, Art Deco, and the Female Form* (New York: Columbia UP, 2003), 206. Ludmilla Jordanova has pointed out (without further elaboration) that the clothes in the film "are not futuristic but contemporary [of the 1920s] or traditional"; see Ludmilla Jordanova, "Science, Machines, and Gender," in *Fritz Lang's Metropolis: Cinematic Visions of Technology and Fear*, ed. Michael Minden and Holger Bachmann (Rochester, NY: Camden House, 2000), 179. In an article for the daily press, the costume designer for *Metropolis* and chief costume designer at UFA, Aenne Willkomm, pointed out that despite their futuristic reference, the clothes in the film reveal "the realism and authenticity of the fantastic"; see Aenne Willkomm, "Metropolis-Moden," *Neue Berliner Zeitung, das 12-Uhr Blatt*, 7 Jan. 1927.

[72] For images of a fashion tableaux in the revues, see Klooss and Reuter, *Körperbilder*, 33–55. For more on the revues as fashion and striptease shows, see Kothes, *Die theatralische Revue*, 76–79.

[73] "Die drei Kleider Sonjas," *Elegante Welt*, 13 Jan. 1926, 11–12.

[74] "The professional association was founded by eighteen of the biggest and most prominent Berlin *Konfektion* companies in 1915, and its first president for many years was Hermann Freudenberg, a co-owner of the Gerson company." See Gretel Wagner, "Die Mode in Berlin," in *Berlin en vogue: Berliner Mode in der Photographie*, ed. F. C. Gundlach and Uli Richter (Berlin: Wasmuth, 1993), 113–46; here, 121.

[75] See "Berlins erste Modekönigin," *Film-Kurier*, 14 Dec. 1925. I came across various spellings of Sonja's last name in different sources: "Sovanowitsch," "Jowanowicz," and, most frequently, "Jovanowitsch." I could not verify which is the correct one. In this book, I am referring to her as Sonja Jovanowitsch.

[76] See "Berlins zweite Modekönigin," *Film-Kurier*, 13 Dec. 1926. See also "Berliner Abende: Fest der Mannequins," *Film-Kurier*, 23 Aug. 1926; "Königinnen der Mode," *Elegante Welt*, 12 Jan. 1927, 36–37; "Asta Offermann, die auf dem Mannequinball zur Modekönigin gewählt wurde," *Die Dame*, Dec. 1929, no. 7, 40.

[77] "Die drei Kleider Sonjas" and "Die Modekönigin Sonja I. in ihrem Krönungsornat," *Elegante Welt*, 13 Jan. 1926.

[78] *Vogue*, German edition, 9 May 1928.

[79] The poster for *Der Fürst von Pappenheim* is reprinted in Peter Mänz and Christian Maryska, *Ufa Film Posters, 1918–1943* (Heidelberg: Umschau Braus, 1998), n.p. See also the cover of this book.

[80] For an extended discussion, see Mila Ganeva, "Fashion Photography and Women's Modernity in Weimar Germany: The Case of Yva," *NWSA Journal* 15.3 (2003): 1–25.

[81] For a discussion of Helm's conflicts with UFA, especially her revolt against her typecasting as a vamp, see Michael Töteberg, "Immer Ärger mit Brigitte. Ein Star muckt auf: Der Fall Brigitte Helm," in *Das Ufa-Buch: Kunst und Krisen, Stars und Regisseure, Wirtschaft und Politik*, ed. Hans-Michael Bock and Michael Töteberg (Frankfurt am Main: Zweitausendeins, 1992), 316–18.

[82] See Hete Nebel, "Ein Filmstar zaubert 'Mode,'" *Die junge Dame*, 18 Jun. 1933, 8–9.

[83] The anonymous reviewer wrote that the film's interest in detailed representation of various interior spaces and the elegance of every day life was determined by the ambition to offer the audience a delight for the eyes, to satisfy its need for a spectacle. See review of "Eine von uns," *Der Film-Kurier*, 21 Oct. 1932.

[84] "Für die Frauen wird sie das Vorbild, nach dem sie sich kleiden und bewegen, nach dem sie lächeln und die Blicke werfen." See Moreck, *Sittengeschichte des Kinos*, 239.

5: The Mannequins

> She is beautiful, cool, detached — but, thank heavens, only a puppet!
> — Franz Hessel, "Eine gefährliche Straße" (1929)[1]

THE FOCUS ON FASHION in Weimar culture brings up numerous direct and indirect references to the mannequin — as living person or inanimate female body — who displayed the latest styles in all kinds of venues: department stores, shop windows, fashion shows, and tea parties. One person looking at the Berlin mannequin was the inquisitive *flâneur*. In a 1929 picture story entitled "Eine gefährliche Straße" (A Dangerous Street), published in *Das Illustrierte Blatt* (Otto Umber provided the photographs), Franz Hessel voiced the common mixture of fascination and anxiety triggered by the sight of dummies in the display windows. Walking down a Berlin street not far from the *Spittelmarkt*, where numerous mannequin factories had their storefronts, he described the "stylized products of display-window artistry" as "the spooky beauties" that appeared in their "thousands all over Germany and around the world in order to demonstrate to us how to wear shirts, dresses, and hats."[2] Indeed, by the end of the 1920s the manufacture of mannequins, as well as fashion in general, was a flourishing business in Germany. There were over a dozen large mannequin factories in Berlin alone, where the thriving *Konfektion* industry counted close to 800 companies and was making huge profits in domestic and international sales.[3]

As he observed the unprecedented proliferation of mannequins in Berlin shop windows, Hessel bemoaned nostalgically the departure of the old-fashioned, realistic wax dummies that resembled "Cleopatra and Gretchen at once." Confronted with the modern dummies, he was frightened by their stylized expressions, their uniform faces, and their "gazes," in which the male observer could only read such human character traits as coldness, corruptness, impertinence, and haughtiness. With his typical provocative irony he concluded: "Their pouted lips challenge us, and they peek at us with narrow eyes from which the gaze oozes like poison. . . . All of them despise us men terribly. They do not wonder what we imagine as we look at them; they simply see through us."[4]

The image of the mannequin in Hessel's essay is paradigmatic of the hesitancy with which the revolutionary changes in appearance of the "real" Weimar woman — her body, her clothes, and her prominent presence in the public spaces of the city — were received by the male public. As another contemporary commentator put it, "this puppet is more than just a clothes-rack. It embodies a desirable fashion type (Modetyp). It confirms the fact that any expression of platonic feelings has been gradually erased from the physiognomy of our working, rational, calculating, speculating, technically savvy, athletic contemporary."[5] It is the aggressive, sexual, non-platonic "Modetyp" rather than the mannequin itself that irritates Hessel. And this reaction is not surprising, since elsewhere in his writing he repeatedly expressed his mixed feelings about the modern Berlin woman — he admired her slim, athletic figure, elegant clothes, and self-confident presence on the street, although at the same time chiding her excessive rationality, her conspicuous pragmatism, and her emphatic embrace of independence.

In "A Dangerous Street" the ambivalence is dramatically exaggerated: the threatening features overcome any original fascination, and the overwhelmingly negative perception of femininity is mapped directly onto the smooth, lifeless body of the mannequin, envisioned as a stand-in for the New Woman. Most audible in Hessel's critique is the voice of the classic *flâneur* in the tradition of Baudelaire and Benjamin, whose ambivalence toward women on the street had been traditionally associated with the dangerous attraction of the prostitute and the rise of commodity consumption in modern societies.[6] Yet even as they were blaming women for the modern condition, *flâneurs* considered their own wandering as something of an erotic adventure marked by the vague yearning to meet the gaze, albeit for a fleeting moment, of a strange woman.[7] Therefore, as the new type of woman emerged in the 1920s — independent, working, with a rational attitude, functional attire, and smart makeup — she had a disenchanting effect on the erotic imagination of the *flâneur* and provoked, as in the case of Hessel, an adverse reaction.[8]

I would like to suggest a way of exploring the Weimar mannequin that in many ways departs from the lasting model established by the *flâneur*, namely taking a close look at mannequins and their viewers as tightly connected to the cultural spaces of the display window (das Schaufenster) and the fashion show (die Modenschau). Both locales are defined by the presence of a female audience and lifeless or living mannequins on stage, and both are variations of what Katharina Sykora has called "urban threshold space" (städtischer Schwellenraum), a space in which images of safe bourgeois interiority blend with fantasies of dangerous, morally ambivalent exteriority.[9] Since it was mostly women on both sides of the Weimar display window and in the fashion show (as mannequins, shop assistants, window-shoppers, audience, and consumers), it would make sense to ask what diverse cultural practices — beyond *flânerie* — emerged in those spaces and what these practices meant to the female observers and participants in the spectacle. In such a reading the display window and the fashion show seem to emerge as settings open to multiple positionalities. In other words, the women in these spaces are not tied to a single role — consumer, commodity, object of observation, opposite of the *flâneur* — but become the subjects of a complex, ambivalent, and constantly shifting experience of metropolitan modernity.

A closer look at the contemporary discourse on the mannequin in Weimar culture — in popular novels and in the press of the time — invites the reader to see the human features concealed under the mask of perfect beauty and elegance, to explore the hidden power games among designers, customers, and mannequins, and to define the meaning of fashion as an everyday cultural practice. Exploring the mannequin inevitably generates an eclectic mixture of historical, sociological, and aesthetic questions: Who were these women who became mannequins? What was their age, social background, and professional status? What was considered particularly attractive about their bodies? What ideal of beauty did they represent? How were they commented upon or fantasized about in contemporary popular literature, magazines, and newspaper columns? But first, a brief overview of the history of the mannequin.

Origins of the Mannequin

The mannequin has always had an auxiliary function. It was born in the artist's studio but was rarely considered art itself; rather, it was meant to be an aid to the artist, stimulating and accommodating his artistic imagination. According to the *Oxford Dictionary of English*, the word "mannequin" dates back to 1570, when Dutch painters named the little figure they used as a model, usually made of wax or wood, a "manekin" — "a little man." Thus from its very inception the term has been endowed with ambivalence: the lay figure resembled a human being but was not a real one; it resembled a work of art, a sculpture or a statue, but was not one in fact, since there was nothing permanent about it and its body parts could be turned and twisted at the whim of its creator. In the eighteenth century the word "mannequin" entered both German and English via French in that very sense of the lay figure, the puppet (in German synonymous with "Gliederpuppe").

The use of the mannequin to present the latest fashions and sell clothes also dates back to the sixteenth century.[10] In the seventeenth century, wooden dolls dressed in miniature versions of couture clothes were sent to the royal courts and wealthy patrons in the capitals of Europe. The first made-to-order wickerwork silhouettes appeared in 1750, and a century later wirework models with wax or papier-mâché heads replaced the unstable basketwork dummies. With the birth of the elegant fashion salons, the large department stores, and the ready-to-wear industry in the nineteenth century, the mannequin was brought into public view in the display window and was designed to be a flattering reflection of the mass customer who would not only buy the latest fashion but also try to emulate fashionable gestures, expressions, and lifestyle. In other words, the mannequin was transformed from a clothes rack — a headless dummy with limbs — into a human-like figure with authentic-looking hair, facial features, and adjustable arms and legs. Then by the late 1920s the dominance of the realistic mannequin was challenged by the appearance of the "stylized mannequin," with neither gender nor individual facial features, and "skin" with a metallic, often silver finish.[11] These anti-mimetic mannequins sought to divert the attention from the female body to the merchandise it was wearing, while at the same time reproducing in abstract form some essentially modern characteristics such as, as one contemporary commentator put it, the "intensified rhythm" of life in the big city.[12] It should be noted that display windows in Weimar Germany featured all different styles of mannequins — from the androgynous-abstract to the wholly naturalistic — and they were all indispensable parts of the street scene.

At about the same time that the big department stores and elegant fashion salons opened their doors in Paris, the dummies' animated doubles — living mannequins — were born. In 1858 Charles Worth, who established his own fashion house in Paris, pioneered a practice to which contemporary fashion is still heir. For the first time brand-new fashions, prepared in advance and changed frequently, were presented to clients in luxurious salons, then made to measure according to the client's choice The fashions — the first seasonal collections — were worn and presented by young women, prototypes of today's mannequins and fashion models, known as *sosies*, "doubles."[13] In France as well as in Berlin, dozens of fashion houses sprang up following Worth's example, and by the beginning of the twentieth century, the use of flesh-and-blood mannequins to model clothes at shows in stores, in hotels, at sporting events, on boats, and in public parks was a popular practice throughout Europe and the United States.[14] By the turn of the century the mannequin had become indispensable to Berlin's thriving *Konfektion* industry, and as numerous classified ads in the Berlin daily press from the 1920s testify, the city's famous fashion salons and central department stores also employed a large number of living mannequins, known by the more dignified title "Probierdamen" or "Vorführdamen."[15]

Drama on Both Sides of the Display Window

The preoccupation of the mass media with the practices of fashion display during the 1920s testifies to the ambiguity conveyed by the term "mannequin." The same word that was commonly used to designate the artificial reproductions of women's bodies in the shop windows (Schaufensterpuppen) was also sometimes used to refer to the women who

Fig. 19: Presentation of fashion for individual clients. *Scherl's Magazin*, Feb. 1930. Staatsbibliothek Berlin.

offered up their bodies to the ritual of the fashion show in order to assist customers in selecting a dress. Both types of mannequins coexisted in a bizarre dynamic that ranged from an uncanny resemblance between the living and the lifeless to stark contrast and mutual exclusion — all intended to entice more passers-by to stop by the store.

It was actually very common for a live person to be made up like the ordinary inanimate mannequins and to "perform" in a display window alongside them, mimicking their expressions. This practice was started by the major department stores in Europe and the United States in the 1890s and reached new heights of ingenuity during the 1920s and early 1930s. A live female model would, for example, disappear and the reappear at intervals as a statue on a pedestal, each time wearing a new hat, shawl, or gloves.[16] The fashion salon of Rudolph Hertzog in Berlin is said to have had the live mannequins in the display window demonstrate a recent invention, a needle used to repair runs in silk stockings.[17] Very often women masquerading as inanimate mannequins would be staged in intimate settings and stay motionless for a long time — as if caught putting on lingerie or stockings. Needless to say, such a display in the store window attracted the masses and even caused traffic jams. In the opening sequence of Joe May's film *Asphalt* (1929), for example, a crowd of curious onlookers is gathered in front of the fictional store Bemberg Strümpfe (Bemberg Hose), gazing in rapture at the brightly illuminated window where a mannequin is trying on a pair of stockings in the "privacy" of her bedroom, oblivious to the numerous observers — and a pickpocket is able to snatch a purse.[18]

Contemporary commentators considered such advertising strategies in line with the intense competition among the numerous garment sellers in Berlin. Reflecting on the perpetual spectacle of fashion in the big city, a short story by Kurt Münzer focuses on the "brilliant idea" of store owner Felix Meier to run a twenty-four-hour display-window fashion show called "Lebende Kleider" (Clothes Come Alive, 1929), which was staged as an inside look into the dressing routines of high-society ladies.[19] This scenario seems to suit star mannequin Anni Drigalski, who hopes to become a film star but has been unsuccessful so far in her auditions for the studios in Babelsberg; it gives her the opportunity to leave behind her relative anonymity as a private model (Vorführdame) for a few clients and to become the agent of her own spectacle — controlling a mass spectatorship and her own boss, who is now dependent on her desire to "perform" in the display window. In addition to serving business purposes, the display window becomes the proto- or quasi-cinematic space in which several sets of scopic desires are fulfilled: those of the mass audience to participate in the visual spectacle of fashion, and those of star mannequin to be seen as an actress.

The appearance of live mannequins in display windows was often perceived as corresponding to the mentality of modern urban dwellers — their desire to be constantly entertained, distracted, and stimulated. In an article in *Scherl's Magazin* entitled "Tausend Lockungen hinter Glas" (A Thousand Temptations behind the Glass, 1930), Ottomar Starke claimed that the window display, a modern-day *Gesamtkunstwerk*, reflected his contemporaries' susceptibility to both voyeurism and narcissism: "We want to see and to be seen."[20] Starke's article featured two photographs as visual examples, implying that it was women who were put on display and, supposedly, "like to be seen." In the first photograph, a scantily dressed woman (her legs, her arms, and part of her back are exposed) demonstrates an electric massage device in the window of a Berlin drugstore; in the second, two young women in rural costumes are washing linen in a spring (an advertisement for soap). In both cases a similar one-way visual dynamic takes place: the objectified bodies of the mannequins clearly become the target of unabashed male voyeurism.

But there is more to this spectacle in and in front of the display window. One cannot avoid the impression that such living tableaux strongly resemble a cinema screen, with the mannequins framed as film stars and

Fig. 20: Fashion show in the display window of a department store. *Scherl's Magazin*, Jun. 1930. Staatsbibliothek Berlin.

the window-shoppers becoming spectators. The mannequins perform for an audience and, to a certain extent, even manipulate that audience — they are in control of the spectacle and choose to look back at the curious onlookers or to avert their gaze. While the audience in the first photograph consists mostly of men (who are obviously less interested in the products being presented than in the live spectacle staged in the window), the second photograph features many women, which suggests further that window-shopping for women may imply consumer contemplation and self-reflective narcissism similar to the way cinema spectatorship suggests distanced fascination and imaginary identification.[21] The woman in front of the glass can indulge in the mise-en-scène even if she cannot enter the store and make a purchase, just as the female spectator can dream of becoming the film icon, even if she cannot enter the screen.

The actual women working in the display windows were typically lower-class, underpaid "shop girls" in the department stores, with no realistic career prospects, which explains why the opportunity to be in the window may have seemed glamorous and lucrative, almost like being chosen for the movies. Contemporary accounts sketch out a collective portrait of these sales assistants. In a 1929 series of three reports on the "Warenhausverkäuferin" (Department Store Saleswoman) for the *Frankfurter Zeitung*, for example, Marie Swarzenski observed how tedious work made the sales girls appear stiff, almost like automatons. The mandatory training in the department stores had taught them to suppress their own personalities and emotions in interactions with customers; it had disciplined their body gestures, straightened their posture, streamlined their appearance, cleansed their language of regional accents, and supplied them with an arsenal of stock phrases. "As a whole," Swarzenski wrote, "[the sales girls] are a true reflection of our times: they are cool, industrious, eager to seek employment outside of the home, but at the same time also indifferent about the future. They are brash but also impassive. All you hear them talk about is 'rates' and 'being fired.'"[22] To another commentator for the *Frankfurter Zeitung*, Siegfried Kracauer, the uniformed female employees of the department store appeared as "its little machines" (seine Apparätchen) and the mannequin in the "sales temple" seemed to be easily confused with a bored little shop girl who conscientiously fulfilled her duty to be decorative.[23]

It is understandable, then, why a sales girl would want to break away from this strictly regimented working environment, which forced her to surrender her personality and to behave like a robot. Paradoxically, she found temporary escape nowhere else but in the display window, where her job was to act precisely as a lifeless body. However, there was an economic difference between pretending to be energetic and lively while in fact being reduced to an automaton (on the sales floor) and pretending to be a wax dummy while in reality you are a person (in the display window): live mannequins received substantial extra pay for their services. Another document of the period, Vicki Baum's 1937 novel *Der große Ausverkauf*, sheds additional light on the practice of live-mannequin display, seen from the point of view of the salesgirl participating in the practice.[24]

At the center of the plot is a campaign to boost the sales of a new garter, and it is decided that "a real girl" should appear alongside sixteen wax figures in a display window of the department store, show her beautiful knees, and demonstrate that the stocking doesn't tear.[25] In order to pick a suitable model, all the professional mannequins are asked to parade in front of a male jury, but none of them is approved, since it is not the "mob of men" but the average "economical housewives" that the store wants to attract in front of the display window (94). Therefore Nina, a humble sales assistant from "China crockery," is selected, a girl with "a pretty face and who looks respectable just the same" (95). Nina accepts the new assignment despite the disapproval of her husband, Eric, a professional window dresser, and despite her own unease about "showing herself in the shop-window" for a week. The prospect of appearing in the display window not only presents a change from her everyday routine (she thought it "was her fate to get saddled with all the tiresome customers") but offers, more importantly, a great financial advantage: "ten dollars extra a day, a stupendous amount compared with the weekly pittance which she had been receiving before her legs were taken into consideration" (93).

Most literary texts of the late 1920s and 1930s that touch upon the theme of the live mannequin in the display window describe the job, not unlike Baum, as "dreadfully tiring," "irritating," and actually reinforcing the young women's sense that they are indeed reduced to "wax figures with a stiff bend in the back and a wooden smile" (101). However, along with providing some realistic descriptions, Weimar popular literature also tended to romanticize the position of the woman as a live mannequin. In Baum's novel as well as in another short story from the time, Curt Krispien's "Das Mädchen vom Blatt IV" (The Girl from Page IV, 1932), the woman in the display windows feels strangely empowered: she is keenly aware of how her presence is generating a huge urban spectacle and forcing all these nervous, rushing, blasé pedestrians to stop in their tracks and forget about their problems and urgent tasks.

In Krispien's piece, a giant fashion journal is displayed in one of the department store's windows. Heads of dummies wearing hats, scarves, and other fashionable accessories pop up from the pages of the journal, and, surprisingly, one of these heads is of a real woman: "[The head] turned smiling left and right and then, every few minutes, retreated behind the page only to reappear with a new hat perched on top of its curly dark-blond hair."[26] The living mannequin takes particular pleasure in the fact that she does not have to return the gaze of all these potential consumers; she can ignore them, "forget that she is being stared at," and fancy herself a performer, an actress.[27] Usually indulgence in such fantasies of control and independence is short-lived and quickly overshadowed by a love affair, for in the plots of all these stories, the appearance of a real woman in the display window serves primarily as a prelude to some sort of romantic entanglement. A rich man may take an interest in the woman behind the glass, then fall in love with her and venture into the store in an attempt to "buy" her (as in Vicki Baum's novel), or a poor man will recognize in the mannequin a girl he had danced with at a party and will launch a desperate chase to regain her (as in Krispien's story). Predictably, a happy ending usually resolves the financial worries of the young couple as well, so that the shop girl will never again be tempted to appear as a live mannequin in a shop window.

The Lives of the Mannequins

The Weimar discourse on the mannequins in shop windows is inseparably intertwined with the profusion of texts (popular novels, critical commentaries, first-person accounts) and images (photographs in the mass media and films) concerning the women who worked as models for department stores, ready-to-wear clothes dealers (Konfektionshäuser), and high-class fashion salons (Modehäuser). According to one succinct definition of the profession in the *Frankfurter Zeitung*, a good mannequin was "like a fata morgana appearing in front of a female customer whose body is quite differently shaped than that of the mannequin and who because of her uncritical self-image can be persuaded to make a purchase."[28] Not unlike the display window, the fashion show — presenting clothes before a large audience or for an individual buyer — had the aura of an artistic performance, with the constantly shifting dynamics between deception and self-deception, identification and manipulation. The women walking in and out of this stage/frame were often referred to as "models" (Vorführdamen), "anonymous fashion actresses" (anonyme Modeschauspielerinnen), and "performers" (Darstellerinnen) in the "theater of fashion."[29] In fact the word "Mannequin" was often despised by the mannequins themselves, especially because its neuter gender in German was perceived as a further validation of their objectification and an affront to their professional dignity. The protagonists of *Ich geh aus und du bleibst da* (I Am Going Out and You Stay Here), Wilhelm Speyer's 1930 novel about Berlin mannequins, offer an alternative term: Gaby and Christa call themselves "cormorants" and provide the following job description, emphasizing, not the appearance of their bodies and their passive behavior, but the skills and aggressive attitude involved in their daily work:

> Cormorants are very skillful at picking fish from the sea with their beaks. In order to prevent them from swallowing their victims, a metal ring is placed around their necks. The cormorant parades its catch in the same way the mannequin parades her dresses. In the end, the fish is taken away from the cormorant in the same way the clothes are stripped from the mannequin.[30]

This description alludes to the mixture of bitter social realities and hidden pleasures implicit in the profession of the mannequin. Every time she demonstrates a new outfit, it is a "game": while seducing the customer, she also indulges the illusion, at least for a few fleeting moments, that these unaffordable clothes are her own and that she is not really who she is, "a fashion-salon girl with a middle-school education" and an empty closet, but rather someone with much higher social status (105). This sense of enjoyment while temporarily forgetting a life of poverty and monotony is also evident in some of the interviews with mannequins published in *Scherl's Magazin*. One of them features a woman employed as a model at a Berlin fashion salon who confessed: "There can't be anything more pleasant than the demonstration of gorgeous clothes. I, at least, enjoy it a lot."[31]

Despite the positive overtone of some accounts, most texts in the popular press reporting on the job of the mannequin focus primarily on the dark side of the glamour — the anonymity, the physical challenges, and the subservient rituals intrinsic to the daily routine. Most revealing in that respect is Katharina von Rathaus's series of reports for the *Frankfurter*

Zeitung on the two weeks she spent in a designer's salon in Paris. In order to gain insight into the workings of the fashion business, Rathaus, a well-known German fashion journalist who published regularly in *Die Dame* und *Elegante Welt*, took a job as a "Habilleuse," or an assistant to the mannequins, the only position within the hierarchical chain of the company that was lower than the mannequin. Helping the models change their attire and hanging up and delivering clothes allowed her to observe the tedious routines, the various social interactions, and the backstage spaces in the theater of fashion. Rathaus's account is especially valuable, not only because of its sober realism, but also because her observations and conclusions for the most part applied to the mannequins' working conditions in Germany as well as in France.

She describes how the young women — who were generally uneducated and poor and often bore the additional burden of raising children on their own — reported to work at nine in the morning. They spent most of their strictly regimented eight-to-twelve-hour workday in a dressing room (die Kabine), where they put on makeup and changed clothes dozens of times in the course of the workday, presenting an entire collection of clothes made to fit them. The mannequins walked out into the official presentation salon for a few minutes per dress and then ran back to the dressing room, changed quickly, and came out to present the next outfit. During the presentation they were forbidden to interact with the public, since only the "Vendeuse," or the sales assistant, was authorized to deal with the customers and collected a commission on each item sold. So it was in the small, hot, stuffy, and incredibly busy back room that the sixteen women modeling for that Paris designer salon actually worked. This space was frequently inspected by Herr B., the director of personnel, who hired and fired mannequins, "a type that can be seen in all fashion salons," but the women preparing for the show learned to ignore "his pasha-like presence" and his voice, which "sounds like the whip crack of a circus manager."[32] Although she found the close physical proximity of bodies uncomfortable, the constant handling of "warm dresses" unpleasant, and the presence of Herr B. intimidating and humiliating, Rathaus admits that there was no better place than the "Kabine" for her to get to know the work of these young women.[33] At the end of her fourteen-day visit, she declares this room an "island of joy amidst a bourgeois commercial enterprise" (Freudeninsel inmitten eines bürgerlich kommerziellen Betriebs), because, paradoxically, it is only here that mannequins are allowed to be human, have conversations, forge friendships, and even read during breaks.[34]

While Rathaus observed the inner workings of the "Kabine," medical student Hanna Helm experienced firsthand what it was to become a mannequin in a typical Berlin clothes company, having chosen the job as a quick way to earn her tuition and fees. In 1930 the magazine *Uhu* published Helm's essay in a series of sobering reports about women working in service industries. When Helm decided to apply for a two-week-long training at the mannequin school (Mannequin-Ausbildungs-Institut), she quickly realized that the very first step on this career path was to accept one's own reduction to a body with an exemplary size. In lieu of an interview or any verbal exchange, she was promptly measured:

> [I go to] a woman who does not even greet me. She sizes me up, loops a tape measure all around me and measures my chest, my waist, and my hips. Several times she glances at the number under her thumbnail on the tape measure. Finally she starts talking: "Yes, young lady, she says, you have potential."[35]

The eager candidate "had potential" because she was (European) size 44; in fact, all living mannequins in Berlin were strictly required to maintain size 42 (44 at the most) or lose their jobs. When she starts working, her colleagues' slimness appears so unnatural, so unhealthy, to Helm that she suspects them of suffering various eating disorders in order to stay thin: "They all have something or they couldn't be so slender. They are living clothes racks."[36] The wax mannequins and the wax figures in the 1920s and 1930s, unlike the live models, came in all possible sizes, since their manufacturers took into account the corporeal variety of the public.[37] Again, a paradox seems to be at work here: one is more likely to find greater variety and realism among the dead puppets than among the living mannequins, who are regarded as mere "clothes racks."

The perfect size for mannequins at that time — European 42 (the preferred size) to 44 (still acceptable) — stipulated that the chest measurement not exceed 92/96 cm, the waist 68/70 cm, and the hips 96/102 cm.[38] In the 1920s these measurements represented a considerable change in the ideal of female beauty, as the slimmer, youthful body was deemed the only one able to demonstrate the elegance of a dress. The new ideal personified by the mannequin targeted primarily the taste and imagination of middle-class and middle-aged female consumers who were not only treated to fashion shows with exceptionally slender models but also confronted with a profusion of advertisements for diets, exercise devices, and slimming undergarments. In reality, however, after looking at the clothes' perfect fit on the slim body of the mannequin, the customers would nevertheless order the dress in the larger size that would best fit them. Thus, if Weimar women in general were subjected to bodily discipline in the abstract, Foucauldian sense of the word, it was the young, lower-class girls employed as mannequins in particular who were the concrete and immediate victims of the practices of bodily control while at the same time actively participating in the mass-cultural practices disseminating this very same ideal.

As soon as a Weimar mannequin was hired, her size (42 to 44), age (20 to 28), and a short, trendy first name (Mia, Hedy, Anny, Hertha, Elli,

Nucki, Asta) became indispensable parts of her new, truncated, and strictly controlled identity. To the contemporary commentators these new short names seemed to correspond to the mannequins' field of work. These "off-the-rack names" (fix und fertig konfektionierte Namen) lacked originality just like the clothes they were displaying, which would soon be circulating on the market in hundreds of almost identical copies.[39] It is not surprising then that for his feature in *Scherl's Magazin* Leopold thought it appropriate to introduce all five women he had interviewed only by their first name, age, size, and hair color: "Minota v. Fr., 25 years old, size 42," "Nita M., 23 years old, size 42, dark blond," "Anita G., 25 years old, size 42, blond."[40] This approach corresponded to the wide practice of addressing mannequins informally, by their first names, even in public, unlike anyone else in the company and contrary to Germany's rigid social etiquette.[41] In addition, as a sign of further displacement of their personality, mannequins would often wear a tag around their neck indicating the name (and some times the price) of the garment they were modeling.[42] In the film *Der Fürst von Pappenheim*, too, Mona Maris's character, Princess Antoinette, puts on a white satin smock like everyone else and adopts a new name, "Tony," when she starts modeling in the fashion salon Pappenheim.

This strict enforcement of body measurements and the uniform guidelines for makeup and hairstyle made the mannequins appear to the outsider as often indistinguishable from each other, deprived of individuality and humanity: "They all belong to the same type: tall, slim, with a hair color that does not stand out," commented a journalist who went on to interview several Berlin mannequins.[43] "They all appear so similar," observed the novice in the business, Hanna Helm. "Blond or chestnut-brown hair, rouged cheeks, black eyeliner — five figures, all the same size."[44] Or as another commentator put it, the Berlin mannequins seemed all to be wearing almost identical masks (uniformierte Masken).[45] But whereas many observers saw this as a lack of personality, individuality, and emotions, mannequins themselves explained it as the consequence of their compliance with the stringent requirements of the job. As has already been pointed out, they were not allowed to talk to or smile at the audience. The blank facial expression also often hid the mannequin's sheer physical exhaustion: Helm reported that very often some of her colleagues would model up to 150 dresses a day, and changes had to be made at a "racing speed," with no breaks in between.[46] One of the mannequins interviewed by Leopold provided even more detail of the daily routine: "You can see how hard we have to work. Each of us models up to 120 dresses on a daily basis: that's our entire collection of twenty outfits five or six times."[47]

Adding to the physical strain of the mannequins' job was the constant realization that for bosses and clients alike they were nothing but lifeless bodies. "I myself do not exist for him," said Helm about the customer inspecting the dress and checking on the quality of the fabric.[48] In time the

Fig. 21: Curt Bois surrounded by mannequins in *Der Fürst von Pappenheim* (Prince of Pappenheim, 1927). Deutsche Kinemathek.

initial pleasure of wearing glamorous clothes and imagining oneself as someone else wore off and was replaced by the "deadly boredom" of salaried employees stuck in the drudgery of the everyday, by "apathy" and by "disdain for the wealthy customers, who do not need to sell themselves."[49]

Perhaps the most comprehensive picture of the life of a mannequin in the late Weimar Republic is found in Elsa Maria Bud's 1931 novel *Bravo, Musch!*, which weaves together many of the motifs already familiar from the short essays on mannequins published in the popular press. The narrative centers on a young woman who calls herself Musch (a shorter and trendier nickname for Margarete). She is an ambitious and entrepreneurial Berlin medical student who temporarily takes on the job of mannequin in a fashion salon in order to save money for her studies, help out her family, and be able to marry her fiancé, also a poor student. From her somewhat privileged position as an astute observer and an educated, "intellectual" mannequin, Musch, like Helm, immediately recognizes the uniformity and artificiality imposed upon the girls working for Berlin's fashion salons. Of one of the mannequins whom she considers typical she remarks: "Petra is the perfect fashionable, skeletal half-boy with long legs, size 42 and dyed, painted, polished and trimmed from one end to the other. The effect is just like a doll; . . . empty porcelain eyes stare slowly left and right."[50]

Musch sees through the underlying material deprivation in the lives of her lower-class colleagues, sympathizes with the hardships of single motherhood, and comments on the sexual harassment and unequal pay common in her workplace. Yet at the same time in a different context she is prone to look at fashion through the lens of national stereotypes and embraces some fairly conventional views of beauty that equate perfect femininity with naturalness. As Musch models for a Dutch fashion salon, she participates in an international contest for the best mannequin and compares herself to her competitors: Antje, the Dutch girl, is "traditionally plump," Mabel from England is "tall and boyishly clumsy," and the French girl "bounces around as if on springs, like a harlequin." It is only Musch, the German, who is naturally charming — "brash, reserved, melancholy, or sober," her expression changing with the clothes she is presenting. Needless to say, it is the German model who is crowned fashion queen.[51] But instead of signing a contract with a film studio, the futile dream of hundreds of her colleagues, Musch — very much like her contemporary and real-life prototype, medical student Hanna Helm — is happy to collect her pay, quit modeling, and take up her studies right away. For lack of any other choice, thousands of other professional mannequins had to continue participating in the incessant parade of fashions.

This overview of the Weimar mannequin in fashion display windows and couture salons demonstrates how easy and compelling it has been for both contemporary male observers and later critics to reduce them to a surface onto which the characteristic markers of Weimar culture — mass production, uniformity, and commercialization — can be projected. Nevertheless, the disparate actual practices of fashion display elude a single, unequivocal classification. The mannequins were more than just a surface; their work life oscillated between live performance and dead artificiality, between intense spectator attention and complete disregard, between stringent body discipline and narcissistic indulgence, and it is this uncanny, multifaceted spectacle that continues to fascinate us.

Notes

An abridged version of this chapter appeared under the title "The Beautiful Body of the Mannequin: Display Practices in Weimar Germany," in *Leibhaftige Moderne: Körper in Kunst und Massenmedien, 1918–1933*, ed. Michael Cowan and Kai Sicks (Bielefeld: transcript, 2005), 152–68.

[1] "Schön, kühl und sachlich — aber gottseidank nur eine Puppe." Franz Hessel, "Eine gefährliche Straße," *Das Illustrierte Blatt*, 15 Jun. 1929, 686.

² "Nichts lenkt dich seidig und tröstlich ab von den gespensterhaften Schönen, den Stilfiguren der Schaufensterkunst, die in Tausenden von Exemplaren von hier durch ganz Deutschland und weiter wandern, um in der Nähe und Ferne Hemden, Kleider, Mäntel und Hüte vorbildlich zu tragen." Hessel, "Eine gefährliche Straße," 686.

³ See Nicole Parrot, *Mannequins* (New York: St. Martins P, 1981), 127.

⁴ "Mit spitzen Mündern fordern sie dich, schmale Augen ziehen sie, aus denen der Blick wie Gift tropft.... Alle verachten uns Männer furchtbar. Sie bestaunen nicht, 'was ein Mann nicht alles denken kann.' Sie durchschauen uns." Hessel, "Eine gefährliche Straße," 686.

⁵ "Die Gliederpuppe ist mehr als nur ein Kleiderständer. Sie ist die Realisirung des Modetyps als Wunschkomplex.... Es ist eine nachdenkliche Feststellung, daß diese arbeitende, rechnende, kalkulierende, spekulierende, diese mit technischem Wissen gesättigte, sportliche Physiognomie des Zeitgenossen allmählich alles verwischt, was platonischen Geist ausdrückt." See Ottomar Starke, "Tausend Lockungen hinter Glas: Zur Physiologie des Schaufensters," *Scherl's Magazin*, Jun. 1930, 609.

⁶ In poem 26 from *Les Fleurs du Mal*, Baudelaire equates the woman who meets the gaze of the *flâneur* with a shop mannequin, whose "eyes lit up like shops to lure their trade." Her eyes also "make use of borrowed power," and this "borrowed power," as Anne Friedberg suggests, is seized from the lure of the luxury item in the shop window. See Friedberg, *Window Shopping: Cinema and the Postmodern* (Berkeley: U of California P, 1993), 34. Benjamin, in his analysis of what Baudelaire first established as a triangular relation between women, commodity, and prostitution, continued to associate women with the modern condition: "Und dieser Reiz [Sexualreiz] wächst wo mit dem reichliche[n] Angebot der Frauen ihr Charakter als Ware unterstrichen wird. Die spätere Revue hat durch Ausstellung von girls in streng uniformierter Kleidung den Massenartikel nachdrücklich in das Triebleben des Großstadtbewohners eingeführt." See Walter Benjamin, *Gesammelte Schriften*, ed. Rolf Tiedemann (Frankfurt amMain: Suhrkamp taschenbuch, 1991), 5:427.

⁷ The most famous example of the *flâneur*'s encounter with a strange woman on the street is provided in Baudelaire's poem "À une passante."

⁸ See Katharina Sykora, *Unheimliche Paarungen: Androidenfaszination und Geschlecht in der Fotografie* (Cologne: Walther König, 1999).

⁹ See Sykora, *Unheimliche Paarungen*, 136.

¹⁰ For extensive details on the history of the production and use of mannequins, see Michael Gross, *Model: The Ugly Business of Beautiful Women* (New York: William Morrow, 1995), 31–42, and Parrot, *Mannequins*. This overview relies mainly on these two sources.

¹¹ See Tag Gronberg, *Designs of Modernity: Exhibiting the City in 1920s Paris* (Manchester, UK: Manchester UP, 1998), 89.

¹² See Janet Ward, *Weimar Surfaces: Urban Visual Culture in 1920s Germany* (Berkeley: U of California P, 2001), 229. For an extensive discussion of the stylized mannequin, see Gronberg, *Designs of Modernity*, 80–113.

¹³ Worth first used his wife Marie Vernet, a former salesgirl in a clothes shop, as a house model in his newly founded salon. Inspired by the success of Vernet in selling the clothes that she showed, Worth hired even more women as mannequins, had Marie Vernet train them, and started the ritual of the fashion show. See Johannes Christoph Moderegger, *Modefotografie in Deutschland, 1929 bis 1955* (Norderstedt: Libri Books on Demand, 2000), 62. See also Lipovetsky, *The Empire of Fashion: Dressing Modern Democracy*, trans. Catherine Porter (Princeton, NJ: Princeton UP, 1994), 57.

¹⁴ The French designer Paul Poiret was the first to take his mannequins on international tours: in 1911–12 to London, Berlin, Vienna, Brussels, Moscow and St. Petersburg; and in 1913 to New York. See Ingrid Loschek, *Die Mode im 20. Jahrhundert: Eine Kulturgeschichte unserer Zeit*, 5th ed. (Munich: Bruckmann, 1995), 23–34. For more on the Poiret show in Berlin, see chapter 4 in this book.

¹⁵ Up until the First World War, the mannequin was known as a "Gelbstern" ("yellow star"), her designation deriving from a system of sizes that used different colors of stars. "Gelbstern" represented the then ideal proportions of 44 cm around the front of the bust and 110 cm around the hips. There were also "blue stars," "white stars," and "red stars," referring to bust measurements of 40, 46, and 48 cm respectively. The stars were made of fabric and attached to the inside of the dress. In the early 1920s the "stars" were replaced by the numbered sizes 42, 44, 46, and so on. In addition to "Gelbstern," other common designations for the mannequin were "Konfektioneuse" and "Probiermamsell." See Moritz Loeb, *Berliner Konfektion* (Berlin: Hermann Seemann, 1906), 72–74.

¹⁶ See Friedberg, *Window Shopping*, 66.

¹⁷ See Brunhilde Dähn, *Berlin, Hausvogteiplatz: Über 100 Jahre am Laufsteg der Mode* (Göttingen: Musterschmidt-Verlag, 1968), 227.

¹⁸ More examples of street crowding or even street riots because of a live mannequin in a display window are recounted in William Leach, *Land of Desire: Merchants, Power, and the Rise of a New American Culture* (New York: Vintage Books, 1993), 66, and Ward, *Weimar Surfaces*, 231. Similar scenes are found in the film *Warenhausprinzessin* (Department-Store Princess, 1926), in which an impoverished Russian princess (played by Hella Moja) finds a job working as a live mannequin in a department-store display window. There are no known copies of this film preserved, but for its critical reception, see the review in *Film-Kurier*, 18 Dec. 1926, and Siegfried Kracauer, "Die Warenhaus-Prinzessin," *Frankfurter Zeitung*, 27 Aug. 1927, repr. in Siegfried Kracauer, *Kleine Schriften zum Film*, ed. Inka Mülder-Bach (Frankfurt am Main: Suhrkamp, 2004) 6/1:393. My references to the content of the film are based on the *Zensurkarte* on file in the German Federal Film Archive (Bundesarchiv/Filmarchiv).

¹⁹ Kurt Münzer, "Lebende Kleider," *Elegante Welt*, 4 Mar. 1929, 56–59. Münzer is also the author of a 1928 novel set in a fashion salon, which comments in detail on the various aspects of the production, advertisement, and retail sale of fashionable attire. See Kurt Münzer, *Salon Rausch* (Leipzig: Josef Singer, 1928). More recently, in 1999, Berlin retailers revived the practice of using live mannequins in the display windows on Tauentzien Street in an effort to attract more customers.

See "Die Schaufensterpuppen am Tauentzien leben," *Berliner Zeitung*, 28 Aug. 1999.

[20] "Wir wollen sehen und gesehen werden." See Starke, "Tausend Lockungen," 606.

[21] See Friedberg, *Window Shopping*, 67–68.

[22] "Als ganzes sind sie ein getreues Abbild unserer Zeit: kühl, erwerbsbedacht, aber gleichgültig gegen die Zukunft, schnoddrig und stumpf zugleich. Die Worte, die ich am meisten hörte, waren 'Tarif' oder 'Kündigung.'" See Marie Swarzenski, "Warenhausverkäuferin," *Frankfurter Zeitung*, 5, 6, and 7 Apr. 1929, 1.

[23] See Siegfried Kracauer, *Schriften: Aufsätze (1927–1931)*, ed. Inka Mülder-Bach (Frankfurt am Main: Suhrkamp, 1990), 5/2:229 and 350.

[24] Although Baum set her novel in New York and published it in 1936, she relied heavily on impressions and data collected in Berlin before her emigration to the US in 1931, by which time she had a script for a film set in a department store to be directed by Ernst Lubitsch. This project fell then through and the script disappeared in the MGM archives. Later on, she used it as the basis for *Der große Ausverkauf*. See Katharina von Ankum, "Rückblick auf eine Realistin," in *Apropos Vicki Baum*, ed. Katharina von Ankum (Frankfurt am Main: Neue Kritik, 1998), 7–46. The exile press praised the novel for its succinct and realistic descriptions of life and mores in the department store. See Fritz Erpenbeck, "Ein Warenhausroman," *Das Wort: Literarische Monatsschrift* 12 (1937): 92–93 and F. C. Weiskopf, "Unterhaltungsliteratur," *Die neue Weltbühne* 46 (1937): 1460–62.

[25] See Vicki Baum, *Der große Ausverkauf* (Amsterdam: Querigo, 1937). All English quotes are from Vicki Baum, *Central Store*, trans. Paul Selver (London: Geoffrey Bles, 1940), with page numbers given in parentheses after the quotation.

[26] "Er drehte sich lächelnd nach links und nach rechts und zog sich in kleinen Abständen hinter das Blatt zurück, um gleich wieder mit einem neuen Hutmodell auf den mattblonden Locken abermals lächelnd zu erscheinen." See Curt Krispien, "Das Mädchen vom Blatt IV," *Scherl's Magazin*, Jun. 1932, 818.

[27] Baum, *Central Stores*, 102.

[28] "Jede ist die Fata morgana einer wesentlich anders geformten Käuferin, deren unkritische Selbsteinschätzung zur Anschaffung verleitet werden soll." See K. v. R. [Katharina von Rathaus], "Ich bin also 'Catherine,'" *Frankfurter Zeitung*, 11 Aug. 1930, 1–2.

[29] See Dr. Leopold, "Die Lockvögel der Mode," *Scherl's Magazin*, Feb. 1930, 189.

[30] "Der Kormoran zeigt seine Geschicklichkeit darin, daß er mit seinem Schnabel Fische aus der See aufzupicken versteht. Aber man hat Maßregeln degegen getroffen, daß er seine Beute etwa aufzehre: ein Metallring an seinem schmalen Hals macht es ihm unmöglich, die Fische herunterzuschlucken. Der Kormoran führt Seefische vor wie 'das Mannequin' die Kleider. Dem Kormoran zieht man die Fische, dem Mannequin die Kleider aus." See Wilhelm Speyer, *Ich geh aus und du bleibst da: der Roman eines Mannequins* (Berlin: Ullstein, 1930), 39–40. Due to the popularity of Speyer's novel, a film by the same title was released in 1931,

directed by Hans Behrendt and featuring film star Camilla Horn in the role of Gaby.

[31] "Es gibt doch nichts Schöneres als herrliche Toiletten vorzuführen. Mir wenigstens macht es sehr viel Spaß." Leopold, "Die Lockvögel der Mode," 192.

[32] See K. v. R., "Arbeit, Zwischenfälle," *Frankfurter Zeitung*, 14 Aug. 1930.

[33] See K. v. R., "Ich bin also 'Catherine,'" *Frankfurter Zeitung*, 11 Aug. 1930.

[34] See K. v. R., "Der Chef; Besucher; Audienz," *Frankfurter Zeitung*, 1 Sept. 1930.

[35] "Eine Frau, die mich erst gar nicht begrüßt. Sie mustert mich nur und schlingt das Zentimetermaß um mich: Brust, Taille, Hüfte. Jedesmal wirft das Auge einen Blick auf den Zentimeterstrich, den der Daumennagel eingeklemmt hält. Dann erst fängt sie an zu reden. 'Ja, Fräulein, sagt sie, Sie haben Chancen.'" See Hanna Helm, "Ich werde Mannequin, um mein Studium zu verdienen," *Der Uhu*, Apr. 1930, 55–56.

[36] "Sie haben eigentlich alle etwas, sonst könnten sie nicht so schlank sein. Es sind lebende Puppenständer." Helm, "Ich werde Mannequin," 59.

[37] See Parrot, *Mannequins*, 22, 44. For more on the garment industry's influence on dieting practices, see also Mary Lynn Stewart with Nancy Janovicek, "Slimming the Female Body? Re-evaluating Dress, Corsets, and Physical Culture in France, 1890–1930," *Fashion Theory* 5.2 (2001): 173–94. On mannequins and beauty ideals in the 1950s, see Adelheid Rasche, *Botschafterinnen der Mode: Star-Mannequins und Fotomodelle der fünfziger Jahre in internationaler Modefotografie* (Berlin: Schwarzkoft & Schwarzkopf, 2001).

[38] See Christine Waidenschlager, "Berliner Mode der zwanziger Jahre zwischen Couture und Konfektion," in C. Waidenschlager and Christa Gustavus, *Mode der 20er Jahre* (Berlin: Wasmuth, 1993), 24–25.

[39] See Dorothea Hofer-Dernburg, "Königinnen Größe 42," *Die losen Blätter: Eine Gratis-Beilage der Dame*, Aug. 1929/30.

[40] Leopold, "Lockvögel der Mode," 189.

[41] References to this practice are found in numerous texts. See Gabriele Tergit, "Modenschau," *Berliner Tageblatt*, 20 Apr. 1927, repr. in Gabriele Tergit, *Frauen und andere Ereignisse: Publizistik und Erzählungen von 1915 bis 1970*, ed. Jens Brüning (Berlin: Das Neue Berlin, 2001), 99–102; Hofer-Dernburg, "Königinnen Größe 42"; and Helm, "Ich werde Mannequin," 58. In the 1920s and 1930s, the credits of fashion photographs in the illustrated magazines did not mention by name who was wearing the piece of attire unless it was an actress or famous society lady. Later, in the 1950s, a magazine such as *Film und Frau* would refer to the fashion models posing for photographs by their first names. See Simone Bergmann, *Make-up: Fotomodelle erzählen aus ihrem Leben* (Ravensburg: Otto Maier Verlag, 1981), 121.

[42] Helm, "Ich werde Mannequin," 57. A two-page spread in *Das Illustrierte Blatt* from 1929 also documents in several photographs the appearance of the mannequin with a price tag in her hand. See "Modenschau am Alex," *Das Illustrierte Blatt*, 26 Oct. 1929, 1230–31.

[43] See Leopold, "Die Lockvögel der Mode," 189.

[44] "Sie sehen sich so ähnlich: kastanienbraun oder blond, alle rosa angemalt, schwarze Striche und weiße Flächen im Gesicht — fünf Figuren in gleicher Größe." See Helm, "Ich werde Mannequin," 56.

[45] See Polly Tieck, "Das Berliner Mannequin," *Der Querschnitt* 5.11 (1925): 985–86, reprinted in *Berlin im "Querschnitt,"* ed. Rolf-Peter Baacke (Berlin: Quadriga, 2001), 99–101.

[46] See Helm, "Ich werde Mannequin," 58–59. Similar observations on the drudgery of the job and the social class of the mannequins are found in Carl Marilaun, "Wienerische Mannequins," *Die Dame*, May 1920, no. 16, 30–32, and in Kasimir Edschmid, "Mannequins," *Münchner Zeitung*, 10 Jul. 1929, and are reflected in some popular poems and cabaret songs of the time. See Mascha Kaléko's poem "Mannequins" (Models, 1933) in *Das lyrische Stenogrammheft* (1933, repr. Berlin: Rowohlt, 1956), 10, and Franz Hessel's "Mannequin-Lied" (Song of the Mannequin, 1930), *Das Tage-Buch*, 6 Sept. 1930, 1446.

[47] "Sie sehen selbst, wie hart wir arbeiten müssen. Jede von uns führt täglich mitunter 120 Keider vor, nämlich fünf- bis sechsmal unsere Kollektion von 20 Kleidern." See Leopold, "Die Lockvögel der Mode," 192.

[48] Helm, "Ich werde Mannequin," 57.

[49] Tieck, "Das Berliner Mannequin," 100.

[50] "Petra ist der modegerechte hundsmagere Halbknabe mit den hohen Beinen, zweiundvierziger Größe, an allen Enden gefärbt, gemalt, poliert und gestutzt. Sie wirkt vollkommen puppenhaft; . . . leere Porzelanaugen starren langsam nach rechts und links." See Elsa Maria Bud, *Bravo, Musch!* (Berlin: Die Buchgemeinde, 1931), 45, 56.

[51] Bud, *Bravo, Musch!* 200–203.

6: Fashion and Fiction: Women's Modernity in Irmgard Keun's Novel *Gilgi*

THE SPECTACLE OF WEIMAR FASHIONS took place not only on the silver screen, in display windows, on the pages of the illustrated press, and in the numerous fashion shows, but also in the imaginary realm of literature by women writers. In works such as Irmgard Keun's novel *Gilgi — eine von uns* (Gilgi — One of Us, 1931) and short stories in women's and fashion magazines, we can find some of the most engaging presentations and discussions of fashion as a mirror of women's conflicted experience of modernity. For Weimar women involvement in fashion, very much like involvement in modern life, meant gaining choice and opportunity but losing roots and certainty. This complexity is captured in the ending of Keun's novel: as the eponymous protagonist is leaving her hometown in the aftermath of a failed relationship and an unwanted pregnancy, she is hopeful that in the big city she can become a professional designer in a fashion salon and manage to combine her professional career with a happy family life. Yet she wonders: Isn't her optimism a mere "fantasy"? Is her move "an escape from reality"? Or is it "an escape into a better reality?"[1] Characteristically, Gilgi's questions remain unanswered: both her life and her love affair with fashion have been marked by an oscillation between reality and fantasy, rationality and daydreaming. This last chapter revisits the Weimar experience of fashion and modernity as it is imagined and discussed in the novel *Gilgi*, a work that foregrounds the New Woman's ambivalent position between prescriptive norms and imaginative practices, between emancipatory potential and constricting reality, between the displays and debates of the time's fashions.

Keun's debut novel is both typical of the literature of the late Weimar period and exceptional in its approach and message. It can be viewed as part of a rising wave of popular novels around 1930 that are all set at the end of the 1920s and with sober language and dry humor tackle the woes and worries of contemporary lower-middle-class office workers (a trend often comprised under the label "Neue Sachlichkeit," or "New Objectivity"). While successful works such as Erich Kästner's *Fabian* (1931) and Hans Fallada's *Kleiner Mann, was nun?* (Little Mann, What Now? 1932) addressed the insecurities of middle-class men in dire times of economic trouble and moral decay, Irmgard Keun, along with Vicki Baum,

Christa Anita Brück, and other popular women writers during the same period, shifted their attention to the dilemmas of Weimar's female white-collar workers, shop assistants, and secretaries, who strove to combine a satisfactory personal life with a professional career. Keun's novel, however, stands out in this particular group. Unlike Vicki Baums's *stud.chem. Helene Willfüer* (1926), a bestseller in the late 1920s, which ends up representing single motherhood as a rewarding path toward progressive femininity on the one hand but, on the other, endorsing marriage as the only way out of trouble, *Gilgi* takes a more realistic approach. Keun avoided Baum's clichéd solutions and happy endings and embraced instead the uncertainty surrounding the image and future of the New Woman.[2] At the same time, *Gilgi* differs radically also from the grim portrayal of women offered in novels such as Christa Anita Brück's *Schicksale hinter Schreibmaschinen* (Destinies behind Typewriters, 1930) and *Ein Mädchen mit Prokura* (A Girl with Legal Power, 1932), as it unequivocally rejects Brück's cultural pessimism and deep aversion toward modernity.[3]

Keun's main character, Gilgi, represents the typical practitioner of fashion in the Weimar years: she self-consciously designs, sews, and wears stylish clothes just as she observes, reads about, and comments on them. At the same time, she contrasts with the male protagonist, Martin, who in many respects resembles the classic *flâneur*. Keun thus suggests that there are two very different modes of reflecting on and negotiating the tensions of modernity. Whereas men in the novel tend to engage in abstract and passive observation of the phenomena of modern life, women, through their immediate, everyday involvement in fashion, are able to explore more actively the various practical and liberating aspects of modern experience: in fashion they discover self-confidence and aesthetic pleasure, as well as potential for professional realization and participation in the public sphere. Moreover, in *Gilgi*, as well as in some other literary works from the same period analyzed in this chapter, fashion enables the female protagonist to step out of the hackneyed image of femininity constructed by men or male-dominated society and reconceptualize specific female perspectives on modernity in terms of women's self-fashioning and self-perception in everyday life.

The Faces of Fashion in *Gilgi*

Irmgard Keun's debut novel became a real bestseller soon after it appeared and had a tremendous impact on the mass public. Between October 1931 and November 1932, *Gilgi* was reprinted six times and sold around 30,000 copies, and in the following two years it was translated into seven languages. In 1932 Paramount released a film version, *Eine von uns* (One of Us, 1932, directed by Johannes Meyer, with Brigitte Helm in the title role) which enjoyed huge popularity in Germany and abroad. The film premiered in Keun's hometown of Cologne (where the novel is also set) on 4 October 1932, and in Berlin on 21 October 1932. Almost at the same time, between August and October 1932, the novel reappeared in serialized form in *Vorwärts*, the central organ of the social-democratic party, as well as in other local social-democratic newspapers such as the *Rheinische Zeitung* in Cologne.[4]

At the center of the novel's plot is Gilgi's life-story, a humorous, ironic, and often self-mocking account, which fluctuates between inner monologue (*erlebte Rede*) and more distanced and sober authorial exposition. The narrative starts on the morning of her twenty-first birthday and ends a few months later with Gilgi's decision to leave her provincial hometown for an uncertain albeit more independent life as a single mother in Berlin. From the very beginning she emerges as a typical representative of the growing social class of female white-collar workers: she is a secretary driven by the bourgeois ambition for social advancement through extra hours of hard work, physical and emotional self-discipline, and adamant self-reliance. Although very young, she has a clear vision of her future life — ordered and strictly regimented — in which success is bound to follow sincere effort and rational planning. But this optimistic scenario gradually falls apart as a result of two unexpected developments. First, on the day she turns twenty-one, Gilgi is told by her parents that she is actually adopted, and her middle-class identity is deeply shaken when she visits her alleged mother, Frau Täschler, a prematurely aged, exhausted seamstress living in a dingy little room. In an additional twist of events the woman confesses that she is not her biological mother either, and that Gilgi had been born to an upper-middle-class family. Gilgi learns that twenty years earlier in exchange for payment Frau Täschler had agreed to put the child up for adoption, pretending it was her own and thereby protecting the reputation of the good bourgeois family and saving the reputation of their daughter on the marriage market.

The second event that changes Gilgi's projected course is her love affair with Martin, whom she find attractive because he represents values diametrically opposite to hers. He is an idle bohemian and *bon vivant* with grandiose plans to travel and write a book, but with neither a stable source of income nor the persistence to accomplish any project. Martin manages to persuade Gilgi to leave her job, abandon her regimented life-style, and adopt much of his bohemian attitude. Gradually Gilgi's romantic involvement is sobered by the grim economic realities of Weimar society after the stockmarket crash in 1929. Her friends Hans and Hertha, who have been driven by unemployment to extreme poverty and hopelessness, commit suicide, and since she is facing an unwanted pregnancy with an unreliable and irresponsible partner, or the humiliation of a costly, illegal and dangerous abortion, Gilgi decides to sever her ties to Martin and depart for Berlin in an attempt to regain control over her life.

Recent critical studies of *Gilgi* have rediscovered the significance of Keun's novel primarily as an evocative "thick description" of Weimar modernity. Barbara Kosta, for instance, reads the main character as representative of young women in the late 1920s "seduced by the promises of a new era and caught within the cultural crisis of modernity and its economic and ideological constraints."[5] Her subtle reading seeks to define the complex parameters of the female experience of modernity by looking at Gilgi's symptomatic relationship to motherhood, sexuality, and the traditional bourgeois family. However, in Kosta's detailed analysis of the female experience of Weimar modernity, one element remains underestimated: the novel's conspicuous preoccupation with the theme of fashion.

The centrality of "the fashionable" in *Gilgi* spurred fierce arguments among Keun's contemporary critics; hence the so called "Gilgi-debate" in the press.[6] Critics tended to two extremes, mirroring prevailing opinions about fashion during the Weimar Republic. On the one hand influential literary critics such as Kurt Tucholsky, Hans Fallada, and Kadidja Wedekind recognized in Gilgi's fashionable appearance a welcome sign of women's emancipation, healthy ambition, and deserved independence. They praised Keun's overall skillful portrayal of modern woman's rational mindset and sober philosophy of life.[7] Additional endorsement of Gilgi's character came from the social-democratic newspaper *Vorwärts*, which reprinted the novel in a serialized version.[8] In an editorial from October 18, 1932, *Vorwärts* called upon its readers to participate in a mass critical discussion:

> And so the novel by a young female author whose social ideas are not quite formed becomes an educational tool. This novel provokes criticism and provides an occasion to think through a problem that affects us all. In this way, we become creative too. But this creative critique should not remain a task of the individual. The public as a whole should be involved and this creative criticism should form a link between the artist and her audience, which what is called for — despite the opinion of the establishment — in a democratic age. The criticism should help form a close relationship between the artist and the public, a relationship that has been prepared by proletarian, socialist efforts.[9]

Uncharacteristically, the leftist newspaper acknowledged the book's empowering effect on the mass public and decided to encourage a debate instead of rejecting offhand any ideologically unacceptable aspects of Gilgi's character. Parallel to the invitation for a wide discussion, the newspaper ran an essay competition in which women readers were urged to describe authentic experiences from their professional and personal life and to submit the essays to the newspaper.

At the other extreme, left-radical and communist writers such as Bernard von Brentano reacted strongly against *Gilgi*, criticizing especially the fact that the mass public was offered a celebration of modernity based on the coupling of obsessive pragmatism with fluency in the idiom of fashion. Such critics condemned the "Gilgi-phenomenon" as an intolerable betrayal of class solidarity and as a sign of dangerous political immaturity. Their criticism often focused on one episode from the book in which the better-dressed and made-up Gilgi snaps up a job under the nose of a rival who is less well-dressed. The leftist critics were particularly resentful of the ways in which, according to their own perception, Keun had chosen to emphasize superficial appearance over real social issues. Journalists like Ingeborg Franke even went so far as to assert harshly that "such over-ambitiousness and pushiness [Strebertum] among white-collar workers constitutes the fascist *Führer*-ideal in everyday life."[10]

Although diametrically opposed, both types of critical reaction tended to reduce the novel to its treatment of fashion, engaging with the text only to the extent that it mediates the triviality and travails of everyday life. Focusing on the level of representation of "reality," namely the highly topical detail and sociologically precise description, none of Keun's critics went beyond either unqualified approval or severe condemnation of the New Woman. Even her most favorable critics — Fallada, Beckmann, and Johst — neglected her conscious use of modernist techniques as a response to a complex experience of modernity, concentrating their praise instead on the author's "honesty," "healthy instincts," and "immediacy," which contributed to a strong realistic effect. Even in such positive reviews, the novel's literary merits remained doubtful and disputable because of its trivial subject matter.

This one-sidedness in the critics' reactions is rooted to a certain extent in the structure of the novel itself. On one hand *Gilgi* constitutes an account that is indeed, as many critics have pointed out, immediate, true in its detail, and faithful to reality. Depending on the critic's ideological stance, it could be praised for portraying life as it is or denigrated for promoting wrong models to emulate. On the other hand, as Vibeke Petersen has noted, like other works of popular literature, this novel operates on a more subtle symbolic level as well, where the porousness and fragmentation of the narrative allows female readers to find "pleasures and alternatives not previously thought of."[11] It is on that level of interpretation that various imaginary, even utopian possibilities for the formation of the New Woman's subjectivity are played out. The different facets of Keun's symbolic representation of fashion shows that Gilgi's variegated and nuanced experience of it draws a complex picture of woman's — real and imagined — modernity.

With regard to so-called realistic, sociologically relevant detail, Gilgi personifies — both in appearance and mentality — the typical, even clichéd, image of the New Woman familiar from magazines, films, and advertisements: young, ambitious, sexy, and elegant. Her obsession with fashion is dictated by her participation in what Kracauer defined as the "culture of the salaried masses" (Angestellten-Kultur). Their painstaking efforts to maintain a distinctly bourgeois social status — through their choice of work, clothes, and lifestyle — coupled with their fear of falling back into a proletarian lifestyle are the dominating sociological characteristics of the everyday life of this group. With her rational, down-to-earth, pragmatic mindset and her distinctively up-to-date look, Gilgi is a typical representative of that class. Her life is efficiently organized around the firm determination to become economically independent. As soon as she finishes her day job as a secretary for Reuter & Weber, Hosiery and Knitwear Wholesale (Reuter & Weber, Strumpfwaren und Trikotagen en gros), she goes to the "room of her own" which she has rented in order to study foreign languages, enhance her skills as a typist, listen to music, or simply enjoy the private space that she has designed and decorated according to her own taste and imagination. Even in times of economic crisis she manages to get a second job at night so that she can earn more money and even save for travel abroad. Gilgi successfully resists becoming a victim either of unemployment or of her boss's sexual advances. Moreover, she is proud of her ability to stay away from any kind of old-fashioned sentimentality: "She is not dumb, she doesn't need anyone, she manages on her own . . . and it is so nice to look at your life as a cleanly solved mathematical problem" (71). This characterization, repeated in many variations throughout the novel, may serve as the summary of Gilgi's modern philosophy of life.

Her physical appearance, too, showcases in all of its details the image of the New Woman as constructed and disseminated by the powerful Weimar mass media. Gilgi has a fashionable short haircut, slender legs, slim hips, a flat stomach, thin and strong limbs, small breasts, and delicate shoulders, and wears elegant clothing; she uses makeup and smokes cigarettes. And for her as for many of her fellow white-collar workers, the conscious cultivation of appearance has not only become an essential part of her self-image and self-esteem but is also inseparable from her prospects for upward mobility. Keun's contemporary Gabriele Tergit, an outspoken journalist, rejected the often voiced accusation that modern women were merely indulging in consumerism and spending too much money on makeup, hair-care, and fashionable clothes. "To look nice today," Tergit wrote in one of her reports from Berlin, "is no longer a matter of coquetry. . . . Silk stockings and permed hair have become weapons in the struggle for survival. . . . Those with better looks and who take good care of themselves have an easier life. They sell more, they type better, they are more likely to be hired as teachers for private lessons. . . ."[12]

This statement is in line with Gilgi's acute observations on how stylish appearance is indeed a weighty factor in the marketability of female employees, especially during the economically turbulent period of the Weimar Republic.[13] On the tram Gilgi carefully examines how her fellow passengers are dressed and recognizes in the various details of their look — a fancy yellow tie, permed hair, colorful beads around the neck — unambiguous signs of the social and professional aspirations of the lower and the "new" middle class. When a female typist applies for a job, according to Gilgi, she has to follow a strategy: "in the right moment, self-confidence should give way to suitable helplessness" (kleidsame Hilfslosigkeit; 83). In the context of staged submissiveness, the adjective used here — "kleidsam" (suitable, fitting) — subtly implies that women employees were expected to use their "Kleider" (clothes) to accommodate the paternalistic self-perception, sexual imagination, and aesthetic tastes of their male bosses. In competition with someone who happens not to have youthful and attractive looks, Gilgi is sure to be the one who gets the job as a typist: "Gilgi glanced at her neighbor out of the corner of her eye: that dark coat has bald spots — perhaps she could have . . ., perhaps I should . . . Nonsense!! She's had the same opportunities I have! Or has she? With that wrinkled old face and that careless demeanor, with those tired, unseeing eyes and those ugly clothes???"[14] Gilgi's pragmatic philosophy suppresses any compassion that she might have with the fate of her rival and undermines the social criticism scattered throughout the novel in various reflections on a woman's experience in the workplace:

> The pale one has messed up her life; earlier she must have had the same opportunities. Or maybe not? Gilgi wasn't sure. The thought that people started out in life with quite different opportunities occurred to her — but then she made up her mind. It wasn't a bit fair, she decided, and if it were up to her . . . but it wasn't up to her, and so she'd have to deal with it.[15]

The emphasis on the pale skin of the unsuccessful job candidate is a typical example of how important looks were for white-collar workers. In his 1930 sociological treatise *Die Angestellten*, Kracauer took issue with the "moralisch-rosa Hautfarbe" which every personnel director considered a decisive part of the candidate's chances for a job: "I know: a morally rosy complexion — this combination of qualities completely unmasks everyday values, which are replete with store-window decorations, white-collar employees, and tabloids."[16] In those instances when Gilgi prefers ruthless conformity to social solidarity or even simple human compassion, and when she chooses to ignore the underlying injustices of the social and economic order, she clearly reveals the "dark side" of society's fashion system. Moreover, Keun's character reinforced those negative aspects of the New Woman's excessive involvement with matters of fashion and clothes; hence the rigorous attacks on the book in the contemporary press.

At the same time, there are other aspects of the character and her relationship to fashion that complicated and partially undermined the stereotypical image of the New Woman. Her embrace of fashionable practices can be seen as an expression of personal determination, and then the spectacle of fashion takes place not in public, where one is competing for jobs or attention, but in private, for just one viewer — oneself. When she is alone in her room in front of the mirror, for example, Gilgi remarks: "Well-groomed is more than pretty" (Gepflegt ist mehr als hübsch), admitting that the narcissistic pleasure of seeing her own image is related not so much to the products that she has acquired (makeup, clothes) but to the efforts she has put into overcoming the givens of nature (7). She sees her fashionable appearance primarily as the product of self-discipline — regular exercise, cold showers every morning — and her own creativity — sewing.

Gilgi's determination to always dress neatly and suitably for any occasion reflects an attempt to dissociate herself from an environment at home and at work that has nothing to do with her own choices and modern ideas. She resents her mother's neglected appearance, makes sarcastic remarks about her obsession with sugar-coated pastry and sentimental movies, and pokes fun at her cousins, whose main goal in life is to find suitable husbands. The contrast between Gilgi's modern views and that of her old-fashioned relatives is revealed most vividly through the costumes they choose to wear during the night of Carnival. The aunt appears in a "highly dramatic shawl" (hochdramatischer Schal) and with three red poppies in her hair — "Carmen after a really successful stay at a spa" (85) — whereas Gilgi adopts the provocative look of a boy in shorts and a tie. Comparing herself with her companions, Gilgi knows that her fashionable costume is definitely neither a means of attracting a sexual partner or future husband nor a sign that she aspires to higher social status. Nor is this a first step to becoming a glamorous film star, for Gilgi clearly distances herself from her many contemporaries who are fascinated by such fashionable images and dream that participation in fashion will lead them to a carefree, affluent life.

Several passages in Keun's novel suggest that fashion has become for Gilgi a source of her own aesthetic pleasure within the framework of modern everyday life. She is aware of her appearance and visibly enjoys being well-dressed even when she is not observed, when she is not in public. In a gesture that very much resembles the character Doris in Keun's second novel, *Das kunstseidene Mädchen* (The Artificial-Silk Girl, 1932), Gilgi indulges in her own image undistorted by the usual expectations and desires placed upon her by male observers. The narrative describes in detail how she comes "home" to her own rented room: she changes from the stylish clothes suited to her work in the office, matching top and skirt (Jumper und Rock), to another piece of fashionable finery, a yellow silk kimono (21).[17] She is doing this to please no one but herself, and the unequivocal narcissism of this gesture represents an act of defiance toward the aesthetic objectification of femininity.

In the same scene, when Gilgi looks at herself in the mirror and gets carried away in dreams of her future, fashion is transformed from a source of purely aesthetic, self-reflective experience into the realm of possible professional realization:

> Maybe one day she just won't go to the office anymore. She has other possibilities after all. She can design and make clothes better than anyone these days. When Little Gilgi goes out in the evening, both men and women turn and look after her, and if she said she buys her clothes at Damm or Gerstel, those people might believe her. But it's all homemade. She owns three evening dresses and not one of them cost more than twenty marks. Maybe later she'll open a small fashion studio in Paris or Berlin — maybe — well, she's still young, and aside from marriage, film, and beauty queen she'll consider any career at all.[18]

This quotation not only reveals how Gilgi's notion of fashion is embedded in a highly rational mindset; it also envisions fashion as a viable and acceptable point of entry into the Weimar public sphere. This idea should be viewed in the context of feminist debate at the time, which promoted creativity in fashion (Modeschaffen) as a venue for women striving for education, independence, and professional realization. In her contribution to a 1931 volume exploring various aspects of women's culture in the twentieth century, Gertrud Dittrich, the presiding chairwoman of the professional organization of German dressmakers at the time, rebutted the commonplace view that a career in fashion (Modeberuf) was suitable only for girls with no particular intellectual capacity. Furthermore, she asserted that women in the modern fashion business, seamstresses and designers, "[were] engaged in a demanding mental and artistic project."[19] Dittrich also emphasized how important it was that professional fashion designers speak foreign languages and travel frequently to Paris. All of these characteristics of the profession resonate with the ambitions and dreams of Keun's Gilgi, whose specific talent for designing and sewing are geared not only toward saving her money but also toward eventually abandoning the life of an office employee to establish her own business.

Gilgi's concept of a stylish appearance is radically different from that of her lover, and it is precisely in this juxtaposition between the male and female protagonists' views and practices of fashion that we discover a full-blown picture of fashion as a distinctively female experience of creativity, independence, and modernity. When Martin enters Gilgi's life, new dichotomies emerge in the narrative and begin to complicate the figure of the New Woman. At their very first rendezvous Gilgi experiences an unfamiliar and awkward feeling: she is dressed up for someone else. In order to attract and please the male's eye, the girl (das Mädchen Gilgi) has suddenly been transformed into a lady (die Dame Gilgi): "hands carefully manicured, eyebrows perfectly drawn, the light georgette collar over the brown silk dress freshly cleaned in benzine and virtually gleaming with self-conscious purity. The bright shawl wafting perfume. That's how elegant the young lady Gilgi is; that's how lovely she is. Does it really make sense to look like this for yourself alone?"[20] Gilgi is obviously disturbed by the anticipation that from now on she will be identified as an object of masculine fetishization. As the love relationship progresses, two diverging modes of viewing and experiencing fashionable appearances become more apparent. While Gilgi is satisfied and proud of herself when she sews and wears stylish clothes because they are the accomplishment of her individual talent and work, Martin considers women's clothes nothing but an external embellishment whose main task is to please his eye and harmonize with his abstract aesthetic concepts. In her Carnival costume Gilgi therefore appears to him as a piece of art, as a "Gainsborough painting" (94).

These differing concepts of fashion correspond to diverging attitudes toward work and lifestyle as well. Gilgi's obsession with fashion is marked by extraordinary pragmatism, and her thriftiness is presented as a necessity if she wants to save enough money to open her own shop. Martin, on the other hand, dismisses her professional aspirations as symptoms of a "psychotic obsession with independence" (Unabhängigkeitspsychose; 161) and would like to prevent her from becoming one of those "desolate clockwork people" (trostlosen Uhrwerkmenschen) that he considers typical of modern times (136). He strives to pull her back into the domestic realm because work, he claims, will destroy her natural beauty and bring wrinkles to her face (103). Indeed, soon after Martin enters Gilgi's life, much of the New Woman identity and rational determination fade away, and sentimentality and romance find their way back into the narrative. She gives up her job and tries in vain to reconcile the ambitions and rationale of the New Woman with the role of a devoted and selfless lover. Overwhelmed by the feeling that her body loses its integrity under her lover's gaze, she is annoyed when he looks at her face or, most notably, her legs (the new sex symbol of the 1920s) as separate parts of herself, as adorable, living art objects (Kunstwerke; 129).

The more the male tastes and desires objectify, construct, and consume the female body, the more alien Gilgi appears to herself; she has a sense of painful self-estrangement, which is intensified in two particular scenes in the novel. The first coincides with Gilgi's failure to reform her lover's lifestyle and to impress her own values on him. Instead, she gives in completely to his wishes and, acting on Martin's request, she dresses in a way that he likes, only to recognize with bitterness in front of the mirror that she looks "unreal": "a white face with dark eyes and a very red mouth — I am very beautiful today — I must say — but I don't belong to myself anymore."[21] The second scene occurs several days later when she puts on expensive fashionable items — fur coat, velvet dress, antique jewelry — not only selected but also bought for her by Martin, and appears even more alien to herself: "A dream of Poiret... *Elegante Welt*, last page... Forgive me, Martin, but I hate looking ordinary... such 'elegance' seems so false.... She is ashamed because she has fallen in love with this false elegance. If I were sitting here in my wrinkled trenchcoat smelling of work, I wouldn't impress you."[22] Feeling shame and a loss of identity, Gilgi runs away in the middle of the night and gradually starts rethinking her life with its new dependencies.

When Keun's protagonist compares her transformed appearance to the exquisite Poiret models or to glamorous images in popular magazines such as *Elegante Welt*, she refers to another dichotomy in the modern notion of fashion established by the novel, namely the split between *haute couture* promoted by male designers and the powerful machine of the press on the one hand and, on the other, women's individualized experience in which fashion served as a means of self-expression.[23] Although Gilgi's acid remarks are more intuitive and associative than consistently analytical, there is no doubt that she deeply resents the showy demonstration of wealth and the artificiality of the "official face" of fashion in Weimar society. She admits to being one of the thousands of consumers of the immensely popular illustrated magazines such as *Der Uhu* and *Die Dame*, but at the same time she is a shrewd reader: she can see through the mechanisms of mass-producing false and commercially successful images of modernity. Gilgi is particularly scornful of those "authoritative" commentators on modern life who lack any immediate experience of it on the everyday level:

> Sure, some write about the sporty youth of today — cars, short skirts, short hair, and jazz — and have an extraordinary talent for *not quite* hitting the nail on the head. . . . And they get all puffed up with a critical talent that they lack entirely. The new generation! Modern times! They act as if "modern times" had genuflected to them: Do please help me, Mr. X, because without you I am nothing. And Mr. X graciously goes along with it and is terribly understanding and generous and now and then conceals a conservative tear.[24]

Gilgi's visit to her biological mother presents another moment of implicit criticism of *haute couture* and the fashion practices of the upper classes. When she meets the stylishly dressed lady who is supposed to be her mother, Gilgi immediately labels her sarcastically "magazine lady" (die Magazindame), because she recognizes in her an accomplished product of the fashion propaganda of the popular press. This woman's house is suffused with the smell of "fine French perfume and Elizabeth Arden cosmetics" (229). Moreover, her trendy look functions as a mark of class superiority and as a mask to conceal unjust and false social norms. In her mother's demeanor Gilgi reads primarily suppressed class animosity: "I find it sad that you look at me with ridicule and even scorn just because you are better dressed than I am right now" (230).

The repeated encounter with the crude economic realities of the end of the 1920s prompts the eventual return of Gilgi's self-determination and the emergence of astute social criticism in her thinking. As she confronts an unwanted pregnancy, financial troubles, and, most notably, the abject existence of her friends Hertha and Hans, Gilgi is forced to rethink both her own unqualified rationalistic optimism as a New Woman and the impossibility of a comfortable or even luxurious quasi-bourgeois existence as Martin's mistress. Again this shift is marked in the narrative by the symbolic reappearance of a piece of clothing: her "black silk kimono with the big yellow sunflowers." At the beginning of the novel, when she was indulging her own image in the mirror, this fashionable outfit signified the aesthetic pleasure accompanying the experience of independence; now, when Gilgi, dressed in the same kimono, meets her unemployed friend Hans at the door, it causes only embarrassment and shame. Suddenly her stylishness signals nothing more than self-alienation: "Gilgi stands in front of him — a spoiled, elegant, sleepy, short woman, wrapped from head to toe in expensive embroidered silk" (187).

Literature vs. Fashion: Different Modes of Reflecting on Modernity

Keun not only turned fashion into a central thematic line in her elaboration on modernity; she also used the notion of fashion to challenge and redefine traditional male concepts of creativity and self-expression, of writing and literature in the Weimar period. Through the lens of the dichotomies established by Simmel in his essays on modern culture — male/female culture or objective/subjective culture — we see the protagonists falling neatly into two categories. On the one hand we have the male characters as representatives of objective culture — Martin, the writer and the man of letters, and Pit, the student of economics, the critical mind, the abstract thinker. On the other are Gilgi, who is good at designing and sewing clothes, and her friend Olga, a successful designer of film and theater posters. The female characters possess specifically female talents, or, to put it Simmels' words, they can endow "even the most abstract idea with a palpable, concrete shape."[25] The narrative maintains throughout the novel a rigid binary differentiation between male and female occupations and activities, and seemingly regards the abstract realm of writing and reading as superior to the concrete forms of fashion and design.

As the romantic relationship develops, Gilgi becomes more and more the object of Martin's educational endeavors (sein Erzieherwerk; 118). She is expected to read and learn to like the books that he considers important and to develop the same aesthetic taste as his. "I'll learn, I'll learn," Gilgi promises, and her "teacher" replies in a patronizing tone: "Yes, you will. There are more stupid and less perceptive women than you. . . . You still have the eyes of a newborn but I'll teach you how to see" (Ich werde dich schon sehen lehren; 118). It is the sphere of visual perception in which the male protagonist claims to be superior to the female, and that claim apparently resonated with some other authors during the Weimar Republic, who resurrected the figure of the *flâneur* as the ultimate, disinterested connoisseur of visual beauty in the metropolis. The very phrases "sehen lehren" or "sehen lernen" in combination with the overall characterization of Martin as *flâneur* evoke leitmotifs in Franz Hessel's programmatic texts on *flânerie* from the late 1920s. For Hessel the aesthetic experience of the modern urban environment was inseparable from the *flâneur*'s ability to distance himself from all pragmatic aspects of reality and be a passive observer on the edge of society's hectic activity. The *flâneur* believes that his "high cultural mission" is to teach rational-minded urban dwellers the pleasures of a slow-paced walk without a goal.[26] And this is not an easy task given the dynamics of everyday life in the big city: "In these parts you have to keep busy; otherwise you're no-account. Here you can't just sit; you have to be going someplace. It's not easy for people like us," Hessel writes, and then he sets forth as a guide through the multitudes of city signs, advertisements, display windows, and fashions.[27]

Chapter 1 made it clear that Hessel's *flâneur* is unequivocally a man (ein Passant) strolling aimlessly along the street (ein eleganter Müßiggänger).[28] If now and then during his city strolls he is accompanied by a female friend, she is usually described very differently: her mind set on a specific, very concrete goal, she walks briskly, and she often must attend to practical tasks such as visiting a seamstress to have a dress mended or shopping for a particular item at the department store: "She's in a hurry, more so today than usually; she has a lot of errands to run. And running errands with her is very interesting. She virtually launches herself into the muddle of a department store and immediately finds what she needs. . . . It all goes faster than I can keep up with. With every movement she's beyond me."[29] Similarly in another short story, "Gespräch mit einer Verkäuferin" (Interview with a Shop Assistant), when Hessel's *flâneur* suggests to a mannequin in a Paris store that she should go for a leisurely stroll after work, she responds: "A leisurely stroll! No, Ihave to hurry to catch the early train."[30]

At first glance *Gilgi* is based on a structure that is very close to Hessel's diagnosis of male and female experience of big-city modernity: the male protagonist behaves like a classic *flâneur*, whereas the female protagonist embraces a thoroughly pragmatic, rational lifestyle. Not unlike Hessel's *flâneur*, Martin refuses to work for money and spends his time in the city's cafés or in long pleasurable walks through the city. Although he feels trapped in provincial Cologne, he has already learned to read the urban landscape with the eyes of the *flâneur* and pursues in his walks the visual sense of an entirely aestheticizable world: "Aimlessly Martin Bruck strolls through the streets. Shitty weather, sticky and wet. . . . Discontentedly the neon signs on the Hohenzollernring peer through the fog. . . . Only a cute little cigarette-boy, proud and status-conscious, unerringly represents the ambition of Cologne's ring-road to emulate Berlin's Kurfürstendamm."[31]

And as for Gilgi, she seems at first to surrender to Martin's desire and makes a sincere effort to adopt some traits of the *flâneur*'s lifestyle: she quits her job, begins to read books recommended by her lover, and accompanies him on his aimless strolls. Even her dreams of traveling abroad change as she defers entirely to Martin's authority in matters of urban perception. Now she cannot imagine going to Paris without Martin, because despite her efforts she hasn't yet mastered all the subtleties of *flânerie* as an art form, or, as she confesses in a somewhat self-deprecating manner, "Without you I don't see anything right; you are my better eyes."[32]

At the same time, however, Keun demonstrated the impossibility of a modern female *flânerie* along the lines of Hessel's definition and mounted a very subtle critique of his polar model. It is mainly through the peculiar narrative position — through the irony and illusive immediacy of the account — that the validity of the *flâneur*'s philosophy is undermined from a feminine perspective. Despite all her laughable attempts to become the perfect companion to the *flâneur*, Gilgi cannot suppress or change her altogether different perception of contemporary reality. Keun allowed her main character to sketch out a specifically female — an alternative to Martin's — experience of the city, compared to which the *flâneur*'s philosophy of a professional idleness and connoisseurship of high art appears anachronistic and completely detached from modernity. Gilgi is good at mimicking an interest in high art and literature just to please her lover: "We look at paintings, listen to concerts. Dressed in a long black gown made of lace, Gilgi . . . tries to assume an interested expression on her face (Man sieht Bilder an, hört Konzerte. Im langen schwarzen Spitzenkleid sitzt Gilgi. . . . Versucht ein stilvoll interessiertes Gesicht zu machen"; 144), but even in moments of complete self-effacement during her love affair she remains remarkably down-to-earth and better able than Martin to picture reality. All "training" is eventually in vain, since Gilgi's eye cannot aestheticize the city the way that Martin's does ("Martin, surely you can't find beauty in these ugly, gray, rotting city gardens?!") and, unlike the *flâneur*, she must have a concrete goal in her strolls ("I like to walk long distances, but I have to be *going someplace*").[33] Finally, she discovers that she loves the city in her own way (auf meine Art), with a particular preference for the familiar, ordinary, and non-poetic features of the landscape — ". . . everyday things, practical things, . . . the gray paving stones" (das Alltägliche hier, das Praktische, . . . die grauen Pflastersteine"; 138).

Describing Martin as a typical *flâneur* and Gilgi as a New Woman who ultimately finds it impossible to adopt the behavior and attitudes of a *flâneur*, Keun presented two different modes of reflecting on the contradictions and tensions of Weimar modernity, modes that are coupled with a gendered specificity of experience. Martin is associated with the mode of passive contemplation and rejection of modern realities, whereas Gilgi, "with her relationship to the street, the dust, the everyday" (135), embodies a more immediate and more sensual interaction with modernity. Following a traditional distinction between male creativity and female reproductivity that was still very common in Germany during the Weimar period, Keun allowed men throughout the novel to be on the side of "true" creativity: they run businesses, compose novels (Martin), or write their memories of the war, like the general for whom Gilgi works as a typist in her spare time (82–83). At the same time, women in her novel have a purely "reflective" function: they (quite literally) reproduce original thoughts by typing them on their typewriters or using patterns to design and sew their own copies of the fashionable clothes promoted by the illustrated press. While Martin may possess genuine understanding of literature and art, Gilgi can only pretend to understand; it seems that her aesthetic visions, tastes, and imagination are entirely preoccupied with and at the same time limited to clothes.

Yet Keun demonstrated how this interaction with clothes — which has both aesthetic and practical dimensions — can open up a narrative space in which a different notion of creativity and modernity can undermine the dominant male perspective. While the romance with Martin obliterates almost every trace of Gilgi's independence and self-determination, the sphere of fashion remains of crucial importance for her identity. Within fashion — and by that she means fashion designed according to her own tastes and views — she is able to keep alive the remnants of her old self. Because she is deprived of work and of any other venue of self-expression, and because she is deeply disturbed by Martin's lavish artistic lifestyle, sewing clothes turns into a happy experience through which she is able to keep up both her fashionable appearance and her rationalistic convictions. In a scene toward the end of the novel — not without irony — Keun juxtaposes the male's literary creativity with the female's presumably inferior creativity in fashion: for three days, Martin experiences an unexpected inspiration to work incessantly on his cryptic novel, but eventually his interest in writing evaporates and his book remains unfinished; at exactly the same time, Gilgi is extraordinarily productive on her sewing machine and succeeds in renewing her spring and summer wardrobe (158–59).

Irmgard Keun's novel *Gilgi — eine von uns* is only one of the literary works of the Weimar Republic that explored the sphere of fashion as a specific and paradoxical space of the female experience of modernity. Other writers from that period also imagined and depicted fashion as fertile ground for female creativity and original self-expression. They also chose female protagonists who vacillated between the search for new identity and defiance of the prevailing norms in writing and lifestyle. Two short stories provide additional examples of the relationship between the New Woman and fashion: Hermynia Zur Mühlen's "Bernice McFadden macht Karriere" (Bernice McFadden Makes a Career for Herself, 1936) and Dinah Nelken's "Einsamkeit and Leichtsinn" (Loneliness and Frivolity, 1933).[34]

In both stories the central characters embody a literary variation on the theme of the female practitioner of fashion. Both stories are set in a modern metropolitan space — Mühlen's in New York and Nelken's in Berlin — and depict young women sitting alone in their tiny "rooms of their own" in a self-reflective mood during a moment of crisis in their lives. Bernice McFadden has just lost her job at a newspaper and in her desperation imagines herself jumping down from her high-rise window into the teeming mass of pedestrians and cars below. Nelken's character, Mary, recently divorced, has just left her husband's roomy, comfortably furnished home and moved with her few belongings into a new apartment in a house that looks like "an enormous box with a flat roof" (a "Neubauwohnung") on the outskirts of Berlin (75). Each story foregrounds a narcissistic moment — a moment in which the character reflects with unconcealed self-content and pleasure on her own appearance. In that, too, Bernice and Mary exhibit similar features and attitudes: they clearly like the "pleasant face," "nice body," and "marvelous legs" — all ostensible attributes of the New Woman — that they see in the mirror.

It is notable that in both stories the actual or imagined solution of the crisis — not unlike that in Keun's novel — is related to professional work in the sphere of fashion. Much to the shock of her mother, a woman from another generation who still cannot swallow the shame of her daughter's divorce, Mary plans to become a fashion illustrator. As she looks at the few objects in the bare apartment that she claims as her own — her books, clothes, and drawings — she decides that the profession of fashion illustrator has been her dream for a long time, and that it would not be too difficult to realize it: "I'll work hard, and perhaps I'll find a job as a fashion illustrator. . . . Up to now I don't need much, and I don't want much. Just my freedom."[35]

The attitude toward a fashion-related profession could be much more critical. For the protagonist of the other short story, Bernice, life does get better after she fulfills brilliantly an unexpected assignment for an essay on what the public is wearing during an opera performance: the publisher is impressed by her writing and offers her a full-time job as a fashion reporter. It becomes clear, however, that for Bernice McFadden, who is not truly interested in fashion, a career in fashion journalism is one of the few available options to be a writer and earn a living. She does not have any choice but to accept this option. In other words, fashion-related activities such as design, drawing, and journalism emerged and established themselves as what Silvia Bovenschen aptly calls "adjoining pre-aesthetic" realms through which women could gain access to the artistic realm.[36]

Thus we can see that fashion was imagined as a specific sphere for the realization of the New Woman's concepts of modernity during the Weimar period, but not always in the same way. Although the New Woman participated in the fashions of the time — she wore outfits with provocative sex appeal — and thus seemed to construct her appearance in conformity with masculine fetishization, there was a concurrent tendency to complicate the notion of fashion, mainly in literary works written by female authors. There the narcissistic pleasure of fashion-conscious women was not merely a substitute for a temporarily missing masculine admiration, but an expression of aesthetic experience determined precisely by the absence of a controlling male gaze. Perhaps the most fascinating aspect of the problem is the way all activities related to fashion were tied to a view of modern urban realities that differed radically from that of the *flâneur*, the emblematic male intellectual observer of metropolitan modernity. While the *flâneur* would prefer to contemplate the paradoxes of modernity from his passive, subtly critical position on the margins of turbulent societal developments, the New Woman emerges as a figure who through her skillful, active, everyday dealing with clothes and appearances manages to give expression to her different experience of modernity. She experiences in fashion the full scale of contradictions that modernity opens up for her — both to affirm herself as an independently acting and reasoning subject and to conform to rules of male-dominated capitalist society, to realize her creative potential and gain access to the public sphere, and to discover the intricate social and institutional restrictions placed upon her professional realization.

Notes

[1] See Irmgard Keun, *Gilgi — eine von uns* (Düsseldorf: Claassen, 1979), 262. All citations are from this edition and the page numbers are given in parentheses following the quotation. All translations are mine.

[2] For an extended discussion of concepts of motherhood in Keun's and Baum's works, see Katharina von Ankum, "Motherhood and the 'New Woman': Vicki Baum's *stud. chem. Helene Willfüer* and Irmgard Keun's *Gilgi — eine von uns*," *Women in German Yearbook* 11 (1995): 175–90. See also Vibeke Rützou Petersen, *Women and Modernity in Weimar Germany: Reality and Representation in Popular Fiction* (New York: Berghahn, 2001), 29–31, and Richard W. McCormick, *Gender and Sexuality in Weimar Modernity: Film, Literature, and "New Objectivity"* (New York: Palgrave, 2001).

[3] Christa Anita Brück, *Schicksale hinter Schreibmaschinen* (Berlin: Sieben Stäbe-Verlag, 1935). After a series of mistreatments and humiliations in the workplace, the narrator in Brück's novel ends up jobless and on the brink of suicide. She decides to leave the big city and opts for a simpler and supposedly more wholesome life in the country. For an analysis of the New Woman in Brück's novel, see Barbara Drescher, "Die 'Neue Frau,'" in *Autorinnen der Weimarer Republik*, ed. Walter Fähnders and Helga Karrenbrock (Bielefeld: Aisthesis, 2003), 163–86.

[4] See Gerd Roloff, "Irmgard Keun: Vorläufiges zum Leben und Werk," *Amsterdamer Beiträge zur neueren Germanistik* 6 (1977): 45–47, and Bruce Murray, *Film and the German Left in the Weimar Republic: From "Caligari" to*

"*Kuhle Wampe*" (Austin: U of Texas P, 1990), 171–72. For more biographical information on Irmgard Keun, see Gabriele Kreis, *Irmgard Keun: "Was man glaubt, gibt es"* (Munich: Heyne, 1991).

[5] See Barbara Kosta, "Unruly Daughters and Modernity: Irmgard Keun's 'Gilgi — eine von uns,'" *The German Quarterly* 68.3 (1995): 283. See also Sabine Falk, "Aufbruch und Stagnation: Zum Frauenbild der 20er und 30er Jahre und seiner literarischen Bearbeitung durch Irmgard Keun," in *Frauenalltag-Frauenforschung*, ed. Anita Chmielewski-Hagius (Frankfurt am Main: Peter Lang 1986), 165–70.

[6] For a very detailed account of the debate on *Gilgi* in the press, see Kerstin Barndt, *Sentimentalität und Sachlichkeit: Der Roman der Neuen Frau in der Weimarer Republik* (Cologne: Böhlau, 2003), 155–65.

[7] Tucholsky gave a particularly favorable critique of Gilgi as a New Woman. See Peter Panter (a.k.a. Kurt Tucholsky), "Auf dem Nachttisch," *Weltbühne* 28.5 (1932): 180. See also Kadidja Wedekind, "Gilgi — eine von uns," *Der Querschnitt* 12.1 (1932): 7, and Hans Fallada, "Fünf Frauen schreiben," *Die Literatur* 34 (1931/32): 249–50. Other favorable reviews include Hanns Johst, "Neues vom Büchertisch: Neue Romane," *Velhagen & Klasings Monatshefte* 46.6 (1932): 621–23, and Anna Beckmann, "Vom Kampf der Geschlechter: Ein Beitrag zur modernen Eheliteratur," *Die Bücherwelt* 29.1 (1932): 29–33.

[8] Bruce Murray claims that the publication of *Gilgi* in *Vorwärts* could be seen as part of its experimental campaign to increase the appeal of the social-democratic party to female white-collar workers and to win them as potential subscribers and voters in the elections to be held in November 1932. See Murray, *Film and the German Left*, 172. For a discussion of the political context, see also Barndt, *Sentimentalität und Sachlichkeit*, 149–54.

[9] "So wird der Roman einer jungen Autorin, deren soziale Blickrichtung noch nicht ganz sicher ist, zum Erzieher: er fordert zur Kritik heraus, er veranlaßt, ein Problem, das uns alle angeht, zu durchdenken, und wirkt so schöpferisch. Aber diese schöpferische Kritik soll nicht die Angelegenheit des einzelnen bleiben. Sie soll die Öffentlichkeit beschäftigen, sie soll an die Autorin herangetragen werden und so ein Bindeglied zwischen Künstler und Publikum schaffen, wie es — trotz aller Barone und aller Kulturreaktion — einem demokratischen Zeitalter angemessen ist. Sie soll jenes enge Verhältnis zwischen Künstler und Publikum schaffen helfen, wie die proletarischen, die sozialistischen Kulturbestrebungen es vorbereiten." "Eine von uns? Wir diskutieren über Gilgi," *Vorwärts*, 18 Oct. 1932.

[10] See Bernard Brentano, "Keine von uns: Ein Wort an die Leser des Vorwärts," *Die Linkskurve* 4 (1932): 27–28; Ingeborg Franke, "Gilgi: Film, Roman und Wirklichkeit," *Der Weg der Frau* 1 (1933): 5–6; and Marianne Gundermann, "Gilgi — eine von 'Vorwärts,'" *Der Weg der Frau* 1 (1933): 7.

[11] See Petersen, *Women and Modernity in Weimar Germany*, 11.

[12] "Das Hübschaussehen, das 'make up,' wie der Amerikaner sagt, das Sichzurechtmachen, wie es in Berlin heißt, ist ja heutzutage keine Sache der Koketterie mehr, geschieht nicht, um einen reichen Mann zu finden, wie in früheren Zeiten, sondern seidene Strümpfe und gewellte Haare sind Waffen im Lebenskampf geworden. Überall haben es die Hübschen und Gepflegten leichter. Die Hübsche verkauft mehr, der Hübschen diktiert der Chef lieber, von einer

Hübschen wird lieber Unterricht genommen und lieber ein Hut bestellt. Das ist grausam, aber es ist so." See Gabriele Tergit, *Atem einer anderen Welt: Berliner Reportagen*, ed. Jens Brüning (Frankfurt am Main: Suhrkamp 1994), 46.

[13] For more discussion on the connections between upward social and economic mobility and the use of cosmetics, see Katharina von Ankum, "Karriere, Konsum, Kosmetik: Zur Ästhetik des weiblichen Gesichts," in *Gesichter der Weimarer Republik: Eine physiognomische Kulturgeschichte*, ed. Claudia Schmölders and Sander L. Gilman (Cologne: DuMont, 2000), 175–90, and Elke Kupschinsky, "Die vernünftige Nephertete," in *Die Metropole: Industriekultur in Berlin im 20. Jahrhundert*, ed. Jochen Boberg, Tilman Fichter, and Eckhart Gillen (Munich: C. H. Beck, 1986), 164–72.

[14] "Gilgi schielt ihre Nachbarin an: der dunkle Mantel hat kahle Stellen — vielleicht hätte man, vielleicht sollte man . . . Quatsch! Die hat ja die gleiche Chance gehabt. So? Hat sie? Mit dem krunkligen, alten Gesicht, der latschigen Haltung, mit den matten, blicklosen Augen und den häßlichen Kleidern???" (84).

[15] "Die [Blasse] hat ihr Leben verpfuscht, früher hat sie doch mal die gleiche Chance gehabt. Oder etwa nicht? Gilgi wird unsicher. Die Tatsache, daß die Menschen mit höchst ungleichen Chancen ins Leben starten, wackelt erst ein bißchen — dann steht sie fest. Eine ganz gemeine Ungerechtigkeit, findet Gilgi. Und wenn's nach ihr ginge . . . aber es geht nicht nach ihr, und damit muß sie sich abfinden" (84–85).

[16] "Ich weiß. Eine moralisch-rosa Hautfarbe — diese Begriffskombination macht mit einem Schlag den Alltag transparent, der von Schaufensterdekorationen, Angestellten und illustrierten Zeitungen ausgefüllt ist." See Siegfried Kracauer, *Die Angestellten: Aus dem neuesten Deutschland*, 3rd ed. (Bonn: Verlag für Demoskopie, 1959), 16–17.

[17] This two-piece outfit — "Jumper" and "Rock" — became fashionable at the end of 1927 and remained so until the beginning of the thirties. See *Metropolen machen Mode*, ed. Barbara Mundt (Berlin: Dieter Reimer, 1977), 72–76. The late twenties also marked the advent of the kimono and of pajamas in women's fashions. See Almut Junker and Eva Stille, *Zur Geschichte der Unterwäsche, 1700–1960* (Frankfurt am Main: Historisches Museum, 1988), 290–93.

[18] "Vielleicht wird sie auch eines Tages überhaupt nicht mehr ins Büro. Sie hat noch andere Möglichkeiten. Sie hat ein Talent, Kleider zu entwerfen und zu nähen wie bald keine. Wenn die kleine Dame Gilgi abends ausgeht, sehen ihr Männer und Frauen nach, und wenn sie erzählte, sie kaufte bei Damm oder Gerstel — man würde ihr's vielleicht glauben. Dabei ist alles selbst gearbeitet. Sie besitzt drei Abendkleider, von denen keines mehr kostet als zwanzig Mark. Vielleicht wird sie später in Paris oder Berlin ein kleines Modeatelier aufmachen, vielleicht — vielleicht — ach, sie ist noch jung, und außer Ehe, Filmschauspielerin und Schönheitskönigin zieht sie jede Existenzmöglichkeit in Betracht" (22).

[19] See Gertrud Dittrich, "Die Frau im Modeschaffen," in *Die Kultur der Frau: Lebenssymphonie der Frau des XX. Jahrhunderts* (Berlin-Frohnau: Verlag für Kultur und Wissenschaft, 1931), ed. Schmidt-Beil, 149. Other articles in the same volume place a similar emphasis on the creative breakthrough of women working in the sphere of fashion illustration (Modezeichnen), fashion journalism,

window-dressing (Schaufensterdekoration), and fashion photography. All authors refer to the specifically female ability to observe the surrounding metropolitan reality as a reason for women's success in those professions. See especially Wally H. Dietrich, "Die Frau im Kunstgewerbe," 288–91; Lotte König, "Die Frau als Photographin," 292–96; and Margarete Edelhein, "Der Journalismus als Frauenberuf," 232–36.

[20] "Die Hände sind säuberlich manikürt, die Brauen exakt nachgezogen, der helle Georgettekragen auf dem braunen Seidenkleid ist heute morgen in Benzin gereinigt worden und strahlt nun in selbstbewußter Sauberkeit. Der bunte Schal duftet nach Chypre. So fein ist die kleine Dame Gilgi, so hübsch sieht sie aus. Hat das denn Sinn, für sich allein hübsch auszusehen?" (81).

[21] "Weißes Gesicht mit dunklen Augen, sehr rotem Mund — Ich bin sehr hübsch heute — jetzt — ich darf sagen ich gehöre mir ja nicht mehr" (134).

[22] "Ein Traum von Poiret... Elegante Welt — letzte Seite... Entschuldige, Martin, aber das reizt mich, ordinär zu werden... ihre Eleganz kommt ihr so verlogen vor. Sie schämt sich, weil sie so verliebt ist in diese verlogene Eleganz.... Wenn ich mit meinem verknautschten Trenchcoat, nach Arbeit riechend, hier säße, ich würde dir nicht imponieren" (163–68).

[23] Paul Poiret's designs were much coveted by Germany's high society, especially before the First World War. After 1918, however, as cheaper synthetic materials (*Kunstseide*) became increasingly popular, as the clothes-manufacturing industry strengthened and fashion transformed into a mass experience for many working women, Poiret's expensive dresses associated with the extravagance and luxurious lifestyle of the upper class were perceived as an attempt to reverse the democratic turn in the history of fashion. See Elizabeth Ewing, *History of Twentieth-Century Fashion* (Lanham, MD: Barnes & Noble, 1992).

[24] "Da schreiben welche von moderner Sportjugend, Autofahren, kurzen Kleidern, kurzen Haaren und Jazzmusik und haben ein kolossales Talent, den Nagel gerad' neben den Kopf zu treffen.... Und blasen sich auf mit einer Urteilskraft, die sie nicht haben. Die neue Generation! Die neue Zeit! Tun so, als hätt' 'die neue Zeit' eine Verbeugung vor ihnen gemacht: ach bitte, kommen Sie doch mit, Herr X, ohne Sie bin ich glatt aufgeschmissen. Und dann ist Herr X gnädig und geht mit. Ist furchtbar verständnisvoll und gütig und zerdrückt hin und wieder eine konservative Träne im Auge" (102–3).

[25] See Georg Simmel, *Philosophische Kultur* (Potsdam: Gustav Kiepenheuer, 1911), 268.

[26] See Hessel, *Ein Flaneur in Berlin* (Berlin: Arsenal, 1984), 145.

[27] "Hierzulande muß man müssen, sonst darf man nicht. Hier geht man nicht wo, sondern wohin. Es ist nicht leicht für unsereinen." Hessel, *Ein Flaneur in Berlin*, 9.

[28] Franz Hessel, *Nachfeier* (Berlin: Rowohlt, 1929), 102 and 111.

[29] "Sie ist in Eile, heut noch mehr als sonst, sie muß schnell viel Besorgungen machen. Besorgungen mit ihr machen, ist sehr interessant. Sie geht im verwirrenden Warenhaus sozusagen querfeldein auf das los, was sie braucht.... Alles geht schneller als ich es wahrnehmen kann. Mit jeder Bewegung überholt sie mein Zuschauen." See Hessel, *Nachfeier*, 62. A similar characterization of his female

companion who is busy "running errands" (Besorgungen machen) appears also in other essays, such as "Der Verdächtige," in *Spazieren in Berlin*, 9–10.

[30] "Flanieren? Nein, ich muß mich eilen, den frühen Zug zu erwischen." See Franz Hessel, "Frühstück mit einer Verkäuferin," *Lose Blätter: Eine Gratis-Beilage der Dame* 16, 1929/30, 249–50.

[31] "Planlos streift Martin Bruck durch die Straßen. Mistiges Wetter, klebrig naß. . . . Mißvergnügt blinzeln die Lichtreklamen auf dem Hohenzollernring durch den Nebel. . . . Nur ein hübscher kleiner Zigarettenboy repräsentiert unbeirrbar hochmütig und standesbewußt die Kurfürstendamm-Ambition der Kölner Ringstraße" (96).

[32] "Ohne dich seh' ich ja nichts richtig, du bist doch mein besseres Auge" (126).

[33] "Martin, also diese häßlichen, grauen, verfaulten Schrebergärten kannst du unmöglich schön finden!? . . . Ich geh' sehr gerne weite Stücke zu Fuß, aber ich muß *irgendwohin* gehen" (141, my emphasis).

[34] In the 1920s and early 1930s Dinah Nelken (1900–1989) published numerous short stories, feuilletons, and poems in Ullstein's widely read illustrated magazines *Der Uhu*, *Die Dame*, and *Tempo*, and in the daily newspaper *Berliner Zeitung am Mittag*. After several years of life in exile and underground during the war, she returned to West Berlin in 1950, where she continued to write. Her works were also published in East Germany, where she won several prestigious literary awards. The short story "Einsamkeit und Leichtsinn" appeared in 1933 and was reprinted in Dinah Nelken, *Die ganze Zeit meines Lebens: Geschichten, Gedichte, Berichte* (Frankfurt am Main: Fischer, 1983) and in *Bubikopf: Aufbruch in den Zwanzigern. Texte von Frauen*, ed. Anna Rheinsberg (Darmstadt: Luchterhand, 1988). For more on Nelken, see the entry in Petra Budke and Jutta Schulze, *Schriftstellerinnen in Berlin, 1871–1945: Ein Lexikon zu Leben und Werk* (Berlin: Orlanda, 1995), 271–72. Hermynia Zur Mühlen (1883–1951) was also a well known and very prolific author in the twenties and thirties who wrote and translated for popular periodicals. She published in the *feuilleton* page of the *Frankfurter Zeitung*, most notably a series of essays on women's culture around 1900. The short story "Bernice McFadden macht Karriere" is taken from Hermynia Zur Mühlen, *Fahrt ins Licht: 66 Stationen* (Leipzig/Wien: Ludwig Nath, 1936) and reprinted in *Bubikopf*. For more on her life and work, see Lynda J. King, "From the Crown to the Hammer and Sickle: The Life and Works of an Austrian Interwar Writer, Hermynia Zur Mühlen," *Women in German Yearbook* 4 (1988): 125–54. See also Jack Zipes's biographical and bibliographical note on Hermynia Zur Mühlen in *Fairy Tales and Fables from Weimar Days*, ed. and trans. Jack Zipes (Hanover, NH: UP of New England, 1989), 21 and 204–5. The quotations from both stories follow the reprints in *Bubikopf*, and the page numbers in parentheses refer to that volume.

[35] "Ich werde sehr fleißig sein, vielleicht finde ich 'ne Stellung als Modezeichnerin. . . . Bis jetzt brauche ich nicht viel. Ich will ja auch nichts. Nichts als meine Freiheit" (80).

[36] See Silvia Bovenschen, "Is There a Feminine Aesthetic?" *New German Critique* 10 (Winter 1977): 111–37.

Epilogue

> It is of course more joyful and more pleasant to stroll through the streets of the rich quarters and observe the colorful crowds of women. The much criticized women's fashion is almost the only creation [in the city] that is lively and dynamic today. Pedants sin against life when they consider fashion a folly because it is transient and hence meaningless. But fashion is a symbol for life itself, for in its continuous passing and change life lavishly pours out its gifts, without calculating in fear whether the expenditure is appropriate to the achievement. . . . It is this wastefulness, this eternal beginning, and this colorful richness that make fashion so enjoyable.
> — August Endell, *Die Schönheit der großen Stadt*[1]

WHEN ARCHITECT AUGUST ENDELL wrote this observation in 1908, a few years after moving to Berlin, he seems to have anticipated and welcomed the rapidly expanding presence of fashion and fashion spectacles in public life in the bustling metropolis. Within the next two decades fashion became transformed into a mass experience in which not only the select few but also middle-class and working-class women participated as both consumers and producers, observers and the observed, commentators and readers. As many women started working outside their homes for the first time, they were earning money and buying off-the-rack clothes or purchasing patterns to create their own outfits. While they had more opportunity to present themselves stylishly dressed in public, they had also to deal with the new pressures created as increasingly they were expected to dress more fashionably and appear more youthful.

For their part, the growing mass media endorsed the democratizing of fashion. Dozens of fashion magazines and the movies gave the women of Weimar Germany plenty of practical advice, provided images to emulate, and shaped taste. And discussing fashion in the popular press became fashionable in itself. As fashion journalist Ea von Allesch reported as early as 1920, "never before has there been so much excitement regarding fashion as in the last few years." She went on to conclude: "Of course, fashion has always been extremely important to women and to the professions that are invested in it. But it is only in our times that this frivolous thing 'fashion' has become involved in artistic, political, national, and ethnic debates, and the focus of all kinds of events. Just as we created the term 'fashion show.'"[2] And it was Weimar German women who played an important role in the discussions that Ea von Allesch talks about, as well as in the displays of fashion.

In this book's kaleidoscopic overview of mass culture — magazines, pulp fiction, and film comedies — and through several detailed case studies, I have attempted to convey in very concrete terms a sense of how self-fashioning, both discursive and literal, became possible for women in the aftermath of the First World War. By taking a closer look at a diverse body of materials, I have sought to reconstruct the multifaceted image of German women in that period as "practitioners of fashion," as participants in and commentators on the spectacle of sartorial display, as eager followers of the most recent styles, but also as original thinkers who offered their own interpretations of modernity and who, by doing so, gained entrance to the public sphere. Indeed, fashion appears as one of the primary sites for women's experience of modernity in Weimar Germany.

The picture that emerges is not entirely positive or negative but always mixed: contradictory and thus fascinating. Emancipation of the New Woman — her freedom to work, vote, and wear clothes that facilitated mobility — went hand in hand with new, sometimes hidden, restrictions and pressures, as for example the expectation to conform to a new ideal of beauty that valued a slimmer and more youthful appearance. At the same time, the widening of the horizon of individual choices and the dominance of functional simplicity were accompanied by a new sense of uniformity and a certain loss of identity. And although she was proud of her self-styled modern femininity, the Weimar woman often encountered accusations that the new fashions made her appear "too masculine," too threatening to the opposite sex. Throughout the 1920s, despite the prevailing cosmopolitan spirit in mass society, critical conservative voices could still be heard claiming that authentic German culture, especially fashion, had fallen victim to corrupt American, French, or Jewish influences.

This study is far from complete or exhaustive. Its primary object is to inspire other scholars to continue to overcome strict disciplinary boundaries and explore fashion at the intersection of traditional lines of inquiry — costume history, art history, women's studies, literary and film studies, and even Jewish studies. There are several areas of research that have not yet received adequate attention, but whose significance has been exposed by the rising interest in women's fashion during the Weimar Republic. It would be instructive, for example, to explore what happened to the inherited fashion discourses in the years after the Nazis' ascendance to power in 1933, during the Second World War, and in the immediate postwar period. What lines of continuity were preserved and where did the breaks occur? Why was fashion — as live practice or as presented in the mass media and films of the 1930s and 1940s — allowed to remain a field of escapist pleasure? In general, what was the prominence of nationalist, racist, or anti-Semitic arguments in the discussions about fashion between 1900 and 1945? Pursuing yet another line of inquiry and taking advantage of vast archival material available, one could also undertake an analysis of how masculinity and men's fashion were affected by modernity in Germany in the 1920s and 30s. Furthermore, a sharper critical attention to both women's and men's fashion could advance the study of stars, stardom, and acting styles within Weimar film and other performance arts.

Although it focuses on a specific historical period, the Weimar Republic, this book offers comparative and analytical paradigms through which we can better understand the shifting tides of gendered identity and self-expression in contemporary media narratives. The case studies presented in the individual chapters are certainly relevant to today's world. To give just a few examples: illustrated magazines on the American market, such as *Marie Claire* and *Elle*, purport to offer style to the emancipated, self-determining woman, while other magazines, such as *Bitch* and *Ms.*, condemn the marketing and presentation of such styles as inherently misogynistic, regardless of the intelligence and talent of the female reporters and editors working for the media. The discussion of the culture of the Weimar mannequin touches on issues of body politics that have recently resurfaced in the fashion industry scandal over size zero models on the runways of Europe and the rather callous responses of male designers, including Karl Lagerfeld. The hottest television show of the recent past, *Sex and the City*, featured self-proclaimed emancipated women who paraded the latest fashions in stiletto heels while pursuing their mind-bogglingly impressive careers. It was followed by a reverse of the tide: fashion as a non-statement is back in with the hot new TV series *Grey's Anatomy*, where sexy, educated, careerist women wear scrubs and supportive shoes throughout most of the show.

Finally, I believe that further research of both historical and contemporary fashion discourses and displays will help overcome the academic prejudice that fashion cannot constitute a field of serious intellectual investigation. Given the fact that modern fashion — with its advertising, shopping practices, image-making, and media presence — encompasses the body and the mind and permeates both public and private domains, it is more than necessary to observe it with a rigorously critical eye. In that respect, I agree with fashion critic and curator Richard Martin and will conclude with his words:

> If fashion is the constructed convergence of our bodies and perceptions, how can we allow this intersection of our most crucial, vulnerable concerns to go unexamined? . . . When we neglect the ordinary, the option for the extraordinary vanishes. If we ignore the quotidian and commercial, we are doomed to speak only of the venerable and awesome. If we cannot consolidate [various] compound languages to address multiple styles, effects, and interests, we are left with mere descriptions in any critical discipline."[3]

Notes

[1] "Lustiger freilich ist es und leichter, in den reichen Vierteln durch die Straßen zu schlendern und dem bunten Gewimmel der Frauen zuzusehen. Die viel gescholtene Frauenmode ist ja beinahe die einzige Gestaltung, die heute lebendig und beweglich ist. Die Pedanten, die Mode für Torheit, eben ihres Vorübergehens wegen für sinnlos halten, versündigen sich am Leben. Denn Mode ist ja Symbol für das Leben selbst, das immer vergehend, wechselnd, verschwenderisch seine Gaben ausschüttet, ohne ängstlich zu berechnen, ob der Aufwand in einem räsonablen Verhältnis steht.... eben diese Verschwendung an Gedanken, dies ewige Beginnen, der bunte Reichtum ist es, der die Mode so vergnüglich macht." August Endell, *Die Schönheit der großen Stadt* (Stuttgart: Strecker & Schöner, 1908); repr. in August Endell, *Vom Sehen: Texte 1896–1925 über Architektur, Formkunst und "Die Schönheit der großen Stadt,"* ed. Helge David (Basel: Birkhäuser, 1995), 196–97.

[2] "Niemals vorher wurde so viel Aufheben um die Mode herum gemacht wie seit ein paar Jahren. Sie war den Frauen und den an Modedingen interessierten Gewerben natürlich stets äußerst wichtig, aber dieses leichtfertige Ding 'Mode' zu künstlerischen, politischen, nationalen, ethnischen Disputationen zu verwenden, sie ins Zentrum aller möglichen Veranstaltungen zu placieren, das bleibt uns und dieser Zeit vorbehalten. Ebenso wie wir das Wort 'Modeschau' kreiert haben.'" Eva [Ea von Alesch], "Die Mode und ihre Mannequins," *Moderne Welt: Illustrierte Halbmonatsschrift für Kunst, Literatur, Mode*, 1920, no. 10, 27.

[3] Richard Martin, "Addressing the Dress," in *The Crisis of Criticism*, ed. Maurice Berger (New York: The New Press, 1998), 70.

Appendix I: Biographical Information on Fashion Journalists and Fashion Illustrators

ALTHOUGH THE NAMES of female fashion journalists and illustrators appear very often in the pages of the Weimar popular press, little is known of their lives and careers during the 1920s and after 1933. Biographical information is scattered and hard to find. Contemporary reference sources rarely list them, since these women were not always considered writers of serious literature or creators of high art. The personnel archives of the publishers for whom they worked were, for the most part, destroyed during the Second World War. The accounts presented below piece together fragmentary facts obtained from newspaper articles, obituaries, archival notes, and interviews. There is no entry on Helen Grund, because a chapter in this book is dedicated to her. There are no entries on Gerda Bunzel, Erica Mohr, Martha Sparkuhl, Julie Haase Werkenthin, and Katharina von Rathaus, since no biographical data could be found on them.

OLA ALSEN (b. 1880 in Bonn, d. 1956 in Munich; real name Henriette Alsberg), daughter of the Jewish merchant Lehmann Alsberg, was one of the best known and most prolific fashion journalists in the 1920s. The 1930 *Reichshandbuch der deutschen Gesellschaft* identifies her as an author of "elegant prose" (elegante Prosa). She was fashion editor of *Elegante Welt*, but she also wrote regularly for *Sport im Bild*, *Die Dame*, *Film-Kurier*, and, from 1921 to 1924, *Der Moden-Spiegel*, a weekly supplement to Mosse's *Berliner Tageblatt und Handelszeitung*. Alsen was a best-selling author of books of advice on cosmetics, makeup, fashion, manners, and beauty. Her novel *Das Paradies der Frau: Berliner Roman* (1919) sheds light on the workings of the Berlin garment industry after the First World War and the role of women as designers and entrepreneurs. Her 1930 documentation *Die Tochter Lots* studies the lives and problems of women in prison. Other novels include *Hier wohnt das Glück* (1910), *Garten der Leidenschaft* (1920), *Charlotte Bell* (1924), *Durch Klippen* (1924), and *Ein Mädchen von heute* (1925). Alsen also wrote the screenplays for several films: *Treibende Kraft* (1921, dir. Zoltan Nagy), *Des Lebens und der Liebe Willen* (1921, dir. Lorenz Bätz), *Monna Wanna* (1922, dir. Richard Eichberg), and *Luxusweibchen* (1925, dir. Erich Schönfelder). Sister of a prominent lawyer, Dr. Max

Alsberg, and married to the editor in chief of the *8-Uhr-Abendblatt* Hanns Schultze, Alsen was a famous socialite who ran one of the most popular salons in Berlin. In 1933, in the hope that she would be spared from persecution, she converted to Christianity. Her brother committed suicide. Shortly thereafter Ola Alsen managed to emigrate to England and later moved to the United States. After the Second World War she returned to Europe, lived in Munich and Zurich, and continued to write on fashion for the Swiss independent daily newspaper *Die Tat*.

Sources: Robert Volz and Ferdinand Tönnies, eds., *Reichshandbuch der deutschen Gesellschaft: Handbuch der Persönlichkeiten in Wort und Bild* (Berlin: Deutscher Wirtschaftsverlag, 1930); Petra Budke and Jutta Schulze, *Schriftstellerinnen in Berlin 1871 bis 1945: Ein Lexikon zu Leben und Werk* (Berlin: Orlanda Frauenverlag, 1995); "Ola Alsen gestorben," *Der Weg: Berliner allgemeine Wochenzeitung der Juden in Deutschland*, 21 Feb. 1956; *Lexikon deutsch-jüdischer Autoren*, ed. Renate Heuer and Andrea Boelke, 1:125–26.

MARIE VON BUNSEN (b. 1860 in London, d. 1941 in Berlin) was a well known writer, critic, and artist. Her fashion commentaries were published in *Die Dame*, the *Vossische Zeitung*, and the *Berliner Tageblatt*, along with numerous other essays, including travelogues. Her best known book was *Im Ruderboot durch Deutschland: Auf Flüssen und Kanälen in den Jahren 1905 bis 1915* (1915).

Sources: *Reichshandbuch der deutschen Gesellschaft*; http://www.luise-berlin.de/lexikon/mitte/b/Bunsen_Marie_von.htm.

ANITA DANIEL (1893–1978). From 1925 until 1933, Daniel wrote in almost every issue of *Die Dame* on topics such as fashion trends and women's emancipation. She signed her humorous poetry, sarcastic commentaries, and witty essays only with her first name. The publication of her photograph "upon numerous requests from our readers" testifies to the tremendous popularity of her writings (see *Die Dame*, 1930, no. 22, 18). In 1933 Daniel left Germany for Switzerland, later emigrating to the United States. As a freelance author in New York, she wrote travel books, a biography of Albert Schweitzer, and occasional essays for the *New York Times*.

Sources: "Feuchtes Klima und trockener Humor," *Die Weltwoche*, 10 Nov. 1967.

JULIE ELIAS (b. 1866 in Berlin, d. 1945 Lillehammer, Norway) was fashion journalist for the daily *Berliner Tageblatt* from 1915 to 1929, but she also published numerous fashion essays and short stories in *Die Dame, Elegante Welt,* and *Styl.* Elias was the author of a popular Ullstein book of essays, *Taschenbuch für Damen* (1924), which contained watercolor illustrations by the famous artist Emil Orlik. She became an expert in giving advice about cooking, dressing, and the modern lifestyle, as exemplified by her bestsellers *Die junge Frau: Ein Buch der Lebensführung* (Berlin: Rudolf Mosse, 1921) and *Kochkunst: Ein Führer durch die feine Küche* (Berlin: Ullstein, 1927).

Source: *Lexikon deutsch-jüdischer Autoren,* 6:282–85.

PETRA FIEDLER (1898–1993), daughter of modernist architect Peter Behrens, joined the staff of *Die Dame* as a graphic artist (Modezeichnerin) around 1923, became a fashion editor, and worked for the magazine until the late 1930s. After the war she left Berlin, moved to Kaiserslautern, and worked for various lowbrow fashion publications.

Sources: Interview with Georg Krawietz, who shared with me some unpublished results from his research for his book *Peter Behrens im Dritten Reich* (Weimar: Verlag Datenbank für Geisteswissenschaften, 1995); Alan Windsor, "Letters from Peter Behrens to P. Morton Shand, 1932–1938," *Architectural Review* 37 (1994): 165–87.

RUTH GOETZ (b. 1886; date of death unknown) was an active contributor to the *Mode-Notizen* in *Die Dame* from 1923 until 1925, when she became editor in chief for *Der Modenspiegel,* where she worked in the late 1920s and 1930s. From 1925 to 1928 she signed her articles as "Ruth von Schüching." Goetz also pursued a career as a writer, wrote novels and advice books, and from 1916 on wrote screenplays for more than 40 silent films, best known among them *Noemi, die blonde Jüdin* (1917, dir. Hubert Moest), *Die Herrin der Welt* (1919, dir. Joe May), *Heiratsannoncen* (1925, dir. Fritz Kaufmann), *Die Kleine aus der Konfektion* (1924, dir. Wolfgang Neff), *Wie bleibe ich jung und schön* (1926, dir. Wolfgang Neff), and *Dirnentragödie* (1927, dir. Bruno Rahn).

Source: Jürgen Kasten, "Populäre Wunschträume und spannende Abenteuer: Das erfolgreiche trivialdramatische Erzählkonzept der Jane Bess und anderer Drehbuchautorinnen des deutschen Stummfilms," in *Das Drehbuch: Geschichte, Theorie, Praxis,* ed. Alexander Schwarz (Munich: Schaudig, Bauer, Ledig, 1992), 17–53.

ELSA HERZOG (b. 1876 in Berlin, d. 1964 in London) was, with Ola Alsen, perhaps the most highly recognized fashion journalist during the 1920s. She received her first writing assignment in 1893 from her father, who was well connected in the textile industry, and wrote initially for the trade publication *Der Konfektionär*. Her association with Ullstein publishing house began in 1905, when she was appointed editor for the recently acquired women's and fashion weekly *Die praktische Berlinerin*. Herzog later became editor in chief for the fashion section of *Die Dame*, but she also wrote regularly for the daily *Berliner Zeitung am Mittag* and for *Sport im Bild*. In 1920 she went to work for Scherl's *Die Woche*. Elsa Herzog is credited for the costume design of one film, *Paradies im Schnee* (1923, dir. Georg Jacoby), and contributed (along with Käthe Krause, Erna Meyer, Marie Gerbrandt, and Gertrud Schnabel) to a popular Ullstein volume, *Ich kann schneidern* (1908). Herzog left Germany in 1938, settled in London, and lived there for the rest of her life. After 1947 she returned to writing fashion articles for the German press. In the early 1950s she contributed regularly to the Swiss women's magazine *Inspiration*.

Sources: *Reichshandbuch der deutschen Gesellschaft: Handbuch der Persönlichkeiten in Wort und Bild*; interview with Elsa Herzog in *Illustrierte Berliner Zeitschrift*, 28 Feb. 1959; "Die Herzogin ist 85," *Der Weg: Berliner allgemeine Wochenzeitung der Juden in Deutschland*; "Mit ihr begann der Modejournalismus," *Die Welt*, 14 Mar. 1964.

LILY VON NAGY (dates unknown) became a fashion correspondent for *Die Dame* from Vienna in 1920 after she won a beauty pageant that same year. She not only wrote commentaries on fashion but was also featured in numerous photographs modeling dresses. She worked for *Die Dame* until 1929.

VALLY REINECKE (dates unknown). A popular fashion journalist and illustrator, she frequently contributed to *Die Dame*. In the early 1920s she was the magazine's fashion correspondent from Paris and costume designer for several films, including *Dr. Mabuse, der Spieler* (1922, dir. Fritz Lang), *Phantom* (1922, dir. F. W. Murnau), *Bardame* (1922, dir. Johannes Guter), and *Die Sonne von St. Moritz* (1923, dir. Friedrich Weissenberg).

MARIETTA RIEDERER (1906–86) began her career in fashion illustration in 1929, when her drawings were published in *Farbe und Form*. At the same time she started collaborating with Helen Grund for the *Frankfurter Zeitung*'s supplement *Für die Frau*. She was the youngest contributor to the newspaper, often reporting from Paris. After the war she was a long-time fashion correspondent for *Die Zeit* and author of several reference works on fashion.

Sources: "Sie erzählte Mode," *Die Zeit,* 10 Jul., 1986; "Marietta Riederer: Eine große Zeichnerin," *Süddeutsche Zeitung,* 12/13 Jul., 1986; Marietta Riederer, *Wie Mode Mode wird* (Munich: Heyne, 1965).

JOHANNA THAL (dates unknown). My research on the run of *Die Dame* from 1918 till 1938 allows me to speculate that Thal was employed by Ullstein as early as 1916 and worked there until 1934. According to Gerd Hartung, who had worked with her, she was Jewish and was forced to leave the publishing house soon after the Nazi takeover. Nothing is known about her life afterwards.

ANNA-PAULA WEDEKIND PARISELLE (1890–1979) began working for the patterns department of Ullstein in 1920 and published fashion essays in *Die Dame.* Later she was promoted to editor in chief of the fashion section of that magazine. After 1945 she founded (with a Russian license) the first postwar fashion publication, *Berlins Modenblatt,* was its editor in chief for almost a decade, and organized the first postwar fashion show in Berlin.

Source: "Ein Leben für die Mode," *Der Tagesspiegel,* 2 Dec. 1979.

Appendix II: A List of German Feature Films about Fashion from the 1910s, 1920s, and 1930s

ALL TITLES MARKED with * are presumed lost. Essential information about them has been obtained from contemporary reviews published primarily in *Film-Kurier*, *Licht-Bild-Bühne*, and the *Frankfurter Zeitung*, and from the plot synopses written by the German board of film censorship, the "Zensurkarten."

1. *Heimgefunden oder Von Stufe zu Stufe: Die Lebensbeichte einer Probiermamsell* (1911, dir. unknown)
2. *Gelbstern* (1912, dir. Otto Rippert)*
3. *Die Firma heiratet* (1914, dir. Carl Wilhelm)*
4. *Der Stolz der Firma* (1914, dir. Carl Wilhelm)
5. *Schuhpalast Pinkus* (1916, dir. Ernst Lubitsch)
6. *Der Blusenkönig* (1917, dir. Ernst Lubitsch),* preserved only in fragments
7. *Die Dame, der Teufel und die Probiermamsell* (1919, dir. Rudolf Biebrach)
8. *Die kleine Midinette (Erlauschtes aus der Konfektion)* (1921, dir. Maurice Turner, pseudonym for Wolfgang Neff)*
9. *Gelbstern: Erlebnisse einer Konfektioneuse* (1921, dir. Wolfgang Neff)*
10. *Yvette, Die Modeprinzessin* (1922, dir. Friedrich Zelnik)*
11. *Das Mädel aus dem Warenhaus* (1923, dir. Franz Hofer)*
12. *Die Kleine aus der Konfektion* (also known as *Großstadt-Kavaliere* or *Das Warenhausmädel*) (1924, dir. Maurice Turner, pseudonym for Wolfgang Neff)*
13. *Luxusweibchen* (1925, dir. Erich Schönfelder)
14. *Der Jüngling aus der Konfektion* (1926, dir. Richard Löwenbein)*
15. *Gräfin Plattmamsell* (1926, dir. Constantin J. David)*
16. *Die Warenhausprinzessin* (1926, dir. Heinz Paul)*
17. *Die drei Mannequins (Die drei Probiermamsells)* (1926, dir. Jaap Speyer)*
18. *Eine Dubary von heute* (1926, dir. Alexander Korda)
19. *Der Fürst von Pappenheim* (1927, dir. Richard Eichberg)
20. *Jennys Bummel durch die Männer* (1929, dir. Jaap Speyer)*

21. *Die Firma heiratet* (1930, remake of the 1914 film, with sound, dir. Carl Wilhelm)*
22. *Moritz macht sein Glück* (1930, dir. Jaap Speyer)
23. *Ich geh aus und du bleibst da* (1931, dir. Hans Behrendt)
24. *Frischer Wind aus Kanada* (1935, dir. Erich Holder, Heinz Kenter)
25. *In letzter Minute* (1939, dir. Fritz Kirchhoff)
26. *Das himmelblaue Abendkleid* (1940, dir. Erich Engels)

Works Cited

Allen, Jeanne. "The Film Viewer as Consumer." *Quarterly Review of Film Studies* 5 (Fall 1980): 481–99.

Altenloh, Emilie. "A Sociology of the Cinema: The Audience." *Screen* 42.3 (2001): 283.

Andrew, Dudley. "Jules, Jim, and Walter Benjamin." In *The Image in Dispute: Art and Cinema in the Age of Photography*, edited by Dudley Andrew, 33–54. Austin: U of Texas P, 1997.

Anita [Daniel]. "Die bevorstehende Männeremanzipation." *Die Dame*, Feb. 1928, no. 10, 14.

———. "Lebensstil 1930." *Die Dame*, April 1930, no. 15, 18.

———. "Mondän ist nicht mehr modern." *Die Dame*, July 1928, no. 21, 44–46.

Ankum, Katharina von. "Karriere, Konsum, Kosmetik: Zur Ästhetik des weiblichen Gesichts." In *Gesichter der Weimarer Republik: Eine physiognomische Kulturgeschichte*, edited by Claudia Schmölders and Sander L. Gilman, 175–90. Cologne: DuMont, 2000.

———. "Motherhood and the 'New Woman': Vicki Baum's *stud. chem. Helene Willfüer* and Irmgard Keun's *Gilgi — eine von uns*." *Women in German Yearbook* 11 (1995): 175–90.

———. "Rückblick auf eine Realistin." In *Apropos Vicki Baum*, edited by Katharina von Ankum, 7–46. Frankfurt am Main: Neue Kritik, 1998.

Apfel, Karl. "In den zwanziger Jahren: Erinnerungen an die Frankfurter Zeitung." *Archiv für Frankfurts Geschichte und Kunst* 55 (1976): 235–53.

Aschke, Katja. "Die geliehene Identität: Film und Mode in Berlin, 1900–1990: Betrachtung einer medialen Symbiose." In *Berlin en vogue: Berliner Mode in der Photographie*, edited by F. C. Gundlach and Uli Richter, 233–76. Berlin: Wasmuth, 1993.

Asper, Helmut. "Neues vom Stummfilm." *Film-Dienst* 53.6 (March 2000): 61.

Banchelli, Eva. "Zwischen Erinnerung und Entdeckung: Strategien der Großstadterfahrung bei Franz Hessel." In Opitz and Plath, *"Genieße froh, was du nicht hast,"* 105–16.

Barndt, Kerstin. *Sentimentalität und Sachlichkeit: Der Roman der Neuen Frau in der Weimarer Republik*. Cologne: Böhlau, 2003.

Barth, Heinz. "Kein ordentlicher Beruf." *Hundert Jahre Ullstein, 1877–1977*. Berlin: Ullstein, 1977. 1:349–55.

Barthes, Roland. *The Fashion System*. 1967. Translated by Matthew Ward and Richard Howard. New York: Hill and Wang, 1983.

Baudelaire, Charles. *The Painter of Modern Life and Other Essays.* Translated by Jonathan Mayne. London: Phaidon P, 1964.

Baum, Vicki. *Der große Ausverkauf.* Amsterdam: Querigo, 1937. In English: *Central Stores.* Translated by Paul Selver. London: Geoffrey Bles, 1940.

———. *It Was All Quite Different: Vicki Baum's Memoirs.* New York: Funk & Wagnalls, 1964.

Becker, Claudia. "Helen Grund." In Opitz and Plath, *"Genieße froh, was du nicht hast,"* 191–209.

Beckers, Marion, and Elisabeth Moortgat. *Yva: Photographien, 1925–1938/ Photographies, 1925–1928.* Berlin: Das Verborgene Museum, 2001.

Beckmann, Anna. "Vom Kampf der Geschlechter: Ein Beitrag zur modernen Eheliteratur." *Die Bücherwelt* 29.1 (1932): 29–33.

Benjamin, Walter. *The Arcades Project.* Translated by Howard Eiland and Kevin McLaughlin. Cambridge, MA: Harvard UP, 1999.

———. *The Correspondence of Walter Benjamin, 1910–1940.* Edited by Theodor W. Adorno. Translated by Manfred R. Jacobson and Evelyn M. Jacobson. Chicago, IL: U of Chicago P, 1994.

———. *Gesammelte Schriften.* Vol. 3. Edited by Hella Tiedemann-Bartels. Frankfurt am Main: Suhrkamp, 1980.

———. *Gesammelte Schriften.* Vols. 5/1 and 5/2. Edited by Rolf Tiedemann. Frankfurt am Main: Suhrkamp taschenbuch, 1991.

———. "On Some Motifs in Baudelaire." In *Illuminations,* edited by Hannah Arendt, translated by Harry Zohn, 155–200. New York: Schocken, 1968.

———. "The Return of the *Flâneur.*" In his *Selected Writings,* translated by Rodney Livingstone, edited by Michael W. Jennings, Howard Eiland, and Gary Smith, 2:262–67. Cambridge, MA: Harvard UP, 1999. German original: "Das unabsehbare Schauspiel der Flanerie, das wir endgültig abgesetzt glaubten." In Walter Benjamin, *Gesammelte Schriften,* edited by Hella Tiedemann-Bartels, 82–84. Frankfurt am Main: Suhrkamp, 1980.

Bergmann, Simone. *Make-up: Fotomodelle erzählen aus ihrem Leben.* Ravensburg: Otto Maier Verlag, 1981.

Berliner Zeitung, "Die Schaufensterpuppen am Tauentzien leben," 28 August 1999.

Berthold, Dr. *Volkswirtschaft in Zahlen und Bildern: Eine Erinnerung an die Ausstellung im Herbst 1929; Was, wie, wo kauft die Hausfrau?* Berlin: Reichsverband Deutscher Hausfrauenvereine e. V., 1930.

Bertschik, Julia. *Mode und Moderne: Kleidung als Spiegel des Zeitgeistes in der deutschsprachigen Literatur (1770–1945).* Cologne: Böhlau, 2005.

———. "Zopf mit Bubikopf: Modejournalismus im Dritten Reich am Beispiel der Zeitschrift *Die Mode* (1941–1943)." In *Reflexe und Reflexionen von Modernität, 1933–1945,* edited by Erhard Schütz and Georg Streim, 273–92. Bern: Peter Lang, 2002.

Bleckwenn, Ruth. "Antimodische Tendenzen in Deutschland." *Waffen- und Kostümkunde* 1 (1977): 66–77.

Boehn, Max von. *Die Mode: Menschen und Moden im neunzehnten Jahrhundert.* Munich: F. Bruckmann, 1924.

Böhm, Andrea. "Brigitte Helm: Heilige und Vamp." In *Grenzgänger zwischen Theater und Kino: Schauspielerporträts aus dem Berlin der zwanziger Jahre*, edited by Knut Hickethier, 194–212. Berlin: Ästhetik & Kommunikation, 1986.

Börne, Ludwig. *Sämtliche Schriften.* Edited by Inge und Peter Rippmann. Vol. 2. Düsseldorf: Melzer, 1962.

Bovenschen, Silvia. "Is There a Feminine Aesthetic?" *New German Critique* 10 (1977): 111–37.

Boveri, Margret. *Verzweigungen: Eine Autobiographie.* Edited by Uwe Johnson. Munich: Piper, 1977.

———. *Verzweigungen: Eine Autobiographie.* Frankfurt am Main: Suhrkamp, 1996.

Brandlmeier, Thomas. "Mit Grazie, Charme und Chuzpe." In *Ich mache alles mit den Beinen . . .: Der Schauspieler Curt Bois*, edited by Sabine Zolchow und Johanna Muschelknautz, 102–33. Berlin: Vorwerk 8, 2001.

Brenner, Peter J., ed. *Der Reisebericht: Die Entwicklung einer Gattung in der deutschen Literatur.* Frankfurt am Main: Suhrkamp, 1989.

Brenner, Vanna. "Gnädige Frau, Sie sind zu intellektuell." *Die Dame*, April 1931, no. 14, 42–44.

Brentano, Bernard von. "Keine von uns: Ein Wort an die Leser des *Vorwärts*." *Die Linkskurve* 4 (1932): 27–28.

———. "Masken und Menschen." *Frankfurter Zeitung*, Abendblatt, 11 February 1926. Reprinted in Bernard von Brentano, *Wo in Europa ist Berlin: Bilder aus den zwanziger Jahren*, 42–44. Frankfurt am Main: Insel Taschenbuch, 1993.

Brück, Christa Anita. *Schicksale hinter Schreibmaschinen.* Berlin: Sieben Stäbe-Verlag, 1935.

Buck-Morss, Susan. *The Dialectics of Seeing: Walter Benjamin and the Arcades Project.* Cambridge, MA: MIT Press, 1989.

Bud, Elsa Maria. *Bravo, Musch!* Berlin: Die Buchgemeinde, 1931.

Budke, Petra, and Jutta Schulze, eds. *Schriftstellerinnen in Berlin, 1871–1945: Ein Lexikon zu Leben und Werk.* Berlin: Orlanda Frauenverlag, 1995.

Bunsen, Marie von. "Kriegszeit und Mode." *Die Dame*, February 1920, no. 10, 10–24.

———. "Männeraugen und Frauenaugen." *Die Dame*, May 1919, no. 16, 2.

C. B. "Die Dame, der Teufel und die Probiermamsell." *Der Film*, 25 January 1919, 36.

Dähn, Brunhilde. *Berlin, Hausvogteiplatz: Über 100 Jahre am Laufsteg der Mode.* Göttingen: Musterschmidt-Verlag, 1968.

Die Dame, "Asta Offermann, die auf dem Mannequinball zur Modekönigin gewählt wurde," December 1929, no. 7: 40.

De Marly, Diana. *Worth: Father of Haute Couture.* London: Elm Tree Books, 1980.

Denscher, Bernhard. *Tagebuch der Straße.* Vienna: Kunstpresse, 1988.

Diethe, Carol. "Nietzsche and the New Woman." *German Life and Letters* 48 (1995): 428–40.

Dietrich, Wally H. "Die Frau im Kunstgewerbe." In Schmidt-Beil, *Die Kultur der Frau,* 288–91.

Dittrich, Gertrud. "Die Frau im Modeschaffen." In Schmidt-Beil, *Die Kultur der Frau,* 145–50.

Dobert, Paul. "Im Reiche der Mode." *Moderne Kunst* 7.11 (1892/93): 137–40.

Dopp, Werner. *125 Jahre Berliner Konfektion.* Berlin: Ernst Staneck, 1962.

Drescher, Barbara. "Die 'Neue Frau.'" In *Autorinnen der Weimarer Republik,* edited by Walter Fähnders and Helga Karrenbrock, 163–86. Bielefeld: Aisthesis, 2003.

Dresler, Adolf. *Die Frau im Journalismus.* Munich: Knorr & Wirth, 1936.

Dryden, Ernst. "Rechtfertigung der Mode." *Die Dame,* November 1929, no. 3, 22–23.

Edschmid, Kasimir. "Mannequins." *Münchner Zeitung,* 10 July 1929.

Eggebrecht, Axel. "Konfektion." *Die Weltbühne* 28.19 (1932): 717.

Elegante Welt, "Asta Nielsen wieder in Berlin," 18 June 1919, 7.

———, "Die drei Kleider Sonjas," 13 January 1926, 11–12.

———, "Königinnen der Mode," 12 January 1927, 36–37.

———, "Die Modekönigin Sonja I. in ihrem Krönungsornat," 13 January 1926.

———, "Der Modentee am Strande von Gatow: Ein Ereignis im sommerlichen Gesellschaftsleben Berlins," 24 June 1929, 26–27.

Elias, Julie. "Die Dame im Sommer." *Styl* 2 (1924): 33–34.

Elsaesser, Thomas. "Early German Cinema: A Second Life?" In *A Second Life: German Cinema's First Decades,* edited by Thomas Elsaesser and Michael Wedel, 9–37. Amsterdam: Amsterdam UP, 1996.

———. *Metropolis.* London: bfi Publishing, 2000.

Endell, August. *Die Schönheit der großen Stadt.* Stuttgart: Strecker & Schöner, 1908. Reprinted in August Endell, *Vom Sehen: Texte 1896–1925 über Architektur, Formkunst und "Die Schönheit der großen Stadt,"* edited by Helge David, 163–208. Basel: Birkhäuser, 1995.

Erpenbeck, Fritz. "Ein Warenhausroman." *Das Wort: Literarische Monatsschrift* 12 (1937): 92–93.

Eskildsen, Ute. "A Chance to Participate: A Transitional Time for Women Photographers." In *Visions of the "Neue Frau": Women and the Visual Arts* in *Weimar Germany*, edited by Marsha Meskimmon and Shearer West, 62–76. Aldershot, UK: Scholar P, 1995.

———, ed. *Fotografieren hieß teilnehmen: Fotografinnen der Weimarer Republik*. Düsseldorf: Richter, 1994.

Eva [Ea von Allesch]. "Modespaziergang in Berlin." *Die Moderne Welt: Illustrierte Halbmonatsschrift für Kunst, Literatur, Mode*, 1920, no. 4: 27–28.

———. "Die Mode und ihre Mannequins." *Die Moderne Welt: Illustrierte Halbmonatsschrift für Kunst, Literatur, Mode*, 1920, no. 10: 27.

Evans, Caroline. "The Enchanted Spectacle." *Fashion Theory* 5.3 (2001): 271–310.

———. "Multiple, Movement, Model, Mode: The Mannequin Parade 1900–1929." In *Fashion and Modernity*, edited by Christopher Breward and Caroline Evans, 125–45. Oxford: Berg, 2005.

Ewing, Elizabeth. *History of Twentieth-Century Fashion*. Lanham, MD: Barnes & Noble, 1992.

Falk, Sabine. "Aufbruch und Stagnation: Zum Frauenbild der 20er und 30er Jahre und seiner literarischen Bearbeitung durch Irmgard Keun." In *Frauenalltag-Frauenforschung*, edited by Anita Chmielewski-Hagius, 165–70. Frankfurt am Main: Peter Lang, 1986.

Fallada, Hans. "Fünf Frauen schreiben." *Die Literatur* 34 (1931/32): 249–50.

Federle, Courtney. "Picture Postcard: Kracauer Writes from Berlin." In *Peripheral Visions: The Hidden Stages of Weimar Cinema*, edited by Kenneth S. Calhoon, 39–54. Detroit, MI: Wayne State UP, 2001.

Feld, Hans. "Der Fürst von Pappenheim." *Film-Kurier*, 8 September 1927. Reprinted in *Die deutsche Filmkomödie vor 1945: Kaiserreich, Weimarer Republik und Nationalsozialismus*, edited by Jörg Schöning, 86–87. Hamburg: Cinegraph, 2005.

———. "Manolescu." *Film-Kurier*, 23 August 1929.

Felden, Tamara. *Frauen reisen: Zur literarischen Repräsentation weiblicher Geschlechterrollenerfahrung im 19. Jahrhundert*. New York: Peter Lang, 1993.

Ferguson, Priscilla Parkhurst. "The *Flâneur* and the Production of Culture." In *Cultural Participation: Trends since the Middle Ages*, edited by Ann Rigney and Douwe Fokkema, 109–24. Amsterdam: Benjamins, 1993.

———. "The *Flâneur* On and Off the Streets of Paris." In Tester, *The Flâneur*, 22–42.

———. "The *Flâneur*: The City and Its Discontents." In Ferguson, *Paris as Revolution*, 80–114.

———, ed. *Paris as Revolution: Writing the Nineteenth-Century City*. Berkeley: U of California P, 1994.

Der Film-Kurier, "Berliner Abende: Fest der Mannequins," 23 August 1926.

———, "Berlins erste Modekönigin," 14 December 1925.

———, "Berlins zweite Modekönigin," 13 December 1926.

———, "Drei Mannequins," 9 August 1926.

———, review of "Eine von uns," 21 October 1932.

———, review of *Gelbstern*, 28 January 1922.

———, review of *Die Kleine aus der Konfektion*, 16 April 1924.

———, review of *Luxusweibchen*, 21 April 1925.

———, "Warenhausprinzessin," 18 December 1926.

Fischer, Lucy. *Designing Women: Cinema, Art Deco, and the Female Form*. New York: Columbia UP, 2003.

Flake, Otto. "Abstrakte Künstler." *Die Dame*, April 1919, no. 14, 4.

Le flâneur au salon, ou M. Bonhomme, examen joyeux des tableaux, mêlé de vaudevilles. Paris: Aubry, 1806.

Flügge, Manfred. *Gesprungene Liebe: Die wahre Geschichte zu "Jules und Jim."* Berlin: Aufbau, 1993.

———. *Letzte Heimkehr nach Paris: Franz Hessel und die Seinen im Exil*. Berlin: Arsenal, 1989.

———. *Wider Willen im Paradies: Deutsche Schriftsteller im Exil in Sanary-sur-Mer*. Berlin: Aufbau, 1996.

Franke, Ingeborg. "Gilgi — Film, Roman und Wirklichkeit." *Der Weg der Frau* 1 (1933): 5–6.

Frederiksen, Elke. "Blick in die Ferne: Zur Reiseliteratur von Frauen." In *Frauen — Literatur — Geschichte: Schreibende Frauen vom Mittelalter bis zur Gegenwart*, edited by Hiltrud Gnüg and Renate Mohrmann, 104–22. Stuttgart: Metzler, 1985.

Freksa, Friedrich. "Mode, Tracht und Möbel." *Die Dame*, November 1918, no. 3, 4–5.

Frevert, Ute. *Women in German History: From Bourgeois Emancipation to Sexual Liberation*. Translated by Stuart McKinnon-Evans, Terry Bond, and Barbara Norden. Oxford: Berg, 1989.

Friedberg, Anne. *Window Shopping: Cinema and the Postmodern*. Berkeley: U of California P, 1993.

Frisby, David, and Mike Featherstone. Introduction to *Simmel on Culture: Selected Writings*. Edited by David Frisby and Mike Featherstone, 3–25. London: SAGE Publications, 1997.

Fritzsche, Peter. *Reading Berlin 1900*. Cambridge, MA: Harvard UP, 1996.

Gaines, Jane. "The Queen-Christina Tie-Ups: Convergence of Shop Window and Screen." *Quarterly Review of Film and Video* 11.4 (1989): 11–35.

Ganeva, Mila. "The Beautiful Body of the Mannequin: Display Practices in Weimar Germany." In *Leibhaftige Moderne: Körper in Kunst und*

Massenmedien, 1918–1933, edited by Michael Cowan and Kai Sicks, 152–68. Bielefeld: transcript, 2005.

———. "Elegance and Spectacle in Berlin: The Gerson Fashion Store and the Rise of the Modern Fashion Show in the Early Twentieth Century." In *Displays: The Places and Spaces of Fashion*, edited by John Potvin. New York: Routledge, 2008. (Forthcoming.)

———. "Fashion Photography and Women's Modernity in Weimar Germany: The Case of Yva." *NWSA Journal* 15.3 (2003): 1–25.

Garelick, Rhonda. *Rising Star: Dandyism, Gender, and Performance in the Fin-de-siècle*. Princeton, NJ: Princeton UP, 1998.

Geiger, Ruth-Esther. ". . . Im verschärften Maße, eine Frauenfrage: Partei- und unabhängige Frauenpresse in Weimar." In *Sind das noch Damen? Vom gelehrten Frauenzimmer-Journal zum feministischen Journalismus*, edited by Ruth-Esther Geiger and Sigrid Weigel, 163–74. Munich: Frauenbuchverlag, 1981.

Gleber, Anke. *The Art of Taking a Walk: Flanerie, Literature, and Film in Weimar Culture*. Princeton, NJ: Princeton UP, 1999.

———. "Die Erfahrung der Moderne in der Stadt: Reiseliteratur in der Weimarer Republik." In Brenner, *Der Reisebericht*, 463–89.

Goebel, Gerhard. "Mode und Moderne: Der Modejournalist Mallarmé." *Germanisch-romanische Monatsschrift* 28.1 (1978): 36–49.

Gohnert, René. "Klassiker deutscher Gebrauchsgrafik." *Neue Werbung* 37.3 (1990): 30–33.

Grazia, Victoria de, ed. Introduction to *The Sex of Things: Gender and Consumption in Historical Perspective*, 1–14. Berkeley: U of California P, 1996.

Gronberg, Tag. *Designs of Modernity: Exhibiting the City in 1920s Paris*. Manchester, UK: Manchester UP, 1998.

Gross, Michael. *Model: The Ugly Business of Beautiful Women*. New York: William Morrow, 1995.

Grossmann, Atina. "Berufswahl — ein Privileg der bürgerlichen Frauen." In Eskildsen, *Fotografieren hieß teilnehmen*, 8–12.

———. "Girlkultur or Thoroughly Rationalized Female: A New Woman in Weimar Germany?" In *Women in Culture and Politics: A Century of Change*, edited by Judith Friedlander, Blanche Wiesen Cook, Alice Kessler-Harris, and Carroll Smith-Rosenberg, 62–80. Bloomington: Indiana UP, 1986.

Grund, Helen. "Aufatmen in Paris." *Das Tage-Buch* 5 (1924): 958–63. Reprinted in Rheinsberg, *Bubikopf: Aufbruch in den Zwanzigern*, 147–55.

———. "Deutsche Mode in Paris: Ein Gespräch mit Renate Green." *Für die Frau*, January 1932, 2.

———. "Für die erste Reise 1928." *Für die Frau*, January 1928, 10–11.

———. "Im Klima der Mode." *Der Querschnitt* 5.6 (1925): 515.

———. "Premiere der Wintermode." *Für die Frau*, September 1930, 8.

———. *Vom Wesen der Mode*. Munich: Meisterschule für Deutschlands Buchdruck, 1935.

———. "Vorzeitiger Abschiedsgruß." *Für die Frau*, May 1928, 9.

———. "Zwischen Abreise und Ankunft." *Für die Frau*, August 1931, 10.

Guenther, Irene. *Nazi Chic? Fashioning Women in the Third Reich*. Oxford: Berg, 2004.

Gundermann, Marianne. "Gilgi — eine von 'Vorwärts.'" *Der Weg der Frau* 1 (1933): 7.

Gunning, Tom. *The Films of Fritz Lang: Allegories of Vision and Modernity*. London: British Film Institute, 2000.

Gustavus, Christa. "Lieselotte Friedlaender und der 'Modenspiegel.'" In Waidenschlager and Gustavus, *Mode der 20er Jahre*, 36–39.

H. W. "Die Bilanz der Mode." *Die Dame*, July 1921, no. 20, 14.

———. "Die nächste Modelinie?" *Die Dame*, July 1921, no. 20, 14.

Haacke, Wilmont. *Handbuch des Feuilletons*. 2 vols. Emsdetten, Germany: Lechte, 1951.

Habermas, Jürgen. *Der philosophische Diskurs der Moderne*. Frankfurt am Main: Suhrkamp, 1985. In English: *The Philosophical Discourse of Modernity: Twelve Lectures*. Translated by Frederick Lawrence. Cambridge, MA: MIT Press, 1987.

———. *Strukturwandel der Öffentlichkeit*. Berlin: Luchterhand, 1971. In English: *The Structural Transformation of the Public Sphere*. Translated by Thomas Burger and Frederick Lawrence. Cambridge, MA: MIT Press, 1991.

Hake, Sabine. "In the Mirror of Fashion." In *Women in the Metropolis: Gender and Modernity in Weimar Culture*, edited by Katharina von Ankum, 185–201. Berkeley: U of California P, 1997.

———. "Das Kino, die Werbung und die Avantgarde." In *Die Spur durch den Spiegel: Der Film in der Kultur der Moderne*, edited by Malte Hagener, Johann N. Schmidt, and Michael Wedel, 193–206. Berlin: Bertz, 2004.

———. *Passions and Deceptions: The Early Films of Ernst Lubitsch*. Princeton, NJ: Princeton UP, 1992.

Hanisch, Michael. *Auf den Spuren der Filmgeschichte: Berliner Schauplätze*. Berlin: Henschel, 1991.

Hansen, Miriam Bratu. "America, Paris, the Alps: Kracauer (and Benjamin) on Cinema and Modernity." In *Cinema and the Invention of Modern Life*, edited by Leo Charney and Vanessa R. Schwartz, 362–402. Berkeley: U of California P, 1995.

———. "Decentic Perspectives: Kracauer's Early Writings on Film and Mass Culture." *New German Critique* 54 (Fall 1991): 47–76.

———. "The Mass Production of the Senses: Classical Cinema as Vernacular Modernism." In *Reinventing Film Studies*, edited by Christine Gledhill and Linda Williams, 332–50. London: Arnold, 2000.

Hauser, Heinrich. "Auto und Frau." *Für die Frau*, July 1927, 11–12.

Hausler, Hermann. *Kunstformen des feuilletonistischen Stils: Beiträge zur Ästhetik und Psychologie des modernen Zeitungsfeuilletonismus.* Stuttgart: Württemberger Zeitungsverlag, 1928.

Hausstedt, Birgit. *Die wilden Jahre in Berlin: Eine Klatsch- und Kulturgeschichte der Frauen.* Berlin: edition ebersbach, 2002.

Helm, Hanna. "Ich werde Mannequin, um mein Studium zu verdienen." *Der Uhu,* April 1930, 54–60.

Herzog, Charlotte. "Powder Puff Promotion: The Fashion Show-in-the-Film." In *Fabrications: Costume and the Female Body,* edited by Jane Gaines and Charlotte Herzog, 134–59. New York: Routledge, 1990.

Herzog, Charlotte Cornelia, and Jane Marie Gaines. " 'Puffed Sleeves before Tea-Time': Joan Crawford, Adrian, and Women Audiences." In *Stardom: Industry of Desire,* edited by Christine Gledhill, 74–91. New York: Routledge, 1991.

Herzog, Elsa. "Die Mode im Frühjahr 1919." *Die Dame,* March 1919, no. 12, 16.

———. "Mode-Notizen." *Die Dame,* October 1918, no. 2, 18.

———. "Mode und Bühne." *Jahrbuch der Berliner Bühnen* 1.1 (1925): 119–23.

Herzog, Peter, and Gene Vazzana. *Brigitte Helm: From Metropolis to Gold: Portrait of a Goddess.* New York: Corvin, 1994.

Hessel, Franz. *Alter Mann: Romanfragment.* Edited by Bernd Witte. Frankfurt am Main: Suhrkamp, 1987.

———. "An die Berlinerin." *Vogue* 13 March 1929, 25. Reprinted in Hessel, *Ein Garten voller Weltgeschichte,* 26–28.

———. *Ermunterung zum Genuß: Kleine Prosa.* Edited by Karin Grund and Bernd Witte. Berlin: Brinkmann & Bosse, 1981.

———. *Ein Flaneur in Berlin* (Berlin: Arsenal, 1984), 258. Reprint of *Spazieren in Berlin.*

———. "Frühstück mit einer Verkäuferin." *Lose Blätter: Eine Gratis-Beilage der Dame,* 1929/30, no. 16, 249–50.

———. *Ein Garten voller Weltgeschichte: Berliner und Pariser Skizzen.* Edited by Bernhard Echte. Munich: dtv, 1994.

———. "Eine gefährliche Straße." *Das Illustrierte Blatt,* 15 June 1929, 686–88.

———. "Das Lederetui." *Die Dame,* September 1934, no. 22: 17–18. Reprinted in Hessel, *Ein Garten voller Weltgeschichte,* 68–73.

———. "Mannequin-Lied." *Das Tage-Buch* 36, 6 September 1930, 1446.

———. "Mitgenommen in eine Modeschau." *Für die Frau,* May 1930, 8.

———. *Nachfeier.* Berlin: Rowohlt, 1929.

———. *Spazieren in Berlin.* Leipzig: Dr. Hans Epstein, 1929.

———. "Von der schwierigen Kunst spazieren zu gehen." *Literarische Welt* 8.6 (1932): 3–4. Reprinted in Hessel, *Ermunterung zum Genuß,* 53–61.

Hessel, Helen. "Berlin in November 1938." In *Letzte Heimkehr in Paris: Franz Hessel und die Seinen im Exil*, edited by Manfred Flügge, 43–66. Berlin: Arsenal, 1989.

Hildebrandt, Dieter. *"Genieße froh, was du nicht hast*: Nie war Franz Hessel aktueller als heute oder warum Berlin der Gegenwart den Flaneur der Vergangenheit braucht." *Die Zeit*, 17 March 1995: 72.

Höfele, Andreas. "Dandy und New Woman." In *Die "Nineties": Das englische Fin-de-siècle zwischen Dekadenz und Sozialkritik*, edited by Manfred Pfister and Bernd Schulte-Middelich, 147–61. Munich: Francke, 1983.

Hofer-Dernburg, Dorothea. "Königinnen Größe 42." *Die losen Blätter: Eine Gratis-Beilage der Dame*, 1929/30, no. 8, 205–6.

Hollander, Anne. "Women and Fashion." In *Women, the Arts, and the 1920s in Paris and New York*, edited by Kenneth W. Wheeler and Virginia Lee Lussier, 109–25. New Brunswick, NJ: Transaction Publishers, 1982.

Huyssen, Andreas. *After the Great Divide: Modernism, Mass Culture, Postmodernism*. Bloomington: Indiana UP, 1986.

———. "The Vamp and the Machine: Fritz Lang's 'Metropolis.'" In Huyssen, *After the Great Divide*, 65–81.

Das Illustrierte Blatt, "Modenschau am Alex," 26 October 1929, 1230–31.

Ivimy, Alice. *A Woman's Guide to Paris*. London: J. Nisbet, 1909.

Jacobeit, Sigrid. "Aspekte der Kleidungsgeschichte im faschistischen Deutschland." In *Sich kleiden*, edited by Gitta Böth and Gaby Mentges, 153–70. Hessische Blätter für Volks- und Kulturforschung 25. Marburg: Jonas Verlag, 1989.

Jazbinsek, Dietmar. "Vom Sittenspiel der Grosstadt zum Sittenfilm: Über die populärkulturellen Zusammenhänge der frühen deutschen Filmproduktion." In *Geschlecht in Fesseln: Sexualität zwischen Aufklärung und Ausbeutung im Weimarer Kino, 1918–1933*, edited by Malte Hagener, 80–101. Munich: Edition Text + Kritik, 2000.

Jelavich, Peter. *Berlin Cabaret*. Cambridge, MA: Harvard UP, 1993.

Johst, Hanns. "Neues vom Büchertisch: Neue Romane." *Velhagen & Klasings Monatshefte* 46.6 (1932): 621–23.

Jordanova, Ludmilla. "Science, Machines, and Gender." In *Fritz Lang's "Metropolis": Cinematic Visions of Technology and Fear*, edited by Michael Minden and Holger Bachmann, 173–97. Rochester, NY: Camden House, 2000.

Jung, Uli, and Walter Schatzberg. *Beyond "Caligari": The Films of Robert Wiene*. New York: Berghahn, 1999.

———. "Robert Wiene's Film Career before 'Caligari.'" In *Before Caligari: German Cinema, 1895–1920*, edited by Paolo Cherchi Usai and Lorenzo Codelli, 292–311. Pordenone: Edizioni Biblioteca dell-Immagine, 1990.

Junker, Almut, and Eva Stille. *Zur Geschichte der Unterwäsche, 1700–1960*. Frankfurt am Main: Historisches Museum, 1988.

K. v. R. [Katharina von Rathaus]. "Arbeit, Zwischenfälle." *Frankfurter Zeitung*, 14 August 1930.

———. "Der Chef; Besucher; Audienz." *Frankfurter Zeitung*, 1 September 1930.

K. v. R. [Katharina von Rathaus]. "Ich bin also 'Catherine.'" *Frankfurter Zeitung*, 11 August 1930, 1–2.

Kaes, Anton. "Cinema and Modernity: On Fritz Lang's *Metropolis*." In *High and Low: German Attempts at Mediation*, edited by Reinhold Grimm and Jost Hermand, 19–33. Madison: U of Wisconsin P, 1994.

Kahlenberg, Hans von. "Pagen." *Die Dame*, August 1919, no. 21, 11.

Kaléko, Mascha. "Mannequins." In *Das lyrische Stenogrammheft*. 1933; repr., Berlin: Rowohlt, 1956.

Kant, Immanuel. *Anthropologie in pragmatischer Hinsicht. Werke*, vol. 12. Frankfurt am Main: Suhrkamp, 1964.

Kaplan, Joel, and Sheila Stowell. *Theatre and Fashion: Oscar Wilde to the Suffragettes*. Cambridge, UK: Cambridge UP, 1994.

Kasten, Jürgen. "Der Stolz der deutschen Filmkomödie: Die frühen Filme von Ernst Lubitsch, 1914–1918." In *Die Modellierung des Kinofilms: Zur Geschichte des Kinoprogramms zwischen Kurzfilm und Langfilm, 1905/06–1918*, edited by Corinne Müller and Harro Segeberg, 301–32. Munich: Wilhelm Fink, 1998.

———. "Verweigerung der korrekten Assimilation: Jüdische Typen, Milieus und Stereotype in Komödien Ernst Lubitschs und Reinhold Schünzels." In *Spaß beiseite, Film ab: Jüdischer Humor und verdrängendes Lachen in Filmkomödie bis 1945*, edited by Jan Distelmeyer, 33–47. Hamburg: edition text + kritik, 2006.

Kästner, Erich. "Bois de Berlin." *Neue Leipziger Zeitung*, 25 May 1929. Repr. in Kästner, *Gemischte Gefühle*, 2:193–95. Zurich: Atrium, 1991.

Kaul, Stephanie. "Beschwingte Sommer-Mode." *Die Dame* March 1930, no. 13, 16–17.

———. "Die frauliche Mode." *Die Dame*, November 1929, no. 4, 90.

———. "Die individuelle Mode." *Die Dame*, September 1930, no. 26, 14–15.

———. "Zur Psychologie der neuen Mode," *Die Dame*, October 1929, no. 1, 82–83.

Kessemeier, Gesa. *Sportlich, sachlich, männlich: Das Bild der "Neuen Frau" in den Zwanziger Jahren; Zur Konstruktion geschlechtsspezifischer Bilder in der Mode der Jahre 1920 bis 1929*. Dortmund: Edition Ebersbach, 2000.

Keun, Irmgard. *Gilgi — eine von uns*. Düsseldorf: Claassen, 1979.

Der Kinematograph, "Der Blusenkönig," 7 November 1917.

King, Lynda J. *Best-Sellers by Design: Vicki Baum and the House of Ullstein*. Detroit, MI: Wayne State UP, 1988.

———. "From the Crown to the Hammer and Sickle: The Life and Works of an Austrian Interwar Writer, Hermynia Zur Mühlen." *Women in German Yearbook* 4 (1988): 125–54.

Klooss, Reinhard, and Thomas Reuter. *Körperbilder: Menschenornamente in Revuetheater und Revuefilm*. Frankfurt am Main: Syndikat, 1980.

Köhn, Eckhardt. *Straßenrausch: Flanerie und die kleine Form; Versuch zur Literaturgeschichte des Flaneurs bis 1933*. Berlin: Das Arsenal, 1989.

König, Lotte. "Die Frau als Photographin." In Schmidt-Beil, *Die Kultur der Frau*, 292–96.

Korff, Kurt. "Die 'Berliner Illustrirte.'" In *Fünfzig Jahre Ullstein, 1877–1927*, 297–302.

———. *Fünfzig Jahre Ullstein, 1877–1927*. Berlin: Ullstein, 1927.

Kosta, Barbara. "Unruly Daughters and Modernity: Irmgard Keun's 'Gilgi — eine von uns.'" *German Quarterly* 68.3 (1995): 271–86.

Kothes, Franz-Peter. *Die theatralische Revue in Berlin und Wien, 1900–1938*. Wilhelmshaven: Heinrichshofen Verlag, 1977.

Kracauer, Siegfried. "Alraune." *Frankfurter Zeitung*, 12 February 1928. Repr. in Kracauer, *Kleine Schriften zum Film*, 6/2:31–32.

———. *Die Angestellten: Aus dem neuesten Deutschland*. 3rd ed. Bonn: Verlag für Demoskopie, 1959. In English: *The Salaried Masses: Duty and Distraction in Weimar Germany*. Translated by Quintin Hoare. London: Verso, 1998.

———. "Berliner Figuren: Das Nummernmädchen." In *Straßen in Berlin und anderswo*, 154.

———. "Berliner Nebeneinander: Kara-Iki — Scala-Ball im Savoy — Menschen im Hotel." *Frankfurter Zeitung*, 17 February 1933. Repr. in Kracauer, *Kleine Schriften zum Film*, 6/3:147–49.

———. "Film 1928," in *The Mass Ornament*, 307–20.

———. "Der Fürst von Pappenheim." *Frankfurter Zeitung*, 29 November 1927. Reprinted in Kracauer, *Kleine Schriften zum Film*, 418.

———. "Kino in der Münzstraße." In *Straßen in Berlin und anderswo*, 92–95.

———. *Kleine Schriften zum Film*. Edited by Inka Mülder-Bach. Vol. 6/1. Frankfurt am Main: Suhrkamp, 2004.

———. "The Little Shopgirls Go to the Movies," in *Mass Ornament*, 291–304,

———. *The Mass Ornament*. Edited and translated by Thomas Y. Levin. Cambridge, MA: Harvard UP, 1995.

———. *Orpheus in Paris: Offenbach and the Paris of his Time*. Translated by Gwenda David and Eric Mosbacher. New York: Knopf, 1938.

———. "Phantasien aus einem Modehaus" (review of *Jennys Bummel durch die Männer*). *Frankfurter Zeitung*, 8 February 1930.

———. *Schriften: Aufsätze (1927–1931)*. Edited by Inka Mülder-Bach. Vols. 5/2 and 5/3. Frankfurt am Main: Suhrkamp, 1990.

———. *Straßen in Berlin und anderswo*. Frankfurt am Main: Suhrkamp, 1964.

———. "Die Warenhaus-Prinzessin," *Frankfurter Zeitung*, 27 August 1927. Repr. in Siegfried Kracauer, *Kleine Schriften zum Film*, 6/1:393.

Kreimeier, Klaus. "Trennungen: G. W. Pabst und seine Filme." In *G. W. Pabst*, edited by Wolfgang Jacobsen, 11–124. Berlin: Argon, 1997.

Kreis, Gabriele. *Irmgard Keun: "Was man glaubt, gibt es."* Munich: Heyne, 1991.

Krengel, Jochen. "Das Wachstum der Berliner Bekleidungsindustrie vor dem Erstem Weltkrieg." *Jahrbuch für die Geschichte Mittel- und Ostdeutschlands* 27 (1978): 206–37.

Krispien, Curt. "Das Mädchen vom Blatt IV." *Scherl's Magazin*, June 1932, 818.

Kupschinsky, Elke. "Die vernünftige Nephertete." In *Die Metropole: Industriekultur in Berlin im 20. Jahrhundert*, edited by Jochen Boberg, Tilman Fichter, and Eckhart Gillen, 164–72. Munich: C. H. Beck, 1986.

Lahmann, Heinrich. *Die Reform der Kleidung*. Stuttgart: Zimmer, 1898.

Larousse: Grand Dictionnaire Universel. 1893 edition.

Latour, Anny. *Kings of Fashion*. Translated by Mervyn Savill. London: Weidenfeld & Nicolson, 1958.

Laver, James. Preface to *The Elegant Woman: From the Rococo Period to Modern Times*, by Gertrude Aretz, translated by James Laver. London: G. G. Harrap & Co., 1932.

———. *Taste and Fashion: From the French Revolution until Today*. New York: Dodd, Mead & Co., 1938.

Lavin, Maud. *Cut with a Kitchen Knife: The Weimar Photomontages of Hannah Höch*. New Haven, CT: Yale UP, 1993.

Leach, William. *Land of Desire: Merchants, Power, and the Rise of a New American Culture*. New York: Vintage Books, 1993.

Lebens- und Arbeitsbedingungen der Journalisten: Studien und Berichte. Reihe L: *Geistige Arbeiter*, vol. 2. Geneva: Internationaler Arbeitsamt, 1928.

Ledermann, Martin. "Die Modenschau — ein erledigtes Kapitel? Führende westdeutsche Konfektionshäuser gründen eine 'Anti-Modenschau-Liga.'" *Der Konfektionär*, 19 October 1927.

Leese, Elizabeth. *Costume Design in the Movies*. Bembridge, UK: BCW Publishing, 1976.

Leopold, Dr. "Die Lockvögel der Mode." *Scherl's Magazin*, February 1930, 189–95.

Ley, Andreas. *Mode für Deutschland: Fünfzig Jahre Meisterschule für Mode*. Munich: Stadtmuseum, 1979.

Lichtbild-Bühne, review of *Die Firma heiratet*, 24 January 1914.

Lipman, Anthony. *Divinely Elegant: The World of Ernst Dryden*. London: Pavilion, 1982.

Lipovetsky, Gilles. *The Empire of Fashion: Dressing Modern Democracy*. Translated by Catherine Porter. Princeton, NJ: Princeton UP, 1994.

Loeb, Moritz. *Berliner Konfektion*. Berlin: Hermann Seemann, 1906.

Loos, Adolf. *Spoken into the Void: Collected Essays, 1897–1900*. Cambridge, MA: MIT Press, 1982.

Loreck, Hanne. "Das Kunstprodukt 'Neue Frau' in den zwanziger Jahren." In Waidenschlager and Gustavus, *Mode der 20er Jahre*, 12–19.

Loschek, Ingrid. *Die Mode im 20. Jahrhundert: Eine Kulturgeschichte unserer Zeit*. 5th ed. Munich: Bruckmann, 1995.

Ludwig, Ruth. "Die Pariserin als modernes Kunstwerk." *Die Dame*, January 1929, no. 7, 53–54.

Lustig, Hanns G. "Die wunderbare Lüge der Nina Petrowna." *Tempo*, 16 April 1929, 20.

Lütgens, Annelie. "Passantinnen/Flaneusen: Frauen im Bild großstädtischer Öffentlichkeit der Zwanziger Jahre." In *Die Neue Frau: Herausforderung für die Bildmedien der Zwanziger Jahre*, edited by Katharina Sykora, Annette Dorgerloh, Doris Noell-Rumpeltes, and Ada Raev, 107–18. Marburg: Jonas Verlag, 1993.

Lützeler, Paul Michael. "Ea von Allesch: Von der femme fatale zur femme emancipée." In *Das Teesdorfer Tagebuch für Ea von Allesch*, edited by Lützeler, 190–222. Frankfurt am Main: Suhkamp, 1995.

Maak, Niklas. "Die blauen Enkel: Das neue Berlin sucht seine Zukunft in den Formen der Vergangenheit." *Süddeutsche Zeitung*, 31 December 1998, 23.

Makela, Maria. "The Rise and Fall of the Flapper Dress: Nationalism and Anti-Semitism in Early-Twentieth-Century Discourses on German Fashion." *Journal of Popular Culture* 34.3 (2000): 183–208.

Mangum, Teresa. "Style Wars of the 1890s: The New Woman and the Decadent." In *Transforming Genres: New Approaches to British Fiction of the 1890s*, edited by Nikki Lee Manos and Meri-Jane Rochelson, 47–66. New York: St. Martin's P, 1994.

Mann, Erika. "Frau und Buch." In Rheinsberg, *Bubikopf: Aufbruch in den Zwanzigern*, 11–12.

Mänz, Peter, and Christian Maryska. *Ufa Film Posters, 1918–1943*. Heidelberg: Umschau Braus, 1998.

Marcus, Paul E. "Manolescu." *LichtBild-Bühne*, 23 August 1929.

Marilaun, Carl. "Wienerische Mannequins." *Die Dame*, May 1920, no. 16, 30–32.

Martin, Richard "Addressing the Dress." In *The Crisis of Criticism*, edited by Maurice Berger, 51–70. New York: The New Press, 1998.

Martinelli, Vittorio. "Kino-Lieblinge." *Giffithiana* 38/39 (October 1990): 9–72.

März, Ursula. *"Du lebst wie im Hotel": Die Welt der Ré Soupault*. Heidelberg: Wunderhorn, 1999.

McCormick, Richard W. *Gender and Sexuality in Weimar Modernity: Film, Literature, and "New Objectivity."* New York: Palgrave, 2001.

Mendelsohn, Peter de. *Zeitungsstadt Berlin: Menschen und Mächte in der Geschichte der deutschen Presse.* Berlin: Ullstein, 1969.

Metzner, Manfred. "Ré Soupault, Neues Sehen, Neues Denken: Vom Bauhaus in die Welt." In *Ré Soupault: Die Fotografin der magischen Sekunde*, edited by M. Metzner, 7–18. Heidelberg: Wunderhorn, 2007.

Michael, Klaus. "Vor dem Café: Walter Benjamin und Siegfried Kracauer in Marseille." In *"Aber ein Sturm weht vom Paradies her": Texte zu Walter Benjamin*, edited by Michael Opitz and Erdmut Wizisla, 203–21. Leipzig: Reclam, 1992.

Moderegger, Johannes Christoph. *Modefotografie in Deutschland, 1929 bis 1955.* Norderstedt: Libri Books on Demand, 2000.

Moers, Ellen. *The Dandy: Brummell to Beerbohm.* New York: Viking P, 1960.

Mohrbutter, Alfred. *Das Kleid der Frau: Ein Beitrag zur künstlerischen Gestaltung des Frauen-Kleides.* Leipzig: A. Koch, 1904.

Moreck, Curt. *Sittengeschichte des Kinos.* Dresden: Paul Aretz, 1926.

MS. "Brigitte Helm." *Film dope* 24 (March 1982): 15–16.

Mülder, Inka. *Siegfried Kracauer — Grenzgänger zwischen Theorie und Literatur: Seine frühen Schriften, 1913–1933.* Stuttgart: J. B. Metzler, 1985.

Mülder-Bach, Inka. "Der Umschlag der Negativität: Zur Verschränkung von Phenomenologie, Geschichtsphilosophie und Filmästhetik in Siegfried Kracauers Metaphorik der 'Oberfläche.'" *Deutsche Vierteljahresschrift für Literaturwissenschaft und Geistesgeschichte* 61.2 (1987): 359–73.

Müller, Robert. "Die Frau aus Marmor: Brigitte Helm — ein deutscher Vamp." In *Schauspielen und Montage: Schauspielkunst im Film*, edited by Knut Hickethier, 15–30. St. Augustin, Germany: Gardez!-Verlag, 1999.

Mulvey, Laura. "Visual Pleasure and Narrative Cinema." *Screen* 16.3 (1975): 6–18.

Mundt, Barbara. "Entwicklung der Mode von 1919–1930." In Mundt, *Metropolen machen Mode*, 25–91.

———, ed. *Metropolen machen Mode.* Berlin: Dieter Reimer, 1977.

Mungenast, Ernst Moritz. *Asta Nielsen.* Stuttgart: W. Hädecke, 1928.

Münzer, Kurt. "Lebende Kleider." *Elegante Welt*, 4 March 1929: 56–59.

———. *Salon Rausch.* Leipzig: Josef Singer, 1928.

Murray, Bruce. *Film and the German Left in the Weimar Republic: From "Caligari" to "Kuhle Wampe."* Austin: U of Texas P, 1990.

Muthesius, Anna. *Das Eigenkleid der Frau.* Krefeld: Kramer & Baum, 1903.

Nagy, Lily von. "Die Frau im Pyjama." *Der Uhu*, March 1925, 48–52.

Nebel, Hete. "Ein Filmstar zaubert 'Mode.'" *Die junge Dame*, 18 June 1933, 8–9.

Nelken, Dinah. "Einsamkeit und Leichtsinn." In Rheinsberg, *Bubikopf: Aufbruch in den Zwanzigern*, 75–86.

———. *Die ganze Zeit meines Lebens: Geschichten, Gedichte, Berichte.* Frankfurt am Main: Fischer, 1983.

Nelson, Carolyn Christensen. Introduction to *A New Woman Reader: Fiction, Articles, and Drama of the 1890s*. Edited by C. C. Nelson, 1–7. Toronto: Broadview P, 2001.

Neumann, Carl, Curt Belling, and Hans-Walther Betz. *Film-"Kunst," Film-Kohn, Film-Korruption: Ein Streifzug durch vier Filmjahrzehnte.* Berlin: Hermann Scherping, 1937.

Neumeister, Sebastian. *Der Dichter als Dandy: Kafka, Baudelaire, Thomas Bernhard.* Munich: Wilhelm Fink, 1973.

Neustätter, Otto. *Die Reform der Frauenkleidung auf gesundheitlicher Grundlage.* Munich: Datterer, 1903.

Nietzsche, Friedrich. *Sämtliche Werke.* Edited by G. Colli and M. Montinari. Vol. 7. Berlin: de Gruyter, 1980.

Noever, Peter, ed. *Ernst Deutsch-Dryden: En vogue!* Vienna: MAK, Österreichisches Museum für angewandte Kunst, 2002.

Oakes, Guy. "The Problem of Women in Simmel's Theory of Culture." In Simmel, *On Women, Sexuality and Love*, 3–62.

Opitz, Michael, and Jörg Plath, eds. *"Genieße froh, was du nicht hast": Der Flaneur Franz Hessel.* Würzburg: Königshausen & Neumann, 1997.

Ortheil, Hanns-Josef. "Der lange Abschied vom Flaneur." *Merkur* 1 (1986): 30–48.

Pänke, Hedda. "Frauen als Mitarbeiter und Leser." In *Hundert Jahre Ullstein, 1877–1977*, 2:367–87. Berlin: Ullstein, 1977.

Panter, Peter. [Kurt Tucholsky]. "Auf dem Nachttisch." *Weltbühne* 28.5 (1932): 180.

Parrot, Nicole. *Mannequins.* New York: St. Martins P, 1981.

Parsons, Deborah L. *Streetwalking the Metropolis: Women, the City and Modernity.* Oxford: Oxford UP, 2000.

Petersen, Vibeke Rützou. *Women and Modernity in Weimar Germany: Reality and Representation in Popular Fiction.* New York: Berghahn, 2001.

Petro, Patrice. *Joyless Streets: Women and Melodramatic Representation of Weimar Germany.* Princeton, NJ: Princeton UP, 1989.

Peukert, Detlev J. K. *Die Weimarer Republik: Krisenjahre der klassischen Moderne.* Frankfurt am Main: Suhrkamp, 1987. In English: *The Weimar Republic: The Crisis of Classical Modernity.* Translated by Richard Deveson. New York: Hill & Wang, 1989.

Poiret, Paul. *Kings of Fashion: The Autobiography of Paul Poiret.* Translated by Stephen Haden Guest. Philadelphia, PA: J. B. Lippincott, 1931.

Pommeranz-Liedtke, G., ed. *Albert Schäfer-Ast, 1890–1951: Gedächtnis-Ausstellung.* Berlin: n.p., 1952.

Prendergast, Christopher. *Paris and the Nineteenth Century*. Oxford: Blackwell, 1992.

Purdy, Daniel. *The Tyranny of Elegance: Consumer Cosmopolitanism in the Era of Goethe*. Baltimore, MD: Johns Hopkins UP, 1998.

Puttnies, Hans, and Gary Smith. *Benjaminiana: Eine biographische Recherche*. Giessen: Anabas, 1991.

Rada, Uwe. "Die Rückkehr des Flaneurs." *taz*, 26 Jun. 1999, 21.

Ramin, Robert. *Brigitte Helm: Geschichte einer glücklichen Karriere*. Berlin: Scherl, 1933.

Rappaport, Erika Diane. *Shopping for Pleasure: Women and the Making of London's West End*. Princeton, NJ: Princeton UP, 2000.

Rasche, Adelheid. *Botschafterinnen der Mode: Star-Mannequins und Fotomodelle der Fünfziger Jahre in internationaler Modefotografie*. Berlin: Schwarzkopf & Schwarzkopf, 2001.

Reeh, Henrik. *Ornaments of the Metropolis: Siegfried Kracauer and Modern Urban Culture*. Cambridge, MA: MIT Press, 2004.

Renk, Elisabeth. *Ernst Lubitsch*. Reinbeck bei Hamburg: Rowohlt, 1992.

Rheinsberg, Anna. "'Alle Risiken auf sich nehmen und für alles bezahlen': Helen Grund." In *Zwischen Aufbruch und Verfolgung: Künstlerinnen der 20er und 30er Jahre*, edited by Denny Hirschbach and Sonia Nowoselsky, 158–64. Bremen: Zeichen + Spuren, 1993.

———, ed. *Bubikopf: Aufbruch in den Zwanzigern; Texte von Frauen*. Darmstadt: Luchterhand, 1988.

Rogowski, Christian. "From Ernst Lubitsch to Joe May: Challenging Kracauer's Demonology with Weimar Popular Film." In *Light Motives: German Popular Film in Perspective*, edited by Randall Halle and Margaret McCarthy, 1–23. Detroit, MI: Wayne State UP, 2003.

Roloff, Gerd. "Irmgard Keun: Vorläufiges zum Leben und Werk." *Amsterdamer Beiträge zur neueren Germanistik* 6 (1977): 45–47.

Roth, Joseph. "Fräulein Larissa, der Modereporter." *Frankfurter Zeitung*, 12 May 1929. Repr. in Joseph Roth, *Panoptikum: Gestalten und Kulissen*, 25–28. Cologne: Kiepenheuer & Witsch, 1983.

Runde, Sabine. *Welt ohne Alltag: Modegraphik der 20er Jahre von Annie Offterdingen*. Frankfurt am Main: Das Museum, 1986.

Schivelbusch, Wolfgang. *Intellektuellendämmerung: Zur Lage der Frankfurter Intelligenz in den zwanziger Jahren*. Frankfurt am Main: Insel, 1983.

Schlüpmann, Heide. "Die nebensächliche Frau: Geschlechtsdifferenz in Siegfried Kracauers Essayistik der zwanziger Jahre." *Feministische Studien* 1 (1993): 38–47.

Schmidt-Beil, Ada, ed. *Die Kultur der Frau: Lebenssymphonie der Frau des XX. Jahrhunderts*. Berlin-Frohnau: Verlag für Kultur und Wissenschaft, 1931.

Schönemann, Heide. *Fritz Lang: Filmbilder Vorbilder*. Berlin: Hentrich, 1992.

Schultze-Naumburg, Paul. *Die Kultur des weiblichen Körpers als Grundlage für die Frauenkleidung.* Jena: E. Diederichs, 1922.

Das Schwarze Korps, 21 Jan. 1937; 29 Sept. 1938.

Seeßlen, Georg. "Das Unterhaltungskino II: Das Spiel mit der Liebe; Aspekte der deutschen Stummfilmkomödie." In *Die Perfektionierung des Scheins: Das Kino der Weimarer Republik im Kontext der Künste*, edited by Harro Segeberg, 95–110. Munich: Wilhelm Fink, 2000.

Severit, Frauke. *Ea von Allesch: Wenn aus Frauen Menschen werden; Eine Biographie.* Wiesbaden: DUV, 1999.

Seydel, Renate, and Allan Hagedorff, eds. *Asta Nielsen: Ihr Leben in Fotodokumenten, Selbstzeugnissen und zeitgenössischen Betrachtungen.* Munich: Universitas, 1981.

Siemsen, Hans. "Die Geliebte Roswolskys." *Die Weltbühne* 47 (1921): 530.

Simmel, Georg. "Female Culture." In *Georg Simmel: On Women, Sexuality and Love*, 70–71.

———. "Die Mode." In *Philosophische Kultur*, 31–64. Potsdam: Gustav Kiepenheuer, 1911.

———. *On Women, Sexuality and Love.* Edited and translated by Guy Oakes. New Haven, CT: Yale UP, 1984.

———. *Philosophische Kultur.* Potsdam: Gustav Kiepenheuer, 1911.

———. *Simmel on Culture: Selected Writings.* Edited by David Frisby and Mike Featherstone. London: SAGE Publications, 1997.

———. *Wirthschaft und Mode: Ein Beitrag zur Theorie der modernen Bedarfsgestaltung.* Wiesbaden: J. F. Bergmann, 1902. Reprinted in *Die Listen der Mode*, edited by Silvia Bovenschen, 81–104. Frankfurt am Main: Suhrkamp, 1986. In English: "Economy and Fashion: A Theoretical Contribution on the Formation of Modern Consumer Demand." In *The Rise of Fashion: A Reader*, edited by Daniel Leonhard Purdy, translated by Kelly Barry, 310–16. Minneapolis: U of Minnesota P, 2004.

Spener, Karl. *Die jetzige Frauenkleidung und Vorschläge zu ihrer Verbesserung: Mit 10 Abbildungen im Text.* Berlin: n.p., 1897.

Speyer, Wilhelm. *Ich geh aus und du bleibst da: Der Roman eines Mannequins.* Berlin: Ullstein, 1930.

Stamm, Brigitte. "Berliner Modemacher der 30er Jahre." *Der Bär: Jahrbuch des Vereins für die Geschichte Berlins* 38/39 (1989/90): 189–203.

Starke, Ottomar. "Tausend Lockungen hinter Glass: Zur Physiologie des Schaufensters." *Scherl's Magazin*, Jun. 1930, 606–9.

Steele, Valerie. *Paris Fashion: A Cultural History.* Oxford: Oxford UP, 1988. 2nd revised ed., Oxford: Berg, 1998.

Stein, Joseph. "The New Woman and the Decadent Dandy." *Dalhousie Review* 55.1 (1975): 54–62.

Stern, Carola. *Die Sache, die man Liebe nennt: Das Leben der Fritzi Massary.* Berlin: Rowohlt, 1998.

Stern, Norbert. *Mode und Kultur.* Dresden: Lemm & Weiss, 1915.

———. *Die Weltpolitik der Weltmode.* Stuttgart: Deutsche Verlags-Anstalt, 1915.

Stewart, Mary Lynn, with Nancy Janovicek. "Slimming the Female Body? Re-evaluating Dress, Corsets, and Physical Culture in France, 1890–1930." *Fashion Theory* 5.2 (2001): 173–94.

Stokes, John. "Wilde the Journalist." In *The Cambridge Companion to Oscar Wilde,* edited by Peter Raby, 69–79. Cambridge, UK: Cambridge UP, 1997.

Stratz, Carl Heinrich. *Frauenkleidung und ihre natürliche Entwicklung.* Stuttgart: F. Enke, 1900.

Suttner, M[arie] von. "Berliner Modenrevüen: Sechs Poiret Kleider der Modenschau bei Herrmann Gerson." *Illustrierte Frauenzeitung,* 1 December 1911.

Swarzenski, Marie. "Warenhausverkäuferin." *Frankfurter Zeitung* 5, 6, and 7 Apr. 1929, 1.

Sykora, Katharina. "Die Neue Frau: Ein Alltagsmythos der zwanziger Jahre." In *Die Neue Frau: Herausforderung für die Bildmedien der Zwanziger Jahre,* edited by Katharina Sykora, Annette Dorgerloh, Doris Noell-Rumpeltes, and Ada Raev, 9–24. Marburg: Jonas Verlag, 1993.

———. *Unheimliche Paarungen: Androidenfaszination und Geschlecht in der Fotografie.* Cologne: Walther König, 1999.

Der Tagesspiegel, "Chronist des Chic: Das Stadtmuseum zeigt eine Hommage an den Modezeichner Gerd Hartung," 7 Jul. 2004.

Tautz, Birgit. "Fashionable Details: Narration in an Eighteenth-Century Travel Account." *Germanic Review* 72.3 (1997): 201–12.

Tergit, Gabriele. *Atem einer anderen Welt: Berliner Reportagen.* Edited by Jens Brüning. Frankfurt am Main: Suhrkamp, 1994.

———. "Modenschau." *Berliner Tageblatt* 20 Apr. 1927. Reprinted in Gabriele Tergit, *Frauen und andere Ereignisse: Publizistik und Erzählungen von 1915 bis 1970,* edited by Jens Brüning, 99–102. Berlin: Das Neue Berlin, 2001.

Tester, Keith, ed. *The Flâneur.* London: Routledge, 1994.

Thal, Johanna. "Empire und 1905." *Die Dame,* October 1929, no. 1, 84.

———. "Kommt ein Modeumschwung?" *Die Dame,* August 1922, no. 22, 55.

———. "Kritisches über die Mode," *Die Dame,* November 1921, no. 4, 13.

———. "Modische und unmodische Beobachtungen." *Die Dame,* January 1924, no. 8, 8–9.

———. "Puppen und Frauen." *Die Dame,* December 1919, no. 6, 7–8.

Tieck, Polly. "Das Berliner Mannequin," *Der Querschnitt* 5.11 (1925): 985–86. Reprinted in *Berlin im "Querschnitt,"* edited by Rolf-Peter Baacke, 99–101. Berlin: Quadriga, 2001.

Todorow, Almut. *Das Feuilleton der "Frankfurter Zeitung" in der Weimarer Republik: Zur Grundlegung einer rhetorischen Medienforschung.* Tübingen: Max Niemeyer, 1996.

Todorow, Almut. "Frauen im Journalismus der Weimarer Republik." *Internationales Archiv für Sozialgeschichte der deutschen Literatur* 16.2 (1991): 84–103.

———. " 'Wollten die Eintagsfliegen in den Rang höherer Insekten aufsteigen?' Die Feuilletonkonzeption der *Frankfurter Zeitung* während der Weimarer Republik im redaktionellen Selbstverständnis." *Deutsche Vierteljahrsschrift für Literaturwissenschaft und Geistesgeschichte* 62 (1988): 697–740.

Töteberg, Michael. "Immer Ärger mit Brigitte. Ein Star muckt auf: Der Fall Brigitte Helm." In *Das Ufa-Buch: Kunst und Krisen, Stars und Regisseure, Wirtschaft und Politik*, edited by Hans-Michael Bock and Michael Töteberg, 316–18. Frankfurt am Main: Zweitausendeins, 1992.

———. "Reklame! Reklame! Reklame!" In *Das Ufa-Plakat: Filmpremieren, 1918 bis 1943*, edited by Peter Mänz and Christian Maryska, 12–16. Heidelberg: Edition Braus, 1998.

Troy, Nancy J. *Couture Culture: A Study of Modern Art and Fashion*. Cambridge, MA: MIT Press, 2002.

Truffaut, François. Introduction to *Jules et Jim*, by Henri-Pierre Roché. Translated by Patrick Evans. New York: Marion Boyars, 1993.

Tucholsky, Kurt. *Gesammelte Werke: 1925–1928*. Edited by Mary Gerold-Tucholsky and Fritz J. Raddatz. Reinbek bei Hamburg: Rowohlt, 1960.

Turszinsky, Walter. "Der Ein-Stunden-Film" (1912). In *Kinometerdichter: Karrierepfade im Kaiserreich zwischen Stadtforschung und Stummfilm*, edited by Dietmar Jazbinsek. http://bibliothek.wz-berlin.de/pdf/2000/ii00-505.pdf.

Der Uhu, "Der siegreiche Bubikopf," December 1925, 89.

Ullstein, Hermann. *The Rise and Fall of the House of Ullstein*. New York: Simon & Schuster, 1943.

Ullstein Berichte. January 1927, July 1929, and January 1931.

Ungeheuer, Barbara. "Helen Hessel." In *Femmes Fatales: 13 Annäherungen*, edited by Ines Böhner, 71–80. Mannheim: Bollmann, 1996.

Vallentin, Frieda. "Ich muß zu Gerson: Erinnerungen an das Modehaus." *Gerson-Brevier* vol 2, Heft 3 (1929): 44–49.

van de Velde, Henry. *Die künstlerische Hebung der Frauentracht*. Krefeld: Kramer & Baum, 1900.

van de Velde, Maria. *Album moderner, nach Künstlerentwürfen ausgeführter Damenkleider, ausgestellt auf der großen allgemeinen Ausstellung für Bekleidungswesen in Krefeld*. Düsseldorf: F. Wolfrum, 1900.

Veblen, Thorstein. "Dress as an Expression of Pecuniary Culture." In *The Theory of the Leisure Class*, 103–15. New York: Macmillan, 1899.

Der Verlag Ullstein zum Weltreklamekongress: Berlin 1929. Berlin: Ullstein, 1929.

Vischer, Friedrich. "Fashion and Cynicism." In *The Rise of Fashion: A Reader*, edited and with an introduction by Daniel L. Purdy, 153–62. Minneapolis: U of Minnesota P, 2004.

———. *Mode und Cynismus: Beiträge zur Kenntnis unserer Culturformen und Sittenbegriffe*. Stuttgart: K. Wittwer, 1879.

Vogue. German edition, 9 May 1928.

Vollmer, Hartmut. "Der Flaneur in einer 'quälenden Doppelwelt': Über den wiederentdeckten Dichter Franz Hessel." *Neue Deutsche Hefte* 34 (1987): 734–35.

Volz, Robert, and Ferdinand Tönnies, eds. *Reichshandbuch der deutschen Gesellschaft: Das Handbuch der Persönlichkeiten in Wort und Bild*. 2 vols. Berlin: Deutscher Wirtschaftsverlag, 1930.

von der Lühe, Irmela. *Erika Mann: Eine Biographie*. Frankfurt am Main: Campus, 1993.

Vorwärts, "Eine von uns? Wir diskutieren über Gilgi," 18 October 1932.

Vromen, Suzanne. "Georg Simmel and the Cultural Dilemma of Women." *History of European Ideas* 8 (1987): 563–79.

Wagner, Gretel. "Die Mode in Berlin." In *Berlin en vogue: Berliner Mode in der Photographie*, edited by F. C. Gundlach and Uli Richter, 113–46. Berlin: Wasmuth, 1993.

———. "'Die Nacht der schönsten Roben': Modische Eindrücke vom Berliner Presseball." *Der Bär von Berlin: Jahrbuch des Vereins für die Geschichte Berlins* (2000): 81–96.

———. "Zeitschriften à la mode." In *Europäische Moderne: Buch und Graphik aus Berliner Kunstverlagen, 1890–1933*, edited by Lutz S. Malke, Michael Hemming, and Christoph Jobst, 191–204. Berlin: Dietrich Reimer Verlag, 1989.

Waidenschlager, Christine. "Aus den Anfängen der Berliner Konfektion." In Waidenschlager and Gustavus, *Berliner Chic: Mode von 1820 bis 1990*, 11–24.

———. "Berliner Mode der zwanziger Jahre zwischen Couture und Konfektion." In Waidenschlager and Gustavus, *Mode der 20er Jahre*, 20–31.

Waidenschlager, Christine, and Christa Gustavus, eds. *Berliner Chic: Mode von 1820 bis 1990*. Berlin: Stiftung Stadtmuseum Berlin, 2001.

———. *Mode der 20er Jahre*. Berlin: Wasmuth, 1993.

Wallach, Edith. "Kunsthandwerk und Mode." *Die Dame*, March 1920, no. 11, 29.

Waller, Margaret. "Disembodiment as a Masquerade: Fashion Journalists and Other 'Realist' Observers in Directory Paris." *Esprit Créateur* 37.1 (Spring 1997): 44–54.

Ward, Janet. *Weimar Surfaces: Urban Visual Culture in 1920s Germany*. Berkeley: U of California P, 2001.

Weber, Marianne. "Das alte und das neue Frauenideal." In Schmidt-Beil, *Die Kultur der Frau*, 17–28.

———. "Die Frau und die objektive Kultur." (1913) In *Frauenfragen und Frauengedanken: Gesammelte Aufsätze*, 95–133. Tübingen: Verlag von T. C. B. Mohr: 1919.

Wedekind, Kadidja. "Gilgi — eine von uns." *Der Querschnitt* 12.1 (1932): 7.

Weigel, Sigrid. "Frauen und Öffentlichkeit: Von den Um- und Irrwegen des Weibes aus den männlichen Räumen zum Ort der Frau." In *Sind das noch Damen? Vom gelehrten Frauenzimmer-Journal zum feministischen Journalismus*, edited by Ruth-Esther Geiger and Sigrid Weigel, 7–12. Munich: Frauenbuchverlag, 1981.

Weiskopf, F. C. "Unterhaltungsliteratur." *Die neue Weltbühne* 46 (1937): 1460–62.

Westphal, Uwe. *Berliner Konfektion und Mode, 1836–1939: Die Zerstörung einer Tradition*. 2nd ed. Berlin: Edition Hentrick, 1992.

White, Palmer. *Poiret*. New York: Clarkson N. Potter, 1973.

Wilke, Charlotte. "Mode, Frauentyp und Zeitgeist." In Schmidt-Beil, *Die Kultur der Frau*, 36–40.

Willkomm, Aenne. "Metropolis-Moden." *Neue Berliner Zeitung, das 12-Uhr Blatt*, 7 Jan. 1927.

Willner, Gustav. "Das Tagewerk der Abteilungen." In *Fünfzig Jahre Ullstein, 1877–1927*, edited by Kurt Korff, 329–362. Berlin: Ullstein, 1927.

Wilson, Elizabeth. "The Invisible *Flâneur*." *The New Left Review* 191 (1992): 93–113.

———. "The Invisible *Flâneur*." In *Postmodern Cities and Spaces*, edited by Sophie Watson and Katherine Gibson, 59–79. Oxford, UK: Blackwell, 1995.

Winter, Helmut. "Pockennarbig von Fallen: Eine kleine Geschichte der Übersetzungen von Nabokovs 'Lolita.'" *Frankfurter Allgemeine Zeitung*, 27 January 1990, 28.

Witte, Bernd. *Walter Benjamin: An Intellectual Biography*. Translated by James Rolleston. Detroit, MI: Wayne State UP, 1991.

Wittkowski, Erwin. *Die Berliner Damenkonfektion*. Leipzig: Gloeckner, 1928.

Wolff, Charlotte. *Hindsight*. London: Quartet Books, 1980.

Wolff, Janet. "The Artist and the *Flâneur*: Rodin, Rilke, and Gwen John in Paris." In Tester, *The Flâneur*, 111–37.

———. "The Invisible *Flâneuse*: Women and the Literature of Modernity." *Theory, Culture and Society* 2.3 (1985): 37–46.

Wurst, Karin. *Fabricating Pleasure: Fashion, Entertainment, and Cultural Consumption in Germany, 1780–1830*. Detroit, MI: Wayne State UP, 2005.

Zipes, Jack, ed. *Fairy Tales and Fables from Weimar Days*. Translated by Jack Zipes. Hanover, NH: UP of New England, 1989.

Zobl, Angele, ed. *Von Wien bis Hollywood: Die Blüte der Mode-Illustration und Werbegrafik: Ernst Deutsch-Dryden (1887–1938) und Max H. Lang (1901–1984)*. Salzburg: Verlag für Kunst und Kultur, 1990.

Zur Mühlen, Hermynia. "Bernice McFadden macht Karriere." 1936. Reprinted in Rheinsberg, *Bubikopf*, 106–11.

———. *Fahrt ins Licht: 66 Stationen*. Leipzig: Ludwig Nath, 1936.

Index

Page numbers for illustrations are in boldface.

Abwege (film), 131, 139
8-Uhr-Abendlatt, 77 n. 8, 198
actresses: as models, 113–41; as suppliers of own costumes, 120. *See also* film stars
Adorno, Theodor, 45 n. 22, 46 n. 39; on Helen Grund, 86
advertising: and fashion, 117, 120–21, 143 n. 18, 156–57, 162–63 (*see also* fashion shows); through fashion farces, 126–27; through film, 141; in the popular press, 52, 54, 73, 113
aesthetics, 74; changing, 10–11, 18 n. 27; and commerce, 118; of the feuilleton, 93; of *flânerie*, 32; gendered concepts of, 184–85; modernist, 117; *vs.* profits, 129; women's, 85
Allesch, Ea von, 1, 42 n. 4, 192
Alraune (film), 131, 134, 137, 139, 148 n. 67
Alsberg, Henriette. *See* Alsen, Ola
Alsen, Ola, 21–23, **22**, 58, 129–30, 197–98
Altenloh, Emilie, 142 n. 4
angst: male, 35, 37, 68–69, 106 n. 26, 151–52; modern, 2
Anita. *See* Daniel, Anita
"Anti-Fashion-Show League," 145 n. 34
Apfel, Karl, 92, 106 n. 29
Arden, Elizabeth, 181
Arme Maria: Eine Warenhaus-Geschichte (film), 146 n. 43
Arnold, Victor, 146 n. 43
artificiality. *See* surface

artists. *See* fashion illustrators
Asphalt (film), 156
Assing, Ottilie, 105 n. 19
audiences: as consumers, 51–52; gendered, 37, 50–51, 85, 92–93, 114, 118, 137–39, 151–52; of live mannequins, 167 n. 18; power of, 40–41; and social class, 50–51, 114, 126
authorship: significance of (and individuality), 41–42; women and, 91
automobiles, 98–99, 181, 186

Balzac and the *flâneur*, 25–26, 29, 43 n. 9
Barthes, Roland, 83 n. 58
Basch, Felix, 114
Baudelaire, 29; and fashion, 26–27, 38, 39; and the *flâneur*, 25–26, 32, 40, 43 nn. 10–11, 166 n. 7; and modernity, 26–27; on women as commodity, 166 n. 6
Baum, Vicki, 56, 67; in *Die Dame*, 38; literary prominence of, 81 n. 37; memoir, 56–57, 78 n. 19; at Ullstein House, 58
Baum, Vicki, works by: *Der große Ausverkauf*, 158–59, 168 n. 24; *stud.chem. Helene Willfüer*, 172
Beardsley, Aubrey, 35
beauty, feminine, 39, 74; changing ideas of, 151–52, 162–63, 165, 193
Becker, Max (designer salon), 148 n. 62
Beckersachs, Karl, 128–29

Beckmann, Anna, 175
Beerbohm, Max, 35, 49 n. 75
Behrendt, Hans, 169 n. 30
Behrens, Peter, 58, 199
Benjamin, Dora, 56, 103 n. 6. *See also* Kellner, Dora Sophie
Benjamin, Walter, 27, 37; on Baudelaire, 166 n. 6; on *flânerie*, 28–30, 44–45 n. 22, 44 n. 21; on Helen Grund, 86; and Siegfried Kracauer, 45 n. 29; on modernity, 29–30, 38; review of Hessel's *Spazieren in Berlin*, 28. *See also* Kellner, Dora Sophie
Berlin: as center of fashion, 1, 4–5; and the *flâneur*, 28–33, 44 n. 18; in the 1920s, 28–33; social life of, 50–51
Berlin, Symphony of a Big City (film), 35, 121–22
Berliner Abendzeitung, 77 n. 8
Berliner Illustrirte Zeitung (BIZ), 52–53, 78 n. 12
Berliner Lokal-Anzeiger, 77 n. 8
Berliner Morgenpost, 52–53
Berliner Morgenzeitung, 77 n. 8
Berliner Tageblatt, 55, 77 n. 8, 197–98
Berliner Zeitung am Mittag, 52–53, 200
Berlins Modenblatt, 201
Das Blatt der Hausfrau: circulation figures, 78 n. 14; compared with *Die Dame*, 54; history of, 53; and the pattern business, 54
Der Blusenkönig (film), 124–27, 146 n. 43
body politics, 74, 194
Boehn, Max von, 16 n. 14, 71
Bois, Curt, 122, 123–24, 145 n. 37, **164**
Börne, Ludwig, 88
"Boulevardfilme," 130
boulevardiers. *See* dandy; *flâneur*
Boveri, Margret, 80 n. 30, 106 n. 29
Brecht, Bertolt, 79 n. 21
Brenner, Vanna, 37
Brentano, Bernard von, 76 n. 1, 85, 174–75

Brück, Christa Anita, 172
Brummell, Beau, 43 n. 11, 49 n. 75
Bubikopf. *See* haircut
Bücher, Karl, 92–93
Bud, Elsa Maria, 164–65
Bud, Elsa Maria, works by: *Bravo, Musch!*, 164–65
Bunsen, Marie von, 39, 67–68, 198
Bunzel, Gerda, 58, 62, 66, 80, 197
Burg, Jacques, 119, 124

camera work, 126–27, 135, 137, 139, 141. *See also* photography
capitalism: and perception, 31; vs. aesthetics, 129. *See also* consumer culture
cars. *See* automobiles
Chanel (designer house), 72, 143 n. 18
cinema. *See* film
cities. *See* urban environment
class, social: boundaries, 76; and fashion, 40–42, 53–54, 72, 94, 157–59, 170 n. 46, 189 n. 13; and fashion farce, 125–26; in *Gilgi*, 173, 174–77. *See also under* women
comedy, 119, 122, 124, 145 n. 36, 147 n. 46. *See also* fashion farce
consumer culture, 82 n. 50, 128, 156–57, 160, 181; classes of consumers, 53–54; deception in, 125; and film, 114, 116–17, 142–43 n. 13; and the New Woman, 36; orchestrated, 73; rise of, 8; and women, 34–35, 166 n. 6. *See also* audiences; women
corsets, 10, 17 n. 27, 71
cosmetics, 181, 189 n. 13, 197
costume: in *Metropolis*, 149 n. 71; and stardom, 143 n. 13; traditional, 7, 16 n. 16. *See also* fashion
costume designers, 80 n. 36. *See also* Herzog, Elsa; Reinecke, Vally; Willkomm, Aenne
"costume tales," 148 n. 63
couture salon. *See* designer salon
creativity: changing concepts of, 182–87; gendered, 185–87. *See also under* women

cross-dressing, 122, 124, 145 n. 37
culture: as gendered, 9; "high" *vs.* "low," 77 n. 6; *vs.* civilization, 31. See also consumer culture; urban environment

Die Dame, 12, **59**, 60, **61**, 63, **64**, **65**, 75; and authorship, 41; compared with *Das Blatt der Hausfrau*, 54; competition with, 55, 79 n. 19; and diversity, 74–75; fashion layouts of, 59, 61; fashion staff of, 58–62, **60**; history of, 53; literary quality of, 55, 79 n. 21; as medium open to women, 37–38; under National Socialism, 100–101; politics of, 66–67; put down, 82–83 n. 52; readership of, 54–55; and the rise of fashion journalism, 38–42; technology and, 55. See also Ullstein House
Die Dame, der Teufel und die Probiermamsell (film), 127–28
Der Damenschneider, 119
dandy, 43 n. 11; defined, 11–12; English, 35; female, 41–42; and female fashion journalists, 40; and mass society, 40; studies of the, 49 nn. 74, 75. See also Balzac; Baudelaire; Flaubert
Daniel, Anita, 39, **65**, 67, 74–76, 81 n. 37, 198
Dawes Plan, 2–3
democratization, 5, 40–41; through fashion, 190 n. 23; through film, 126, 131, 133; of social life, 2
department stores: and advertising in newsreels, 124; and designer salons, 121; fashion shows in, 80 n. 34, 129; and mannequins, 153–55, 159; and mass produced fashion, 4, 73; and patterns, 54; as setting for fashion farces, 13, 123; and urban environment, 26, 34. See also display windows
designer house. See designer salon
designer salon: and actresses, 120, 148 n. 62; and fashion farces, 126,

129, 137; German, 79 n. 20; and mannequins, 80 n. 34, 153–55, 160, 165, 167 n. 19. See also department stores; individual salons listed
designer store. See designer salon
"Deulig-Wochenschau," 124, 137. See also newsreels
Deutsch, Ernst. See Dryden, Ernst
Die deutsche Elite, 55
Dietrich, Marlene, 80 n. 36
directrice (chief dressmaker), 97, 126
display windows, 1, 13, 89, 151–57, 158–60, 171, 183; live mannequins in, 156–57, **157**, 159, 165, 167 nn. 18–19
Dittrich, Gertrud, 179
Döblin, Alfred, 79 n. 21
dolls, 13, 69, 153, 165
Doucet (designer salon), 72
Dr. Mabuse, der Spieler (film), 114, 142 n. 8
Drecoll (designer salon), 113, 142 n. 2, 144 n. 25
Drei Mannequins (film), 130
Dresler, Adolf, 80 n. 29
dress-reform movement, 10–11, 17 nn. 26–27, 24, 35
Dryden, Ernst, 66, 74, **75**, 80–81 n. 36
Durchreise (semi-annual trade fair), 120, 145 n. 34, 147 n. 46
Durieux, Tilla, 120

economics, and fashion, 7–8, 114, 176–77
Edschmid, Kasimir, 87, 170 n. 44
Eichberg, Richard, 122, 137
Eine von uns (film), 131, 137–39, 140–41, 161, 172–73
Elegante Welt, 55, 113, 128, 130–31, **136**, 139, **140**, 181, 197, 199; Asta Nielsen interviewed in, 113
Elias, Julie, 62, 88, 198–99
emancipation *vs.* misogyny, 194
"Emelka-Woche," 124. See also newsreels
Endell, August, 192

entertainment, public: demand for, 53, 124; fashion and, 121, 156–57; and the feuilleton, 92; and the *flâneur*, 27; and the mass press, 44 n. 17. *See also* audiences
eroticism, 114; in fashion farce, 125–26; in *Metropolis*, 133–34. *See also* legs; stockings
escapism, film as, 116, 122, 171
Eva. *See* Allesch, Ea von
Eva, Evi, 128–29

fabric shortage, 67–68
fabrics, synthetic, 1, 190 n. 23
Fallada, Hans, 171, 174, 175
Fascism, 175. *See also* National Socialism
fashion: and aesthetics, 10, 18 n. 27, 27, 67–68; changing status of, 192; and consumerism, 8; daytime *vs.* evening, 74; defined, 5, 7; democratization of, 192; as democratizing, 120–21; as distinctly women's sphere, 9, 38–39, 179–80; and economics, 7–8; as escapist pleasure, 19, 125–26, 128; as everyday experience, 153; fiction and, 14; as field of serious intellectual investigation, 194; and film, 13, 113–18, 125, 194, 203–4; as folly, 192; and foreign influence, 3–5, 16 n. 16, 72, 100, 193; and health, 10–11; and historical necessity, 68; and individuality, 7; as instrument of oppression, 11; as interdisciplinary, 5; key to development of publishing, 53; male perspective on, 7–11, 71–72; masculinization of, 68–69, 193; and mass media, 2, 192; mass-produced, 1, 4; and the metropolis, 1, 9; and modernity, 1–2, 7–11, 26–27, 53; and nationalism, 16 n. 16, 17 n. 27, 100–102; opposing views of, 174–75; post-1918, 68–70; post-1930, 193; and practicality, 68–69, 72; as practice, 5, 6, 11, 193; as sociological phenomenon, 8–11, 9, 42 n. 4; spectators *vs.* practitioners, 38–39; and sports, 35; as surface value, 6–7; symbolic use of, 181–82, 192; and television, 194; as theme, 122; trends in the 1920s, 76; 20th-century continuity of, 3; *vs.* high art, 116–17; *vs.* traditional costume, 7, 16 n. 16, 71–72. *See also haute couture*
fashion and travelogue, 106 n. 26
fashion competitions, 1, 11, 13, 31, 115, 135–38; international, 165
fashion contests. *See* fashion competitions
fashion debate, course of, 74
fashion design, 41, 58–59, 79 n. 20; as prestigious male occupation, 16 n. 19; and social principles, 94. *See also* fashion illustrators; Green, Renate; Reich, Lilly; Reinecke, Vally
fashion discourse, 18th-century, 106 n. 26
fashion editors. *See* fashion journalists, female
fashion farce, 122–41; defined, 13; as democratizing influence, 123; mixed message of, 130; pre-Weimar, 122–27; standard characters in, 123–24; staples of, 125–26; Weimar, 127–30
fashion house. *See* designer salon
fashion illustrators, 80 n. 28, 197; women as, 38, 48 n. 67, 58, 62, 66. *See also* Bunzel, Gerda; Dryden, Ernst; Fiedler, Petra; Goerke, Hanna; Haase-Werkenthin, Julie; Hartung, Gerd; Mohr, Erica; Nathan, Steffie; Riederer, Marietta; Sparkuhl, Martha
fashion industry, French. *See haute couture*
fashion industry, German: history of, 4–5, 15 n. 7; institutional reorganization, 109 n. 52; and journalism, 72; and National Socialism, 123–24; in the 1920s, 151, 154; and salon Gerson, 144 n. 29
fashion journalism: and class, 40–42; competing magazines, 55; early days

of, 21, 42 n. 4; foreign influence on, 77–78 n. 10; importance of, 21–24; as mirror, 50–51, 55; overview of, 77 n. 3; the rise of, 38–42; as springboard to literary career, 84; as women's public sphere, 50–51
fashion journalists, female, 56–66; affinity with the *flâneur* and the New Woman, 11–12, 24–25; as authors and creators, 69–70 (*see also Mode-Notizen*); as authors and models, 62; biographies, 197–201; changing attitudes toward, 91; collective cultural portrait of, 58–67; and dandyism, 40; as intellectuals, 42; as media celebrities, 21; as models, 41; relative prestige of, 67; rise of, 21–24; as script writers, 129; self-presentation of, 97–98; social history, 80 n. 29; and stardom, 67; studies on, 42 n. 4; women as, 189–90 n. 19. *See also* Alsen, Ola; Bunsen, Marie von; Daniel, Anita; Elias, Julie; Goetz, Ruth; Grund, Helen; Herzog, Elsa; Kaul, Stephanie; Nagy, Lily von; Rathaus, Katharina von; Reinecke, Vally; Riederer, Marietta; Thal, Johanna; Wedekind-Pariselle, Anna Paula; Wilke, Charlotte
fashion journalists, male, 21, 71–72, 82–83 n. 52, 101; and the *flâneur*, 27
fashion models, 59, 61; as changing profession, 62; status of, 80 n. 34. *See also* mannequins
fashion parades. *See* fashion shows
fashion photography. *See* photography
fashion plays: development of in Paris and London, 143 n. 21; emergence of, 119–20; as theatrical genre, 143–44 n. 23. *See also* fashion farce
fashion press. *See* fashion journalism; Ullstein House
fashion queens, 135–38. *See also* Jovanowitsch, Sonja; Offermann, Asta; Zimmermann, Hilde
fashion reporters. *See* fashion journalists
fashion salons, **123**, **155**; configuration of, 121. *See also* designer salons
fashion shows, **157**; and fashion journalism, 59, 66; and film, 13, 115, 122–24, 126–30, 133, 135–39, 141, 145 n. 38, 146 n. 40; history of, 73, 118–22, 143 n. 17; mannequins in, 80 n. 34, 152–53; in newsreels, 124, 137, 145 n. 39, 146 n. 40; as performance, 160; postwar, in Berlin, 201; at the races, 118–19. *See also* department stores; display windows; Press Ball
fashion store. *See* designer salon
fashion tableaux, 135, 149 n. 72
fashion vignettes. *See Mode-Notizen*
female body as spectacle. *See* women, objectification of
femininity: concepts of, 3; demonization of, 133–34; and Franz Hessel, 103 n. 8; negative perception of, 152; return to, 74; vs. practicality, 74. *See also* women
feminism, early 20th-century, 179
feminist scholars, on *flânerie*, 33–35
femmes fatales, 131
Feuchtwanger, Lion, 79 n. 21
feuilleton as genre, 12, 27, 84–85, 92–94, 102 n. 2
fiction and fashion. *See under* fashion
Fiedler, Petra, 58–59, **59**, 62, **64**, 66, 199
film: the canon, 122; and capitalism, 116–17, 125; and the city, 35; and consumer culture, 115–18, 142–43 n. 13; as democratizing influence, 116–17, 126, 131, 133; early German, 145 n. 36, 147 n. 46; as escapism, 116; as fashion display, 113–14, 124, 131; increasing length of, 124; and photojournalism, 53; practical application of, 118; as visual experience, 116–18. *See also* specific titles of films; visual culture
film stars, 21, 50–51, 62, 141, 142–43 n. 13, 194. *See also* actresses
Film und Frau, 169 n. 41

Film-Kurier, 113, 129, 147 n. 54, 148 n. 55, 148 n. 56, 148 n. 58, 149 nn. 75–76, 150 n. 83
films, German fashion, 1910–1940, listed, 203–4
Die Filmwoche, 113
Die Firma heiratet (film), 124–27, 146 n. 43
Flake, Otto, 82–83 n. 52
flânerie; aesthetic pleasures of (*see* Hessel); as art form, 33; defined, 11–12; female, 35, 84, 184–85 (*see also flâneuse*); ideological implications of (*see* Benjamin, Walter; Kracauer, Siegfried); imaginary, 35; male, 11–12, 32–33; and modernization, 30; return of, 27–33; as sociological and journalistic practice, 30–32. *See also under* Benjamin, Walter; urban environment
flâneur, 24–25, 25–33; and aestheticism, 32, 46 n. 42; as author, 84; as authority, 183; as badly dressed, 25; and Berlin, 28; and the city, 25–26, 43 n. 10, 89; and class, 40; defined, 25–26, 28–29, 34; economic status of, 27, 30; evolution of, 45 n. 22; female, 24–25; and the feuilleton, 85; and Marxism, 30; metamorphoses of, 25–26; and modernity, 25; as nostalgic, 32–33, 46 n. 42; and politics, 32; redemptive qualities of, 28; return of the, 28, 44 n. 18; roles of, 25, 27–28, 31; vs. dandy, 43 n. 11; vs. *flâneuse*, 89, 99; as walker, 32–33. *See also flânerie*; *flâneuse*
flâneur-as-dandy, 11–12, 24
flâneuse: defined, 12; and the feuilleton, 85; as impossible, 33–34; vs. *flâneur*, 89, 99; as word, 34. *See also* New Woman, the
Flaubert and the *flâneur*, 43 n. 10
Fleck, Jakob, 139
Fleck, Luise, 139
Fleißer, Marieluise, 56

Franke, Ingeborg, 175
Frankfurter Zeitung, 87, 106 n. 29, 106 n. 30, 148 n. 57, 148 n. 67, 157–58; attitude toward women and fashion, 91–92
freedom of choice. *See* individuality
Freksa, Friedrich, 71–72
French fashion, influence in Berlin, 121. *See also* Chanel; Doucet; Drecoll; *haute couture*; Lanvin; Paquin; Paris; Patou; Poiret, Paul; Rouff; Worth
Freudenberg, Hermann, 140 n. 84
Freudenberg, Philipp, and salon Gerson, 121, 144 n. 29
Friedländer, Regina (designer salon), 79 n. 20
Für die Frau, 55, 94; and Helen Grund, 87, 94, **95**, 96, 98–99
Der Fürst von Pappenheim (film), 122–24, **123**, 137, 163, **164**; critics on, 145 n. 35, 145 n. 37

Galeen, Henrik, 131
garment industry. *See* fashion industry
Die Gartenlaube, 77 n. 8
Gebrandt, Marie, 200
Gelbstern (film), 119, 124, 125–26, 148 n. 55
Die Geliebte Roswolskys (film), 114, **115**
gender: and appearance, 76; competition, 35, 70; and fashion farce, 125–26; identity, 74; and narrative technique, 89–90; and observation and perception, 88; perspectives, 51, 106 n. 26; roles, 2, 7, 8, 10–11, 11–12, 16 n. 19, 32–33, 33–34, 39, 46 n. 43, 70, 72, 76
gender roles: changing, 182–87; *flâneur* vs. New Woman, 24; in journalism, 58, 66 (*see also* Ullstein House)
genres, literary, 27; *Modeplauderei*, 93. *See also* feuilleton; *Mode-Notizen*; travelogue
Gerla, Alois, 119
Gerson (designer salon), 15 n. 6, 79 n. 20, 135, 141, 149 n. 74; costumes

for *Der Fürst von Pappenheim*, 122;
history of, 15 n. 6; and Poiret, 121;
Poiret as trendsetter, 121
Gerson, Herrmann (founder of the
  designer salon), 4, 144 n. 29
Gerstel, M. (designer salon), 79 n. 20
Gilgi, 138–39; the character, 172;
  literary merits of, 174–75; plot, 171,
  173; publishing history, 172–73;
  social class in, 174–77; social
  criticism in, 177. *See also* Keun,
  Irmgard
"*Gilgi*-debate," 174–75
Girardin, Emile de, 44 n. 17
Girl, *vs.* the lady, 72, 75, 189
Glaser & Goetz (designer salon), 126
Goerke, Hanna, 58
Goetz, Ruth, 62, 128, 199
Goldmann (designer salon), 146 n. 40
Gordon, Lady Duff. *See* Lucile
Gralla, Dina, 122
Grand, Sarah, 47 n. 51
Green, Renate, 94, 107 n. 39
Grey's Anatomy, 194
Grund, Helen: biography, 87, 104 n.
  12; characterized by Erika Mann,
  99–100; compared to Walter
  Benjamin, 94; conscious of
  professional status, 97–98; earliest
  publications, 87–90, 104 n. 14;
  essays from Paris, 85, 88–90; in
  fashion journalism, 12–13; and the
  feuilleton, 93; and the *Frankfurter
  Zeitung*, 90–100; in *Für die Frau*,
  95, **96**; her audience, 85, 88; in
  Franz Hessel's writing, 86, 104 n. 9;
  and *Jules et Jim*, 85–86, 103 n. 7;
  and Dora Sophie Kellner, 103 n. 6;
  on mannequins, 94, 97; under
  National Socialism, 100–102; and
  notions of modernity, 85; political
  mission of, 100–101
Grund, Helen, works by: *Vom Wesen
  der Mode*, 101–2

Haase-Werkenthin, Julie, 58, 59, **60**,
  62, 66, 197
Hahn-Hahn, Ida, 105 n. 19

haircut, 3–4, 118, 176
Hartung, Gerd, 79 n. 19, 201
Hauser, Heinrich, 98–99
Hausler, Hermann, 93
Haussmann, 26
haute couture, 4; authority of, 70–71;
  history of, 82 n. 50; influence of on
  women's self-conception, 72–74;
  invention of, 16 n. 19; and male
  designers, 181
Hausvogteiplatz, 15 n. 7
Hearst press, 77 n. 6
Heine, Heinrich, 88
Der heitere Fridolin, 53
Heller, Ludwig, 119
Helm, Brigitte, **132**, **133**, **140**; in
  Alraune, 148 n. 67; conflicts with
  UFA, 150 n. 81; her costume
  designers, 148 n. 62; in *Eine von uns*,
  172; her film career, 148 n. 59; in
  Metropolis, 149 n. 71; as model, 113;
  as star and fashion icon, 130–41
Helm, Hanna, 161–63, 165
Hertzog, Rudolph, 4, 155
Hervé, Melitta, 126
Herzog, Elsa, 21–23, **23**, 40, 68, 120,
  199–200
Heß (designer salon), 135, 146 n. 40
Hessel, Franz, 37; on *flânerie*, 32–33,
  46 n. 42, 183; on mannequins,
  151–52; rediscovery of, 46 n. 42; as
  writer, 103 n. 8
Hessel, Franz, works by: "A Dangerous
  Street," 151–52; *Spazieren in Berlin*,
  28, 84
Hessel, Helen. *See* Grund, Helen
history, the present as part of, 31–32
Hitler, Adolf, 50. *See also* National
  Socialism
Höch, Hannah, 48 n. 58
Hoffmann, E. T. A., 29
Hollywood in the 1930s, 143 n. 13
Horn, Camilla, 169 n. 30
Hubert, René (designer salon), 148 n.
  62
Hugenberg, Alfred, 77 n. 8. *See also*
  UFA
Hutter, Francis, 54, 78 n. 15

Ich geh aus und du bleibst da, 160, 168–69 n. 30
Die ideale Gattin (film), 146 n. 43
identity: female, and fashion, 89; gendered, 3, 193; personal, 74–76. *See also* gender; women
Ihering, Herbert, 144 n. 27
Das Illustrierte Blatt, 151, 169 n. 42
Illustrierte Frauenzeitung, 53, 119, 144 n. 31
individuality: and fashion, 7, 39, 62, 66–67, 69–72, 74, 76; modern cult of, 70; women's experience of, 181. *See also* identity
intellectuality, modern, 29–30, 31–32, 91; and Ullstein House, 55–56; and women, 37–38, 98
international fashion. *See* fashion, and foreign influence

Jacobi, Emil (designer salon), 126
Jennys Bummel durch die Männer (film), 148 n. 57
Jews: in fashion farces, 122, 125; and the fashion industry, 4, 123, 125, 144 n. 29; in fashion journalism, 66; in Nazi propaganda, 145 n. 37; persecution of, 109 n. 51, 198, 201. *See also* Bois, Curt; Gerson, Herrmann; Lubitsch, Ernst
journalism: difficulties of women in, 80 n. 30; discrimination against women, 106 n. 29; and the *flâneur*, 29–30; genres of, 27. *See also* fashion journalism
Jovanowitsch, Sonja (first fashion queen), 135–36
Joyless Street (film), 6, 113
Jules et Jim (film), 85–86, 103 n. 7
Die junge Dame, 139

Kahlenberg, Hans von, 68–69
Kaléko, Mascha, 38, 170 n. 46
Kant, Immanuel, 8
Kästner, Erich, 145 n. 35, 171
Kaul, Stephanie, 40, 62, 67, 72, 74
Kaus, Gina, 56

Kellner, Dora Sophie, 103 n. 6. *See also* Benjamin, Dora
Keun, Irmgard, 14, 35, 56, 138–39; vs. Hessel on *flânerie*, 184–85
Keun, Irmgard, works by: *Das kunstseidene Mädchen*, 178. *See also* Gilgi
Kleidergeschichten. *See* "costume tales"
Die Kleine aus der Konfektion (film), 128–29, 147 n. 54
Kleist, Heinrich von, 88
Konfektion. *See* fashion industry, German
Der Konfektionär, 119, 145 n. 34
Konfektionskomödie. *See* fashion farce
Konfektionsposse. *See* fashion farce; fashion plays
Korff, Kurt, 53, 66, 67, 78 n. 13
Ein Kostüm, 119
Kracauer, Siegfried, 27, 44 n. 17, 177; biography, 30–31; and the feuilleton, 85; on *flânerie*, 30–32, 45 n. 33; friendship with Walter Benjamin, 45 n. 29; on mannequins, 158; on mass culture, 175–76; on modernization, 30; as reviewer, 148 n. 57, 148 n. 67; "theory of the surface," 31–32
Kracauer, Siegfried, works by: "Film 1928," "Kino in der Münzstraße," 36–37, 116; *The Salaried Masses*, 3–4, 14 n. 4
Krause, Käthe, 200
Krispien, Curt, 159
Kriwitz, Martha, 146 n. 43
Krüger, Charlotte, 144 n. 29
Kunstseide. *See* fabrics, synthetic

Lagerfeld, Karl, 194
Landshoff, Ruth, 56
Lang, Fritz, 114, 130, 133–34
Lanvin (designer salon), 72
La Roche, Sophie von, 105 n. 19
Lasker-Schüler, Else, 79 n. 21, 87
Le Falconnier, 87
Léger, Ferdinand, 87
legs, eroticized, 3, 35, 158–59, 180. *See also* beauty, feminine

leisure, modern women's experience of, 98–99
Leux, Lori, 120
Levin, David Leib, 4
Lewald, Fanny, 105 n. 19
Life, 78 n. 13
Lindau, Carl, 119
literature: as commodity, 55; high *vs.* low, 40–41, 92–93, 197; modern, 84; popular, 159–65; and the urban environment, 92; *vs.* fashion, 182–87
loitering. *See flâneur*
Loos, Adolf, 17 n. 25
Löwental, Martha (designer salon), 79 n. 20
Lubitsch, Ernst, 122, 124–27, 146 n. 43, 168 n. 24
Luce, Henry, 78 n. 13
Lucile, London's premier couturier, 145 n. 33; and theater, 120–21
Luxusweibchen (film), 129–30, 148 n. 56

Mack, Max, 146 n. 43
Mahrenholz (designer salon), 131, 148 n. 62
makeup, 4, 35, 118, 152, 161, 163, 176, 178, 197
male gaze, the, 2, 34, 39, 135, 151, 156–57; and mannequins, 151; in *Metropolis*, 133–34. *See also* women, objectification of
male perspective on fashion. *See under* fashion
Mann, Erika, 99–100, 108 n. 48
Mann, Thomas, 79 n. 21
mannequin, the German, 127–28
mannequins, 73, 94, 97; as actresses, 156–57, 159; ambiguity of the term, 13–14, 153–54, 160, 167 n. 15; ambivalent position of, 162–65; and the beginning of the fashion show, 73, 120–21; in fashion plays, 119; in film, 122–30; live, in display windows, 154–59, 167 n. 18, 167 n. 19; manufacture of, 151; mentality of, 157–58; names of, 162–63, 169 n. 41; as a national type, 165; new type of in the 1920s films, 129–30; origins of, 151, 153–54; in poems and songs, 170 n. 46; as role models, 127; romanticized in popular literature, 156, 158–59; and sexuality, 152; social class of, 97, 157–59, 170 n. 46; as social type, 147 n. 53; as stand-ins for the New Woman, 152; working conditions of, 159–65
Mannheimer, Valentin (designer salon), 4, 79 n. 20
Manolescu (film), 113, 131, 139
Maris, Mona, 122, 163
marketing, fashion. *See* advertising
Marxism, 29, 30
masculinization, 37, 59, 61, 66, 68–69, 81 n. 41. *See also* New Woman, the
Massary, Fritzi, 120, 144 n. 25
mass consumption. *See* consumer culture
mass culture, 27, 175–76; creation of, 51–52; and modes of vision, 39; and the New Woman, 36; phenomena of, 30–31; readers, 44–45 n. 17. *See also* audiences; consumer culture; popular culture
mass media: commercialization of, 44 n. 17, 77 n. 6; concentration and centralization of, 77 n. 6; and fashion, 41–42, 154, 192; female fashion journalists as representative of, 98; and the feuilleton, 92; modernization of, 53; and the New Woman, 36; Paris and, 44 n. 17; and public entertainment, 44 n. 17; and transformation of the public sphere, 51; Ullstein House's contribution to the rise of, 55–56. *See also* publishers
May, Joe, 156
McCall's Patterns, 78 n. 15
media giants, 52, 77 nn. 7–8
Meinert, Rudolf, 113
men: resistant to change, 39; response to mannequins, 151; and the tradition of fashion, 2
Mendelssohn, Peter de, 77 n. 7

"Messter-Woche," 124. *See also* newsreels.
Metropolis, 133–35; as Art Deco, 149 n. 71; Brigitte Helm in, 130; as paradigm of modernity, 92; women's experience of, 88–90
Meyer, Erna, 200
Meyer, Johannes, 131, 172
misogyny *vs.* emancipation, 194
mobility. *See under* women
Modehaus. *See* designer salon
Modekonkurrenz. *See* fashion competitions; fashion queens
Modenball. *See* fashion competitions
Mode-Notizen, 38, 61–62, 66–70, 76; in the *Frankfurter Zeitung*, 84; as genre, 40; and modernity, 69–72
Modenschau um Mitternacht, 119
Der Modenspiegel, 128
Modentee, 1, 51, 121. *See also* fashion show
Modeplauderei, *vs.* feuilleton, 93
Moderennen. *See* races as sites for fashion display
Moderne Kunst, 144 n. 29
Die Moderne Welt: Illustrierte Halbmonatsschrift für Kunst, Literatur, Mode, 195 n. 2
modernism: and Helen Grund, 86–87; theory of, 6–7; and Ullstein House, 52–53. *See also* feuilleton
modernity: defined through fashion, 1–2, 26–27, 38–39, 53–54, 67–76; definitions of, 85; demonstrated by fashion models, 62; experience of, 24–25, 115–18, 141, 171–88; and the First World War, 67–69, 70; and the *flâneur*, 25; gendered perspectives on, 51; and the mass media, 51; men's experience of, 33–34, 183–87; modes of reflecting on, 182–87; the New Woman's experience of, 36; personified by Parisian women, 89–90; and popular culture, 130; and socio-historical disruption, 67–69; and sports, 4; theory of, 38; and visual modes of perception, 26–27; in Weimar Germany, 2–7; woman driver as symbol of, 98–99; and women, 33; women's experience of, 1–4, 67, 74–76, 153, 174, 193 (*see also Gilgi*; New Woman). *See also under* Benjamin, Walter; democratization
Mohr, Erica, 58, 62, 197
Moja, Hella, 167 n. 18
Moreau, Jeanne, 85, 103 n. 7
Moreck, Curt, 114, 141
Mosse, Rudolf, 77 n. 8
Mosse press, 52, 77 n. 8
Mossner, E. (designer salon), 79 n. 20
motherhood, 81, 165, 172, 174, 187 n. 2
movie stars. *See* film stars
Mühlen, Hermynia Zur, 185–86, 191 n. 34
Muenzer, Auguste (designer salon), 126
Münzer, Kurt, 156, 167 n. 19

Nabokov, Vladimir, 87
Nagy, Lily von, 40, 62, **63**, 69, 200
names, use of mannequins', 169 n. 41. *See also* authorship
narcissism, 156–57, 178
Nathan, Steffie, 58, 59, 66, 80 n. 33
National Socialism, 79 n. 29, 100–102, 109 n. 52–53, 110 n. 57; and the fashion industry, 123–24; on Jewish decadence in film, 145 n. 37. *See also* Hitler; Jews
Nelken, Dinah, 38, 56, 185–86, 191 n. 34
Neue Frau. *See* New Woman, the, German
die neue linie, 55, 79 n. 19
Neue Sachlichkeit. *See* New Objectivity
Neumeister, Heddy, 106 n. 29
New Objectivity, 171–72
New Woman, the, 24–25, 33; ambivalent position of, 14, 171–72; before 1926, 59, 61; constrained by tradition, 179–81; creating her own image, 117–18; defined, 11–12, 35–36; emancipation of, 193;

English *vs.* German, 35, 47 n. 55;
evolving myth of, 66; and fashion,
185–87; German stereotype of,
35–36; Franz Hessel on, 152; image
of, 62, 176–78; as intellectual, 37,
52; in literature, 35; and mass
culture, 36–37; studies of, 36–38;
the term, 47 n. 51. *See also*
masculinization
newspapers, increasing popularity of,
92–93
newsreels: and fashion competitions,
137; and fashion parades, 124,
145 n. 39, 146 n. 40
Nielsen, Asta, **115**; as fashion icon,
139; her audience, 142 n. 4;
influence of, 113; in *Joyless Street*
Niemeyer, Erna. *See* Green, Renate
Nietzsche, Friedrich, 17 n. 20
Northcliffe press, 77 n. 6
nostalgia, as male phenomenon, 71–72

Offenbach, Jacques, 30
Offermann, Asta (third fashion queen),
135
originality, and social conventions, 40
Orla, Resl, 126, 146–47 n. 43
Orlik, Emil, 199
Osborn, Max, 79 n. 21
Die östliche Göttin, 119

Pabst, G. W., 131, 148 n. 63
Paquin (designer salon), 72, 143 n. 18
Paramount, 172
Paris: as fashion center, 59, 66, 72–74;
and the *flâneur*, 25–27; influence on
German *Konfektion*, 4, 109 n. 53;
and the mass press, 44 n. 17; and
the press, 27; as travel destination,
88. *See also* Grund, Helen; *haute
couture*
Parry, Lee, 129
Pathé fashion shows in newsreels, 124,
145 n. 39
Patou (designer salon), 72, 94
patterns, sewing: advent of, 1;
development and appeal of, 54;
relative distinction of, 66. *See also*
Ullstein House
Pfeiffer, Ida, 105 n. 19
photographers and photojournalists,
62, 66; models for, 80 n. 34
photography, 21, 127, 139; and female
stereotypes, 48 n. 58; and mass
media, 41; in *Metropolis*, 135;
techniques of, 133–34; Weimar
women in, 48 n. 67
photojournalism, development of, 53
Poe, Edgar Allan, 28, 29
Poiret, Paul, 73, 143 n. 18, 167, 181,
190 n. 23; in Berlin, 144 n. 30,
145 n. 32; and filmed fashion shows,
124, 145 n. 38; and theater, 120–21
Popper, Otto Reinhard, 119
popular culture: and modernity, 130;
neglected, 5; *vs.* high art, 6
popular literature and fashion, 171–72
popular press: and advertising, 52; and
fashion tradition, 2; and women, 2.
See also fashion journalism;
feuilleton; mass media; travelogue
Porten, Henny, 127–28
practicality, *vs.* feminine image, 74. *See
also* dress-reform movement
Die praktische Berlinerin, 103 n. 6. *See
also* Herzog, Elsa; Kellner, Dora
Sophie.
Press Ball, tradition of the, 50, 76 n. 1
price tags, 163, 169 n. 42
public sphere, 49 n. 74; literary,
40–41; and the mass media, 50–51;
women's, 51, 77 n. 4, 85
publishers: modern production and
marketing, 52; modernist self-
identity, 77–78 n. 10. *See also* Mosse,
Rudolf; Mosse Press; Scherl, August;
Ullstein, Hermann; Ullstein House
Putti, Lya de, 113

Der Querschnitt, 88, 137, **138**

races as sites for fashion display,
118–19
Rathaus, Katharina von, 160–61, 197
Ré. *See* Green, Renate

reading public, the, 27; power of, 65
ready-to-wear, 4, 131, 153, 159
reform dress. *See* dress-reform movement
Reformkleidung. *See* dress-reform movement
Reich, Lilly, 41
Reichsfilmblatt, 113
Reichshandbuch der deutschen Gesellschaft, 21, **22**, **23**, 58
Reinecke, Vally, 58–59, **61**, 62, 66, 80 n. 33, 142 n. 8, 200; designer for *Dr. Mabuse, der Spieler*, 142 n. 8
Reinhardt, Max, 125
Renee. *See* Green, Renate
revues, 119–20, 135, 143 n. 22; fashion tableaux in, 149 n. 72; in Metropol Theater (Berlin), 144 n. 22
Riederer, Marietta, **96**, 109 n. 50, 200–201
Rippert, Otto, 125
Roché, Herni-Pierre, 85–86, 87, 103 n. 7
Rössler, Carl, 119
Roth, Joseph, 85, 87, 88, 90–91
Rouff (designer salon), 72
Ruttmann, Walter, 35, 121–22

Sachs, Nelly, 56
Sandten, Thea, 125
sartorial social codes, 1, 11, 24, 117
Schäfer-Ast, Albert, 80 n. 33
Schenker, Karl, 62
Scherl, August, 52–53, 77 n. 8, 200
Scherl's Magazin, **155**, 156, **157**, 160, 163
Schlemmer, Oscar, 134
Schmidt-Beil, Ada, 70
Schnabel, Gertrud, 200
Schopenhauer, Johanna, 105 n. 19
Schüching, Ruth von. *See* Goetz, Ruth
Schuhpalast Pinkus (film), 124–27, 146 n. 43
Schultz, Clara, 144 n. 25
Schultze, Hanns, 198
Schünzel, Reinhold, 128–29
Schwarz, Hanns, 131
Das Schwarze Korps, 100–102

screenplay writers, 128–30. *See also* Alsen, Ola; Goetz, Ruth; Turszinsky, Walter
Seligo, Irene, 106 n. 29
Sex and the City, 194
Simmel, Georg, 2, 7, 8–11, 182; and Benjamin, Walter, 86; critique by Marianne Weber, 17 n. 24; and gender roles, 70; on surface, 31
sizes: perfect, 125, 162–63; standard, 4, 54; system of, 167 n. 15
Sofar-Film, 113
Sombart, Werner, 2, 7–8, 16 n. 18
Soupault, Ré. *See* Green, Renate
sources, 167 n. 18; biographical, 80 n. 36; Bundesarchiv/Filmarchiv in Berlin, 146 n. 40; Film Museum Berlin, 146 n. 40; missing, 79 n. 29, 197
Sovanowitsch, Sonja, 149 n. 75. *See also* Jovanowitsch, Sonja
Sparkuhl, Martha, 58, **60**, 62, 80 n. 33, 197
Speyer, Wilhelm, 160, 168–69 n. 30. See *Ich geh aus und du bleibst da*
Sport im Bild, 107 n. 39
sports: and modernity, 4; and the New Woman, 24, 35; as venue for fashion display, 154
stardom, birth of, 120
Starke, Ottomar, 156
Steffie. *See* Nathan, Steffie
Stern, Norbert, 16 n. 16
stockings, 3, 114, 134, 139, 155–56, 176. *See also* legs
Der Stolz der Firma (film), 124–27, 146 n. 43
strolling. *See flânerie; flâneur*
Styl, 88. *See also* Verband der deutschen Modeindustrie
styles: functional, 3; turn-of-the-century, 3
subjectivity, female, 35, 36–37, 38–42. *See also* women
suffrage, women's, 2
surface: literal and conceptual expressions of, 6–7; the New

Woman as, 36. *See also under* Kracauer, Siegfried
Swarzenski, Marie, 157–58
Szafranski, Kurt, 78 n. 13

Das Tage-Buch, 87, 104 n. 14
technology, advancing, 25, 53, 55, 85, 99
Tempo, 108 n. 48
Tergit, Gabriele, 56, 176
Thal, Johanna, 39, 40, **60**, 69–70, 74, 201
Tieck, Polly, 38, 56
Tourjansky, Viktor, 131
traditional costume, and nationalism, 16 n. 16. *See also* dress-reform movement; fashion
travelogue, 12; compared to feuilleton, 92; 18th-century, 106 n. 26; as genre, 88, 105 n. 19
Truffaut, François, 85–86, 103 n. 7
Tucholsky, Kurt, 55, 79 n. 21, 174; reviews of Franz Hessel, 86, 103 n. 8
Turszinsky, Walter, 119, 124, 128, 147 n. 51

UFA (Universum Film-Aktiengesellschaft), 139, 150 n. 81; and Brigitte Helm, 130–31; importance of costumes to, 148 n. 62
Uhde, Anna-Marie, 87
Der Uhu, 12, 51, 161–62, 181
Ullmann, Regina, 56
Ullstein, Hermann, 52–53, 77–78 n. 10
Ullstein House: advertising, 54, 78 n. 16; in female fashion journalism, 12; history of, 52, 57–58, 77 n. 7; as an institution, 51–56; literary reputation, 79 n. 21; and literature, 55; most successful publications, 53; as pioneer, 41–42; readership, 54–55; and rise of mass media, 55–56; sewing patterns, 54; and women, 55–58, 62
Umber, Otto, 151
Die Unschuld im Tailor-made, 119
"unter dem Strich," 84, 102 n. 2. *See also* feuilleton

urban environment: effects of, 31–32; in films, 35; and the *flâneur*, 25–26, 27, 29, 32, 44 n. 18; and literature, 92; modernization of, 30; and women, 34

Valéry, Paul, 86
vamp, 35, 139, 141. *See also femmes fatales*
Veblen, Thorstein, 2, 7, 8
Verband der deutschen Modeindustrie, 79 n. 20, 135
Vernet, Marie, 143 n. 18, 167 n. 13
Vienna, 1, 17 n. 25, 42 n. 4, 66, 101, 119, 200
Vischer, Friedrich Theodor, 7, 8, 86
visual culture, 141, 150 n. 83, 156–57; Asta Nielsen and, 113–14; development of, 53; and fashion farce, 125–26; and the feuilleton, 84. *See also* film; photojournalism
visual modes of perception: as gendered, 39; and modernity, 26–27, 39
Vogue (German ed.), 131, **132**, 137, 149 n. 78
Vorwärts, 174, 188 n. 8
Vossische Zeitung, 52, 198
voyeurism, 2, 156–57. *See also flâneur*

Wallach, Edith, 41
Walser, Robert, 79 n. 21, 87, 103 n. 8
Das Warenhausmädchen (film), 119
Warenhausprinzessin (film), 167 n. 18
Weber, Marianne, 17 n. 24, 70
Wedekind, Kadidja, 174
Wedekind-Pariselle, Anna Paula, 62, 66, 201
Weimar Germany: economy of, 4, 15 n. 7; social and economic conditions in, 2–3; social structure of, 57; sources on, 14 n. 2; tensions within, 5
Weisse, Hanni, 146–47 n. 43
Wiene, Robert, 128, 146 n. 43, 147 n. 51
Wilde, Oscar, 35
Wilke, Charlotte, 70
Willkomm, Aenne, 134, 149 n. 71

window-shopping, 123, 156–57, 166 n. 6
Die Woche, 21, 53, 77 n. 8, 200
Wolff, Charlotte, 108 n. 44
Wolff (designer salon), 141, 146 n. 40, 148 n. 62
womanhood. *See* women, stereotypical
women: as active, creative, 6, 12, 38–42, 51, 53, 62, 66, 101–2; as anti-modern, 33; changing lives of, 51, 57, 67–76, 68–70, 76, 151–52, 182–87, 192, 193 (*see also* democratization; Ullstein House, double standard); as consumers, 16 n. 19, 34–35, 47 n. 49, 54 (*see also* consumer culture); and domesticity, 68–69, 81 n. 41; and education, 35; entering the workforce, 2–3, 14 n. 1; expectations of, 192, 193; experience of fashion, 50–51; experience of modernity, 1–4, 67–76, 85, 193; as fashion practitioners, 6; and independence, 38; and individuality, 69–72; and intellectuals, 37–38; as intellectuals, 24–25, 61, 66, 98; and mobility, 34–35, 47 n. 49, 98–99; modern characteristics of, 54; and the modern metropolis, 88–90; objectification of, 2, 9, 24, 34, 51, 97, 135, 141, 156–57, 160, 163–65, 166 n. 6, 178, 179–80; objectification of in *Metropolis*, 133–34; objectification of in the 1920s, 97; and photography, 48 n. 58, 48 n. 67; as photojournalists, 62, 66; and politics, 56, 188 n. 8; and professional realization, 186–87; and the public sphere, 77 n. 4, 193; social and economic status of, 4, 35, 62, 67–68; stereotypical, 6, 9, 10, 39, 48 n. 58, 102; technology and, 134; as viewed by Ullstein House, 55–56; as writers, 84, 91, 197 (*see also* popular literature)
Worth (designer salon), 72, 94, 145 n. 38
Worth, Charles Frederick, 16 n. 19, 118, 143 nn. 17–18, 154, 167 n. 13. *See also* Vernet, Marie
Die wunderbare Lüge der Nina Petrowna (film), 131, 139

Die Yacht der sieben Sünden (film), 133, 139
Yva, 80 n. 34, 139

Zimmermann, Hilde (second fashion queen), 135–36, **136**, 137, **138**
Zuckmayer, Carl, 79 n. 21
Zweig, Stefan, 79 n. 21

Ganeva's carefully researched and clearly written study is not only interesting to film studies scholars for the part that deals explicitly with film. Instead, the entire book works out parallels between the societal perception of fashion and film, both components of popular culture that promised unmatched brilliance and glamour and were medial systems that mirrored the experiences of Modernity in a very direct way and formed a feminine niche in mass culture.
FILMBLATT

[T]his important and innovative work . . . makes a significant contribution to the emerging literatures of fashion and modernity with respect to gender.
H-NET REVIEWS

Mila Ganeva has demonstrated the special meaning of fashion in the discourse on modernity between 1918 and 1933, and particularly has analyzed the intricate role of women between self-empowerment and objectification. Her work [is] an indispensable contribution to research in this area.
QUERELLES-NET

www.ingramcontent.com/pod-product-compliance
Lightning Source LLC
Chambersburg PA
CBHW060948230426
43665CB00015B/2114